Linda Brotherton                              Kim Ward

# COMMUNICATING IN BUSINESS:
## Key to Success

## Fourth Edition

# COMMUNICATING IN BUSINESS: Key to Success

## Fourth Edition

## William H. Bonner, Ph.D.

*Professor of Business Management*
*Tennessee Technological University*

**1986**

**dame publications, inc.**
*P.O. Box 35556*
*Houston, Texas 77235-5556*

**Typographer:**  Jan Tiefel
**Designer:**  Stephen Emry

© 1986 by DAME  PUBLICATIONS, INC.
P.O. Box 35556
Houston, Texas  77235-5556

ISBN 0-931920-90-6
Library of Congress Catalog Card No. 82-72152

*Printed in the United States of America.*

**To my wife and sons**

**Martha Sue, Andy, and Kent**

# PREFACE

In this fourth edition, the material has been expanded and up-dated to reflect current practices and trends and to incorporate changes suggested by users of the earlier editions. The book has been reorganized so that all chapters pertaining to writing are in sequence; oral communication is in the final chapter. This edition is presented in these five parts: theory and style, letters, reports, word processing, and oral communication.

This sequence of parts makes the book easier to adapt to courses in which letters are emphasized, to courses in which reports are emphasized, or to courses in which both letters and reports are emphasized. Oral communication and word processing can be included easily in any of these courses.

Among the features that have been retained is the progression from the easiest-to-write business messages to those that are the most difficult. Liberal illustrations are included as another special feature.

The chapter on employment letters and interviews has been up-dated to reflect the latest practices. This chapter contains information on not only application letters and data sheets but also other letters relating to employment. Among them are letters confirming interviews, following up interviews, accepting offers, declining offers, and resigning. Suggestions for preparing for employment interviews are also included.

The most significant changes have been made in the business reports section and in word processing and computers in communication. Some of the chapters have been completely rewritten, and new problems have been added to most chapters. The problems are the types college students have adequate background for handling, and they require application of the guidelines to be used later when writing letters and reports and making oral presentations to solve actual problems in business. Numerous other problems are in the study guide.

For many of the ideas presented in this book I am indebted to convention participants, teachers, and business executives with whom I have discussed business communication. I am indebted to New York Life Insurance Company for ideas from the pamphlet "Making the Most of Your Job Interviews."

I give a special note of gratitude to my wife and two sons for their interest in this writing project and for their encouragement.

*1986*                                                 *William H. Bonner*

# CONTENTS

# PART TWO
# LETTERS

Interview Confirmation
Interview
    Before
    During
    After
Job-Offer Acceptance
Job-Offer Rejection
Resignations

Substitutes or Alternatives
    Substitutes
    Alternatives
    Delayed compliance
Need for More Information
Another Source
Outright Refusals

Seeking Information About Applicants
Inviting to an Interview
Offering Employment
Welcoming a New Employee
Rejecting an Applicant
Accepting a Resignation
Dismissing an Employee
Recommending an Employee
Writing Other Messages

# PART THREE
# REPORTS

Primary
    Experimenting
    Observing
    Interrogating
    Sampling
    Processing information
Secondary
    Organization files
    Publications
    Data bases
    Note taking

Footnotes
    First reference
    Second reference
    Placement
Bibliography

Constructing Graphics
    Informal table
    Formal table
    Other graphics
Using Computers
Interpreting Graphics

# PART FOUR
# WORD PROCESSING

Pointers for Beginners
Recording Mediums
    Stenographer
    Machine
Dictating Efficiency
    Collection of information
    Outlines
    Machine requirements
    Names and addresses
    Knowledge of content
    Special instructions
    Style
    Numbers
    Follow-up
Word Processing Center

Letters
    Uses of form letters
    Advantages of form letters
    Disadvantages of form letters
    Types of form letters
    Preparation of form letters
Routing Slips
Records of Calls
Word Processors

# PART FIVE
# ORAL COMMUNICATION

Listening
    Barriers
    Tips for effective listening
Seeing
Touching
Speaking
    Conversations
    Interviews
    Telephone calls
    Demonstrations
    Instructions
    Briefings
    Meetings
    Discussions
    Speeches
Conclusion

# PART SIX
# REFERENCE SECTION

Punctuation
      Period
      Exclamation mark
      Comma
      Semicolon
      Colon
      Question mark
      Hyphen
      Apostrophe
      Parentheses
      Dash
      Quotation marks
      Ellipses
      Brackets
   Spacing with Punctuation Marks
   End-of-Line Divisions
   Capitalization
   Numbers
   Abbreviations
   Sentence Types
      Simple
      Compound
      Complex
      Compound-complex
   Special Addresses and Salutations for Special Correspon-
      dence
   Confusing Terminology

# PART ONE

# THEORY AND STYLE

# Chapter 1
# Effective Communication

Everyone has to communicate, for no one can survive as an isolated individual. A normal human desire and genuine need is to share joys, successes, failures, and frustrations. Business people have occasions for sharing feelings of almost all classifications.

When friends, relatives, or business associates receive awards, are promoted to higher positions, or are elected to offices in organizations, we like to share this good fortune with them. We, therefore, congratulate them orally or in writing. If those people experience a tragedy, we want to try to console them by making oral or written statements or by using nonverbal communication mediums.

Sometimes in business transactions, errors are made that create disappointments, major inconveniences, and financial losses. These errors can lead to irate tempers and other displays of emotions that require the use of finesse and the very best communication skills to restore goodwill. Fortunately, though, a high percentage of business communication activities pertain to conditions that are pleasant. While some business situations create highly emotional feelings, most business situations are on an even-tempered level. Some are routine.

A successful business enterprise has to be staffed by adequately trained personnel who obtain materials for producing, handling, or selling the products or services the enterprise provides. Only through effective communication can the necessary personnel be employed, and only through effective communication can the personnel perform the duties necessary to make the enterprise succeed. Business personnel must, in addition to communicating successfully within an organization, communicate with consumers. Conversely, all consumers—whether they are employed, retired, disabled, or wealthy enough to live a life of leisure—have to engage in business communication activities in order to exist.

To communicate effectively, business people and others need at least a partial understanding of the communication process.

## THE COMMUNICATION PROCESS

Communicating is the sharing of information, ideas, or feelings. Always, therefore, at least two people—a sender and a receiver— are involved in the communication process. Information or ideas can be transmitted verbally (with spoken or written words) or nonverbally (without words). Words are usually used to transmit information or ideas. Words or nonverbal mediums such as gestures or facial expressions are used to indicate that the information or the ideas have been received.

Words can be used in expressing feelings; but generally, feelings are expressed more effectively by nonverbal means such as the tone of voice and the facial expressions used with words. Perhaps you have heard a comment such as this one: "It's not what he said; it's the way he said it." Words spoken in one tone and with certain gestures indicate one feeling, yet the same words spoken in another tone and with other gestures indicate an entirely different feeling. And, of course, the context in which a communication medium is used has a major bearing on the effect that medium has on the communicators.

Words—whether spoken or written—should be chosen carefully to fit the particular situation at hand and the communicators involved. Because of backgrounds and experiences, people tend to perceive different meanings of words. The owner of a Lincoln

Continental and the owner of a Subaru, for example, may listen to a salesman's description of a Cutlass. One listener would perceive the Cutlass as a little car; the other, a big car.

To communicate effectively in social situations and at work, we choose words carefully and combine them with nonverbal communication mediums. We use these mediums to share information, ideas, and feelings so that sound decisions can be made and appropriate actions can be taken.

## THE SELECTION OF A COMMUNICATION MEDIUM

Communication mediums are chosen to fit existing situations and to accomplish desired objectives. Nonverbal communication mediums serve well for transmitting some simple messages and are often used spontaneously. For complex messages, though, words are combined with nonverbal mediums. Both nonverbal and verbal mediums merit thought and discussion.

### Nonverbal

Some of the frequently used nonverbal communication mediums are sound, sight, and touch. Only a few illustrations of each of these three categories are given here.

**Sound.** Firing a blank revolver to tell swimmers to begin a race, speaking in a pleasant tone of voice to indicate approval or speaking in a sarcastic tone of voice to signify disapproval, and ringing a bell to indicate the end of a planned period are among the many uses of sound as a nonverbal medium of communication.

**Sight.** Visual forms of nonverbal communication mediums are illustrated in these examples: A person attending a group meeting usually raises a hand or uses facial expressions to indicate to the presider a desire to participate orally. College students sometimes start looking at their watches to remind the professor that it is time for the class period to end. A traffic director holds a hand up with the palm toward the motorists to tell them to stop and waves an arm to tell them to proceed or to turn. An interviewer may stand to signify a desire to end an interview.

People making oral presentations may have their confidence reinforced by listeners who smile or nod in a way that indicates approval of the manner in which the oral presentation is being made. Such gestures are especially reassuring to speakers who believe the persons making the gestures are competent to judge the quality of the oral presentation. Using words as a medium of expressing approval would not be appropriate in an instance such as this, yet these nonverbal mediums can be used quite effectively. Speakers may indicate their reception of the nonverbal message by relaxing or by exhibiting greater self-confidence or enthusiasm. They can exhibit these characteristics through a change in the tone of voice or a change in posture.

Such factors as posture and eye contact tend to suggest—but not to prove—self-confidence and strong character.

Among the many nonverbal communication mediums that can be combined with written words to transmit a message effectively are punctuation marks, underlines, color, spacing on a page, stationery quality, and type style or handwriting style. An exclamation mark at the end of a sentence may indicate the mood of the writer, or it may draw attention to the importance or the severity of a situation. Underlining a word or a group of words calls attention to that part of a message. Varying the line lengths accomplishes the same purpose.

**Touch.**   A handshake—a gesture given little thought by many people—is an example of touch as an effective nonverbal communication medium. A firm handshake by people who are being introduced to each other suggests warmth or amicable personality. A handshake used with congratulatory remarks to a person whose accomplishment you are genuinely proud of is probably firm, and it helps you to share the feeling of elation. On the other hand, a handshake given because of obligation, such as to congratulate an opponent who won the contest, is likely to express a feeling that is somewhat less cordial.

Touch can be an effective communication medium in other situations. A grief-stricken person, for example, seldom derives much consolation from words that are spoken or written, regardless of the degree of sincerity that is felt by the person who attempts to console. The person in distress does, though, receive some degree of consolation from knowing that a friend sympathizes because of the unfortunate circumstances. A warm handshake or other simple gesture such as placing a hand firmly on the person's shoulder may do more than words (spoken or written) could do to express sympathy or to console.

The nonverbal mediums mentioned here, as well as many others, can be combined with words to produce effective oral and written communication.

## Verbal

Verbal messages can be sent by speaking or by writing. Most oral communication is carried out in face-to-face situations either on a one-to-one basis or within a larger group. Telephone conversations also are used extensively, of course, in transacting business. Among other instances in which oral communication predominates are training sessions and committee meetings.

Letters and memorandums are perhaps the most frequently used forms of written business communication. Fill-in forms, manuals, brochures, catalogs, advertisements, newsletters, and reports of various kinds are also used widely. These written messages, as well as oral presentations, are given thorough coverage in this book.

Technological developments have greatly expanded the mediums of effective communication. Among the mediums that are growing in popularity—but are still used less frequently than the traditional ones—are communicating word processors, electronic copier/printers, facsimile, mailgrams, and radio and television. These mediums are discussed in later chapters.

The mediums or vehicles used in communicating effectively are so numerous that an attempt to mention all of them would be a mammoth task indeed, even if completing such a task were possible. An awareness that various mediums are used in a variety of ways is, however, important. The medium to use should be appropriate for the existing situation. Here are some of the questions to be answered when choosing a medium for transmitting a message:

1.  Is a copy needed for the files of the sender and/or the receiver?

2.  Must the message be transmitted instantly?

3.  Is an immediate response needed?

4.   What communication equipment or facilities does the intended receiver have?

5.   Are gestures and facial expressions vital to effective transmission?

6.   Is cost a major factor?

For whatever communication medium you use, you can apply the information presented in this book to prepare effective messages.

## REQUIREMENTS FOR EFFECTIVE COMMUNICATION

A primary requirement for communicating effectively is at least a partial understanding of, as well as an appreciation for, the communication process. Other attributes, which can be attained if you do not already have them, follow:

1.   Right attitude

2.   Thorough knowledge of the problem or situation that leads to the need for communication

3.   Adequate vocabulary and good grammar usage

4.   Adaptability and eagerness to break bad habits

### Right Attitude

When sending a message, remember that at least two people— you and the receiver—are involved and that the receiver, as far as that person is concerned, is the most important person in the world. Regardless of the person's social status, financial condition, political affiliation, or level of intelligence, the receiver of your message is someone who deserves to be treated with dignity and who wants to be respected. No one should ever, therefore, intentionally embarrass anyone by speaking or by writing caustic or accusing remarks or by making statements that cannot be readily understood.

When speaking or writing, try to put yourself in the receiver's place by looking at the situation from that person's point of view.

### Knowledge of the Problem

A thorough knowledge of the situation leading to communication helps you to understand the statements others make orally or in writing, and it helps you to decide what to say or write. In business you usually understand the conditions that exist, and you have access to information about the receivers of your message. Completing the exercises and the problems in this book, though, will require you to use your imagination to a greater extent than in real situations.

### Vocabulary and Grammar

You need to be familiar with the terms used in connection with the business transactions you handle so that you can transmit your ideas in an appropriate way and so that you can interpret precisely the ideas you receive by listening or by reading. Strive always to increase your knowledge of words, especially those pertaining to your field of work. Since people think in words, the larger the vocabulary you have, the better you can formulate and express ideas.

To communicate accurately, use good grammar. Errors in sentence structure, in spelling, in punctuation, and in pronunciation can make a message convey ideas or information different from what is intended.

You can enhance the quality of your business messages by studying the following chapters and the reference section of this book. You can, of course, get further help by referring to any one of the many grammar books or reference books that are available.

### Adaptability

To communicate well, we need to be adaptable and eager to break bad habits. Perhaps all of us pick up a few bad habits from other people, for a tendency to imitate to some extent seems to be a natural trait of all human beings. We learn to talk by imitating. Accents, pronunciations, word choices, and idiomatic expressions are learned from family and friends. As we associate with more and more people, we become aware of the bad habits we have acquired by the natural inclination to imitate. We do not become aware of some of them, however, unless someone calls our attention to them.

Here are three requirements for breaking a habit:

1. Become aware that it exists and that a change is desirable.

2. *Want* to break it.

3. Do enough conscientious practice to break it.

Many habits of using certain expressions and of organizing oral and written messages need to be broken. For example, often when people reply to a letter, they begin by saying, "Thank you for your letter"—not because the main reason for writing is to express appreciation—but because they are imitating other writers. Also, this ending or a variation of it, "If I can be of further assistance to you, please do not hesitate to contact me"—which is a poor ending for a letter—is used only because the writers often see letters that end this way.

As you study this book, you will learn that many expressions are trite and should not be used; and you will read many suggestions you will want to use to make your oral and written messages clear, interesting, and effective.

## QUESTIONS FOR DISCUSSION

1. How can silence coupled with the absence of gestures and facial expressions be a medium of communication?

2. What are some of the communication mediums that were not mentioned in this chapter?

3. What are some of the fastest ways of transmitting written messages?

4. What steps can people take to improve their ability to communicate?

# Chapter 2
# Style
# of Expression

Style of expression is the way in which a message is conveyed. The way we express facts, ideas, and feelings is important— whether we express them orally, nonverbally, or in writing. For oral communication, expression style is made up of combinations of words, tone of voice, and gestures and facial expressions. For written communication, expression style is made up of combinations of words and such factors as punctuation, spacing, and underlining.

A primary objective of all speakers and writers should be to transmit messages *so clearly that they can~~not~~ be ~~mis~~understood*. For messages to be effective, we should make them interesting and should transmit them in a way that enables the receivers to concentrate on the content of the messages rather than on the way we transmit them.

As you study business communication in college, you can improve your style of expression by giving special consideration to conversational tone, positive and specific statements, sentence structure, paragraph development, and mechanics of communication.

## CONVERSATIONAL TONE

The tone of letters, memorandums, informal written reports, and oral presentations should be conversational. Use the same first- and second-person pronouns, contractions, idioms, personal references, contemporary expressions, word choices, courtesy expressions, and concise wording that you use in oral conversation.

### Personal Pronouns

When using letterhead stationery, you write as a representative of the organization that is identified in the letterhead. The pronouns *we*, *us*, *our*, and *ours* mean the group that makes up the organization the letterhead identifies. Use these personal pronouns, therefore, instead of such expressions as *our firm*, *our company*, and *our organization*.

Eliminate the use of such wordy, impersonal, outmoded third-person expressions as "The Smithfield Wholesale Company welcomes the opportunity to supply your paper products" when you are writing as an employee of the Smithfield Wholesale Company. Instead, write "*We* welcome the opportunity to supply your paper products."

Use second-person pronouns to refer to the reader of your message. When the reader represents a particular organization, use such expressions as "We welcome *you* as a customer" instead of stilted expressions such as "We welcome *your company* as a customer" or "We welcome *the Wright Manufacturing Company* as a customer."

Use the personal pronoun *I* when it contributes to conversational tone. The tone of your message should express an interest in the listener or reader. This interest, frequently referred to as the *you attitude*, can be established more naturally by using *I* and *we* than by omitting these pronouns and thus creating a telegraphic style. "Appreciate your writing to me on April 17" contributes less to displaying the *you attitude* than does "I appreciate your writing to me on April 17."

## Contractions

Contractions, provided they are used discreetly, help to add a natural, conversational tone to business messages. Contractions can be used in congratulatory letters to a business friend or associate; in sales letters for inexpensive, widely used products; in routine letters to people with whom you correspond regularly; and in memorandums, which are used for people within your organization. In many business messages more formal than these, contractions are good when used sparingly.

Choose contractions carefully. Such contractions as *don't*, *doesn't*, *it's*, and *won't* seem natural and in good taste for informal business messages. On the other hand, do not write such contractions as *I'd* and *you'd* since they are not commonly used in written messages.

Ordinarily, do not use contractions in letters about employment; in those to a person whose background is not familiar to you; and in those to older, conservative people.

When deciding whether to use contractions, keep the reader in mind. You want the reader to concentrate on the content of the message rather than on the writing style. If you believe the reader would like contractions, use them.

## Idioms

Well-known idiomatic expressions contribute to the conversational tone of business messages. When writing to someone who requested your help because of having business financial problems, the expression "When you are on your feet again" sounds not only conversational but also positive and pleasant. This idiom expresses the feeling you wish to convey. Countless other similar expressions can, when well chosen, contribute to the tone you want the message to have.

Keep these points in mind when using idioms:

1.  A reader who is not familiar with the idiom may be confused by your message.

2.   If the idiom can have different meanings in different contexts, the reader may misinterpret your expression and thus make your otherwise well-written message convey an idea entirely different from the one you intended.

Be especially careful about using idiomatic expressions in messages pertaining to contracts, topics about which people are especially sensitive, and other situations in which goodwill may be adversely affected.

## References to People

People are the most interesting creatures on earth. Refer to people, therefore, by using well-chosen nouns and pronouns.

Common nouns such as banker, president, secretary, and assistant can be used liberally. By the same token, the personal pronouns *he, she, they, I, you, we,* and so on can be used to add interest and conversational tone to messages. Frequently, readability of written messages can be improved by including proper names—Mr. Booth, Mary Harris, Miss Robbins, for example.

Do you often use the name of the person with whom you are talking? If you do, use the reader's name in a letter or a memorandum just as you use it when talking. Excessive use of a person's name (especially a person who is not a close friend), though, can lead the listener or reader to think you are insincere and are trying to use flattery or possibly even trickery to accomplish a selfish objective.

NEVER use the reader's name in the first sentence of a letter when you use a salutation. By reading aloud the following illustration, you can readily recognize the inappropriateness of this practice: "Dear Mr. Jackson: I congratulate you, Mr. Jackson, on the success of your end-of-the-year sale."

If you seldom use people's names when talking with them, avoid using their names in the body of a letter or a memorandum. To do so would make your message sound unnatural rather than conversational.

Whether or not you use a person's name frequently in conversation, do use the reader's name in the salutation of a letter!

**Contemporary Expressions**

Some people hesitate to change their preferences for types of clothing. They become accustomed to wearing certain styles, and they resist changes that are necessary for them to dress fashionably. Also, some people become set in their ways of transmitting business messages and decline to update their style of expressing ideas. Some writers continue to use outdated writing styles only because they are not aware of better ways of writing.

Compare the following two columns (*outdated* and *up-to-date*) of frequently used business expressions. As you can see, the expressions in the *up-to-date* column are better for conversational tone. They are clear, short, and tactful.

| Outdated | Up-to-Date |
|---|---|
| Enclosed is | Here is |
| Enclosed herewith | Here is |
| Due to the fact that | Because *or* Since |
| Enclosed please find . . . | . . . is enclosed |
| Attached you will find . . . | . . . is attached |
| advise *or* inform | tell |
| self-addressed envelope | addressed envelope |
| to be of service to you *or* to be of assistance to you | to help you |
| at the present time | now |
| Respectfully yours *or* Yours truly | Sincerely *or* Cordially |
| can be found on page 6 | is on page 6 |

The *up-to-date* expressions are more effective; and they save time for the dictator, the transcriber, and the reader. These lists are by no means exhaustive. They merely represent the numerous frequently used business expressions that affect the impression writers make on the readers of their messages. What type of impression do you want to make?

## Word Choice

Properly chosen words help the reader or listener to interpret accurately the ideas, the opinions, the feelings, and the information you wish to convey. They help you to develop the tone you want the letter, the memorandum, the report, or the oral presentation to have. When choosing words, consider these factors:

1.   The receiver's vocabulary

2.   Your personality

3.   Preciseness of meaning

4.   Appealing words

5.   Use of verbs

**Receiver's vocabulary.**   The reason for sending a message is to convey information, ideas, opinions, or feelings. You attempt to speak or write *so clearly that your message cannot be misunderstood*, and you want the receiver to be favorably impressed by the message. Therefore, use only those words you believe the receiver will readily understand. A listener or reader who has to ponder the meaning of a word or has to consult a dictionary to determine its meaning focuses attention on that particular word rather than on the content of the message. Avoid using any word that would divert a receiver's attention from the message content.

Technical or specialized words not familiar to the receivers require them to spend time interpreting the message rather than listening to or reading it easily and taking quickly the steps you want them to take.

Occasionally, specialized, technical words should be used. For example, a physician communicating with another person in the medical profession should use medical terms. By using this terminology, the sender achieves clarity of expression and maintains the natural tone of a conversation the two might have. A physician communicating with someone outside the medical profession, however, should not use medical terms the receiver does not readily understand. The people in other fields—engineering, mathematics, and so on—should apply these same guidelines for using technical terms.

In choosing words, consider the receiver. Use specialized terms and other words that help you and your listener or reader to communicate clearly and easily. Remember, too, that you can use simple words and still maintain the respect of the message receiver. Big ideas are much more important than big words.

**Your personality.**    Even though you have characteristics that are common to all people, you are different in some respects from all others. No two people look exactly alike. No two people do or say the same things in the same ways under identical circumstances. When you attempt to communicate through the medium of words—in writing as well as in speaking—choose words that best fit *your* personality.

A young man who had driven with his family to New York City from a distant state had an opportunity to participate in a live TV show. In rehearsing for that show, the young man was asked among other questions, "How was your drive to New York?" He was instructed to answer, "It was lovely." He refused, even after considerable prompting, to say his trip was lovely. He said he never used this word, it did not fit his personality, and his friends who would see the show would realize he was not being himself. He was then permitted to choose another adjective to describe his enjoyable drive to New York City.

Many words that can be used naturally by some people cannot be used by others. Continue building your vocabulary, but study the words you learn and decide whether they can be adapted to your personality. Use the same vocabulary for writing that you use for talking.

**Preciseness of meaning.**    To transmit a message so clearly that it cannot be misunderstood, you have to choose words that express precisely the idea you wish to convey. Saying *"There are* slightly more than 24,000 people in Laramie, Wyoming" is less exacting than "Slightly more than 24,000 people *reside* in Laramie,

Wyoming." Incidentally, a sentence beginning with *There* is usually wordy and less precise than if it begins with another word. Avoid, therefore, beginning a sentence with *There is*, *There are*, *There was*, *There were*, and so on.

Instead of saying "We look forward to *serving* you again," substitute a word that states specifically the type of service or product you look forward to supplying. Here are examples:

> We look forward to providing bimonthly service for your factory generators.

> We look forward to sending you another shipment of building materials.

Instead of saying "The manager *went* to New York yesterday," say "The manager *flew* to New York yesterday."

Countless other words can be substituted to give the precise meaning you want your written messages to convey.

**Appealing words.**   The words you use can have a psychological effect on the receivers of your messages. Combine psychology with grammar and communication mechanics, therefore, to help get favorable reaction to your messages. Knowing the purpose of a message and studying the receivers will help you to decide which words to use. Choose words you believe will appeal (consciously or subconsciously) to your listeners or readers.

Here is a list of words that appeal to many people:

| | | |
|---|---|---|
| achieve | crisp | excel |
| clear | eager | sharpen |
| competent | enhance | success |
| complimentary | energetic | tact |
| confident | enthusiastic | win |

Will this brief list help you to choose other words you can use to enhance the effectiveness of your business messages? Adding life and interest to your messages will pay rich dividends.

**Use of verbs.**   People like action. They like to observe others acting (they like to attend football games and other sports events) and to participate in activities (dance, swim, and so on). They also enjoy reading and hearing about action. Therefore, make ample use of verbs (words that express action or a state of being) to add to the zest and interest of your messages.

The verbs that express action are stronger than those that express a state of being, but often the verbs that express a state of being are needed. Here are examples:

The manager *will be* in his office from 9 a.m. until I p.m. tomorrow.

The maintenance cost for this computer *is* low.

Unless a verb that expresses a state of being is needed, do not use it. These examples are worth studying:

| Instead of Saying | Say |
| --- | --- |
| John is working in Seattle. | John works in Seattle. |
| I will be looking forward to hearing from you. | I look forward to hearing from you. |
| Lisa had been wishing she could buy the car. | Lisa had wished she could buy the car. |

Verbs in active voice (the subject of the verb does the acting) are preferred in most instances over the passive voice (the subject of the verb receives the action). Not only are the sentences that are written in active voice more interesting, but also they are shorter in most cases. Here are examples:

| Passive Voice | Active Voice |
|---|---|
| The three letters were dictated by the personnel manager. | The personnel manager dictated the three letters. |
| The suggestions were accepted by the committee. | The committee accepted the suggestions. |

Verbs that could be used effectively are often hidden in derivatives. Words ending with *ment* and *tion* are examples.

| Hidden | Verb |
|---|---|
| Accomplishment of their objective required teamwork | Accomplishing their objective required teamwork. |
| Completion of the task required two hours. | Completing the task required two hours. |
| A description of the table is on page 4. | The table is described on page 4. |

Using a verb instead of a derivative strengthens the sentence and also shortens it. A short sentence is superior to a long one, provided the short sentence is as courteous, as interesting, and as nearly complete and accurate as the longer one.

Use verbs to eliminate such weak, overused expressions as "at your earliest convenience" and "as soon as possible." Instead, use "as soon as you can." By substituting "as soon as you can," you improve your message in four ways:

1.  Eliminate the trite expression.

2.  Include a verb—*can.*

3.   Use the pronoun *you*, which may help project the "you at-
     titude."

4.   Use a shorter expression—more words, but fewer syllables.

**Courtesy Expressions**

   Courtesy contributes to success in business. Gestures, facial expressions, tone of voice, and choice of words help to portray
courtesy in oral communication; but only words can express
courtesy in a written message. Choose words carefully and use
them in the proper places.
   "Thank you," "please," "grateful," and "appreciate" are
courtesy expressions frequently used in business messages. Even
when ordering an item you know the supplier is eager to sell,
"Please send . . . ." seems considerably more courteous than does
"Send . . . ." Men and women in prestigious positions know the
value of using "courtesy words," and they use them freely. They
know, however, that excessive use of these expressions leads the
receivers to believe the speaker or writer is insincere and is using
flattery or perhaps trickery or is "talking down" to them. A
listener or reader who suspects the sender has used courtesy expressions for any of these purposes may doubt the sender's sincerity.
Therefore, the effectiveness of the message may be nil.
   Excessive use of courtesy expressions can also make the listener
or reader think the sender has limited self-respect or backbone.
The person who can be firm yet tactful, diplomatic, and open-
minded possesses the strong character that wins friends and com-
mands respect.
   Many well-intentioned writers spoil what would otherwise be a
good business message by poor usage of courtesy remarks. Some
of these writers append a terse "Thank you" to the ends of their
letters or memorandums when nothing has been done for which
the readers should be thanked. This ending for a message is poor.
The ending "Thank you" is often used for a letter or a memorandum asking a favor. This usage is a major violation of good letter-
writing guidelines. Never thank people before they grant a favor.
   A poorer ending than "Thank you" that is used frequently is
"Thank you in advance." And one of the poorest possible endings

is the following sentence fragment or a variation of it: "Thanking you in advance, I am." This poorest-of-all endings violates these four basic rules for writing a good business message.

1. Write complete sentences.

2. Thank a person for a favor only *after* the favor is granted.

3. Only in very rare instances end a letter or a memorandum with a sentence beginning with a participle.

4. Eliminate trite expressions.

Here are three of the numerous good endings that tell the reader you will appreciate compliance with a request:

Your returning the completed form will be appreciated.

I will be grateful for your help in locating the missing manuscript.

We will appreciate your suggestions.

Your personality, your style of expression, and other sentences in the message help you to express gratitude at the ends of requests for favors.

**Conciseness**

Conciseness—a desirable characteristic of business letters, memorandums, reports, and oral presentations—differs from brevity. Brevity usually means incomplete. A brief message includes only the most significant points. Conciseness means all essential elements are covered adequately without excess words. Concise speaking or writing is direct and forceful, and it should be tactful. Study these examples:

| Wordy | Concise |
|---|---|
| The study was made for the purpose of determining . . . . | The study was made to determine . . . . |
| I am looking forward to . . . . | I look forward to . . . . |
| They are making plans to . . . . | They are planning to . . . . or They plan to . . . . |
| They learned that two programs are in existence. | They learned that two programs exist. |
| Twenty people were in attendance at the meeting. | Twenty people attended the meeting. |
| This is a subject that . . . . | This subject . . . . |
| Their office is located on Sixth Avenue. | Their office is on Sixth Avenue. |
| You will be able . . . . | You can . . . . |
| In the event that . . . . | If . . . . |
| . . . in an easy manner. | . . . easily. |
| In the near future . . . . | Soon . . . . |

   To communicate tactfully and specifically, you sometimes have to use more words than are essential for transmitting the general information. In these situations, using the extra words to create the desired impression is worthwhile. Study the contrasting examples in these two columns:

| Weak | Specific and Tactful |
|---|---|
| Thank you for your recent letter. | Thank you for writing to me on October 18. |
| We are glad to serve you. | We are glad to ship the No. 10 envelopes to you. |
| We appreciate the opportunity to serve you. | We appreciate the opportunity to clean and adjust the machines in your factory. |
| We will ship your order promptly. | We will ship the stationery the day we receive your order. |
| We shipped your order today. | We shipped your two Model 8 electric typewriters by UPS this morning. |

Words that add to the smoothness or readability of sentences can be justified, too. For example, a sentence flows more smoothly when a date is preceded by a preposition or an adjective, as in these examples:

| Acceptable | Preferred |
|---|---|
| The group met Tuesday. | The group met *on* Tuesday. |
| The letter was mailed Friday. | The letter was mailed *on* Friday. |

Do not use the telegraphic style of writing that is exemplified in the following list.

Received casters from factory today. Shipping same tomorrow.

Will attend meeting in Boston January 18.

Contacted Mike this morning. He will mail contract Tuesday.

Using *former* and *latter* is false economy of words. Sometimes using one of these words saves time for the writer, but it requires unnecessary time for the reader. The reader almost always has to reread at least one sentence, and often a whole paragraph, to recall the idea to which *former* or *latter* refers.

Do not begin written sentences with the indefinite pronouns *this*, *these*, *that*, *those*, and *such*. Often the reader has to reread the preceding sentence to identify the specific idea to which the indefinite pronoun refers. These five words are good sentence beginnings, however, when they function as adjectives. Here are examples:

| Indefinite Pronoun | Adjective |
| --- | --- |
| *This* is the one you should read. | *This* pamphlet is the one you should read. |
| *Those* have been recorded. | *Those* receipts have been recorded. |
| *Such* should not be filed. | *Such* letters should not be filed. |

Avoid beginning a sentence with *it*. Beginning a sentence with *it* adds unnecessary length, as in these illustrations:

| Instead of Saying | Say |
| --- | --- |
| It is the purpose of this meeting to elect officers for next year. | The purpose of this meeting is to elect officers for next year. |
| It was assumed the budget would be approved. | They assumed the budget would be approved. |
| It was a pleasure talking with you. | Talking with you was a pleasure. |

The guidelines to which the examples in this section pertain merit careful study. Do practice word economy; but do not hesitate to add length when the addition improves the quality of a letter, a memorandum, a report, or an oral presentation.

## POSITIVE AND SPECIFIC STATEMENTS

Good communicators know that positive, specific statements enhance the effectiveness of business messages.

### Positive

The power of positive thinking is great indeed. Most people think positively and are more favorably impressed by positive words or comments than by negative words or comments. When a good rapport exists between two persons, one has a tendency to do what the other suggests. A writer who wishes to call attention to a specific item in a catalog, a pamphlet, or any other publication may profitably write "Turn to page 4 and read the description of the . . . ." The reader is more likely to read the description than if the writer used the weak, worn-out wording "A description of the . . . can be found on page 4."

*Find* and *found*, which are good words when referring to research data or items that have been lost, are frequently misused. Such expressions as "can be found" and "you will find" are seldom effective. People who are intelligent enough to comprehend your message are intelligent enough to *find* whatever you call their attention to, provided it is in the proper place.

Just as the positive suggestion "Turn to page . . . ." encourages the reader to turn to that page, the phrase *why not* tends to make the reader think of reasons for not doing whatever is suggested. Avoid, therefore, using *why not* when suggesting that someone take positive action. Also, avoid using negative words such as *sorry*, *regret*, and *unfortunately*. As is true with other negatives, though, occasionally—but seldom—there are times when these words can be used advantageously.

Positive expressions are usually shorter than negative expressions. They can be understood more easily, and they have greater appeal. Compare the expressions in these two columns:

| Negative | Positive |
|---|---|
| why not come in to see us | come in to see us |
| do not forget the meeting | remember the meeting |
| please do not hesitate to write us | please write us |

Like the other examples in this book, this list is representative rather than exhaustive.

Use positive words and statements in most instances. An occasional negative expression does, however, attract the desired attention or provide the change of pace needed to enhance the interest quality of a message.

## Specific

If you have thought about a situation sufficiently to determine the real purpose of the message—letter, memorandum, report, or oral presentation—you are getting ready to convey, you should be able to use words and statements that are specific. Specificity helps to make a good impression on the receivers. They know that only those people who can think clearly can express their ideas specifically. Conversely, they know that vague or indefinite words or expressions in a business message indicate that the speaker or writer was poorly prepared for it. Vagueness or rambling detracts from the effectiveness of a business message almost as much as does poor grammar. The examples in the following two columns are presented to help you convey messages specifically.

|          Vague           |          Specific          |
| ------------------------ | -------------------------- |
| your recent letter       | your letter of September 2 |
| I appreciate your contacting me. | I appreciate your writing me. or I appreciate your calling me. |
| Thank you for your inquiry | Thank you for your letter. or Thank you for writing. |
| as soon as possible      | by October 8               |
| under separate cover     | by parcel post             |
| in the near future       | before July 1              |

When you want a reader of your message to do something promptly, you may specify the date by which you want it done. Saying an action is to be taken within two weeks is better than saying it is to be taken "as soon as possible" or "at your earliest convenience." But because the reader may not know whether you mean two weeks from the date the letter was written or two weeks from the date it was received, specifying a date such as "by November 12" would be even better.

Keep these points in mind when specifying a date on which something is to be done:

1.  If you specify a date that is too far in the future, the reader may lay your request aside with the thought that there is plenty of time and may then forget to respond.

2.  If you specify a date that is too close at hand, the reader may not have an opportunity to comply by that particular time and would therefore disregard your request. The reader may be out of town when your request arrives and therefore would not be aware of the request before the date you specified.

On some occasions specifying a date is impossible, or at least it is not feasible. In those cases "as soon as you can" is as nearly specific as you can write. Use specifics almost always; however, just as negative words or statements are occasionally superior to positive words or statements, generalities are occasionally better than specifics. Some occasions for which generalities are recommended are discussed in Chapter 7.

## SENTENCES

Even though much intelligent conversation—personal and business— consists of sentence fragments, use complete sentences when communicating in writing. Write sentences that are clear, correct, and concise.

"Variety is the spice of life." Variety in sentence structure—length and type—adds to the interest and readability of a business message.

### Length

Sentence length depends somewhat on the expression style of the message sender. Some people compose rather long sentences that are clear and easy to comprehend, yet other people use shorter sentences. Length alone is not a good criterion for judging sentence quality. Variety of written sentence length contributes to the interest, the readability, and the overall effectiveness of a message. Some short, some medium, and some rather long sentences are desirable in many business letters, memorandums, and reports. The average length of the sentences should be from thirteen to nineteen words. Certainly, some sentences should be shorter than average; and others should be longer. Restricting sentence lengths to within the thirteen-to-nineteen-word range would be as senseless as placing well-adjusted executives in straightjackets when they enter their offices each day.

When considering average sentence length, remember the little old lady who could not swim but thought she could safely wade across a river. She was 5 feet 2 inches tall, and the river had an average depth of only 4 feet. She drowned.

As a river has shallow areas and deep areas, most well-written business messages have short sentences and long ones.

Consider the background of the listener or reader. When sending a message to a poorly educated person, use shorter sentences than when communicating with a person who is well educated on the particular subject the message covers. Regardless of the receiver's background and the knowledge of the subject, you can use sentence length to emphasize any specific point. In messages that have several long sentences, a very short sentence can be used to emphasize a point. In other messages a longer-than-average sentence emphasizes an idea or thought. Vary the lengths, as well as the types, of sentences.

### Type

Variety in sentence types is just as important as variety in lengths. While in short messages there is little need for variety in sentence types, many business messages are sufficiently long to merit the use of variety of sentence types—simple, compound, complex, and compound-complex—to make those messages interesting and effective. A majority of the sentences in effective messages are simple.

For a review of the four types of sentences, turn to the reference section of this book.

### TRANSITION

Once you have chosen words carefully and have arranged them into well-constructed sentences, you need to make certain that you have good transition from one idea to the next. Good transition can be achieved by numerous ways. Some effective ways—which are illustrated in the next few paragraphs—are sentence structure, pronouns, conjunctions, and conjunctive adverbs.

### Sentence Structure

The ideas in the following two simple sentences could be joined in various ways:

> The manager was late in arriving at his office this morning. The electrical service was interrupted at his apartment last night.

One way to join these ideas with good transition is to use a complex sentence:

> Because the electrical service was interrupted at the manager's apartment last night, he was late in arriving at his office this morning.

## Pronouns

Pronouns oftens serve as good transition, as in these examples:

> The employees like the new recreation center. *They* use it often.

> Steve returned from a two-week vacation last night. *He* feels refreshed and is eager to go to work again tomorrow.

## Conjunctions

Conjunctions also serve often to join thoughts naturally, as in these examples:

> The vice-president would like to speak to your group on October 8, *but* he has another commitment that day.

> She received your first order on Wednesday afternoon, *and* she received your second one this morning.

> He will write to you on Thursday, *or* he will talk with you on the telephone on Saturday.

## Conjunctive Adverbs

Conjunctive adverbs can be used effectively to show the relationship you wish to show for two clauses or sentences. Observe the use of a conjunctive adverb as a time connector in each of the following sentences:

> The administrative assistant had to wait for the questionnaires to be returned; *meanwhile*, he wrote the computer program for analyzing the responses.

> Mike liked Melba's joke about the stone-faced computer; *thereafter*, he referred to the computer as the "stone face."

The conjunctive adverbs in the next sentences express similarity:

> Joan completed the mailing list this morning; *likewise*, Robert brought the charge-customer list up to date.
>
> Carl sends monthly payments on the lot he bought last summer; *similarly*, Brent makes monthly payments on a car.

The conjunctive adverbs in the following sentences serve as cause-and-effect connectors:

> The wholesaler's supply of paper was exhausted; *consequently*, he could not send our stationery when he intended to send it.
>
> We received your order before our original supply had been used; we could, *therefore*, send your merchandise immediately.

The conjunctive adverbs in the following sentences serve as contrast connectors:

> Margaret B. Leatherwood has had only two years' experience in that type of work; *nevertheless*, she is the best-qualified applicant for the job.
>
> Tim Atkins has taken several college courses that relate specifically to this type of work; *on the other hand*, he has had no practical work experience.

Transitional words such as those in the preceding illustrations can be used at the beginning of new sentences as well as within sentences. Here are examples:

> Samuel E. Ledbetter has not completed the work for a college degree. *For that reason*, we did not invite him to come for an interview.
>
> Our computer is being repaired. *Therefore*, we must wait until tomorrow to process the questionnaire responses.

Many other words can be used within or at the beginning of a sentence to provide good transition.

Transition is an important aspect of a good style of expression. Usually, thoughts expressed in well-constructed sentences—even the short simple ones—flow smoothly from one to the other in carefully planned paragraphs.

## PARAGRAPHS

A paragraph consists of one or more statements about a major idea or topic.

Generally, a paragraph is introduced with a topic sentence, which presents the major idea. The topic sentence can be, however, at the end or at any other place in the paragraph. In business letters and memorandums, it is best to have the topic sentence first. Then the following sentences support the main idea by giving evidence or by giving explanations. In other words, the added statements develop the major idea.

Short paragraphs are easy to read. Because the beginning of a letter or a memorandum is the most important part and the ending is the second most important part, write short (four or fewer typewritten lines) first and last paragraphs of most multiple-paragraph business messages. The other paragraphs should not exceed eight to ten typewritten lines. If the idea cannot be developed in a paragraph of this length, use a good breaking point to start another paragraph.

Be sure that every sentence in the paragraph follows the preceding one in logical meaning or that it introduces the next sentence.

Letters, memorandums, and reports have a more attractive appearance when the length of paragraphs is varied. Write some longer paragraphs to develop an idea fully, and write some shorter paragraphs for special emphasis. Varying the length of paragraphs helps to create interest and to improve the readability of business messages.

## MECHANICS

The expression style suggestions in this chapter can be used effectively only when the mechanical details are correct. Correct spelling, punctuation, word choice, and sentence structure are essential to achieve competency in writing business letters, memorandums, and reports. A dictionary, a thesaurus, and a good English handbook should be used often by anyone who wants to prepare business messages of good quality.

Some of the mechanical details—spelling, punctuation, expression of numbers, and so on—are presented in the reference section of this book. Refer to that section for special help.

More suggestions for improving your writing style are presented in other chapters of this book. The suggestions for improving writing style apply to oral communication also.

## QUESTIONS FOR DISCUSSION

1. What are some exceptions to the guideline "write the way you talk"?

2. What are some idiomatic expressions you hear frequently?

3. What is meant by "contemporary expressions"?

4. How can you improve your vocabulary?

## EXERCISES

Improve the following sentences.

1. Our organization will be glad to make the adjustments you requested in your recent letter.

2. We shall be happy to supply your company with automotive parts.

3.  Am grateful for your help in the completion of the writing project.

4.  Will you please give our representative an opportunity to give you a demonstration of our company's sanding machine?

5.  A description of the motor can be found on page 4 of our catalog.

6.  Due to the fact that the form must be returned before October 16, I am enclosing herewith a self-addressed envelope for your use.

7.  In order to be of further assistance to you, I will come to your office in the near future.

8.  Enclosed you will find a set of special instructions.

9.  We look forward to an opportunity to be of service to you.

10. There are 227,000 people in Louisville.

11. The sale was made by the representative.

12. Organization of the group can be accomplished during the month of October.

13. I shall appreciate your sending the merchandise as soon as possible.

14. The book you ordered has been mailed under separate cover.

15. Your order was shipped this morning.

16. You can complete this assignment in a short period of time.

17. Why not visit our store during our special sale, which begins on October 21.

18. Please do not hesitate to get in touch with me.

19. It is a pleasure to visit you again.

20. Twenty-five people were in attendance at the meeting.

## PROBLEMS

1.   Rewrite the following letter:

> Mr. Hugh M. Stults, Manager, Hayes Manufacturing Company, 1142 Bethlehem Road, Wyndotte, PA 00632
>
> Dear Mr. Stults:
>
> Enclosed is a copy of our operations report for the month of July. You asked, when you telephoned me last week, that this report be sent to you before Monday of next week. This report, which is thirty-four pages in length, was written by Edith Downs and Wayne E. Combs.
>
> I believe that you will be especially interested in reading a description of the results we obtained by instituting the new procedures for handling the materials in the warehouse. You will find those results described on page 17.
>
> It is my opinion that Miss Downs and Mr. Combs have done a fine job of the preparation of this report. If, however, you have any questions concerning the contents of this report, please do not hesitate to contact me.
>
> Cordially, Helen S. Camp, Production Manager, Enclosure

2.   Rewrite the following letter:

> Mrs. Ada M. Hatfield, 1221 Stoneview Road, Vinona, WI 54876
>
> Dear Mrs. Hatfield:
>
> I want to take this opportunity to thank you for calling my attention to the defect in the carrying case for the portable typewriter that we sent to you last Monday. You should receive a replacement for it in the near future. We wrote to our supplier under the date of May 8 and requested that a new case be mailed to you as soon as possible to replace the defective case that you received.
>
> Ordinarily, we would have another case in stock; but due to the fact that this particular typewriter has been so popular, our supply is depleted at the present time.
>
> We are confident you will be pleased with your portable typewriter.
>
> Cordially, Niles F. Williams, Order Department Manager

**3.** Rewrite the following letter:

Ms. Judy L. Rothchild, Assistant Manager, Walls-Hillis Department Store, P.O. Box 1034, Hastings, NV 89417

Dear Ms. Rothchild:

In reference to your letter of April 9, I am glad to tell you that we would be glad to have you visit our factory on May 14, the date you specified. Kindly tell us how many salesclerks you plan to bring with you.

We have several employees who conduct tours of our factory, but we have asked Ms. Amy Harrell to serve as your hostess and to conduct your tour that day. You and your employees will be guests of ours for lunch.

We look forward to your visit with us on May 14.

Cordially, Kenneth L. Edwards, Public Relations Director

# PART TWO

# LETTERS

# Chapter 3

# Letter-Writing Guidelines

Communicating can be easy when the process involves the oral exchange of words and such common symbols as smiles, frowns, and handshakes that achieve immediate responses. The communication process becomes rather complex, though, when the only medium is written words with several days passing between sending a message and receiving a response.

Because business transactions are carried on over long distances, a large portion of business communication must be in writing. Business employees have to decide whether to send a message. Often, this decision is easy to make; for example, a letter is received containing a request for a reply. Some letters must be written to confirm agreements that were expressed orally. Other letter-writing decisions that are easy to make involve ordering merchandise and inquiring about a product, as well as numerous similar situations. Letters such as these can be written easily and rapidly.

Letters about a delicate problem in human relations require a high degree of skill and finesse. No formula can be devised for writing them. Some guidelines, however, can be adapted to the specific situations with which you are working. A careful study of the following guidelines will help you to write good business letters of all kinds:

1.  Write promptly.

2.  Determine the purpose of the letter.

3.  Begin with good news.

4.  Omit obvious statements.

5.  Subordinate the telling of information you believe the reader already knows.

6.  Tell *first* what you *can* do when you cannot do what the reader wants you to do.

7.  Write the way you talk.

8.  Economize on words.

9.  Say "thank you" only *after* something has been done.

10.  End with something pleasant and specific.

These guidelines are discussed as they apply to numerous circumstances described in this book.

**Write promptly.**   As revealed in the following two stories, promptness in writing letters is important. A young woman sent letters to two companies to inquire about a moderately expensive item she wanted to purchase. One company replied immediately; the other waited about a week to reply. The first company to reply quoted a slightly higher price than did the second one. Because the young woman was eager to receive the item, she sent the order to the company that replied first to her letter.

An organization had a position to be filled, and only two people applied. The applicants were equally well qualified for the job. One applied on the day the vacancy was announced; the other waited several days to apply. The one who applied immediately received attention first; and although the second applicant's qualifications were equal to the first one's, the first applicant was hired.

Ordinarily, a letter calling for a reply should be answered within twenty-four hours from the time of its receipt. Obviously, such promptness is not always feasible. For example, the information needed for a reply may not be available for three days. In most such instances waiting three days would be appropriate. If, though, the information needed will not be available for a longer time (perhaps two weeks), a short letter should be written telling the date on which the desired information will be sent.

Promptness in writing helps people in business to compete efficiently and to make the favorable, businesslike impression needed for the greatest degree of success. A thorough understanding and appreciation of the guidelines discussed in this chapter will help you to write good letters; and, therefore, you will want to write them promptly. Remember, a person who writes promptly has an advantage over one who does not.

**Determine the purpose of the letter.** Ask yourself, "Why am I writing this letter?" Keeping in mind the specific purpose or purposes of a letter helps you to present the contents clearly, concisely,and effectively.

When writing to thank someone for something that has been done, begin with a note of gratitude. The following two sentences are examples:

> Thank you for sending me the two chairs.

> I appreciate your sending me the two chairs.

When requesting information, determine the specific questions you wish to have answered. State the questions clearly and arrange them in a logical order. You may tabulate them, as in this example:

> Please answer these three questions for me:
>
> 1.  How many people do you employ?
>
> 2.  With what company do you have a health insurance plan for your employees?
>
> 3.  What portion of the health insurance premium do the employees pay?

There are, of course, other ways to begin a letter requesting information. In some cases it is wise to give the reasons for the request and then ask for the specific information you desire.

Many letters have more than one purpose. For example, you may wish to thank the reader for a favor and to send materials you were requested to send. Before beginning to write a letter that has more than one purpose, decide the order in which you will arrange the contents. Usually, the item of greatest interest to the reader should be written first. Other factors to be considered are presented later in this book.

By all means, know the purpose for writing before you attempt to write a letter of any type.

**Begin with good news.**   Most letters can contain some good news. Begin with good news when you can. When you know the reader wants to know something you can tell, tell it first. The reader, when seeing the envelope containing a reply to a letter, thinks about the type of information that was requested. By starting your letter with that information, the reader will be pleased and will likely read the rest of the letter with a receptive attitude.

Suppose someone invites you to speak to a group and you accept the invitation. Begin your letter by accepting and then add anything you wish to include, as in this example:

> Yes, I will speak to your first-line supervisors at 9 a.m. on October 9.
>
> Can the room in which the group will meet be darkened so that I can use an opaque projector effectively? I want to show some illustrations that help to clarify the points you mentioned in your letter of July 31.

Do not waste words in getting started. Participial beginnings and prepositional phrase beginnings such as these are too slow and wordy:

> Referring to your letter . . . .
>
> Concerning our agreement . . . .
>
> Pursuant to your request . . . .

In reply to your letter . . . .

In reference to your inquiry . . . .

In regard to your . . . .

The frequently used beginning "Thank you for . . . ." is *ineffec-tive* for most letters. Many writers use this beginning because of habit or because they do not know how to apply letter-writing guidelines to their tasks. "Thank you . . . ." is a good beginning for only those letters that are written for the primary purpose of *thanking* the reader for a favor. Instead of thanking a reader for sending you an order, begin by saying you have sent the merchandise and *then* include the "thank you," as in this illustration:

We shipped two green secretarial chairs to you by Kenland Freight Lines this morning. Thank you for sending us the order.

Not every letter can contain good news. Suggestions for writing that type of letter are in Chapter 9, "Disappointing News."

Remember, the *beginning* is the most important part of a letter. Make it good.

**Omit obvious statements.**    Omit such obvious statements as these:

I have received your letter.

I should like to take this opportunity to write you about our high-speed drill.

You will find the enclosed copy of the brochure you requested.

Please find the enclosed check for $28.

If your reply is well written, obviously you have received the reader's letter. Not only is such an expression as "I have received your letter" absurd, it is also a time-wasting element for the dictator, the transcriber, and the reader.

When you are writing about a high-speed drill or anything else, you are obviously taking the opportunity.

When you are writing about a high-speed drill or anything else, you are obviously taking the opportunity.

A person who is intelligent enough to read your letter is also intelligent enough to find any properly enclosed item. Do not risk embarrassing yourself and insulting the reader by asking the reader to "Please find the enclosed . . . ." Do, however, *refer* to an enclosure.This reference can be very important for records. For example, an enclosed check is not filed with the letter. Sometime later the files may be consulted to determine when the check was mailed.

Instead of writing "Please find the enclosed check for $28," write "A check for $28 is enclosed," "I am enclosing a check for $28," or some other sentence that has a conversational tone.

Tell only those facts that are not obvious to the reader.

**Subordinate the telling of information you believe the reader already knows.**  Busy people make many assignments and requests, and they cannot be expected to remember the exact details—dates, mediums of requesting or assigning, persons to whom requests or assignments were made, or the procedures used in making the requests or assignments. A person complying with a request or completing an assignment does the reader a favor by referring to pertinent details. These references, however, are to be subordinated. Here are examples of poor ways and good ways to tell readers what they already know:

| *Poor* | *Good* |
|---|---|
| You wrote to me on May 6 and asked me to make a list of our professional journals. I am enclosing that list. | Here is the list of our professional journals you asked for in your letter of May 6. |
| When you wrote to me on May 6, you asked me to make a list of our professional journals. That list is enclosed. | The list of professional journals you asked for in your letter of May 6 is enclosed. |

The statements in the second column are courteous, businesslike ways of referring to requests.

Although busy people cannot be expected to remember all details of assignments and requests, some people who do remember almost all details take pride in remembering. They would dislike intensely being told (unless the telling were subordinated) the details they remember. Occasionally, however, those people forget specific items. They would be disturbed if the details they had forgotten were not included in your letters. Do, therefore, include all pertinent details in your letters; but when you tell readers something they already know, subordinate the telling.

**Tell _first_ what you _can_ do when you cannot do what the reader wants you to do.**   Sometimes you must say NO. Always catering to the whims of individuals is not expected. When you must decline a request but can grant another favor (and often you can), begin by mentioning what you _can_ do for the reader. The thing you can do will depend, of course, on the situation about which you are writing. You may offer to send a substitute, you may offer to provide a service at some time other than the date for which the service is requested, or you may recommend another source for the desired product or service. Study these examples:

| _Instead of Saying_ | _Say_ |
| --- | --- |
| Our stock of No. 26 tape recorders has been depleted. | We can send you six No. 32 tape recorders the day we receive your approval to send them. |
| I have another engagement on November 1; therefore, I cannot discuss office furniture with your employees that day. | I could discuss office furniture with your employees on November 9. |
| We do not stock the pottery you requested in your letter of June 16. | Cottage Furnishings, Inc., in Memphis can probably send you the pottery you requested in your letter of June 16. |

Explain early in your letter the reason for not complying with the request. If you precede that explanation with a cordial offer to do something else worthwhile for the reader, the reader will more readily accept your explanation without the loss of goodwill.

Telling the reader *first* what you *can* do is extremely important. This guideline is applied in later chapters of this book.

**Write the way you talk.**   With a few minor exceptions, the wording of your letter should be the same as that of a message you would send orally. A letter should parallel the writer's oral comments in tone, vocabulary, and organization. Here, however, are three exceptions to this practice of writing the way you talk:

1. Since you have an opportunity to edit what you write, your written sentences should be constructed more precisely. Fragments should be avoided even though they are acceptable in oral communication. There are, however, some fragments such as *Congratulations*, *Happy Holidays*, and *Good Luck* that are acceptable.

2. Traditionally, most letters contain a salutation (Dear Ms. Gray, Dear Mr. Carmichael, and so on) and a complimentary close (Cordially yours, Sincerely, and so on). These letter parts perform the same function as do oral greetings and parting remarks.

   A person who would say "Dear Mr. Hayes" instead of saying something such as "Good Morning" or "How do you do?" when starting a conversation would be considered eccentric. A person would seem to be equally odd by using "Sincerely yours" or another familiar letter ending instead of "Goodbye," "So long," "See you later," or another frequently used parting remark when leaving the presence of another person.

   Just as tradition binds us to some degree in fashions for the clothing we wear and the automobiles we drive, tradition governs to some extent the mechanics of business letters.

3. When communicating orally, you have gestures, tone of voice, facial expressions, and immediate responses to help in transmitting ideas. Because words carry greater weight as a

vehicle in written communication and because the response is delayed, you must exercise more care in choosing words and in constructing sentences and paragraphs than when communicating orally.

**Economize on words.**   A letter should be long enough to be courteous, to cover the topic adequately, and to be worded interestingly. A concise, well-written letter may very well be longer than one full page; but any word that does not contribute to good quality should be omitted. Length is not a good criterion for judging the quality of a letter.

Excess words not only lessen the effectiveness of a letter, but they also waste time for the dictator, the transcriber, and the reader. Exclude, therefore, redundancies and wordy phrases from all messages. Examples of redundancies and wordy phrases with suggestions for improving them follow:

| *Instead of Saying* | *Say* |
| --- | --- |
| subsequent to | after |
| prior to | before |
| a long period of time | a long time *or* a long period |
| for the purpose of selecting | to select *or* for selecting |
| can be found on page 6 | is on page 6 |
| a check in the amount of $5 | a $5 check *or* a check for $5 |
| due to the fact that | because |
| I should like to order | please send |
| for the month of October | for October |
| we are able | we can |
| inasmuch as | since *or* because |
| in order to | to |
| . . . she is a person who is well qualified . . . . | . . . she is well qualified . . . . |

**Say "thank you" only after something has been done.** "Thank you" is a courteous expression to use in business letters, but only at appropriate times. Thank people *after*—NEVER *before*—they do something. Many well-intentioned letter writers request that certain products be shipped or that certain favors be granted and then end their letters with "Thank you." Those writers are being presumptuous. They are presuming that the request will be granted, yet it may not be granted. This ending may also make the reader feel pressured.

To let the reader know you will appreciate a compliance with your request, end your letter with a statement such as these:

> Your sending the package by railway express before June 30 will be appreciated.

> I will appreciate your writing to me about the schedule.

Because no one likes to be taken for granted, do not say "thank you" before the reader complies with a request.

**End with something pleasant and specific.**   The ending is the second most important part of a letter. Only the beginning is more important.

The letter ending should be pleasant and specific, and it should contain a note of goodwill. Usually, any action that is requested in a letter is mentioned—either the first time or as a repetition—at the end of the letter.

*Do not* use the trite ending:

> If I can be of further assistance to you, please do not hesitate to contact me.

This sentence is wordy, overused, and almost always meaningless. When you would honestly like to give the reader additional help, you could use this version:

> When I can help you again, please write me.

The trite version of this ending contains sixteen words; the suggested version, only nine words. *When* is positive, whereas *if* is negative. Usually, a specific word—write, call, and so on—is better than *contact*. If, however, you believe the reader may likely choose any of a variety of ways to request help, use *contact*.

Seldom should you end letters by offering further help. After all, when you have given courteously the help you should give, you do not need to encourage the readers to ask for more. They will ordinarily realize you would be willing to help them again. Therefore, end with another positive, specific idea. For example, if you supply merchandise that was ordered, you may end with a sentence such as these:

> An up-to-date catalog of our maintenance supplies is enclosed.
>
> Here are forms for your next orders.
>
> We can ship any of our merchandise within twenty-four hours after we receive your order.

If you have supplied products, service, or information for a special occasion, a sentence or a fragment such as these may be a good ending:

> I wish you the best of luck with your special sale.
>
> Good luck with your convention plans.
>
> Have a good vacation.

A few people still end letters with a sentence fragment such as this one:

> Looking forward to hearing from you, I am,

*Do not* end a letter with this type of fragment; instead, say specifically what you mean. For example, if you are requesting information, you could write:

> I look forward to hearing from you.

If you are granting a request for travel information, you could write:

> We are glad to help you with your travel plans.

The next chapter explains letter formats you can use when you apply the letter-writing guidelines that are presented in this chapter.

## QUESTIONS FOR DISCUSSION

1.  Which guidelines are adhered to and which ones are violated in these opening sentences for business letters? Explain.

    ✓ a.  Yes, you may use our mowing machine free of charge for a period of one month's time.

    ✗ b.  Unfortunately, our supply of the four-ply tires you ordered is exhausted.

    ✗ c.  This letter is in reply to your request of October 6 for a copy of our catalog.

    ✓ d.  Here is the pamphlet you requested on August 4.

    ✗ e.  I should like to tell you that I will gladly send the information you requested in your letter of June 17.

    f.  Although we cannot send you a copy of the report you requested, we would be very glad to have you read the report when you come to our office next month.

    ✗ g.  You said you need a secretary who can take dictation at a high rate of speed.

2.  Which guidelines are violated in these closing sentences for business letters?

    ✗ a.  In closing, I should like to apologize again for failing to send the materials so that they would reach you by the date you specified.

    ✓ b.  We look forward to your visit with us on November 9.

    c.  I sincerely regret that I cannot accept your invitation to speak to your group on October 11.

    ✗ d.  I am sorry we cannot supply the stationery you ordered.

3.    Which guidelines are adhered to and which ones are violated in these seven letters?

September 26, 1985

Mr. Harry B. Brown
Box 1183, Tennessee Tech
Cookeville, TN  38505

Dear Mr. Brown:

Thank you for your letter of September 24. The two pamphlets you requested were mailed to you by parcel post this morning. Please accept them with our compliments.

The chart on page 3 of the pamphlet entitled "Financial Management" contains some figures that should be especially helpful in writing your term paper. You have our permission to reproduce any of the charts in these two publications.

If I can be of further assistance to you, please do not hesitate to contact me.

Cordially yours,

\* \* \* \* \*

September 29, 1985

Miss Mary Bramblett
P.O. Box 411
Sheffield, AL  35660

Dear Miss Bramblett:

I mailed to you by parcel post this morning the two books you requested in your letter of August 1. I believe these books contain a good deal of information that will help you with the term paper you are writing.

Will you please return the two books as soon as you have completed your term paper. We expect to receive other requests for them before the end of the month.

Thanking you in advance, I remain,

Sincerely yours,

\* \* \* \* \*

October 1, 1985

Dr. Milton O. Haney
Director of Admissions
Temple Community College
Roanoke, Virginia

Dear Dr. Haney:

In compliance with your request of September 30, I am sorry to tell you that the catalogs for 1985-1986 will not be available until the first of December. I am, though, submitting herewith a copy of the booklet entitled "Earn While You Learn." You stated that you would like to use the information in this booklet when counseling students who are making plans to enroll in a senior college next term. In the event that any of the students in your school would like to secure further *recieve* information in regard to this subject, please so inform them that they should get in touch *Contact* with the placement office at our school.

If I can be of further assistance to you in the future, please do not hesitate to contact me.

Cordially,

\* \* \* \* \*

July 31, 1985

Mrs. Robert E. Holland
187 Freeze Street
Billington, VT  05042

Dear Mrs. Holland:

I mailed to you by parcel post this morning the three No. 6 calendar bases that you ordered on July 29. As the color of these bases is the same as the pencil holders you ordered last month, they will match perfectly.

An up-to-date copy of our catalog of office supplies is enclosed.

Cordially,

December 8, 1985

Mr. Clement H. Wainwright
P.O. Box 347
Mason, MT  59469

Dear Mr. Wainwright:

Pursuant to your request of November 28, I am more than happy to comply. You asked me to recommend three good books pertaining to the subject of letter writing. The names of the books that I would like to recommend follow. The names of the authors and the publishers are also given.

WRITING FOR BUSINESS by Hall T. Marcrum, Webster Publishing Co., 1817 Ridgeway Road, Laurel, TX  76785

PRINCIPLES OF LETTER WRITING by Marianne Davis and Mark L. Fowler, Standard Publishers, Inc., 1827 Park Avenue, Macy, NY 12145

LETTER WRITING SIMPLIFIED by Bradley O. Romine, Hastings Publishing Corporation, P.O. Box 247, Conley, OR  97016

I believe this is the information you need.

Sincerely,

August 1, 1985

Whitfield Office Supply Company
1148 Market Street
Wheeling, DE  19775

Gentlemen:

I should like to place an order for the following three items:

| | |
|---|---:|
| Model No. 3 electric stapling machine,<br>Catalog No. 42207 . . . . . . . . . . . . . . . . . . . . . . . . . . . . . | $4.87 |
| Tan paper clip dispenser, Catalog No. 38706 . . . . . . . . | 1.19 |
| Desk blotter, 15 x 20 inches, Catalog<br>No.  25813 . . . . . . . . . . . . . . . . . . . . . . . . . . . . . . . . . | 2.89 |
| Total . . . . . . . . . . . . . . . . . . . . . . . . . . . . . . . . . . . | $8.95 |

Please charge this merchandise to my account (No. 38743) and ship it by parcel post to reach me by August 11.

Thank you.

Cordially,

\* \* \* \* \*

April 26, 1985

Miss Carolyn Wisner
Route 3
Marblehead, MD  21101

Dear Miss Wisner:

I am sorry that I cannot send the seventy-five ball-point pens that you requested for favors for the secretaries who will attend your meeting on May 19. Our stock of that item has been depleted. I can, however, send you seventy-five attractive paperweights that I believe your meeting attendants would like to have.

I hope that you will have a very enjoyable, worthwhile meeting.

Sincerely,

## EXERCISES

Improve the following sentences.

1. In the event that the chief clerk resigns, we will have to employ a replacement.

2. Please ask your assistant to make an analyzation of the data.

3. In order to complete the project on time, they will need to use the computer tonight.

4. It is the purpose of this meeting to discuss the two proposals.

5. Enclosed herewith are the two drawings you requested.

6. The telephone call was made subsequent to our conversation.

7. We will be glad to be of service to you.

8. This is the copier our representative told you about.

9. They are trying to make some improvements in the situation.

10. A revision will be made in the plans in the near future.

# Chapter 4

# Letter Format and Parts

The purpose of a letter is to persuade the reader to react in some way. Obtaining the desired reaction requires effective communication; and every characteristic of your letter, from the format to the written message, says something to the reader.

Neatness, format, and adherence to business writing standards or conventions are important. A neat letter tends to impress the reader favorably. A poorly written or poorly typed letter implies a lack of respect for the reader.

Following letter-writing conventions serves two other purposes. First, it tells the reader that you know and understand business correspondence practices and take the time and effort to maintain business standards. Second, it allows the reader to concentrate on the content of the letter. Any deviation from standard practices would divert the reader's attention from the message. The reader may even be irritated. Originality and imagination are extremely valuable in business; observing standard practices is too. Make sure that any deviation from convention serves an important and specific purpose.

## FORMAT

The format of the letter is the first thing the reader notices. The letter should be centered on the page; that is, the left and the right margins should be about equal, and there should be about as much space below the letter as above it. All margins—side, top, and bottom—should be *at least one inch*. The top and bottom margins and most side margins should be somewhat more than one inch for typewritten letters.

The typewriter ribbon should be dark, and the keys should be clean. If a letter is handwritten, the ink should be dark and the writing must be legible. Use a good quality bond paper for both typewritten and handwritten letters.

## STATIONERY

White, 20-pound bond paper of 25 percent rag content is the most popular business stationery. This paper is good for letterheads, memoramdums, reports, additional pages of letters that are longer than one page, personal business letters, and envelopes.

Twenty-pound paper is strong enough to be handled easily and to make a good appearance, yet it is thin enough to permit the typist to make clear carbon copies. Corrections can be made quite satisfactorily on this paper. Other somewhat lighter paper that contains less rag content, or no rag content, also can be used for business letters, memorandums, reports, and envelopes.

Thinner, 7-pound, paper is good for carbon copies.

When choosing business stationery, consider not only weight, but also size, color, letterhead makeup, and envelopes.

### Size

The standard size for business stationery is 8½ by 11 inches. Among the advantages of using paper of this size are:

1.   The letters fit nicely in the standard-size folders and file cabinets.

2.   Stationery in this standard size is less expensive than in other sizes.

3. Letters can be folded well for mailing in business envelopes.

4. Pages fit into the folders for business reports.

5. Typists, because they use more stationery of this size than of any other, can easily place the message properly on the page.

6. Readers of business letters and reports are familiar with this size and therefore tend to like it.

Some top-level executives like to use smaller stationery for short letters that probably will not be filed. Smaller stationery has an advantage of attracting attention and may be thought of as prestigious.

The dimensions of popular sizes of small stationery are 7¼ by 10½ inches, 5½ by 8½ inches, and 8 by 10½ inches.

## Color

Pastel colors are appropriate for some business stationery. Because colored stationery attracts attention, it is especially good for sales letters.

## Letterheads

Most businesses use printed letterhead stationery. The letterhead, which ordinarily extends less than two inches from the top of the paper, contains the name and the address of the organization and something to indicate the nature of the business. Often, the name indicates the nature of the business. Frequently, other elements are included. Popular elements are department designation, telephone number, names of officers, slogans, and drawings or photographs.

Avoid including so much detail that the letterhead becomes cluttered, thus detracting from its attractive appearance. The examples on the next page seem appropriate.

The letterhead style and contents as well as the quality of the stationery should be appropriate for the type of group and the product or service it provides. For example, the stationery for a non-

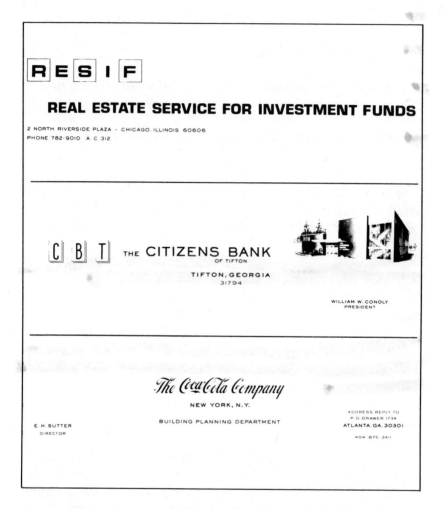

profit group or for a small business should be simple in design and of conservative quality. Large organizations that stress quality and prestige should use more elaborate stationery. A resort hotel is an example of an organization that could use a high-quality stationery (possibly a linen finish) with a colorful, yet dignified, letterhead design. Simplicity in design can be combined with expensive materials to provide stationery of the highest quality.

Sporting goods businesses, chewing gum companies, and other organizations that handle products used in informal situations would wisely choose an informal design for their letterheads.

## Envelopes

Two standard sizes of business envelopes are the No. 10, which is 4⅛ by 9 inches, and the No. 6¾, which is 3⅝ by 6½ inches. The No. 10 is used for most business letters. This size is recommended for one-page letters that transmit small enclosures and for two-page letters. Many people use only one size—except, of course, for the letters that are accompanied by enclosures that are too large for envelopes of this size. In these cases large manila envelopes are used. Because of economy, some people prefer the No. 6¾ envelopes for one-page letters.

The name and the address of the organization are printed in the upper left-hand corner of the front of the business envelope. This information is printed in the same style and color as those appearing on the letterhead sheets, but frequently the print is smaller on the envelope. Plain envelopes are used for personal business letters.

## STANDARD PARTS

Traditional letter formats include the following parts, which are identified in the letter in Figure 4-1:

1. Return address

2. Date

3. Inside address

4. Salutation

5. Body

6. Complimentary close

7. Signature

### Return Address

Because a letterhead contains the name and the address of the organization for which it was printed, do not repeat the address

**Figure 4-1**

Modified Block Style with No Paragraph Indentions

129 Pine Avenue
Return address ──▶ Hattisburg, IL 62643
February 8, 1985

Date

Mr. James T. Holmes, Manager
Harrison's Department Store
1129 Market Street ◀─────── Inside address
McMinnville, IL 60909

Dear Mr. Holmes ◀─────── Salutation

Please send a representative to my home within the next
two weeks to demonstrate the Lectromatic vacuum cleaner
you advertised yesterday in The McMinnville Times.  I am ◀── Body
especially interested in seeing how well the Lectromatic
cleans shag carpets.

Let me know when he can give the demonstration so that I
will be at home when he arrives.

Complimentary close ──▶ Cordially

Signature ──▶ *Mary M. Taylor*
Mrs. Mary M. Taylor

above the date. When writing a letter on plain paper, though, be sure to include *your* address. Include all information—except your name, which will appear below the complimentary close—that the recipient would need to address a reply to you. Ordinarily, these items are needed: (1) house or apartment number; (2) street, avenue, route, or post office box number; (3) city; (4) state (two-letter abbreviation); and (5) ZIP code. Here are examples:

245 East Tenth Street          P.O. Box 748
Dayton, WI  53529              Huntsville, KY  42251

In most business offices the mail is opened by clerks who remove the letters and the enclosures and then discard the envelopes. Unless the return addresss is on the letter, therefore, the recipient may not be able to reply. Numerous inconveniences have resulted from omitting return addresses on letters.

A man who applied for a job wrote to the college from which he had been graduated several years earlier and asked that a transcript of his college work be sent to him. He did not include his return address. The registrar attempted to locate the man by writing to his home address at the time he was a student, but the letter was returned. The alumnus sent a second request and again omitted his address. Finally, he wrote a third letter and explained that his getting the job for which he had applied depended on his receiving the transcript; and he expressed anger because of the delay. Fortunately, he included a return address on that letter. The registrar sent the transcript immediately and explained why it could not be sent earlier.

In another case a woman wrote for a room reservation in a hotel that was hosting a convention she planned to attend. Even though she requested a confirmation, she did not receive it. The night before she was to drive about 450 miles to the convention city, she called the hotel to inquire about the reservation. The clerk who answered the telephone told her a room had been reserved for her. When she asked why the reservation had not been confirmed, he explained that she had not included her return address on the letter. She stated indignantly, "I clearly remember typing '127 Vine Avenue' on the letter!" The clerk replied, "Yes, you did, lady; but you did not include the city and the state." She examined the carbon copy she had kept and found that he was correct. Omitting part of her return address caused her some expense, irritation, inconvenience, and embarrassment.

## Date

Include the date—month, day, and year—on which the letter is written. Among the reasons for including the date are these:

1. Either the receiver or the writer of the letter may wish to refer to the date in later communications.

2. Letters are usually filed by date.

3. When a letter arrives after a delay in the mail, the receiver understands why the letter arrived late.

## Inside Address

Begin the inside address at least four lines below the date. Include in the inside address the same information you write on the envelope. You should usually include the addressee's (1) name; (2) house or apartment number; (3) street, avenue, route, or post office box number; (4) city; (5) state (two-letter abbreviation); and (6) ZIP code. The job title and the company name are needed in some addresses. In some large organizations two or more employees have the same name, and the job title helps the mail clerks to get the letter to the right person quickly.

Good business etiquette and common courtesy dictate the use of a courtesy title (*Miss, Mr., Mrs., Ms.,* and so forth) before the person's name in the inside address, as in these examples:

| | |
|---|---|
| Mr. Boyce L. Williams<br>859 Maple Avenue<br>Lexington, KS 67552 | Ms. Judy Y. Arnett, Manager<br>Simms Department Store<br>P.O. Box 1193<br>Hastings, MN 49058 |

The courtesy title is omitted when the writer does not know whether the addressee is a male or a female.

## Salutation

When addressing a letter to a person rather than to an organization, you should in most instances use a three-word salutation—Dear + courtesy title + surname. If, however, you and the the addressee are on a first-name basis in oral communication, you may use a two-word salutation—Dear + first name. Do not use *Dear Sir*; it is outdated.

For many years *Gentlemen* has been used as a salutation for a group of men or for a group of both men and women. Either *Mesdames* or *Ladies* has been used for a group of women. *Dear Gentlemen* or *Dear Mesdames* should never be used. To eliminate sexist words, many writers today use various other salutations such as *Dear Customers*, *Dear Committee Members*, and *Dear Friends* for letters addressed to groups. When you choose a salutation, the main idea to remember is that your objective is to persuade the reader to concentrate on the letter content rather than on the mechanics of presentation. Use a salutation, therefore, that will not offend a reader; or eliminate the salutation and the complimentary close by using the simplified letter form illustrated in Figure 4-2 or the functional form illustrated in Figure 4-3.

You will observe that the functional form includes no subject line. For some letters, especially those that transmit disappointing news, omitting the subject line is advantageous. Also, omitting it saves time.

The simplified and the functional forms are rapidly gaining favor among business correspondents.

## Body

In typing a letter, single space the paragraphs and double space between them. Indenting the first line of a paragraph is not necessary. When writing the letter in longhand, however, indent the first line of each paragraph. Indenting the first lines of handwritten paragraphs contributes to easy reading

A handwritten letter is shown in Figure 4-4.

**Figure 4-2**
AMS Simplified Style

Haskins Wholesalers, Inc.
P. O. BOX 1184
RUSSELL, CA 93101

July 19, 1985

Mr. John B. Clardy
Northfield Department Store
1246 Market Street
Marietta, CA 95902

FRINGE BENEFITS SURVEY

Here, Mr. Clardy, are answers to the three questions you asked
in your letter of July 18:

1.  Each employee is entitled to two weeks' vacation each year.

2.  An employee pays only half the premium for life insurance.

3.  We pay the tuition for employees who take college courses.

Yes, do send us a summary of your survey findings.

*Michael C. Rucker*
MICHAEL C. RUCKER, MANAGER

trm

**Figure 4-3**
Functional Style

August 19, 1985


Order Department
Broadway Bookstore
P. O. Box 786
Walker, MS 38161


This morning we sent by parcel post two copies of AN EFFICIENT
ORGANIZATION, which you ordered on August 17.  As I mentioned
earlier, this book is quite popular.  Our supply was exhausted
twice before the printing company could reprint the book on
July 15.

We have a good supply of all the titles on the list we mailed
to you last week.  Prices of some of the paperbacks are lower
than they were a year ago.

When you need more books, just let us know.  We can send them
immediately.


Howard J. Aiello
Manager

bc

**Figure 4-4**
Modified Block Style with Paragraph Indentions

976 Morningside Drive
Cookeville, TN 38501
January 25, 1985

Mr. Max W. Stein
Vice-President
Hartford Publishing Co.
1122 Second Avenue
Lebanon, OH  42131

Dear Mr. Stein:

Please send me your brochure "Executives
Must Communicate." I want to use some
of the information in your publication for
a term paper I am writing.
Since the paper is due on February 28,
I will appreciate your sending the brochure
by February 15.

Cordially yours,

Shelia L. Key

Shelia L. Key

## Complimentary Close

*Cordially*, *Sincerely*, *Cordially yours*, and *Sincerely yours* are the most popular complimentary closes. *Yours truly*, *Very truly yours*, and *Respectfully yours* are outdated.

## Signature

When typing a business letter, type your name about four lines below the complimentary close or about four lines below the last line of the letter if a complimentary close is not included. In a handwritten letter, you may print your name in that position. Remember, a man does not include a courtesy title (*Mr.*, *Dr.*, and so forth) in his signature; a woman may if she so desires.

*Sign* each letter with a *pen* above your typed or printed name.

## SPECIAL PARTS

In addition to the seven letter parts described in the preceding paragraphs and illustrated in Figure 4-1, these special parts are frequently needed:

1. Attention line

2. Subject line

3. Position title

4. Enclosure notation

5. Special mailing notation

6. Postscript

7. Other

These special parts are illustrated in the letters in Figures 4-5 and 4-6.

**Figure 4-5**

## IDLEWILD INSURANCE AGENCY
245 West Sixth Avenue
Hanover, DE  19721


July 16, 1985


Mr. Stephen H. Phillips
1224 Hamilton Street
Bloomington, DE 19711

Dear Mr. Phillips

Accident Report Form

Please complete the enclosed form and return it before
August 1.  We can then file the necessary report on the
automobile accident in which you were involved on July 8.

I am glad to know that no one was injured and that only
minor repairs are required for your car.  You can expect
high-quality work by any of the three body shops you
mentioned on the telephone.

Cordially

*Robert E. Davis*

Robert E. Davis
Adjustor

jgh

Enclosure

Be sure to have the two witnesses sign the form.

**Figure 4-6**

```
                                    1224 Hamilton Street
                                    Bloomington, DE 19712
                                    July 20, 1985




CERTIFIED MAIL


Idlewild Insurance Agency
245 West Sixth Avenue
Hanover, DE 19721

Attention:  Mr. Robert E. Davis

Gentlemen

Here is the completed form you asked me to send to you
before August 1.  As you will notice, it contains signa-
tures of three witnesses.

I appreciate your prompt processing of this claim.

                        Cordially

                        Stephen H. Phillips
                        Stephen H. Phillips


Enclosure
```

## Attention Line

Usually, a letter is addressed to a specific person. When, however, you address a letter to an organization but wish to direct the letter to a particular person within the group, type an attention line between the last line of the inside address and the salutation. Even though you use an attention line, always use a salutation that is appropriate for the first line of the inside address, as in this example:

Sheely Manufacturing Company, Inc.
P.O. Box 1214
Helena, GA  31037

Attention:    Mr. Stephen M. Mitchell

Gentlemen:

## Subject Line

So that the reader can see at a glance the subject of the letter, you may place key words in a subject line. By including account numbers, policy numbers, and similar references, you can assist the addressee and others who handle correspondence. The subject line helps in filing a message and in finding one that has been filed. Place this line between the salutation and the body of the letter. The word *subject* is optional. Here are examples:

Cumberland Printing Company
1441 Grandview Road
Joplin, NE  68378

Gentlemen:

SUBJECT:   Procedures for Submitting Manuscripts

---

Mrs. Frances M. Wilson, Manager
Haynesville Grocery Co., Inc.
P.O. Box 126
Denver, WA  99007

Dear Mrs. Wilson

Policy No. 32-787531

## Position Title

When using a letterhead and writing as a representative of the organization for which the letterhead was designed, show the title of your position on the line immediately below your typewritten name or on the same line, as in these examples:

Sincerely

*Elizabeth S. Minnear*

Mrs. Elizabeth S. Minnear
Personnel Director

---

Cordially

*John R. Luckett*

John R. Luckett, Credit Manager

## Enclosure Notation

If you place an item with the letter inside the envelope, type or write the word *Enclosure* flush with the left margin and a line or more below the signature line. When sending more than one enclosure, use the word *Enclosures* followed by the number of items you are sending. Itemizing or describing the enclosures is desirable when they are especially important or when you believe the person opening the envelope may overlook an item. Examples follow:

Cordially

*Whewon Cho*

Whewon Cho


Enclosures 2

Sincerely

*Shirley G. Claborn*

Ms. Shirley G. Claborn

Enclosures 3—$15 check
               Revised manuscript
               Addressed envelope

## Special Mailing Notation

When sending a letter by any method other than regular first-class mail, place the notation for the special mailing (REGISTERED, CERTIFIED, and so on) either above the inside address or as the last item below the signature. Even though the postal employees do not see this notation, it tells the recipient the letter was sent by a special method. Also, this notation on the file copy provides a record of the mailing method.

## Postscript

If you use a postscript, place it two lines below the last part of the letter. The original purpose of the postscript was to present ideas that were inadvertently omitted in the body of the letter or ideas that occurred to the writer after dictating the letter. The postscript is still used occasionally for these reasons, but the chief reason today for using it is to emphasize an idea. Because it is short and in a position that makes it stand out from the rest of the letter, it gets special attention. Use postscripts sparingly.

You may use or omit the abbreviation *P.S.* Here are examples:

Enclosure

P.S. The Lectromatic vacuum cleaner sells for only $259.95.

Enclosure

The Lectromatic vacuum cleaner sells for only $259.95.

## Copy Notation

You may send a copy of a letter to a third person. Usually, you would like the addressee of the letter to know you are sending a copy to another person. If so, type two spaces below the final notation on the page the words "Copy to" followed by the name of the person who is to receive the copy. Here is an illustration:

Cordially,

*Barry E. Woodcock*

Barry E. Woodcock

bfr

Enclosure

Copy to Mr. Arnold Kemp

---

If you prefer that the addressee not know you are sending a copy to another person, omit the copy notation from the original, but type *bc* (blind copy) on the copies only, as in this illustration:

Cordially,

*Barry E. Woodcock*

Barry E. Woodcock

bfr

Enclosure

bc   Mr. Arnold B. Kemp

## MULTIPLE-PAGE LETTERS

Include these three items on the second and succeeding pages of a multiple-page letter:

1.  Addressee's name

2.  Page number

3.  Date

Begin these items about one inch from the top of the page. Space down about three lines to continue the body of the letter. These three items may be arranged horizontally, as in Figure 4-8, or vertically, as in Figure 4-9. Either arrangement is acceptable for the formats that have indented opening and closing lines. Use the vertical arrangement in Figure 4-9 for the block, the functional, or the AMS simplified format.


## PUNCTUATION STYLES

Use conventional punctuation for the body of a business message. Punctuate the salutation and the complimentary close of a letter according to either of two styles — *mixed* and *open*. For *mixed* punctuation use a colon after the salutation and a comma after the complimentary close.

For *open* punctuation use no punctuation mark after the salutation or the complimentary close.


## ENVELOPE

Regardless of how well a letter is written, it is of no value until it is delivered. For mail that is to be processed by hand (no computers), the envelope addess can be identical to the inside address of the letter and should be in the approximate horizontal center of the lower half of the envelope. The return address should be in the upper left-hand corner.

**Figure 4-7**

## SOUTHERN BUSINESS EDUCATION ASSOCIATION
### RICHLAND, KY 40171

April 12, 1985

Dr. Robert B. Comer
Radford Research Institute
126 Frederick Street
New York, NY 10031

Dear Dr. Comer

Here are the answers to the three questions you asked in your letter of
April 10 about the leadership development seminar for the Southern Business Education Association:

1. You can choose the hours for beginning and ending the
   seminar. Beginning registration at 8:30 and the seminar
   at 9:00 has worked well in the past; and since you suggested these times in your letter, perhaps they are the
   best we could use.

   As you will notice when you look at the enclosed copies
   of previous programs, the closing times have varied.
   Close when you wish. We do not want to shortchange you
   on time; neither do we want to overburden you with an
   excessive amount of time.

2. For each of the two earlier seminars, we had thirty-six
   official participants (three from each of the twelve
   states in this region). Members of the executive board
   and a few visitors also attended. The total last year
   was fifty-five. I suspect about fifty will attend this
   year.

3. I should know by the end of September the names of the
   thirty-six official participants, and of course I already
   know the names of the executive board members who will
   attend. In the past we have not known the names of some
   of the participants until the day of the seminar. We may
   not know all the names this year.

You have complete freedom in planning this seminar. I am enclosing copies
of the previous programs merely to let you know what has been done earlier.
I believe no two seminars should be alike.

**Figure 4-8**

Dr. Robert B. Comer                    2                    April 12, 1985

Please send me one of your photographs for use in the convention program
booklet.  The SBEA president would like to have the program materials ready
to send to the printer by May 15.  I will forward your photograph to her.

I'll help you in any way I can in conducting the seminar.

                              Cordially

                              Ray A. Hawn
                              Ray A. Hawn
                              Past President

dfg

Enclosures 2

P. S.  A single room has been reserved for you at the Ridgeway Hotel for
Tuesday and Wednesday nights, November 26 and 27.

**Figure 4-9**

Dr. Robert B. Comer
Page 2
April 12, 1985

Please send me one of your photographs for use in the convention program
booklet. The SBEA president would like to have the program materials ready
to send to the printer by May 15. I will forward your photograph to her.

I'll help you in any way I can in conducting the seminar.

Cordially

Ray A. Hawn
Past President

dfg

Enclosures 2

A single room has been reserved for you at the Ridgeway Hotel for Tuesday
and Wednesday nights, November 26 and 27.

Each year more automatic scanning devices (computers) are being used in post offices. So that your mail will not be rejected by these computers and thus require slower hand sorting, the United States Postal Service has requested that these instructions be followed when addressing business envelopes:

1. When no attention line is used, the wording for the envelope address should be the same as the wording for the inside address of the letter.

2. If the address contains an attention line, type it as the second line of the address.

3. Use only capital letters, eliminate all punctuation, and use block format (see Figure 4-10).

4. Include the city, two-letter abbreviation for the state, and the ZIP code in the last line.

5. For a No. 6¾ (short) envelope, begin the address twelve lines from the top and two and one half inches from the left edge of the envelope. For a No. 10 (long) envelope, begin the address twelve lines from the top and four inches from the left edge of the envelope.

6. When you use a plain envelope, type *your* address in the upper left-hand corner.

7. Type special notations such as PERSONAL or CONFIDENTIAL two lines below the return address and three spaces from the left edge of the envelope.

8. Type special mailing notations such as SPECIAL DELIVERY, REGISTERED MAIL, and CERTIFIED MAIL in the upper right-hand corner immediately below the stamp area. Type the notation nine lines from the top and be sure it ends at least one half inch from the right edge of the envelope.

**Figure 4-10**

TENNESSEE TECHNOLOGICAL UNIVERSITY
COLLEGE OF BUSINESS ADMINISTRATION
OFFICE OF THE DEAN
Cookeville, Tennessee 38501


MS MARGARET R KELLY
PRODUCTION MANAGER
WILDS PUBLISHING CO. INC.
PO BOX 1121
PHOENIX KY 40411


CHARLES E RAINS
1151 PINE STREET
DOVER TN 38712


REGISTERED MAIL


GENERAL PROCESSING COMPANY
ATTENTION MR R M WATERS
1222 MARKET STREET
RICHMOND AL 35563

## FOLDING

For an attractive letter to retain its good appearance, it must be folded properly if it is to be mailed in a long (No. 10) or a short (No. 6¾) envelope.

### Long Envelope

Three ways of folding letters for long envelopes are standard, overlap, and back fold.

**Standard.**   Only two creases are needed for folding a letter for a long (No. 10) envelope:

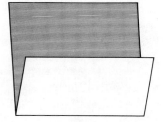

1.    Place the letter face up on a desk and bring the bottom edge of the letter up toward the top edge so that roughly one third of the page is left uncovered, as shown. Crease the letter at this point.

2.    Bring the top edge of the letter down over the bottom one third of the letter that has already been creased. The top edge should come to within about one quarter of an inch from the crease you have already made. Hold the top edge in this position as you make the second and final crease in the letter, as shown. The folded letter is now slightly smaller than a long (No. 10) envelope and, therefore, can be placed easily into the envelope.

**Overlap.**   Only two creases are needed for folding a letter by the overlap method for a long (No. 10) envelope:

1.   Place the letter face up on a desk and bring the bottom edge of the letter up toward the top edge so that slightly more than one third of the page is left uncovered, as shown. Crease the letter at this point.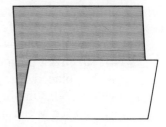

2.   Bring the top edge of the letter down over the bottom one third of the letter that has already been creased. The top edge should overlap the first crease by about one quarter of an inch. Hold the top edge in this position as you make the second and final crease, as shown. The folded letter is now slightly smaller than a No. 10 envelope and, therefore, can be placed easily into the envelope.

**Back fold.**   Only two creases are needed for folding a letter by the back fold method.

1.   Place the letter face up on a desk and bring the bottom edge of the letter up toward the top edge so that about one third of the page is left uncovered, as shown. Crease the letter at this point.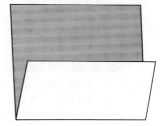

2.  Turn the top edge of the letter backward so that this edge touches the crease you have already made. Hold the top edge in this position as you make the second and final crease in the letter, as shown. The folded letter is now slightly smaller than a long (No. 10) envelope and, therefore, can be placed easily into the envelope. This method of folding may be used when mailing a letter in any type of No. 10 envelope; it is the required folding method for mailing in a window envelope unless an address slip is also inserted into the envelope.

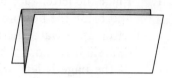

**Short Envelope**

Three creases are required for folding a letter to be mailed in a short (No. 6¾) business envelope:

1.  Place the letter face up on a desk and bring the bottom edge of the letter up toward the top edge so that the bottom edge is within about one quarter of an inch of the top edge. Crease the letter, as shown here.

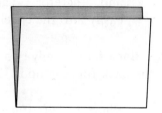

2.  Bring the right edge of the letter over toward the left side so that about one third of the width of the letter remains uncovered by the portion that extends from the second crease you have made, as you see here.

3. Bring the left edge of the letter over toward the right so that the left edge is within about one quarter of an inch from the second crease you have made, as shown. The folded letter is now smaller than the short (No. 6¾) envelope and, therefore, can be placed easily into the envelope.

The appearance of a correctly folded letter for either of the two popular sizes of business envelopes is as good as it was before being folded. Improper folding would have an adverse effect on the appearance of a well-spaced letter. A correctly folded letter can be opened easily and fits into the files as it should. Easy handling of correspondence is especially important in large offices where dozens (and possibly hundreds) of letters are opened each day.

## QUESTIONS FOR DISCUSSION

1. Even though usually business letters should be typewritten, for what reasons should some of them be handwritten?

2. How does the appearance of a letter contribute to the effectiveness of the contents of the letter?

3. What do the block style and the AMS simplified style have in common?

4. How is the modified block style different from the block style?

## PROBLEMS

1.   Assume you composed the following letter. Type it or write it in proper form on a sheet of plain white 8½ by 11-inch paper.

> I am enclosing the book *The Executive Must Communicate* that you mailed to me on January 27. Some of the information in it was just what I needed to complete a term paper for a business communication course.
>
> Thank you for lending me your only copy.

The person to whom the letter is to be addressed is Harold L. Baker. He is the general manager of the Hartford Printing Company. The address of that company is 1122 Second Avenue, Lebanon, OH 42133.

2.   Address a No. 6¾ or a No. 10 envelope for the letter in Problem 1.

3.   Address an envelope for each of these addresses:

> Mr. Robert F. Jones, Manager, Johnson Manufacturing Company, 1122 Market Street, Florence, AL 35630
>
> Mr. Thomas L. Winningham, Public Relations Director, Wright Finance Corporation, Jackson, TN 37111
>
> Miss Margaret Ann Hitchcock, Secretary, Office Services, First National Bank Building, Helena, ND 58001

# Chapter 5

# Good-News Letters

Good-news letters have one common characteristic: they contain information the receivers are happy to receive. They are, therefore, easy to write. The three types of good-news letters discussed in this chapter pertain to:

1. Complying with requests

2. Showing gratitude

3. Ordering

Promptness in writing these letters is important.

## COMPLYING WITH REQUESTS

Of all business letters, those written to comply with requests are perhaps the easiest to write. You know that when the person who made the request receives an envelope with your return address in the upper left-hand corner, that person hopes the letter contains a compliance with the request. You know, therefore, how to begin. You know what the reader wants to read, and you are prepared to give that information. *Begin* the letter by telling the reader that you *are* complying or that you *have already* complied with the request.

Here is one way to begin a reply to a request for a book you published:

A complimentary copy of *Shortcuts for Sales Managers* is enclosed.

If you are replying to a request for a $5 adjustment because of an overcharge, you could begin:

Here is a $5 check to adjust your account.

A reply to a request for permission to take a vacation earlier than usual may begin with this sentence:

Yes, you may take your vacation from June 14 through June 27.

When you have enclosed materials or supplied the information the reader asked for, the reader can readily see you *have already* complied with the request. Frequently, though, you must send the requested materials in a separate mailing or shipment. All people realize that sometimes they cannot do the things they intend to do. Even though you intend to send an item at a specific time and you have good reasons to believe you can, circumstances can—and they frequently *do*—prevent your sending it as scheduled. You should, therefore, first mail or ship whatever materials you cannot send with the letter and *then* write a letter saying you *have* sent them.

Be specific in telling the reader about the action you have taken. Do NOT use the trite phrase "under separate cover." DO tell the reader the method (parcel post, railway freight, first-class mail, or others) you used to send the materials.

The following opening sentence of a business letter is a good illustration:

> The two 3-ring notebook binders you ordered on January 26 were sent to you by parcel post this morning.

We are not expected to do everything we are requested to do. Some requests are unreasonable; and others, though reasonable and quite ordinary, cannot be granted because of existing circumstances. Only those requests that *are granted* are discussed in this chapter. The requests that are declined are discussed in Chapter 9.

When requested to do something, do it *cheerfully* or not at all. By beginning a letter with a granting of the request, you promote goodwill, you make a good impression, and you put the reader in a good mood for reading the rest of the letter.

The *beginning* is the most important part of a business letter; but even though the beginning is good, the tone can seem to be somewhat curt unless there is a follow-up that helps the reader realize you are complying cheerfully. Here are follow-up sentences for the letter beginnings that have just been presented:

> A complimentary copy of *Shortcuts for Sales Managers* is enclosed. The four points discussed on page 14 apply specifically to the term paper you are writing.
>
> I wish you much success in completing your paper.

* * *

> Here is a $5 check to adjust your account. I appreciate your writing so that we could correct the overcharge of April 16, which we would not have otherwise discovered.
>
> The latest edition of our catalog of sporting goods is enclosed. We can ship any of these items the day we receive your order.

* * *

> Yes, you may take your vacation from June 14 through June 27.

The work on the assembly line can be adjusted easily so that production will not be affected during that time. In fact, the adjustment can be made more easily then than later in the summer.

Drive carefully and enjoy the Colorado scenery.

* * *

The two 3-ring notebook binders you ordered on January 26 were sent to you by parcel post this morning.

Because so many other people have placed repeat orders for this particular binder, I believe you will be especially pleased with it. Orange is the most popular color for all styles of the loose-leaf folders.

I am enclosing five forms for your use when ordering more office supplies.

Even though the preceding four letters are short, they contain enough information to show the readers they have been given courteous consideration. In each letter the request is granted in the first sentence, and sincere concern for the reader is shown in the rest of the letter.

People who have applied to you for credit want to read that you have approved their requests. They realize, of course, that your complying with their requests will make it possible for them to transact business with you conveniently; and they feel complimented by knowing you have made routine investigations and are favorably impressed by the information you received. Telling them you have approved their requests is the best way to begin the letters.

Having read good news in the first sentence, the readers are receptive to any sales talk you include as long as the sales talk is of possible benefit to them. High-pressure tactics, however, alienate readers. Follow up your compliance with the requests by letting the readers know you are genuinely interested in transacting business with them. Tell them you provide prompt, reliable, and courteous service as well as merchandise they will want to purchase.

In Figure 5-1 the writer granted credit to the customer and then stated positively the amount of credit. Note that instead of saying "Your credit purchases must be limited to $600 a month," the writer said, "You may charge purchases up to $600 a month." Such positive wording tends to make the reader feel complimented.

More details are required for a letter accepting an invitation to speak to a group. The time, the date, and the place of the meeting should be specified in addition to a definite acceptance of the invitation. The person who invites a speaker likes to know that these details are clear to the person who accepts the invitation. *Verify the date carefully*; for example, make sure May 26 is *Friday* rather than Thursday or Saturday. An error of this nature can cause anxiety, and it usually requires additional correspondence or a telephone call. Mentioning the length and the topic of your speech is also helpful. The time you expect to arrive at the meeting place and your mode of travel—especially when tight scheduling is involved—should also be included in your reply. Remember to tell the reader the special facilities (screen, overhead projector, tape recorder, and so on) you will need for the speech. A letter illustrating some of these points is in Figure 5-2.

When replying to some types of requests, you may have additional information, publications, or sample merchandise you think would be helpful to the reader. Send these items along with those requested. Refer specifically to these additional items. Any items enclosed with a letter should be mentioned.

Resist the temptation to end any letter with the trite *"If I can be of any further assistance to you, please do not hesitate to contact me."* Many otherwise good letters have been *spoiled* by this type of ending. When you have done as much as you should do for the reader, do not suggest a request for more assistance. When you feel, however, that it is probable you *can* help the reader in the future and you would *like* to help, refer in a positive way to your offer to help.

Here are positive statements of offers to help:

We will be glad to send you copies of our other publications if you should need them for another term paper.

**Figure 5-1**

# Delta Department Store
## JACKSBORO, MISSISSIPPI 39011

May 17, 1985

Mrs. Steven L. Hampton
259 Riderwood Road
Mason, AR 72180

Dear Mrs. Hampton

Your credit application has been approved.  All you have to do
to charge a purchase at our store is to present the enclosed
card to the salesclerk and sign the sales slip.

We are happy to have you as a credit customer.  You may charge
purchases up to $600 a month.  The people whose names you gave
as references for our routine credit investigation complimented
your prompt-pay practice.

When you wish to shop by mail, please include your account number (A-26734) in your letter so that the clerk can process your
order speedily.  The merchandise you request will be shipped
within twenty-four hours after we receive your order.

Cordially yours

*Robert G. Norred Jr.*

Robert G. Norred, Jr.
Credit Manager

vmc

Enclosure

**Figure 5-2**

**LOUISIANA PUBLISHING COMPANY**
Hopkins, Louisiana 71121

February 15, 1985

Mr. Randy M. Thomas, Jr.
President, Marketing Club
Lakeland University
Sheffield, GA 30306

Dear Mr. Thomas

I will be glad to speak to your group at 6:30 p.m. (EST) on
Tuesday, March 26.  Thank you for inviting me.

Will you please have a small screen and an overhead projector
ready.  I will use some transparencies to introduce the subtopics of the speech, which is entitled "Sales Talk for the
Twentieth Century."

Since my plane (Delta Flight No. 685) is scheduled to arrive
in Sheffield at 3:35 p.m., there should be ample time to get
to your administration building before the meeting begins.

I look forward to seeing you on March 26.

Cordially

W. Mark Cross
Sales Manager

bhw

> Just let me know when I can help you again.
>
> When I can help you again, please write me.

The most important thing to keep in mind is that providing whatever assistance you feel should be provided in complying with a request is almost always enough to offer. Sometimes an offer to give further help suggests that you are incompetent or that you may be withholding some assistance you should provide.

Sales talk such as that in the letter adjusting the $5 overcharge and the letter stating that the notebook binders have been sent is appropriate when writing to customers. Be discreet, however, in including sales talk when writing to people who do not buy from you. Including sales talk in letters complying with requests from persons who are not your customers can detract greatly from the courtesy you are showing by complying with the requests. The readers may believe your primary motive in granting the requests was to try to sell your merchandise or services rather than to assist the readers in their endeavors.

When you have reason to believe sales information would be appreciated by the recipient of your letter, you may add the person's name to a list to receive sales talk later. Be careful never to make a person feel obligated to do business with you because you complied with a request.

Try to reply to a letter within twenty-four hours from the time you receive it. In some instances, though, such quick responses are not feasible. For example, you may have to wait three or four days to receive the information or the materials you were requested to send. In such cases, delaying your reply until you can comply with the request may be the best course of action. If, however, you must wait somewhat longer (five days or more) to supply the requested items, reply within twenty-four hours and give the date on which you can comply with the request.

Replying *promptly* makes a favorable impression on the reader.

## SHOWING GRATITUDE

Everyone is called upon from time to time to help someone else. Also, everyone must be helped by others occasionally. Sometimes assistance is given voluntarily; at other times it must be requested.

No one is completely self-sufficient. Certainly, you should use your own resourcefulness and ingenuity to accomplish your objectives; but when you realize you need advice, direction, or tangible materials from someone else, ask for the help confidently and courteously.

When you help someone, do you appreciate an acknowledgment and an expression of gratitude? Of course you do, even though you were glad to help and you did not want the person to feel obligated to you. Other people feel the same way. When someone grants you a favor, therefore, express your sincere appreciation promptly.

Frequently, an oral "thank you" or "I appreciate your helping me" is sufficient expression of gratitude. When you cannot make an oral comment promptly or when the favor you receive is somewhat out of the ordinary—or a big one, so to speak—write a letter. This letter is easy to write. You know the purpose for writing, and you know the addressee will be pleased to receive the letter. Begin immediately with a statement of appreciation for the *specific* favor.

The following sentences illustrate appropriate ways of beginning a letter of this type:

Thank you for lending me your copy of *Executive Decision Making*.

I appreciate your help in solving the records storage problem in our office.

Although one sentence may be all that is needed, additional comments enhance the effectiveness of the letter. The person who granted the favor obviously has a special interest in you or in the particular matters with which you were helped; therefore, a comment about the *specific* ways you were benefited, the present status of the project, or the expectations may reveal your sincere appreciation and convince the person that the assistance was beneficial.

Expressing a desire to return the favor is sometimes good for this type of letter.

These letters were written to express appreciation:

> Thank you for lending me your copy of *Executive Decision Making*. I will use information from some of the charts in Chapter 6 when speaking to the management professors of Utah State University next month.
>
> I mailed the book to you by parcel post today.
>
> * * *
>
> I appreciate your help in solving the records storage problem in our office. The transfer cases you suggested are superior to any others we have used.
>
> Please come by to see us when you come to Athens next month. I would like to show you the new office layout.

Writing the way you talk, beginning with good news, and economizing on words are among the guidelines that apply specifically to letters showing gratitude. Some people, unfortunately, waste words and still never actually say what they mean because they began with such wordiness as:

> I wish to thank you for . . . .
>
> I should like to thank you for . . . .
>
> I should like to take this opportunity to thank you for . . . .

Simplicity, directness, and sincerity are desired qualities of a letter expressing appreciation.

Letters have several advantages over oral communication. Repeated oral expressions of gratitude can become boring to the listener, and excessive repetition can lead the listener to believe that the person talking is insincere or is insecure. Chances are good, though, the recipient of a letter of appreciation will read it several times. Repetitious reading will have a desirable effect on the recipient because the letter is read voluntarily and only when the recipient is in the proper mood to read it.

Letters that express gratitude promote good feelings. Write letters when you feel grateful and when you feel that the readers will not think you are attempting to apple-polish.

## ORDERING

A supplier of any type of merchandise is obviously pleased to receive an order. An order is, therefore, good news. Generally speaking, the more merchandise that is sold, the greater are the profits. Some suppliers provide forms to simplify the ordering process for both the customer and the supplier. When an order form is available, no letter is necessary. Simply fill out the form *accurately* and mail it. Quite often, however, no order form is available. You must, therefore, write a letter to obtain the desired merchandise.

The four essential items of information in an order letter are: (1) identification of the merchandise desired, (2) cost, (3) delivery instructions, and (4) method of payment.

### Identification

The types of information necessary to identify the merchandise you desire vary depending on the situation. When a *catalog number* is available, specify that number in your letter. State the name of the item, the desired size, color, style, weight, and any other variable characteristics of the items you are ordering. Also, specify the desired quantity.

Special features such as monograms should be stated clearly in the letter.

### Cost

Specify the cost of each item in the order.

### Delivery

Tell the supplier the method—parcel post, railway freight, truck, air express, or other—to be used in sending your merchandise. If you wish to have the package insured, include these instructions. Generally, the person ordering the merchandise pays the delivery costs. Include this amount in your check when sending payment with the order letter.

If items you are ordering are to be delivered to different destinations, give the name and complete address to which each item is to be sent. When merchandise is needed by a specific date, be sure to mention the date and possibly the occasion; for example, ". . . for our annual spring sale, which begins on April 7."

### Payment

Tell the supplier *how* you will pay for the merchandise. You may enclose a check, a money order, or a bank draft for the payment. Refer to the exact amount of the payment you are enclosing so that the supplier can readily see you have sent the correct amount. Be sure to refer specifically to the check, money order, or other type of payment you enclose.

If you have a charge account with the supplier, you can request that the entire amount for the merchandise, the sales tax, and the delivery expenses be charged to your account.

Use a *format* that makes your letter easy to read. When ordering several items, try to tabulate the information. When tabulating is inappropriate, you can space all information that pertains to one item of merchandise in paragraph form. Two good formats are illustrated in the letters in Figures 5-3 and 5-4.

Spacing the contents of the order letter so that the prices are in a column on the right-hand side of the letter will enable the supplier to verify quickly the total amount for the merchandise, the sales tax, and the delivery charges. Show this total clearly in the letter.

Regardless of the format you choose, arrange the information so that it can be read easily and accurately. Such an arrangement helps the supplier to fill your order quickly and helps ensure that you receive each item ordered.

Remember, the addressee will be pleased to receive your letter. You can, therefore, begin immediately with a courteous request that the merchandise be sent. End your letter with a note of goodwill. A courteous, positive reference to your belief that the supplier will fill your order promptly can be a very good ending.

**Figure 5-3**
Order Letter with Items Tabulated

## MAYFIELD HANDICRAFTS, INC.
Mayfield, NC 28071

April 26, 1985

Miller Office Supply Company
1181 Broad Street
Austin, TN 37136

REQUEST FOR MERCHANDISE

Please send me the following merchandise by parcel post:

| Quantity | Description | Price | Total |
|---|---|---|---|
| 4 reams | Onionskin, 8½ by 11, 7-lb. | $ 3.30 | $13.20 |
| 3 reams | Bond paper, 8½ by 11, 20-lb., white | 6.50 | 19.50 |
| 2 boxes | Envelopes, No. 10, white | 5.40 | 10.80 |
| 2 dozen | Pencils, No. 2, black lead | 1.20 | 2.40 |
| 1 dozen | Typewriter ribbons, black, cotton for Royal electrics | 18.00 | 18.00 |
| | Postage | | 3.60 |
| | Sales tax | | 3.20 |
| | Total | | $70.70 |

A check for $70.70 is enclosed.

*Jeffrey K Klinstiver*

JEFFREY K. KLINSTIVER, CHIEF ACCOUNTANT

bac

Enclosure

**Figure 5-4**

## The Farm and Garden Shop

BRENTWOOD, AL 35360

July 3, 1985

Pick-Wick Wholesalers, Inc.
1226 First Avenue North
Birmingham, AL 35200

Please send us the three following items and charge the total
for them and the shipping cost to our account--No. 386670:

Harvey 25" Riding Mower, No. 3-46-4, 5 H.P.,
B & S 4-cycle engine, 25" cut, 3 speeds forward
and reverse parking brake                              $979

Robin Tiller, 5 H.P., Cobb and Rainey engine,
recoil start                                            489

Steel Wheelbarrow, 3 cubic feet                          27

I will appreciate your sending these items by motor freight to
arrive at our store before July 8.

Jimmy W. Suiter
Manager

rtm

## QUESTIONS FOR DISCUSSION

1.  Why is format more important for order letters than for some other types of business letters?

2.  Why should you thank a person for calling your attention to an error you have made?

3.  Why is it important that letters complying with requests, showing gratitude, or submitting an order be written promptly?

4.  What kinds of information would a new customer like to receive in addition to being told the request for credit has been approved?

## EXERCISES

Improve the following sentences.

1.  I should like to take this opportunity to thank you for sending the catalog that I requested October 6.

2.  The installation of the machine is a simple job.

3.  In reply to your letter of June 16, I am enclosing a copy of the report that was written by our sales manager.

4.  I wish to thank you for sending me a copy of the book entitled YOUR FIRST ADVENTURE IN BUSINESS.

5.  It is our policy to be prompt and fair to our customers.

6.  I have received the check for which I thank you.

7.  They should like to be of assistance to him in some way.

8.  Please do not hesitate to get in touch with me at any time that I may be able to help you.

9.  Enclosed is my check for $9 in payment of invoice No. 7673.

10. The second pamphlet you requested will be mailed to you at a later date.

## PROBLEMS

1.   Which letter-writing guidelines are adhered to and which ones are violated in the following letter?

> Enclosed you will find two copies of the report entitled "Your Future in Advertising" that you requested in your recent letter.
>
> Although this report usually sells for 75 cents a copy, we are glad to send two copies to you without charge. On page 17 you will find a list of the companies for whom we have prepared advertising copy within the past three years. I believe you will enjoy reading this unusual report.
>
> If I can be of further assistance to you, please do not hesitate to contact me.

Rewrite the letter. Add any specific information you wish to add without changing any of the facts that are presented in the letter. Supply the inside address and other necessary parts.

2.   In what ways can the following letter be improved?

> Miller Office Supply Co.
> 1181 Broad Street
> Athens, Ohio
>
> Attention: Mr. James L. Miller
>
> Dear Mr. Miller:
>
> I am interested in obtaining several items of merchandise for use in a class that I shall begin teaching soon. If you carry these items in stock, will you please send them as soon as possible.
>
> I will need 4 packages of onionskin, 3 packages of bond paper, 2 dozen pencils, 100 plain envelopes, and 2 dozen typewriter ribbons. If you need additional information to ship this order, please do not hesitate to get in touch with me.
>
> Cordially yours,

3.  What are some of the good characteristics of the letter that follows? What are the trite or wordy expressions that should be revised? What letter-writing guidelines are violated?

> Please send me two flashlights (catalog No. 30455) and two boxes of No. 2 pencils with red lead (catalog No. 3096).
>
> My check in the amount of $14.00 to cover the cost of this merchandise and the postage is enclosed herewith.
>
> Please send the above items as soon as possible.
>
> Thank you.

4.  You are Professor Mosley, who conducted a short correspondence workshop last Saturday morning for the Tuscaloosa chapter of the Professional Secretaries International. Since you have taught business communications courses for several years, you have a large up-to-date library. Recommending a book on letter writing will, therefore, be an easy task for you. Reply to the following letter that you received this morning. Recommend a book and send Miss Long the information she will need to obtain a copy. Do NOT send her a book. Include any comments that would be appropriate for this letter.

**T.L. PATRICK AGENCY**
FIRST NATIONAL BANK BUILDING
624 Market Street
Tuscaloosa, Alabama 37402

October 5, 1985

Dr. William W. Mosley
Department of Business Administration
Foothills University
Gatlinburg, Tennessee

Dear Dr. Mosley

Enjoyed your correspondence workshop so very much at the Secretarial Institute this past Saturday at the YMCA, and feel that I gained from it.

I am wondering if you have the time to give me the name of a good book on letter writing and if you could, I would appreciate it so very much.

Very truly yours

(Miss) Annette Long

5. Order these items from the McDearman Wholesale Supply Company. The address is P.O. Box 2187, Walker, PA 19171. 4 dozen No. 2 pencils @ 72 cents a dozen, 8 dozen blue ball-point pens @ $3.60 a dozen, 2 dozen red ball-point pens @ $3.60 a dozen, and 5 boxes plain white No. 10 envelopes @ $9.75 a box

   Ask that these items be charged to your account. Supply additional information you will need to write a good order letter.

6. You are the president of a club, a fraternity, or a sorority. You asked an administrative assistant to the president of your college or university to speak to your group at a special meeting last night to tell those attending about the plans for landscaping the residence halls section of the campus.

   Write to the administrative assistant and thank him or her for speaking to your group. Refer to a specific item in the presentation so that the reader of your letter will know you are not sending a form letter that you send to all the speakers you invite.

7. Your first job after you were graduated from college was that of copy editor for the *Morningside Times*, a daily newspaper in Phoenix, Nevada. Your immediate supervisor, Ms. Margaret R. Phillips, helped you a great deal during the twenty-two months you worked for the *Morningside Times*. Although she was sorry to lose you as an employee, she was happy to know that you received a better job in another state. You and she have corresponded with each other occasionally during the two years since you left her office, and she continues to be interested in your progress.

   Last week you were promoted to the job of sports editor for the newspaper for which you now work. Ms. Phillips would be pleased to know about your promotion. And, of course, you are interested in her continued success. Write to her.

8. Miss Irene M. Jackson, who worked as a receptionist for you from 1980-1982, wrote to you and asked that you recommend her for a job as sales representative for a textbook publishing company. You had told her earlier that you would be glad to recommend her for employment. You have written the recommendation letter. Now write to Miss Jackson.

9. Order four of the following items from the Smithfield Sporting Goods Store, 5104 Carlton Pike, Ridgeway, Connecticut:

   a. Ragsdale Golf Cart, deluxe bag brackets, 10½" cast wheels $29.98.
   b. Roomy vinyl golf bag, $18.44, colors: green, black, beige.
   c. Men's suede golf shoes, $21.96, colors: olive, tan, gray, sizes 6-12.
   d. "Bobby Sampson" golf clubs (starter set—3 woods, 4 irons, putter) $82.88 (men's).
   e. "Under Par" golf balls, $8.96 a dozen.

10. Order these two items from the Charleston Discount House, P.O. Box 872, Billington, Vermont: 1 doz. bottles Prim Shampoo at 67 cents a bottle and ¼" Gray and Smiley electric drill, $12.88, with extra long electric cord. The drill is for your brother, whose address is 1151 Walton Road, Brotherton, Massachusetts. Ask that the drill be mailed to him.

11. You are the assistant manager of Fairview Office Supply Company, 124 Main Street, Littleton, IA. 50153. Today you received from Frank R. Scofield an order for an Oliver portable electric typewriter and a Swingway 500 stapling machine. You can ship these items immediately. This order is the first one you have received from Mr. Scofield, whose address is Route 8, Lincoln, IA. 50652. Write to him. In your letter let him know that you are glad to have him as a customer.

12. When you applied for a part-time job on your college campus, you gave as one of your references the name of your high school principal. You were offered the job for which you applied and were told that the principal had given you an excellent recommendation, which was a strong factor in the decision to hire you. Write a letter to your high school principal and thank him for helping you get the job.

# Chapter 6

# Public Relations Messages

People like to be remembered. Sending greeting cards or writing letters to show you think of people can be rewarding for them and for you. Casual as well as intimate friendships, both personal and business, are strengthened by good public relations experiences.

A letter—whether it is an order, an inquiry, a refusal of a request, or any other type—should establish, re-establish, maintain, or promote goodwill. Some messages are sent for the sole purpose of goodwill or good public relations. Messages of that type are discussed in this chapter.

*Sincerity* is the key to good public relations. Any message that is sent solely for public relations, therefore, should be sent only when the writer is sincerely interested in the addressee. True enough, the writer may have the ulterior motive of increasing business or receiving other benefits; but fair-minded people realize they cannot continue to succeed when their success is achieved at the expense of someone else. When an experience is mutually beneficial, the two communicators can reap genuine rewards.

Everybody appreciates compliments, and people of average intelligence usually can sense the difference between compliments and flattery. Do not, therefore, risk embarrassing yourself or insulting the person with whom you are communicating by attempting to flatter.

The message you send should be in keeping with the characteristics of the people involved and the occasion that prompts you to send it. You can present a message in a handwritten or a typewritten letter or by means of a printed greeting card.

Printed cards and letters can be sent on numerous special occasions. Birthdays, holidays, anniversaries, special programs, sales, and the time of moving into a new location or into a new business venture are among the occasions on which special public relations messages are sent.

Whether you send cards and letters as an individual or as an officer of an organization, pay careful attention to the content, the vocabulary, and the mechanics of these messages. Sign with ink a card or a letter you mail as a goodwill gesture. A personal signature contributes a great deal to the warmth and effectiveness of the message—whether it is handwritten, typewritten, or printed.

## GREETING CARDS

The number of people or groups to whom an individual or a group wishes to send special greetings may be so great that sending individual letters is impractical. In these instances printed cards can be sent. In still other situations printed cards may be better than letters.

The choice of message and card design should be made on the basis of the relationship between the sender and the receiver, the nature of the group sending the card, and the characteristics of the recipient. The message to clients, customers, or other business friends should not be as personal as the one to relatives or personal friends. The message should, however, let the recipients know the sender is thinking of them as persons and not just as names in an accounts file or on some other impersonal list.

Because printed messages are sent to many people, you are wise to group the recipients according to common characteristics and then choose messages to fit each group. The more similar the people are in a group, the easier it is to select an appropriate card. For example, a card that would appeal to adults may not appeal to children. Obviously, the greater the differences are within the group, the more general the message should be.

The selection of a card also depends upon the type of organization sending it. Ordinarily, stationers and printers send a card of high-quality printing on equally high-quality paper. Other organizations, especially the smaller ones and the nonprofit groups, usually send less expensive cards. Banks and similar institutions may very likely send a conservative card, whereas an organization such as a resort hotel or a large restaurant would probably prefer a more elaborate greeting card. A novelty shop could appropriately send an unusual or novel form of greeting.

Some card layouts include designs, emblems, or pictures that represent the group sending the message. The layouts can include pictures of the region in which the group operates.

The address on the envelope of a printed greeting card should be handwritten, and *the card should be signed in ink*. One person or a group may sign. For example, the owner, the officers, or all the employees—provided the number is small—may sign the card. The signatures can be in random order, in alphabetic order, in rank order by the offices held, or in still some other order. Quite likely, the people who sign the card use their own pens; and each person may use a color of ink different from the others. Such variety contributes to the "personal touch" of the message. The signatures do not have to be carefully aligned; but when several signatures are in a scrambled arrangement, locating a particular name is difficult.

Examples of signed greeting cards are in Figures 6-1, 6-2, and 6-3.

Cards are used extensively for birthdays, holidays, anniversaries, special programs, and sales as well as other occasions.

### Birthdays

A birthday greeting is usually a welcome piece of mail. This message is appreciated especially by youngsters and elderly people. Cards rather than letters are usually sent on this occasion.

When you send a birthday card to a business or professional acquaintance, limit the message to the birthday greeting only; do *not* make any reference to a business transaction. The inclusion of such an item as advertising literature or an announcement of a sale would spoil an otherwise *good* public relations gesture.

The birthday card in Figure 6-1 was designed to be used by an insurance company for any of its clients. Maintain records of the cards you send to each customer, and use a particular card design only *once* for any one recipient.

**Figure 6-1**

HAPPY BIRTHDAY

The front of this greeting card has a picture of the insurance company office building.

## Holidays

Some business or professional men and women send greeting cards to their clients, customers, or other business friends during holiday seasons. Under certain circumstances this practice is good. While no one objects to receiving a greeting during a holiday season, most people receive so many greeting cards at those particular times they pay little attention to those from businesses. Unless you have a special reason to believe clients or customers would be pleased to receive a greeting card at holiday time, choose another occasion for sending them greetings.

For business or professional relationships that do not ordinarily afford a good occasion on which you can send a special message, you may send a holiday card.

The holiday card in Figure 6-2 was mailed by the manager of a ski club; it was signed by the manager and two office assistants. The card in Figure 6-3 was mailed by the owner of an automobile agency and was signed by the owner, two office assistants, and three salesmen.

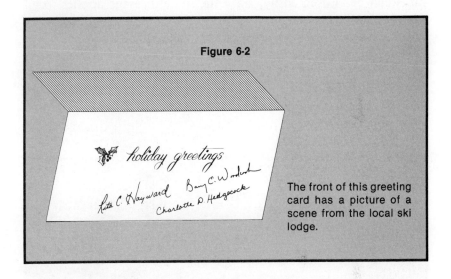

**Figure 6-2**

The front of this greeting card has a picture of a scene from the local ski lodge.

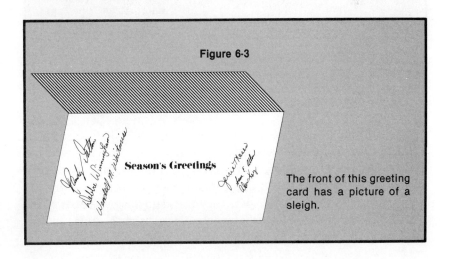

**Figure 6-3**

The front of this greeting card has a picture of a sleigh.

## Anniversaries

Some businesses such as jewelry stores and department stores keep a record of wedding anniversaries of their customers and send greeting cards on that occasion. This practice is not practical, however, for all stores. When the list of regular customers is quite large, the store may send greetings for only the special anniversaries such as the silver or the golden anniversary. Anniversary cards can be chosen easily, since the same message applies to all who celebrate this occasion.

The card in Figure 6-4 was sent by a jewelry store.

Some organizations send messages to their clients or customers on the anniversary of their becoming associated with the organization. While cards can be used for this event, letters are often more desirable. Letters written at such times are discussed later in this chapter.

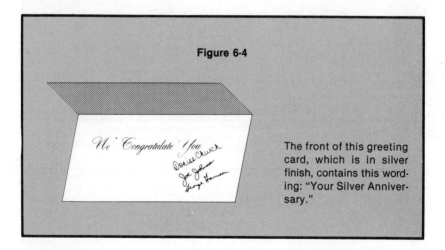

**Figure 6-4**

The front of this greeting card, which is in silver finish, contains this wording: "Your Silver Anniversary."

## Programs

From time to time organizations sponsor a special program for which they issue invitations to a large group. Among these programs are appliance or equipment shows or demonstrations by manufacturers or distributors, fashion shows by department stores, and parties or concerts by schools or other groups. Invitations sent for these programs are usually engraved or printed.

The invitation should include information about the nature of the event, the time and date, the exact location, and a specific invitation to attend. If it is desirable, but not a requirement, that you know the number of people who expect to attend, request a reply. In some instances simply adding the letters R.S.V.P. or please reply in the bottom left-hand corner of the invitation will serve adequately to get the needed replies. Chances are good that a few of the people on the list to receive an invitation will not reply as promptly as they should. To make it easy for the recipient of the invitation to reply and to make it easy for you to process the replies, enclose a card that is to be returned. If accommodations are limited, ask the recipient to make a reservation by returning the card by a specified date. Then if some of the cards are not returned by that date, other people can be invited to attend the event.

The invitation in Figure 6-5 was engraved for mailing to a list of selected purchasers of high-quality merchandise.

Include whatever information is necessary for the recipient to reply to the invitation. You may need to include directions (a map may be helpful) on how to reach the site; and under certain circumstances, you may need to instruct the recipient to present the invitation on arrival at the event.

Be sure to write so clearly that your message cannot be misunderstood.

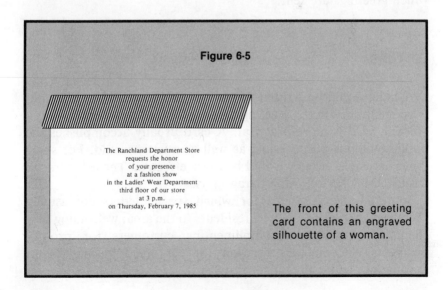

**Figure 6-5**

The Ranchland Department Store
requests the honor
of your presence
at a fashion show
in the Ladies' Wear Department
third floor of our store
at 3 p.m.
on Thursday, February 7, 1985

The front of this greeting card contains an engraved silhouette of a woman.

## Sales

Notifying customers of special sales is a courteous, considerate, and smart thing to do. This announcement can be sent on a printed postal card or on a card similar to the other greeting cards discussed in the preceding paragraphs.

The postal card probably would be best for large sales of general merchandise (low-, medium-, and high-priced items). For the high-priced exclusive or luxury items, though, the greeting card style of announcement sent to a list of *preferred* customers would create a better impression.

Sales announcements are discussed further in the next chapter.

## Other

The special occasions (birthdays, holidays, anniversaries, programs, and sales) mentioned in the preceding paragraphs of this chapter do not comprise an exhaustive list. Numerous other occasions—special as well as holidays—afford an individual or a group opportunities to send greetings to clients, customers, fellow workers, and other friends.

The ideas discussed in this chapter apply to all occasions for which greetings are sent.

## LETTERS

A letter could be written for any of the special occasions that were mentioned in the greeting cards section of this chapter, but a greeting card is more practical. A card usually accomplishes the public relations purpose just as well as a letter would. For some other occasions a letter would be more effective. Those letters are discussed in the following paragraphs.

Some of the situations for which special letters are usually preferred are welcoming new residents to the area, welcoming new clients or customers, complimenting customers for prompt payments, showing appreciation for continued business, congratulating, and expressing sympathy.

## New Residents

New residents may be potential clients or customers of your organization. Cultivate potential business. If a new resident is not yet acquainted with a banker or a department store, for example, persons in one of these establishments have a golden opportunity to add the newcomer to their family of clients or customers. By offering your services, you can help the person who has recently moved into the community; and you can increase your own business volume. What would be better than an opportunity to provide a service or a product and thereby benefit both you and another person?

An officer of one of the four banks in a small college town secures a list of the names and addresses of new faculty members for the college and new personnel on the management level for the various local factories. He writes letters to these people before they move into town. He no doubt uses the same letter, or possibly similar letters, for all of these people but has each letter typewritten. (Using form letters is discussed in Chapter 18). In the letters the officer welcomes the newcomers and offers the services of the bank. He mentions only briefly the routine services—checking accounts, savings accounts, loans, and so on—but stresses special services such as helping the newcomers locate suitable housing. He invites the newcomers to come to the bank when they arrive in town.

For people who move into the town in the summer or the fall, the banker encloses a wallet-size card containing the football game schedule for the local college. He could include other information such as a schedule of local concerts.

Numerous people have said this letter influenced them to do business with that particular bank rather than with one of the three other local banks. The letter in Figure 6-6 is typical of those mailed to new residents.

## New Customers

Everyone likes to be appreciated and likes to be given special consideration within acceptable limits. New customers for a department store, for example, do not expect to be granted discount rates higher than those for other people; but the new

## Figure 6-6

*Raleigh National Bank*

RALEIGH, VIRGINIA 23673

May 27, 1985

Mr. Juan L. Lopez
276 Vine Avenue
Mattson, SC 29065

Dear Mr. Lopez:

We welcome you to Raleigh and offer you the services of our all-purpose bank.

Can we help you locate living accommodations?  A few houses are for sale or for rent inside the city as well as in the suburbs. Mr. Harry W. Allen, who has located houses for eighty-seven new residents during the past two and a half years, would be glad to help you with this task.  Just write to him here at the bank.

You can write without charge as many checks as you wish when the balance in your checking account with us is above $100.  We offer money market certificates as well as regular and Golden savings accounts.  The loan department will gladly work with you in any way.

As I am confident you already know, Raleigh College plays an important role in the lives of our residents.  We appreciate the contributions the college faculty, staff, and students make to the city; and we like to become acquainted with each newcomer. Please come by the bank for a visit when you arrive later in the summer.

                              Cordially,

                              *Charles R. Brown*

                              Charles R. Brown
                              Public Relations Director

wsh

customers appreciate the store personnel's thinking of them as individuals—not just as names on a customer list. Some store managers, therefore, write letters welcoming new customers.

Very little needs to be said in a letter welcoming new customers. As a manager, tell the new customers that their business is appreciated; and mention any existing discount policies and special sales conditions. Also outline the procedures for opening a charge account if you believe a customer qualifies for credit. Your having enough interest to send an individually typed, personally signed letter is often sufficient to encourage the new customer to continue to purchase from your store rather than from a competitor unless, of course, the competing store offers better prices, better services, or better merchandise.

A form letter designed so that minor changes can be made quickly and easily is usually effective for this type of communication. Each letter should be typed either personally or by an automatic typewriter. These letters can be worded so that they sound as if they were composed especially for the recipient. What you, as a fair-minded store manager, would write to one new customer is what you would write to others. Use a direct, friendly style of writing and avoid any references to what your "records show" about the addressee.

Contrast the sentences in the two columns that follow:

| Poor | Good |
|------|------|
| I was pleased to learn, when glancing through our records, that you have purchased merchandise from us four times since January 1. | We appreciate the four purchases you have made at our store since January 1. |
| According to our records, your first purchase at our store was on June 26. | Since your first purchase at our store on June 26, we have added a new line of clothing that will appeal to your family. |
| Our records show you purchased $347.86 worth of merchandise at our store on May 16. | Your $347.86 purchase on May 16 is appreciated. |

Customers realize the employees of any large business must refer to records to recall the details of purchases. They are not favorably impressed, however, by a writer's referring to the records when the reason for sending a letter is good public relations.

A letter welcoming a new customer should be written within a few days after the first purchase is made. This letter, which is comparatively short, can be followed by sales announcements and other sales materials at whatever intervals seem best for the occasion. That type of item, however, should not accompany this letter.

The letter in Figure 6-7 was written to a customer four days after her first purchase at a large department store.

## Prompt-Paying Customers

Praise is a *positive* motivating device. Use it freely and sincerely to promote goodwill. All people like to know they or their performances are recognized and appreciated.

Although all customers are expected to pay their accounts promptly, your letting them know you appreciate their fine paying habits can mean a great deal to them. Write them a letter from time to time to compliment them. Make these letters short, direct, sincere, and friendly. Mail them at *irregular* intervals. Mailing them at obviously scheduled times such as every five years would detract from the effectiveness of this thoughtful gesture. The readers would probably sense the routine handling of records that prompted you to write.

Too frequent mailing of letters of this type to any person would detract from their effectiveness. The frequency of writing to customers may be determined by:

1.  The length of time they have transacted business with you

2.  The frequency of their purchases

3.  The size of their purchases

4.  Their personalities

5.  A combination of these factors or one of several others

**Figure 6-7**

## Ranchland Department Store
### Spring City, Kansas 66012

October 4, 1985

Miss Alice Coleman
2715--22 Street
Billings, NE 68015

Dear Miss Coleman

Miss Geraldine Northcutt enjoyed helping you make clothing
selections when you visited our store last Friday.  Any of
the salesclerks will gladly help you choose from our large
variety of high-quality merchandise.

Your name has been added to the list of persons to receive
announcements of special sales.  Please remember that the
2 percent discount you received by paying cash last Friday
will apply to any purchase you make from us.

We look forward to your visiting us again soon.

Sincerely

Brad J. Sexton

Brad J. Sexton
Manager

glm

Regardless of the system you use to schedule these public relations letters, write in a way that the readers will realize you are genuinely interested in them. The letter in Figure 6-8 was used for this purpose.

Form paragraphs, which are discussed in Chapter 18, can be devised to serve as parts of many of these letters. Special, individually dictated paragraphs can be added to the form paragraphs at the time the letter is typewritten.

## Continued Business

Some customers do not pay their accounts as promptly as you would like them to, yet they always pay their accounts in full without having to be prompted. These customers are valued too. When they have been buying from you for several years and are satisfied with your products and your services, you want to encourage them to continue buying from you.

A letter similar to the one you mail to compliment the customers who always pay promptly can be sent to these valued customers also. Omit, of course, any reference to their paying habits; but let them know you appreciate their business. Write these short letters in a direct, sincere, and friendly style. The letter in Figure 6-9 is an example.

Any letter mentioned in this chapter is more appealing to the recipient if it is typewritten than if it is duplicated. The number to be mailed can be so great, however, that you have to duplicate them. Chapter 18 contains more information on mailing identical or similar letters.

## Congratulations

*Congratulate* is a good word. Any of its forms connotes pleasantness. A person who receives an honor or succeeds in some endeavor—is elected to an office, is promoted to a higher-level job, and so forth—has reason to be happy. Human nature's being what it is, people want to recognize the successes of their friends and associates and to share the thrill of accomplishment. This eagerness to share happiness is frequently expressed by using some form of the word *congratulate.*

**Figure 6-8**

*Ranchland Department Store*
Spring City, Kansas 66012

August 20, 1985

Mr. Burton M. French
1126 Hazelhurst Road
Fleming, NE 68539

Dear Mr. French

You know, of course, your bill-paying habits are of the highest
calibre; and we want you to know we realize that too.

We surely do appreciate having you as a regular customer.  Your
clothing selections represent us well, and we will continue to
provide high-quality merchandise that will appeal to you.

Because you are one of our "preferred" customers, you can purchase any item we sell by simply signing the sales slip.

Cordially

C. Bruce Posey
Credit Manager

cfy

**Figure 6-9**

*Ranchland Department Store*
**Spring City, Kansas 66012**

March 8, 1985

Mr. Elliot W. Sawyer
267 West Sixth Street
North Plains, KS 66651

Dear Mr. Sawyer

We like transacting business with you and your family.  To keep
you as regular customers, we will continue to offer only the
highest-quality merchandise.  We will offer it at competitive
prices and provide the same courteous, efficient services you
have come to expect since you opened your account with us six
years ago.

Your signature is as good as cash in any department of our store.

Sincerely

*C. Bruce Posey*
C. Bruce Posey
Credit Manager

cfy

When congratulating a person with whom you are closely associated, an oral statement is usually the most appropriate way to express congratulations. This statement may be combined with a smile, a firm handshake, a slap on the back, or another gesture.

When you want to congratulate someone you do not expect to see within the next few days *or* when the accomplishment is an unusual one, write a letter. Write immediately and make your congratulatory remarks in the first paragraph.

Here are examples of beginnings:

> Congratulations on doing a fine job of writing the article "Dilemmas of the Purchasing Officer" for the October issue of the *Office Executive*.

> \* \* \*

> I congratulate you on passing the Certified Professional Secretary's examination.

In most situations you have enough interest in the accomplishment to write more than just a one-sentence letter. After all, you write because you are interested and want to make the reader feel good. In the sentences that follow the beginning, say something *specific* about the accomplishment that will let the reader know you have thought about it.

Read these examples:

> Congratulations on doing a fine job of writing the article "Dilemmas of the Purchasing Officer" for the October issue of the *Office Executive*. I am especially interested in your proposed solution to the human relations problems that arise because bids are mailed after the date announced for opening them.

> I look forward to seeing you at the convention in Kansas City in December.

> \* \* \*

> I congratulate you on passing the Certified Professional Secretary's examination.

Because only 3 percent of the people who take that examination pass all six parts on the first attempt, you have justification to be proud of your accomplishment. Your hard work in preparing for the examination obviously paid rich dividends.

I wish all the graduates of this department would set the CPS rating as one of their goals.

Your superiors are just as much human as you, your peers, and your subordinates. They, too, appreciate recognition. Congratulating superiors is a fine practice, provided your remarks are sincere and are stated in a way that the readers do not think you are apple-polishing. Be careful not to volunteer *advice* or appear to try to direct their activities.

Just about all congratulatory messages should be short. The following example contains a congratulatory comment, a specific reference to the accomplishment, and an expression of confidence.

Congratulations! I was pleased to read in the *News-Sentinel* yesterday that you were elected president of the Jackson Chapter of the Rotary Club.

I am confident you will perform the duties of that office in your usual efficient manner.

Repetitious oral statements of congratulations for any occasion would bore the listener and may seem to be insincere. The person who receives a congratulatory letter, however, reads it several times before discarding it and often shows it to others. Because the repetitious reading is voluntary, it has a good effect on the reader.

Use letters advantageously. By writing sincere congratulatory messages, you boost the morale of the reader, make yourself feel good, and make a good impression on the reader. You make this good impression in an ethical way.

Write a congratulatory letter when you believe the reader will appreciate it.

## Sympathy

Anyone may experience a misfortune. A misfortune affecting either directly or indirectly the business or the personal affairs of the individual can be minor. Sometimes, unfortunately, major tragedies occur. A mature, fair-minded person not only wishes to share the thrill of the accomplishments of friends, but also has concern for their misfortunes. When misfortune strikes one of your friends, you probably want to express condolence in some way—possibly by writing a letter.

Under certain circumstances you could offer to help in a specific way. For example, suppose a friend's warehouse is destroyed by fire. If you have space that could be used temporarily, your offering the space at a reasonable rate (or possibly without charge for a short period) could help the victim overcome a severe hardship. If you do not have space to offer, telling where some is available could be equally helpful. Regardless of whether the person uses the space you mention, chances are good that your thoughtfulness and your willingness to help will be appreciated.

Write the way you would want someone to write to you if you had a misfortune. When you offer assistance, make your letter sound positive and optimistic. Study the following letter that was written by one businessman to another whose tobacco warehouse was heavily damaged by fire:

> The 2,000 cubic feet of space that was added this fall to our warehouse on Highway 61 is not being used. We would be glad for you to use it without charge until November 15, the date Mr. James L. Hall's lease will become effective.
>
> I am sorry the fire damaged your warehouse on Pinehurst Street. No doubt, though, the repairs will be completed before November 15.

A personal tragedy such as the death of a business partner or a member of the family is so great and of such nature that the only assistance you can provide is an expression of sympathy. Sympathy is expressed by making personal visits, sending a representative to visit, sending flowers, contributing to a special fund, mailing a printed card, or writing a letter. One never knows exactly which action would be best. Often, a letter is appreciated most. Usually, writing a letter is more appropriate than sending a printed card.

The main idea to bear in mind about letters written to express sympathy because of a death is that you can accomplish only one

**Figure 6-10**

627 Market Street
Handley, KS 66581
February 5, 1985

Mr. and Mrs. Ray M. Gold
286 Fifth Avenue
Hazel, KS 66121

Dear Mr. and Mrs. Gold:

I realize that at a time such as this there is little I can say that would be very comforting to you, but I want you to know you have my deepest sympathy.

Sincerely,

Kermit M. Hayes

objective: let the readers know you are thinking of them. Seldom can you write anything that would be especially comforting. Do not add to the reader's anguish by reminiscing or by referring to sentimental experiences.

The letter in Figure 6-10 was handwritten to an associate whose daughter was killed in an automobile mishap. Handwriting is probably preferred to typewriting for letters of this nature.

*Simplicity* is the key word for letters expressing sympathy.

## QUESTIONS FOR DISCUSSION

1. What are sources of names and addresses of people whose names are not in your records?

2. You could delegate to your secretary the handling of some public relations messages. What are some of them that your secretary could handle as well as (or perhaps even better than) you could?

3. What are some of the advantages of sending personally written letters instead of printed cards?

## EXERCISES

Improve the following sentences.

1. I hope that you will be able to be in attendance at the fair June 6.

2. Please return the enclosed card as soon as possible.

3. Why not visit our store during the annual sale?

4. Ms. Brown will be glad to be of service to you.

5. We are looking forward to your future orders.

6. Do not forget the meeting October 12.

7. Development of the outline was a challenge.

8. Mr. Riley W. Holtsman is the party who called you this morning.

9. You will find a description of Model No. 634 on page 8.

10. May we take this opportunity to congratulate you on your 25th wedding anniversary.

## PROBLEMS

1. You are the manager of the production department of Phillips Manufacturing Company. You learned when reading the local newspaper this morning that Jerry E. Hutton, who was your capable assistant manager more than three years, was elected this year's chairman of the United Way Fund in your city. You know he was elected to this office because he is well organized and is well liked and admired by many civic leaders and business personnel.

    Write to him; congratulate him; wish him luck; and assure him you are confident he will have a successful fund-raising campaign this year. His address is 2627 White Road, Deerfield, MI 48112.

2. James C. Martin and Thomas A. Gresham, owners of a large successful department store in a city of some 450,000 people, have been buying house furnishings from your company for resale since 1948. You have known both men since you became president of your company in 1957. You have maintained a fine working relationship. This morning you learned that Mr. Gresham died one week ago.

    Write a letter to Mr. Martin and express sympathy in the loss of his close friend and business partner. The name of the department store is Martin-Gresham, and the address is 109 Second Avenue North, Whitfield, OH 45101.

3.  You heard an unusually good presentation last night when you attended a regularly scheduled monthly meeting of the Administrative Management Society. The speaker, Ms. Inez M. Missling, talked about psychological effects that office technology is having on today's office workers.

    Ms. Missling, a consultant with Anderson, Radford, and Smith Consultants, Inc., has done extensive research on this topic. Not only is she well informed, but also she presented her many worthwhile ideas clearly, convincingly, and entertainingly.

    Write to Ms. Missling at Anderson, Radford, and Smith Consultants, Inc., 1148 Water Valley Road, Houston, TX 77211. Tell her you enjoyed the presentation and congratulate her on doing an outstanding job of presenting her ideas. Mention a specific point or two that you learned from her remarks.

4.  You are the manager of the production department of a manufacturer of sports equipment. A manufacturer of sports equipment in a city 200 miles away installed some special automation equipment about three months ago. You had an opportunity to talk briefly with Mr. James M. Roberts, the production manager for the company; and you asked him whether you and your assistant could visit his factory to observe the new equipment in operation. He seemed eager to show you the equipment.

    Yesterday you and your assistant visited that factory and were given a tour and courteous treatment. Write to the manager and thank him for giving you the tour.

5.  Ms. Maria M. Crisp bought $471.96 worth of clothing from one of your efficient salesclerks eleven days ago. The salesclerk was helpful, but used no high-pressure tactics in selling the clothing. You were surprised, therefore, when you learned this morning that Ms. Crisp had returned a jacket and two of the dresses without giving a reason for returning them. Send her a refund check for $241.94. Encourage her to return to your store for future purchases. You are the manager of the women's clothing department of your store.

6.   You are a first-line supervisor in a large manufacturing company. A young man, Jason O. Kline, who entered the company training program at the same time you entered it two years ago has been promoted to the position of assistant manager of the transportation department. He is a likable person and is quite competent. You are, therefore, happy to learn of his recent promotion.

Because the organization for which you work is large, you usually see Jason only about once a month. Write a letter and congratulate him on being promoted.

7.   You are the manager of a department store in a city of about 100,000 residents. Mr. and Mrs. Harlan J. Cope moved to your city when they were married 25 years ago. Since that time they have been two of your best customers. They buy almost all their clothing, as well as many other types of merchandise, from you. You have had an opportunity to talk with them occasionally. You have learned the exact date of their silver anniversary next month. Write a letter to them and congratulate them.

8.   As manager of Independent Wholesale Foods, write a letter of sympathy to one of your regular customers, Big Foods of America, whose basement was flooded during the storm we had last Monday. Although the water did not reach the main floor of the grocery, many food items totaling several thousand dollars that were stored in the basement were destroyed. Mr. David Allen Winston is manager of Big Foods. The store is in your city.

9.   You are the owner and manager of Ramsey's Furniture Store, 57 West Broad Street, Century, CT 06011, which opened two months ago. Your grand opening was a great success, but business has slackened a little now. You have decided to send letters to all new property owners inviting them to visit your store and buy any furniture they need to furnish their new houses or to replace worn-out pieces they have. Emphasize the fact that your store offers 20 percent off when cash is paid or will establish credit accounts for all qualified customers. Of course, your Drexwell and Thomasburg furniture is nationally known. Delivery is made within two days to anyone within a 100-mile radius of Century.

10. You are the owner and operator of a laundry and dry cleaning establishment in Greenwich, Maryland. The home of one of the Greenwich residents who has been one of your regular customers for several years was destroyed by fire yesterday. You know that Mrs. Louise F. Riddle, whose home was destroyed, had very little insurance on the property. Write a letter of sympathy to her. She is a teller in the First National Bank of Greenwich.

11. As public relations director of the Bank of Sterling, Montana, write a letter congratulating one of your customers, Mr. Paul Wilson Bryant, on passing the Montana Bar Examination, which was held last month. You read about his achievement in the *Sterling Public Dispatch*.

# Chapter 7

# Persuasive Letters

The ability to persuade can contribute to success in business. A degree of persuasion is involved in any leadership role. Executives, as well as personnel on the lower levels of the organization chart, know that much more can be accomplished through persuading (convincing—but not begging) people than through attempting to drive them.

Self-confident people *sell* their ideas to others—superiors, subordinates, prospects, customers, and so on. They display their leadership ability by convincing others that whatever they are trying to sell is worthwhile, and they do this diplomatically. Fair-minded as the successful business people are, they think of the ways others could benefit by *buying* the concept, the service, or the product they are trying to sell. They point out these benefits in a simple, specific way; and they omit flattery.

A salesclerk in a clothing store may stress, among the other attributes of a garment, the quality of the material, the tailoring, and the way the garment enhances the appearance of the prospective purchaser. A salesclerk, who obviously expects to make a profit for the store, concentrates on the benefits to be derived by the prospective purchaser and mentions these benefits in a sincere, cheerful manner. Obvious flattery in a sales situation would probably tempt the prospective customer to go elsewhere to purchase a similar or an identical item.

When persuading a person to accept an assignment (with or without pay) use the same techniques you would use to make a sale in a department store or in other situations.

For persuasive letters use the same principles that are used for face-to-face selling. A degree of persuasion is required in letters that are written to invite, to request, to ask for an adjustment, to solicit, to collect, and to sell a product or a service.


## INVITING

When you invite people to speak to a group, to serve on a committee, or to submit suggestions or recommendations, you compliment them. Inviting them lets them know you believe they have the ability to do what you are asking them to do. You can, therefore, extend invitations in a straightforward manner without feeling in any way apologetic. Frequently, though, persons you invite have to be sold on the idea of accepting the invitations. You have to convince them they have the ability to carry out the assignments you are asking them to accept, or you have to convince them their completing the assignment will benefit them or someone else.

Write invitations so clearly that the readers know exactly *what* you are asking them to do and *when*, *where*, and *how* they are to do it. Facts are almost always more useful than opinions in persuading people to accept invitations. Therefore, give one or more reasons for selecting them as participants. State the benefits, which may be monetary, they can expect to receive and possibly explain how their participation will contribute to the success or welfare of others. Write persuasively, cordially, and confidently. When you use the positive approach, the recipients are more likely to accept. Study the letter in Figure 7-1.

**Figure 7-1**

ADMINISTRATIVE MANAGEMENT SOCIETY
P. O. BOX 26    RILEY, NE 89301

October 11, 1984

Mr. Wendell W. Robbins
General Manager
Johnson Wholesale Company
Hastings, CO 81041

Dear Mr. Robbins

The four members of our organization who heard you speak at the
Administrative Management Society meeting in Athens on August 22
have recommended you so highly that we would like you to be the
speaker for our dinner meeting on Thursday, February 14, 1985.
We will meet at 6 p.m. in the Walnut Room of the Riley Motel.
About fifty-five men and women will attend.

Could you give the same speech, "Cutting Administrative Costs,"
you gave at the Athens meeting?  Our four representatives liked
the content of that speech and the manner in which you presented
it.

We will pay your expenses and give you an honorarium of $150.  I
will be glad to reserve you a room at the Riley Motel, the newest
motel in Riley, for the night of February 14.

Please let me know soon whether you can speak to our group.

Cordially

*Cheryl R. Williams*

Cheryl R. Williams, Chairman
Program Planning Committee

pac

## REQUESTING

Requests are a part of the normal business operations of our economy and are made by business personnel, homemakers, and others. Many requests—routine and special—are made by writing letters.

### Routine Requests

When requesting something that is generally available, you have to use very little persuasion. A courteous tone is all that is needed. Make courtesy a characteristic of every letter you write.

In making routine requests, show proper consideration for the reader and at the same time do yourself a favor by making it easy for the reader to understand your letter and to reply to it. If your request is for a product, provide all the details needed to identify the specific item you want to receive. Specify the quantity, the size, the color, and any other variable that is applicable. This letter is similar to an order letter (see Chapter 5) except that it does not mention a payment method and probably does not specify a method of delivery.

If the supplier has indicated you are to send a stamped, addressed envelope, enclose it. And, of course, follow the good practice of referring to the enclosure. Often, an organization that supplies free materials prefers to use its own envelopes for mailing these materials. As more people see the name and address on the envelopes, the organization becomes better known. Banks, department stores, and some other organizations use their own envelopes when answering *routine* or *special* requests.

The letter in Figure 7-2 is an example of a routine request for a product that is supplied at no cost.

Write requests for services in the same way you request products. Include the specifics of the services desired and the time, the date, and the exact location where the service is to be performed. The service requested in the letter in Figure 7-3 was paid for by a maintenance contract between the two companies.

Letters that request more than one item should be organized so well that the reader can easily see the number of items you want. This good arrangement of the letter helps the reader, and it helps to ensure that you receive each item requested. The letter in Figure 7-4 is presented in an easy-to-read format.

**Figure 7·2**

519 North Oak Street
Pine Hill, NC 28060
June 18, 1988


Woodley Furniture Company
1222 State Street
Radford, NC 27961

REQUEST FOR "DECORATOR'S GUIDE"

Please send me the ten-page "Decorator's Guide" you advertised
yesterday in the Pine Hill Times. This booklet should help my
husband and me in selecting the furnishings for our house that
is to be completed this fall.

Your sending the "Decorator's Guide" so that it will reach me
before we leave on a two-week vacation trip on July 1 will be
appreciated.

Jean K. Job
MRS. JEAN K. JOB

**Figure 7-3**

# Hastings Shirt Company, Inc.
Hastings, CO 81041

October 7, 1988

Mr. Herman C. Waters
Colby Office Supply Company
402 East Broadway
Hampton, CO 81632

COMPUTER REPAIR

Please ask one of your servicemen to come to our factory
this week to repair the ribbon mechanism on a Wellington
computer.  This machine, which is covered by a service
agreement with you, is in Room 110.

Our offices are open from 8:15 a.m. until 4:45 p.m. each
day.

*Kandy K. Brown*
KANDY K. BROWN, ADMINISTRATIVE ASSISTANT

**Figure 7-4**

1151 Pebble Beach Road
Santa Fe, CA 93406
June 26, 1985


Dr. Raphael L. Wickleman
Director of Admissions
Central California College
San Juan, CA 95125

Dear Dr. Wickleman

So that I can decide which college to attend next fall, will
you please answer the following questions:

1.  Is a first-quarter freshman who lives in a men's
    dormitory permitted to operate an automobile on
    campus?

2.  If I decide to move into a private home at mid-
    term, will the unused portion of the rent I must
    pay when I register be refunded?

3.  When must I register for the private golf lessons
    that are offered during September and October?

I will appreciate your prompt answers to these questions.  All
the other questions I had were answered by the printed materials you sent me on June 18.  Thank you for sending them.

Sincerely

Steve Duncan

Steve Duncan

## Special Requests

More persuasion is required in special requests than in those that are routine. When sending a special request to an acquaintance or to someone else who is likely to ask a similar favor of you, less persuasion is needed than in other situations. You may profitably express your willingness to return the favor, as in the letter in Figure 7-5. The writer of that letter did not anticipate a particular request from the addressee, but she realized a possibility did exist. Notice the arrangement of that letter; the addressee could reply easily.

Often, the effectiveness of special request letters can be enhanced by telling how the addressee will profit by complying. For example, some letters that are mailed to ask that a questionnaire be completed and returned contain promises to send summaries of the findings of the questionnaire survey. Since the writer sends the questionnaire to only those people who have a genuine interest in the survey, the writer can logically assume the recipient would like to have a summary of the findings.

In some instances a product is offered as a reward for complying with a special request. Do not write in a way that the reader could logically interpret your offer as a bribe, but making an offer as a token of appreciation can be appropriate and in good taste.

Enclose a stamped, addressed envelope for the reply to a special request.

## SEEKING ADJUSTMENTS

Asking for an adjustment is actually making a special request; but because adjustment requests are so important, they are treated in this separate division.

Even in the most efficient organizations, errors are made sometimes. "To err is human." Merely acknowledging the fact that an error was made through normal human behavior without making a genuine attempt to correct the error is inexcusable. Repeated actions such as that could cause business persons to lose the respect of their associates (and rightly so). The loss of respect through such actions could lead to business failure. Alert, successful business people recognize the importance of correcting

**Figure 7-5**

## CENTRAL HIGH SCHOOL
Spokane, OR 97067

April 4, 1985

Miss Ramona Ashbury
Chairperson, Business Department
Ragland Senior High School
Ogden, OR 97644

Dear Miss Ashbury:

Mr. Robert Waverly, the McFarland Publishing Company representative who visited your school last Friday, made some very
complimentary statements about your model office arrangement.
We are drawing plans for a layout that is similar to the description he gave of yours.  To help us with these plans, will
you please answer these questions:

   1.  How many work stations are in your classroom?

   2.  How much aisle space is between each two rows
       of stations?

   3.  What types of filing equipment do you use to
       illustrate the three filing systems that are
       covered in Study Guide 275?

Because our classrooms are similar to yours in size and design,
your answering these questions will be helpful.  I will welcome
an opportunity to assist you in some way.

            Cordially,

            *J. Lynn Greeson*

            J. Lynn Greeson
            Chairperson, Business Department

jst

errors. Although they dislike making errors, they appreciate the "injured" person's calling an error to their attention so that a satisfactory correction can be made.

Fair-mindedness is needed for success. People are obligated to be fair to themselves and to those with whom they communicate. When, as the result of an error, you suffer financially or suffer an inconvenience, you owe it to yourself and to the person who made the error to call it to that person's attention. Generally, fair-minded people believe most other people are also fair-minded. Their first communication with another person is based, therefore, on the assumption that they are associating with an honest, upright citizen. They know, however, that a small percentage of people cannot be trusted.

When errors are made or acts that appear to be unjust are committed, call these errors or injustices to the attention of the persons responsible. Give them an opportunity to make a satisfactory adjustment or a proper restitution. Quite possibly those persons are not aware that the errors have been made. They may know some particular thing has been done, but they may not realize it is unfair. When such an error or act is brought to their attention, they (if they are fair-minded) not only correct the error; but they also appreciate your calling their attention to it, thus enabling them to avoid doing the same thing again.

Sometimes people feel that errors have been made or that they have been treated unfairly only to learn later that they themselves were at fault because of a misinterpretation. Discuss misunderstandings so that good public relations can be restored.

Give a person who makes an error an opportunity to correct it. If a waitress gives you a check for $9.65 that should total only $9.45, ask *her* to correct it. Do not wait until presenting the check to the cashier to ask for a correction. Give salesclerks in department stores opportunities to correct any errors they make. Do not report errors to department managers or to any other employee unless the salesclerk declines to correct them.

Publicizing errors to outsiders—people who are not employees of the organization in which an error is made—is one of the most inappropriate things that can be done. Not only is such an act a waste of time and energy, but it is also unethical. Be ethical in all your communications. When you do not know the name of the person who should make an adjustment, address the letter to the adjustment manager.

As a tactful, diplomatic writer, choose words carefully in order to maintain goodwill. When requesting an adjustment, therefore, avoid using negative, unpleasant words such as *error*, *mistake*, *failed*, and *failure*. Put yourself in the reader's place. Compare the expressions in the two columns that follow and ask yourself how you would react to any one of them if it were in a letter asking you to make an adjustment.

| Negative | Positive |
| --- | --- |
| Please correct the error on the enclosed statement. | Please adjust the total on the enclosed statement. |
| Please correct the mistake on the enclosed statement. | Please correct the total on the enclosed statement. |
| Please credit my account with the $45 check you failed to record last month | Please credit my account with the $45 check I sent to you on May 2. |

Positive statements are almost always more pleasant and more effective than negative statements.

Request an adjustment only when you honestly believe the adjustment is due you. And when you do believe an adjustment is due, you owe it to yourself and to the other person or group to ask for it. Request the adjustment confidently and courteously. The factors that led to your decision to write a letter should enable you to decide on the best way to organize the letter contents. Present the request first or the explanation first, or present the message according to the time sequence of events.

**Request First**

When you feel reasonably sure the reader will readily agree that your request should be granted, begin your letter by asking for the adjustment. Then give your reason. Make your explanation clear and sufficient to justify the request, but do not include unnecessary details. A tone of goodwill should permeate this message. The end of the letter may very well refer confidently to the request and mention appreciation for prompt action. The following letter is an example of a successful adjustment request.

> Would you please adjust the balance of our account (No. 30762). As was mentioned in my letter of June 7 ordering ten reams of letterhead stationery, our account had a $12 credit balance at that time. The current balance should, therefore, be only $18 instead of $30.
>
> We will appreciate your sending a corrected statement of our account before the end of the month.

Notice that the tone of the preceding letter is positive and that goodwill is evident from the beginning to the end. Contrast with that letter the following message, which contains negative wording.

> Please correct a mistake you made in our account (No. 30762). The balance of $30 is the correct amount for the ten reams of letterhead stationery we ordered on June 7, but you failed to give us credit for the $12 credit balance we had before placing the June 7 order.
>
> We will pay the account after you correct your error and send us another statement.

Would the second letter do much to maintain or to promote goodwill? Although the facts are accurate and the letter is concise and well organized, the message contains nothing that contributes to good public relations.

Because the adjustment that was requested in each of the two preceding letters was unquestionably due, the writer of either letter would receive the adjustment. The courteous tone of the first letter, though, promotes goodwill. Such letters frequently help to establish a relationship that is beneficial to the writer in unexpected future situations.

While the writer of the letter with the negative wording would obtain the requested adjustment, a letter of that type can influence the reader to react negatively to future business transactions.

## Explanation First

The nature of some situations is such that an explanation of the problem is needed to set the stage for an adjustment request. A reader who understands a problem usually reacts favorably to the request. The letter in Figure 7-6 illustrates the explanation-first approach.

That letter brought a quick response stating that a new pair of shoes (the same size, style, and color) had been mailed to replace the defective pair. The response also included a note of appreciation for being given an opportunity to make an adjustment.

## Time Sequence

In seeking some adjustments, the writer may be wise to relate all the factors pertaining to the problem in the order in which they occurred. Such a plan is to be avoided, however, because it leads to wordiness. In this plan more details than are required to obtain the adjustment are usually included. The letter in Figure 7-7 is an example.

## SOLICITING

Letters are used frequently for soliciting funds or services. When soliciting funds or services for an organization that is well known to the reader, the letter-writing task is much easier than when you have to describe the organization and its activities. A reader who has already been convinced that the organization is worthwhile needs little more than enough information to learn the kind of help you are seeking. The reader usually helps when it is feasible to do so.

The following letter was mailed to a civic-minded businessman who had contributed on several occasions to the group that mailed the letter.

The local Homemakers Club is soliciting the help of the business people in our city again this year to send children of low-income families to summer camp.

**Figure 7-6**

509 North Cedar Avenue
Wheaton, ND 58201
July 5, 1985

Adjustment Manager
Floorshine Shoe Store
1104 Broad Street
Boise, ND 58201

DEFECTIVE SHOES

For no apparent reason the sole has separated from the upper portion of one of the Floorshine shoes I purchased from you on May 6.
I mailed the pair of shoes to you by parcel post this morning.

I am confident that when you examine the shoes, you will realize
they have been worn only a few times.  You will, of course, also
notice the defect in the left shoe.

Having worn Floorshine shoes for the past twelve years (I have
bought at least five pairs at your store), I am surprised this
difficulty has developed.  I realize, however, that occasionally
an item in any top-quality line of merchandise may be less satisfactory than its "peers."

I believe you will appreciate my calling your attention to these
"10½ C's," and I will appreciate your making an adjustment.

COLLIE B. JARED, JR.

**Figure 7-7**

1151 Hammond Road
Molaree, WS 54548
October 31, 1988


Adjustment Manager
Kerley Vacuum Cleaners, Inc.
248 Willow Street, N.E.
Lanier, MI 49946


REQUEST FOR ADJUSTMENT


On September 6 I purchased a Kerley vacuum cleaner and a rug
renovator unit from Mr. Terry Wolf, your representative in the
Molaree area.  I am quite happy with the vacuum cleaner; when
I used the rug renovator, though, it did not do a satisfactory
job.

I took the renovator to the Kerley office and discussed it with
Mr. Wolf's assistant.  He suggested that I leave the renovator
so that Mr. Wolf could check it out and call me the next day
either to explain why the renovator was not doing a satisfactory
job or to refund my money.  Since I did not hear from him for
several days, I tried to call and discovered that the office
had been closed.

On October 14 I called Mr. Wolf's wife, and she explained that
the family was moving out of town and that everything in the
office had already been moved.  She promised to ask her husband
either to bring a renovator to my home or to refund the purchase
price when he would be in town during the weekend of October 26.

When I tried to reach her by telephone yesterday, I discovered
that her telephone had been disconnected.

Will you please send me a refund of $78.16 for the rug renovator
unit ?


*Becky P. Hull*
MRS. BECKY P. HULL

> As you already know, this two-week program includes educational and recreational activities especially planned for the group. We have received applications from 36 deserving boys and girls from nine to eleven years of age. To permit all of them to participate, we must increase our existing fund by $700 before May 1.
>
> Can you help again this year? Any contribution you make will be appreciated as much as ever.

Obviously, more information is needed for a letter to a person who is not already familiar with the organization or its activities. Keep the letter short yet complete, courteous, and interesting. Business people, as well as other citizens, receive so many letters of this nature they may not read the entire letter if it is long. On the other hand, they do not contribute the help that is solicited unless the letter contains adequate information in a well-written style.

Typewritten letters are much more effective than duplicated letters for soliciting. Frequently, form letters must be used, however, when many people are asked to contribute. (See Chapter 18 for more information on preparing form letters.)

An attention-getting device of some kind is needed for a letter that solicits. The attention-getting device is especially important when form letters are used. Among the devices used to get the reader's attention are these:

1.   Pictures

2.   Cartoons

3.   Slogans

4.   Questions

5.   Colored stationery

6.   Special placement on the page

One large university alumni office has used special placement and a special color for the letter *u* as an attention getter:

"We must have U for a f nd."

Attention getting is obviously not enough. To be successful, messages must hold the readers' interest and convince them that the purpose for which the solicitations are made is worthy of their help. Once you have convinced a reader you are soliciting for a worthwhile cause, make it easy to contribute. Give the exact name to whom the check should be written. Or if a service is to be contributed, give complete instructions on *where*, *when*, and *how* the service is to be performed. To encourage a quick response, enclose an addressed, stamped envelope.

## COLLECTING ACCOUNTS

A major portion of today's business is transacted on a credit basis. Water, electric, and telephone services are provided on credit and are usually paid for once a month. Services of professional people—dentists, physicians, and attorneys—are usually paid for on a monthly basis or when a series of services has been completed. An item as small as a greeting card, or even smaller, can be purchased on credit in a store where the buyer has a charge account. Large items such as houses, farms, and ranches are seldom bought on a cash basis; instead, they are purchased on credit from an individual or a bank or another financial institution. Consumable goods—groceries, beverages, meals in restaurants—may be charged to an account. Buyers can have items charged to their accounts, or they can use a credit card to defer payment. Rental plans on typewriters, large electronic computers, and other office machines are forms of credit.

The size, the price, or the nature of an item or a service would not prohibit the user from obtaining that item or service on credit.

A credit arrangement is a convenience for consumers, and it helps suppliers simplify their paperwork. Using credit eliminates the need to carry large sums of money or a checkbook. Also, by paying for services, rentals, or products only one time each month, consumers can easily maintain accurate records of their payments. Suppliers can keep records of accounts due, mail periodic statements, and record receipts more easily than they could handle all the busywork that would be created by cash payments. Maintaining a system for cash payments rather than extending credit for such services as electricity and water would be almost impossible.

A major advantage to suppliers is that the credit system expands business volume because more people can avail themselves of services or products. A major advantage to consumers is that they can enjoy the ownership of clothing, automobiles, houses, and other items before they pay for them. Retailers profit by being able to purchase merchandise and then sell part, or even all, of it before having to pay for it.

The advantages of credit are so numerous that an attempt to mention all of them is beyond the scope of this book.

Why can credit be used so extensively? Because a high percentage of people are honest, one can assume that most accounts will be paid.

So that creditors can meet their own financial obligations and make a satisfactory profit, they must receive payments from their debtors when the payments become due. Credit plans require creditors to establish collection procedures. An effective procedure for collecting payments includes one or more of these steps:

1.   Issuing invoices

2.   Sending statements

3.   Sending duplicate statements

4.   Mailing friendly reminders

5.   Sending form letters

6.   Sending typewritten letters

7.   Issuing ultimatums

**Issuing Invoices**

Issuing an invoice is the first step taken by creditors to collect an amount that is due. To encourage prompt payments, many creditors issue invoices bearing a notation that a discount is allowed if the merchandise or service is paid for within a specified time. A popular notation on an invoice for merchandise reads, "2/10, n/30," which means that debtors are permitted to deduct 2 percent from the invoice total by paying for the merchandise within ten days after the invoice is issued or that they must pay the total amount within thirty days after the invoice date.

Because most good business people take advantage of these prompt-pay discounts, issuing the invoice is frequently the only step necessary to collect the amount due. For any one of various possible reasons—oversight, pressure created by peak workloads, illness, and others—gilt-edge debtors (those of unquestionable integrity and good business practices) occasionally do not make their payments on the due date. When a payment is late, the creditor has to decide what action to take.

### Sending Statements

When the payment is not made in time for the discount, the creditor mails a statement at the end of the billing period (usually at the end of a month). Mailing the statement may be considered the second step in collecting the account. If payment is not made at the end of thirty days, the creditor thinks of possible reasons for the tardiness. The creditor realizes that "to err is human" and, therefore, assumes the tardiness in paying is the result of an honest error. The creditor should be constantly aware that the objective is *to collect the money and at the same time maintain the goodwill of the debtor*. The creditor may, therefore, decide to delay taking action of any kind with the hope that the debtor will pay the account without receiving any type of reminder.

### Sending Duplicate Statements

Creditors may have so many debtors who are tardy in making their payments that they cannot afford to wait many days to receive some of the payments. Under these circumstances a courteous and helpful step is the mailing of a printed (nonpersonal) reminder to each debtor that payment should be made promptly.

When you find yourself in this predicament, you can mail to each of the debtors a duplicate copy of the statement of the amount due. This type of reminder is frequently all that is necessary to collect the money.

## Mailing Friendly Reminders

If the account is not paid soon after the duplicate statement, another subtle reminder may be effective. You can mail another duplicate statement bearing a brightly colored sticker containing such comments as "REMINDER," "JUST A REMINDER," "YOUR FRIENDLY REMINDER," or "FOR YOUR ATTENTION."

## Sending Form Letters

If, after mailing the invoice, a statement at the end of the billing period, a duplicate copy of the statement, and a duplicate of the statement with a sticker notation attached, the debtor still does not pay, at least one further step is obviously required. This next step may be a form letter that has been reproduced with blank spaces provided for filling in these items:

1.  Address and salutation for the debtor

2.  Amount due

3.  Date on which the amount should be paid

4.  Possibly the dates on which previous reminders were mailed

Seldom is the receipt of a form letter of this type rightfully considered to be insulting to the addressee.

Make the tone of the form letter positive, friendly, and courteous. Including a sales pitch for some of your products or services can be quite appropriate at this stage of a collection attempt. Often, a sales pitch serves one or both of these two purposes: (1) to increase sales volume and (2) to help maintain the goodwill of the debtor at the same time that you increase the pressure on the debtor to pay the account.

Because the letters are duplicated rather than typewritten, the receivers realize the sender is giving the same treatment to all others who are delinquent with their payments. This evidence of identical treatment helps to maintain goodwill and to eliminate possibilities of embarrassment for the debtor.

The letter in Figure 7-8 has been effective at this stage of a collection process. The second paragraph would have to be revised to suit the occasion.

### Sending Typewritten Letters

A second and even a third duplicated letter could conceivably be mailed as further steps in the collection process. A more frequently taken step, however, is the mailing of a typewritten letter that has been composed especially for a specific debtor. In this letter you may wisely review the status of the past-due account and the steps that have already been taken to collect it. Omit resale or further sales promotion content in this letter. Concentrate more on collecting the overdue account than on attempting to make more sales to that particular debtor. An appeal to the debtor's pride and good credit standing is ordinarily more effective than other appeals. Tactful yet firm references to the necessity of paying promptly should characterize this letter.

Read the letter in Figure 7-9.

### Issuing Ultimatums

Successful business people realize that in some instances they fare better by losing a small debt than by collecting the account and at the same time creating unfavorable publicity for their organization. Being fair-minded, they go to great lengths to avoid ill will for the debtor and the unpleasantness that would be generated for themselves if they were to turn an unpaid account over to a collection agency or take action against the debtor.

Successful business people are characterized not only by fair-mindedness but also by intelligence. They know that even though a high percentage of people are honest, some are not and that those who are dishonest have to be treated differently. Successful business people—considerate and intelligent—realize that no one thinks more highly of them than they think of themselves. They must take the steps necessary to protect themselves and their associates. They resort to strong measures, therefore, when necessary to collect accounts that are owed by dishonest people.

**Figure 7-8**

# Williamson Wholesale Company
### MUNCIE, OHIO 46362

Dear

Perhaps you have already mailed your check for $_____ to pay
your account that became due on _____.  If you have
mailed your check, please disregard this reminder.

This month we're having a special sale on outdoor items for the
home.  The prices, which are shown on the enclosed leaflet, have
been reduced as much as 20 percent on lightweight lawn furniture,
charcoal grills, children's wading pools, and badminton sets.
Perhaps you would like to send your order right away for a good
supply of these items for your customers.

A stamped, addressed envelope is enclosed for your use in sending
your next order and your check for $_____ if you have not yet
mailed it.

Cordially

*Pamela D. Birdwell*
Pamela D. Birdwell
Collection Manager

rne

Enclosures 2

**Figure 7-9**

# Williamson Wholesale Company
## MUNCIE, OHIO 46362

Dear

You have reason to be proud of your fine reputation for paying
your accounts promptly, and I am confident you want to maintain
that reputation.  Receiving a check for $_____ from you
before _____ would enable us to continue selling to you
on the basis of your signature as well as for cash.

Until after we wrote to you on _____--the third reminder
that your account is overdue--we thought perhaps your payment
had been delayed because of illness, a vacation, or a business
trip.  We are convinced now, though, that one of your capable
assistants would have sent a check if you had been out of the
office for an extended time.

So that we can meet our own obligations and so that we can earn
the profit to which we are entitled by supplying high-quality
merchandise at fair prices, we must have your check for $_____
before _____.

Please use the enclosed envelope.

Cordially

*Pamela D. Birdwell*
Pamela D. Birdwell
Collection Manager

rne

Enclosure

As a business person, remember that *your objective is to collect the overdue account and retain the customer*, provided the customer is trustworthy and therefore the type of person with whom you wish to transact business. In some instances, taking strong action to collect an account makes the debtor respect the creditor. After legal action, the debtor may become a better customer than before. This reaction cannot be expected, however. Many debtors will not want to transact further business with you. Delay turning an account over to a collection agency or an attorney until you are convinced you would rather lose the customer than the money that is due you. If you are confronted with this situation, you have to become involved in some degree of unpleasantness.

State an ultimatum firmly and clearly without any threat or any comment that could rightfully be interpreted as slanderous. Word your letters carefully and keep copies for possible use during the collection process.

A smart thing to do is to prepare a series of messages to be mailed for various steps of the collection process. Do not, however, use the same steps more than once for a customer; and do not use identical steps (beyond the initial phase) for any two customers. Depending on the situation, you may logically omit one or more of the steps you have prepared. You may also add one or more steps to the prepared series. When some customers believe from their past experiences or from the experiences of your other debtors that you have a set procedure for collecting past-due accounts, they tend to wait to pay their accounts until they receive a certain type of letter in the series. Their waiting for this message can cost you a considerable sum in mailing costs and in the use of the money if you had received it when it became due.

Vary not only the steps but also the intervals between them. Debtors who are less considerate than they should be become aware of the same intervals as well as the various steps when a set pattern is followed in a collection process. Numerous factors help you to use good judgment in determining which steps to use and the time intervals to follow. You would obviously use more steps and longer intervals between the mailings for the first time a debtor has been late in paying an account than you would for a large sum that is owed by a customer who has been late on other occasions.

Legal action can be taken against you if because of your negligence a third person reads your comments that reflect on the addressee's character or practice of paying accounts. For your own legal protection, therefore, send by *first-class mail* any reminder that an account is due. Send even the first friendly reminder by *first-class mail*!

## SELLING PRODUCTS AND SERVICES

Selling is a basic business function. To attain the sales volume required for efficient operation, suppliers must publicize their products and services. They can do this through advertising in periodicals, on radio and television, and with billboards; distributing catalogs; and mailing announcements and letters.

Techniques of selling by mail are discussed in the paragraphs that follow.

A first step in selling by mail is acquiring a list of names of potential buyers. Some effective ways of acquiring this list are:

1. Use your list of present customers.

2. Solicit names from your sales representatives and your other employees.

3. Refer to telephone directories.

4. Rent or purchase a list from one of the many organizations that prepare mailing lists of various types. The Department of Commerce publishes a directory of these organizations.

The first three of these sources may be adequate for a small geographic area. If, though, you wish to mail letters to a large area, you can use the last source. Since mailing costs are high, it is important that the names and addresses be correct. Be selective. Mail only to those people who you believe can be persuaded to try your product or service.

## Letters

Letters are used successfully to sell some low-priced items. The lower the price, the greater is the effectiveness of a letter in making a direct sale. Items priced at $10 or lower can be sold readily by mail, provided the sales message is well written. Higher-priced items also can be sold by mail. As the price increases, however, the effectiveness of direct-mail selling diminishes.

Letters are effective for selling subscriptions to periodicals and memberships in book clubs.

People are reluctant to read long, duplicated letters; and most sales letters must be duplicated. Keep your sales letters as short as you can and still include the information that is essential to accomplish the objective. The objective may be to get the readers to:

1.  Place an order

2.  Visit your showroom to see a product or a demonstration

3.  Ask that a representative visit a home or a work place to demonstrate a product or a service

4.  Request additional information about the item you are selling

Informality is a desirable characteristic of a good sales letter. You can use contractions. Write in a clear, direct, cordial style. For the sales letters that obviously must be form letters, there is no need to try to personalize them by typing the name and address of the recipient. Merely use a salutation or other attention-getting remark that is appropriate for all recipients and have your signature duplicated along with the letter. Determine as many traits as you can that are common to the people whose names are on your mailing list. The greater the number of these traits, the easier it is to write a letter that appeals to the readers.

Make certain the letter does these three things:

1.  Gets attention

2.  Creates interest in and a desire to obtain the item you are selling

3.  Motivates action and makes it easy for the reader to act

**Getting attention.** Because people are reluctant to read duplicated letters, use an attention-getting device to motivate recipients to read your short, informal, well-written sales letter. Attention-getting devices are limited only by the imagination of the letter writer. Choose a device you believe will appeal to the particular group to whom you are writing. Among the almost unlimited number of devices are headlines, letter formats, alterations, attachments, and enclosures.

For some sales letters you can use a catchy slogan, a question that creates interest, or another type of headline to get the recipient's attention. These headlines may be near the top of the page, in the margin, in a diagonal position, or in any other position that will stand out. You can use a special color to make a headline more prominent.

Use your imagination in planning a format to get immediate attention and create a favorable impression. You may conceivably type your sales letter in an "up-side-down" manner (accomplished by inserting a sheet of carbon paper backward) so that it must be held before a mirror for easy reading. Send a letter in this format to only those people who can spare the time for this reading arrangement and who you believe would be fascinated by it. Restrict the length of a letter in this unusual format.

One letter writer obtained the desired attention by having his secretary burn the upper right-hand corner of the letter that began with the headline "This letter contains HOT NEWS!"

A piece of brightly colored yarn was attached to the letter in Figure 7-10. Copies of that letter were mailed to a large number of homemakers.

Notice the simple puzzle arrangement of the letter in Figure 7-11. That letter was written to induce youngsters to go to a neighborhood park to purchase a ticket at a special price. A note written on a bright yellow sheet of paper called each recipient's attention to the puzzle pieces that were enclosed to make up the sales letter.

A well-chosen attention getter is of utmost importance in a sales letter; but that device alone cannot accomplish the purpose of the letter, which is to sell a product or a service. Follow the attention-getting device with a carefully written message that creates interest in the item you are attempting to sell.

**Figure 7-10**

# PAULETTA'S HANDICRAFTS, INC.
### CITRUS ROW, FLORIDA 32011

Brightly colored yarn

September 4, 1985

Dear Homemaker

Two 40-yard skeins of this 100 percent virgin wool yarn in neutral, white, or beige will be placed in your mailbox at <u>no cost</u> within <u>three</u> days after we receive your order for any needlepoint pattern that is described in the enclosed leaflet.

From this large assortment you can select the pattern that you believe will do most to enhance the charm of your living room, bedroom, dining room, or den.　Your choice may be a picture to be framed, a bellpull, or a bench cover.

Use the color scheme of your own imagination, or choose from the recommendations that our talented artists have included in the descriptions in the leaflet.　The special hard-to-believe <u>low prices</u> on these needlepoint patterns <u>are in effect through October 17.</u>

Your relatives and friends would treasure a needlepoint piece as a gift for Christmas or for any other occasion.　They would treasure it not only because of its aesthetic value but also because of the sentimental value they would place on your handiwork.

Just place a check mark by the catalog number for each one you choose, specify the color of yarn you prefer, and return the enclosed order form that already bears your name and address.　You may enclose a check, or we will bill you next month.

And remember, <u>two skeins</u> of the yarn in the <u>color of your choice</u> will be mailed to you <u>without cost the day we receive your order.</u>

Cordially

*Bonnie C. Sparkman*

Mrs. Bonnie C. Sparkman
Sales Representative

crs

Enclosures 2

**Figure 7-11**

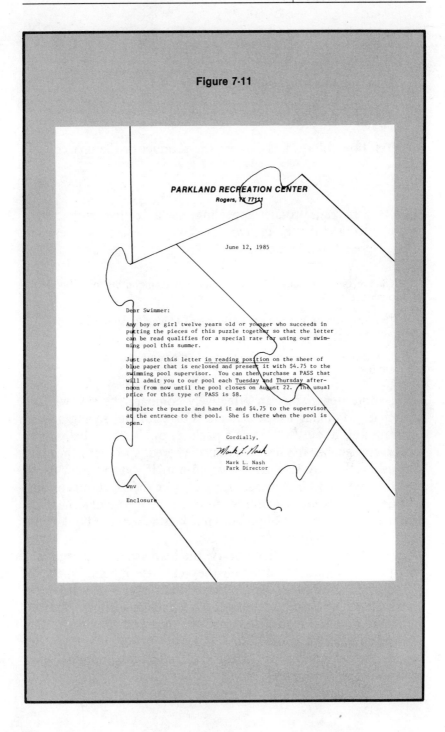

PARKLAND RECREATION CENTER
Rogers, TX 77111

June 12, 1985

Dear Swimmer:

Any boy or girl twelve years old or younger who succeeds in
putting the pieces of this puzzle together so that the letter
can be read qualifies for a special rate for using our swimming pool this summer.

Just paste this letter in reading position on the sheet of
blue paper that is enclosed and present it with $4.75 to the
swimming pool supervisor. You can then purchase a PASS that
will admit you to our pool each Tuesday and Thursday afternoon from now until the pool closes on August 22. The usual
price for this type of PASS is $8.

Complete the puzzle and hand it and $4.75 to the supervisor
at the entrance to the pool. She is there when the pool is
open.

Cordially,

Mark L. Nash

Mark L. Nash
Park Director

mv

Enclosure

**Creating interest and a desire for the item.**  To create interest in and a desire for a product or a service:

1.  Describe the appearance of the product.

2.  Tell about novel features (if any).

3.  Tell how the readers can use the product or the service.

4.  State the price.

To help make a product appealing, use adjectives and adverbs carefully to describe the *appearance* (colors, designs, shapes, and sizes). Here are illustrations:

> London tan continues to be a popular color among distinguished businessmen.
>
> The soft yellows and pinks have promise of being favorite colors for women next season.
>
> The back that tilts slightly contributes to the comfort of this colorful patio chair.

For some items you can effectively compare the size with an item that is familiar to the readers. For example, saying a transistor radio is about the size of a package of cigarettes helps most readers to visualize the size of a radio, whereas specifying the exact dimensions—$2\frac{1}{8}$ by $3\frac{1}{2}$ inches—would not. If, on the other hand, the product is to fit into a specific place, give the exact dimensions.

If an item has *novel features*, describe them to make them appeal to the readers. A ribbon bookmark attached to a book could be described to help create interest.

Tell the readers how they can *use* the item you are selling. Give examples of situations in which they can use it; and when appropriate, tell how other people use the item. Mention well-known persons when you can. You can usually enclose leaflets, pictures, and other material to help describe the appearance of a product and to show how it is used.

State the *price* and convince the readers you are quoting a good price for the product or service. Make fair comparisons with similar, comparable items.

**Motivating action.**   Motivate the readers to take action: place an order, visit your showroom, send for a representative, request more information, and so on. In some types of promotion letters, you may include a toll-free telephone number or a number the readers could call collect. For most sales letters, however, enclose an addressed, postage-paid card or envelope. You may even prepare the information on the order blank or card so that all the readers have to do is place check marks by the color, size, and other variables to indicate their choices. When you simplify the ordering process to this degree, be sure the customer's name and address are on the order form; or *highlight* the importance of the customer's adding that information.

Enclose a card for the readers to use only when you are willing to charge the item to their accounts or to mail the item c.o.d. If you do not sell the product on these terms, enclose an envelope rather than a card; and include clear, simple instructions on whether you will accept personal checks or whether the readers must enclose money orders.

The letter in Figure 7-12 was written to announce plans for a representative to visit a customer's office.

Keep sales letters short and minimize the number and the length of enclosures. Do, though, use whatever enclosures are needed to describe adequately the product or service. You can advantageously use pictures, drawings, and descriptive writing on carefully chosen colored paper to supplement the sales information in the short, carefully written letter.

Keep a record of the people who respond by purchasing. Later, send the same enclosures and a similar letter to the people who do not respond to the first mailing. The same information, but stated differently, can be included in the third, fourth, and additional mailings.

## Announcements

Suppose you are planning to conduct a sale for a retail store. You may increase the volume significantly by mailing special announcements to regular customers. These announcements can be short, simple fliers or duplicated letters.

**Figure 7-12**

## North Plains Printing Co., Inc.
North Plains, Texas 77222

_____

_____
_____
_____

Dear _____:

With the new equipment that was installed last week, we can
produce high-quality copy (the enclosed leaflet is an example)
on any size paper up to 17 by 22 inches.  The copy can be on
any weight paper with as many colors as you wish.

Please study the prices in the second column of the leaflet.
You will realize, I am confident, that these prices are lower
than those that are quoted by any other printer for the same
quality of work.

Ted Raulston, one of our representatives, will stop in to see
you a few minutes next week and will show you more samples of
our work.  He will also tell you more about the operation of
our business and the three-day service we provide for almost
all printing jobs.

Cordially,

*Mindy L. Booth*

Mindy L. Booth
Manager

trm

Enclosure

**Fliers.**   Short, simple fliers are appropriate for sales of inexpensive merchandise or a large variety of merchandise—some inexpensive and some rather expensive. Send these announcements to a large number of people. Send them to those customers whose names and addresses you know and to addresses in the region even though you do not know the names of the persons who live there.

These announcements—which can be in various forms, colors, and designs—can contain a variety of information. Use a headline to call attention to the sales place and dates. To stimulate interest in the forthcoming sale, include a list or a partial list of the items to be sold and pictures of some of the items. Also send prices.

An announcement for a department store mid-winter sale is in Figure 7-13.

**Letters.**   Mailing a letter to each charge-account customer can increase sales of exclusive, high-priced merchandise. Also, it is wise to send letters to let those customers know about regular sales before the general public is informed. Customers appreciate your giving them special attention.

Make the letter short enough to encourage the recipients to read it, yet long enough to create interest and a desire to purchase. To minimize the length of the letter, enclose supplementary information on colorful leaflets.

Use a duplicating process that produces high-quality copies; or for announcing sales of exclusive merchandise, use an automatic typewriter so that you can mail letters that are individually typewritten.

**Figure 7-13**

# SPECIAL SALE!

## SNOW AND PRICES

...WE PREDICT          ...WE PROMISE

WILL FALL

LINENS

POTTERY

JAN. 7 - 11
9 - 5

STAINLESS STEEL

HOUSEWARES

*CHOOSE FROM OUR GREATEST ASSORTMENT EVER OF HOUSEWARES!*

## and CLOTHING

### RANCHLAND DEPT. STORE

SPRING CITY, KANSAS

## QUESTIONS FOR DISCUSSION

1. What steps can you take to make it easy for the recipient of your letter to respond to your *special* request?

2. What are advantages of writing letters instead of making telephone calls or personal visits to collect accounts?

3. What are some of the items that can be attached to sales letters to attract attention?

## EXERCISES

Improve the following sentences:

1. I extend this invitation to you to attend the meeting that will be held on the 28th.

2. You will be able to complete the task in fifteen minutes' time.

3. I am writing this letter to ask you to be the speaker for our annual spring banquet April 16.

4. Why not use the self-addressed envelope for mailing your check in the amount of $14.00?

5. On page 2 of the pamphlet, you will find a description of the new calculator.

6. You can reply by writing to the above address.

7. I will appreciate your returning the completed form as soon as possible.

8. Send a serviceman to repair our copier immediately.

9. We humbly request that you send a serviceman to repair our copier soon.

10. These folders are not expensive.

## PROBLEMS

1.  For the past eleven years you have been a co-owner and the manager of McCready Nurseries. This year you realize you have many more shrubs—Japanese holly, upright yews, pfitzer junipers, and English boxwood—than you usually sell in one season. These shrubs have grown rapidly, and you want to sell them so that you can use the space for other nursery items.

    Write a sales letter that you can reproduce on your word processor and send to homeowners within a 75-mile radius of your office. Describe the shrubs, offer delivery service for a nominal fee, and emphasize the ease with which the shrubs can be set out. For orders that reach certain amounts (you specify the amounts), you will give free forsythia bushes, iris bulbs, or daffodil bulbs.

    Write a one-page sales letter. You may enclose an order blank and an addressed envelope. Use no other enclosures for this letter.

2.  You and two of your friends are building five chalets on a 12-acre tract in the beautiful Skyland Mountains. These chalets are in a secluded wooded area near a stream that several fishermen have referred to as "the fisherman's paradise," and they are about 40 miles from the nearest city, which has about 60,000 residents. Excellent ski slopes that are used by avid skiers from distant places provide entertainment during the winter. Other recreational facilities are also available.

    The chalets will be ready for use by June 1. Each chalet will accommodate six people. Each one is attractively furnished and has the modern conveniences of city living. You will rent them on a weekly or a monthly plan. Because of their attractiveness, their location, and the beauty of the surrounding area, you expect them to be used most of the year. Reservations for them will have to be made several months in advance.

    Write a letter to be reproduced on your word processor and mailed to 200 skiers and fishermen who have enjoyed the ski slopes and the stream at Skyland Mountain the past eight years. You may enclose a folder of photographs, but put most of the essential information in the letter.

3.    You and your family have spent your two-week summer vacation at Sandy Beach four of the past six summers. You have enjoyed an efficiency apartment at the "Sun Light Inn" each time you have gone to Sandy Beach. Two years ago the entire building needed to be repainted, and your apartment needed minor repairs. You observed when you arrived for a two-week stay this summer that the outside of the building had not been repainted, but your apartment was clean and attractive. A faucet that started leaking in the bathroom the third day you were there was an annoyance throughout the rest of your stay even though the assistant manager assured you it would be repaired. And even though you reported a problem with ants, nothing was done to eliminate them.

Residents of some of the other apartments at "Sun Light Inn" experienced similar problems. You are disappointed. You would like to return to "Sun Light Inn" for another two-week vacation in two more years, but you will find other living accommodations at Sandy Beach if the "Sun Light Inn" is not maintained better.

Write a letter to the manager and persuade him to improve the physical conditions of his motel.

4.    You are the collection manager of a department store. The James M. Wilham family started buying clothing, furniture, and other items from your store in 1979. Three months ago Mr. Wilham applied for credit. He had an excellent record, and you gladly approved his request. He bought $200 worth of merchandise the week after you approved his credit request, and his wife made a $166 purchase the next week. You have sent them two statements and another reminder that they have an overdue account. You have not heard from them. Write them a letter.

5.    You are responsible for obtaining a speaker for the annual spring banquet for athletes at your college. Invite a coach from a college in a neighboring state. Use your imagination and supply any information that you need to write a persuasive letter.

6.  You are the manager of a bicycle factory that employs 275 people. If the existing parking area were used properly, it would accommodate all the cars the employees drive to work. Several groups of employees have formed car pools. Because the area is not properly used (some cars are parked so that they use more space than is needed for one car), parking has become a problem for many workers. You have decided to appoint a committee of five people to study the problem. Write a letter to Dennis V. O'Neal, the supervisor of painting operations, and ask him to assume the responsibility of chairman of the committee. Make whatever suggestions you wish to make and convince him you believe he is especially well qualified to be chairman of the committee. Tell him the names of the four other people you will ask to work with him on this committee.

7.  As program chairman of the Franklin, Maryland, chapter of the Administrative Management Society, invite Mr. Sam T. Collier to speak at your monthly chapter meeting three months from now. Because he has done a great deal of work in the word processing area, you want him to talk on that subject. Many of the executives in your region have expressed an interest in learning more about this popular concept. Mr. Collier is vice-president of Office Consultants, Inc. His address is 1125 Park Avenue, Bennington, NY 12783. Add any information that is necessary for you to write a good letter inviting Mr. Collier to speak to your group.

8.  As chairman of the United Fund drive for Davis County, write a letter to Mr. Jerome P. Stinger, President of the United Laborers, asking for a donation from his group. Last year the United Laborers pledged $1,000 and gave over $1,400. This year your goal is a 10 percent increase over last year's gifts. Mr. Stinger's address is P.O. Box 672, Frederick, Delaware 19937.

9.  You are the manager of the Abrams Wholesale Company in New Havelon, CT 06775. For the past seven months you have been selling merchandise on 2/10, n/30 terms to the Y and L Department Store, 247 Market Street, Stamps, CT 06809. The first five months that store paid its account within the 10-day period and took advantage of the 2 percent discount. Last month you received payment at the end of 12 days. The 2 percent discount had been deducted, and the check had been dated two days before the end of the discount period. Even though mail has always arrived within two days from the Y and L store, you assumed that possibly the check had been delayed in the mail. Yesterday, five days beyond the final date of the discount period, you received payment for merchandise. Again, the discount had been taken; and the check was dated within the discount period. The envelope had been postmarked two days ago. You have justification to believe the Y and L Department Store should not have taken the discount. Write the store manager a letter and ask him to send you another check for the amount of the 2 percent discount on $742.81 worth of merchandise. You want to maintain his goodwill, but you must insist that he take the discount only when he pays within the 10 days. Write a firm, courteous letter to the store manager, Thomas E. Sells.

10. Write a letter to sell subscriptions to *Weekly Reporter*, a magazine that contains a variety of features (hints for consumers, short stories, gardening guides, and so on). Add any other details you need for an effective sales letter. (This magazine is fictitious.) Assume your letter will be duplicated and mailed to several hundred people across the country.

11. Two of your classmates and you have decided to establish a cleaning service. You will work nights and on Saturdays to clean offices, stores, and restaurants. You will clean floors, windows, and so on. Write a letter to be duplicated and mailed to the businesses within a 25-mile radius of your campus. Add any details you need for an effective sales letter.

12. You are working for the owner of a new nine-hole golf course, which is to be used primarily by the students in your college. Write a letter to sell season tickets for the golf course. Assume the letter is to be duplicated and sent to the entire student body.

# Chapter 8

# Letters About Employment

What kind of job do you want when you leave school? What skills and abilities do you have that will help you to get a job and to do your work well?

Employers screen applicants carefully to determine those who can contribute significantly to the employers' goals. To compete successfully with others who will apply for the job you want, you owe it to yourself to do as much as you can through study and part-time work to make yourself ready to produce for an employer. What can you offer? Study your background—education, work experience, and personal traits—so that you can present your qualifications in a way that will convince an employer you will be a valuable member of the work force.

As you prepare to seek employment, remember that employers' primary interest in you as an applicant is what you can do to help them accomplish their objectives. Learn what the job for which you wish to apply requires and then present your qualifications that fit those requirements.

You may know an organization or a person you would like to work for, or you may search for jobs that are available. You can learn about employment possibilities from various sources. Here are some of them:

1.  Present or former teachers

2.  The school placement office

3.  Present or former employers

4.  Friends and relatives

5.  Newspaper and journal advertisements

6.  Inquiries to individuals

Before you send an application letter to an organization, learn some of the important facts about it. Find out how long it has been in business, its location, the types of products or services it provides, its recent growth, and its prospects for the future. Here are some of the sources of information about various types of organizations:

1.  College Placement Annual by the College Placement Publication Council

2.  Company annual reports

3.  Dun & Bradstreet Middle Market Directory

4.  Dun & Bradstreet Million Dollar Directory

5.  Moody's manuals

6.  Standard and Poor's Corporation Records

7.  Thomas' Register of American Manufacturers

What will you look for in a job? Some of the factors to consider are opportunities for advancement, the type of work in which you are especially interested and for which you are well qualified, location, salary, fringe benefits, and opportunity to continue formal education.

An important point to keep in mind is that if the job is good enough for you to seek, it is good enough for other well-qualified people to seek. And that is the way you want it to be. You would not want a job that nobody else wants. Competition for good jobs is strong; therefore, put forth your best efforts when applying. *Submit your application as soon as you can after you learn the job opportunity exists.* When two or more people who are somewhat equally well qualified for a job apply for it, the one whose letter gets there first is usually the first to be invited for an interview.

Most jobs are obtained through written communication plus interviews. When you write an application letter, therefore, your objective is to present effectively enough information to impress the reader favorably so that you will be invited for an interview. Send a data sheet along with the letter. By enclosing a data sheet, you can keep the letter short and still present adequate information in a neat, orderly arrangement. Prepare the data sheet before you write the letter.

## DATA SHEET

Data sheets are often called résumés, vitae, and qualification sheets. Although there are technical differences among these forms, each serves these purposes: (1) enables applicants to give in an easy-to-read form a great deal of information about themselves without having to write long letters and (2) enables prospective employers to get a good idea of the applicants' ability to organize and to determine what is important for the job. Sample data sheets are shown in Figures 8-1 through 8-6. None of them are ideal; but studying them carefully will help you to determine the format to use and the information to include for the particular job you are seeking.

The traditional form of data sheet includes information in these four categories: *education*, *work experience*, *personal*, and *references*. You can make these headings more interesting and lively by adding adjectives or by substituting words that go well with your

## Figure 8-1

SUSAN ELIZABETH FAIRCLOTH
234 West Ninth Street                                    Telephone:  (503) 571-5509
Spokane, OR 97639

professional    1984-1988  Edgewood State University, Edgewood, OR 97343
education       B. S. in Marketing

                Special Related Courses:  salesmanship, advertising, business
                law, business communication

                Extracurricular Activities:  Marketing Club, President; Alpha
                Delta Pi social sorority; University Committee on Faculty
                Evaluation

                1980-1984  Clearwater High School, Clearwater, OR 97016

applicable      1985-1988  Edgewood State University, 1601 High Street,
work            Edgewood, OR 97343  Clerk in business office (part time)--
experience      typed memorandums, letters, reports; filed correspondence,
                checks, tapes; assisted with payroll preparation (immediate
                supervisor:  Mr. Max M. Stein)

                1982-1984  June's Fashion Shoppe, 128 Pine Street, Clearwater,
                OR 97016  Salesclerk (part time)--assisted customers in
                selecting clothing, helped arrange displays (immediate
                supervisor:  Miss Elise T. Holbrook)

                1981-1982  Burger Princess, 126 Willow Avenue, Clearwater,
                OR 97016  Waitress (part time)--accepted orders at the drive-in
                window (immediate supervisor:  Mr. Samuel T. Hakes)

personal        Health:  For five years no absences      Pastime:  Reading, golf,
information               from school or work                      snow skiing

references      Dr. Samuel R. Davidson, Associate Professor of Marketing,
(with           Edgewood State University, 1601 High Street, Edgewood, OR 97343
permission)     (503) 524-7216

                Dr. Margaret M. Callis, Associate Professor of General Business,
                Edgewood State University, 1601 High Street, Edgewood, OR 97343
                (503) 524-7142

                Mrs. Harriett L. Jeffries, Assistant Business Manager,
                Edgewood State University, 1601 High Street, Edgewood, OR 97343
                (503) 524-7165

**Figure 8-2**

STEVEN RAY THOMAS

School:  Box 118, Jackson College          Home:  126 Pine Street
        Florence, TN 38151                        Macon, AL 36156
        (615) 526-7686                            (205) 983-9655

Career Objective

To do accounting that leads to possibilities for advancing to managerial
work for a Big Eight firm

Professional Education

1980-1984  Jackson College, Florence, TN 38151  (B. S. in Business
           Administration)

           Major:  Accounting                              Average:  B+

           Courses of Special Interest:  Theory and Practice of Auditing,
           Operational and EDP Auditing, Advanced Accounting Information
           Systems, Accounting Theory, Accounting and Decision Making,
           Accounting for Policy Decisions, Managerial Accounting

           Related Courses:  Legal Environment of Business, Business
           Applications of Microcomputers, FORTRAN Programming for
           Business, COBOL Programming for Business, Personnel Management,
           Business Policy, Business Communication

           Extracurricular Activities:  Accounting Club; Alpha Kappa Psi,
           President; Intramural Basketball

Practical Work Experience
(part time)

1983-1984  Research Assistant (collected data from library sources and
           processed data by computer)  Accounting Department, Jackson
           College, Florence, TN 38151

1980-1983  Laborer (drove truck and poured concrete)  Hayes Construction
           Co., Inc., Marshall, TN 37116

1975-1979  Carrier (delivered daily newspaper before 6 a.m. and collected
           accounts weekly)  Montgomery News, Macon, Alabama

Earned 90 percent of college expenses

References

References sent when requested

**Figure 8-3**

```
              MARLENE RUTH MOORE'S QUALIFICATIONS
                   FOR SECRETARIAL WORK
                  FOR MEMPHIS PLASTICS, INC.

                     205 Windham Avenue
                     Sioux City, SD 57472
                       (605) 673-2256


                   Academic Preparation

Sioux City Community College, Sioux City, SD 57472        1982-1984
Associate of Arts Degree

Major:   Secretarial Administration

Special Skills:   Typing--75 words a minute
                  Shorthand Dictation--120 words a minute

Extracurricular Activities and Honors:  President, Phi Beta Lambda;
Treasurer, Professional Secretaries Club; Outstanding Secretarial
Student of the Year--1984

Central High School, Sioux City, SD 57471--diploma        1978-1982


                   Related Work Experience

Jameson, Heinke, and Wright Law Firm, Sioux City, SD 57471  1982-1984
Part-time Secretary--took dictation, typed letters and
abstracts, filed correspondence, researched property titles

Central High School, Sioux City, SD 57471 (part time)      1980-1982
Receptionist in the principal's office--greeted visitors,
answered the telephone, typed reports


                   Personal Characteristics

Initiative:  Earned 100 percent    Interests:  Designing clothes, play-
             of college expenses               ing bridge, and swimming


                   References (by permission)

Dr. May L. Herd, Chairperson, Department of Secretarial Administration,
Sioux City Community College, Sioux City, SD 57472   (605) 673-1919

Mr. John C. Jameson, Attorney-at-Law, 418 First National Bank Building,
Sioux City, SD 57472   (605) 673-2376

Mr. James M. Hay, Principal, Central High School, Sioux City, SD 57472
(605) 673-9127
```

**Figure 8-4**

WALTER BAYNE RAMSEY'S QUALIFICATIONS FOR THE JOB
OF PLANT MANAGER
FOR THE HILTON MANUFACTURING COMPANY

836 Fifth Avenue
Richland, VA 23216

Telephone (703) 653-1185

SUCCESSFUL WORK EXPERIENCE

1977-present    Manager, Production Department, Hallmark Manufacturing Co.,
                Richland, VA 23216

1972-1977       Assistant Manager, Production Department, Randall Products
                Co., Newman, NJ 07312

1968-1970       Management Trainee, Williams Manufacturing Co., Inc.,
                Greenville, VA 24011

1963-1968       Laboratory Assistant in the Management Department (did
                research and helped prepare teaching materials for under-
                graduate courses in management), Wheatley State College,
                Wheatley, MO 63121

PROFESSIONAL EDUCATION

1967-1968       Littleton State University, Littleton, WV 25113
                M.S. Degree

                <u>Major</u>: Management    <u>Thesis</u>:  "Quality Control in
                                                   Morgantown Manufacturing
                                                   Companies"

1963-1967       Wheatley State College, Wheatley, MO 63121
                B.S. Degree

                <u>Major</u>: Management    <u>Minors</u>:  Accounting and English

                <u>Extracurricular Activities</u>:  Beta Gamma Sigma, Honor
                Society; Alpha Kappa Psi, Professional Fraternity;
                Delta Tau Delta, Social Fraternity

1956-1960       Columbus High School, Columbus, MO 63212  (diploma)

MILITARY SERVICE

1960-1963       United States Army (Infantry--in England and in France)
                Honorable Discharge

**Figure 8-4 Continued:**

WALTER BAYNE RAMSEY                                                                    2

COMMUNITY ACTIVITIES

    Member, Ryan County School Board, Richland, VA 23216--1979-1985
    Former President, Rotary Club, Richland Chapter
    Member, Parent Teacher Organization

REFERENCES

    References supplied when requested

**Figure 8-5**

DAVID RALPH MADISON

P. O. Box 121
Walton State University
New Market, OH 45714

(614) 871-2786

Career Objective

To advance rapidly to the level of senior electrical engineer by starting
with a job that provides experiences on which a sound foundation can be
built

Professional Preparation

1982-1987   Walton State University, New Market, OH 45714
            B. S. in Engineering

            Major:  Electrical Engineering          Average:  3.68  B+

            Courses of Special Interest:  Electrical Energy Systems, Research
            and Design, Design of Feedback Control Systems, Communication
            Theory, Electromagnetic Wave Propagation and Antennas, Electro-
            physical Devices

            Other Relevant Courses:  Applications of Microcomputers, Oral
            and Written Communication, Industrial Psychology

            Extracurricular Activities:  Eta Kappa Nu (honor society); Tau
            Beta Pi (honor society); President, IEEE (local student chapter);
            Intramural Basketball and Soccer

1978-1982   Bradford High School, Scioto Falls, OH 45141--diploma

Practical Work Experience

1986-1987   Research Assistant--supervised two other students in conducting
(part       experiments in energy conversion projects under the guidance of
time)       two professors--College of Engineering, Walton State University,
            New Market, OH 45714  (immediate supervisor: Dr. Jane E. Byland)

1985-1986   Engineering Assistant--designed (with supervision) a feedback con-
and         trol system; drew plans for electrical energy systems--Weiland
1983-1984   Electronics, Inc., Duluth, OH 45281  (immediate supervisor:
(co-op)     Mr. George C. Reynolds)

1978-1982   Kitchen Assistant--washed dishes, mopped floors, peeled potatoes,
            sliced onions, helped maintain accurate inventory of food items--
            Hollingsworth Restaurant, 65 Bypass, Merton, OH 45217  (immediate
            supervisor:  Mr. Lewis R. Flemming)

**Figure 8-5 Continued:**

DAVID RALPH MADISON                                          2

References (with permission)

Dr. Margaret E. Harrison, Professor of Electrical Engineering, Walton State
University, New Market, OH 45714   (614) 871-2114

Dr. Hunter E. Whitfield, Associate Professor of Electrical Engineering,
Walton State University, New Market, OH 45714   (614) 871-2195

Mr. Thomas A. Hedgecoth, Chief Engineer, Weiland Electronics, Inc.,
P. O. Box 824, Duluth, OH 45281   (614) 421-2086

Mr. Hobart E. Brown, Assistant Manager, Hollingsworth Restaurant, 65 Bypass,
Merton, OH 45217   (614) 382-1145

**Figure 8-6**

KELLY WILLIAM McKINNEY

416 Maplewood Road
Plymouth, KS 66013

(913) 732-9488

Objective

To assist the director of university development in raising funds

Fund-Raising Activities

Collected $2,794.75 when serving as chairman of the annual "Heart Fund
Drive" in my hometown in 1982

Organized in 1980 the drive that raised $78,116.50 of the funds needed
to purchase a new organ for a local church

As activities chairman of a social fraternity in college, organized in
1974 the annual "Help-the-Handicapped" bike-a-thon, which has raised at
least $2,600 a year

Leadership and Supervisory Roles

Coordinated the work of twenty-three line operatives and one secretary
when directing each step in automating the handling of raw materials and
scheduling baseball glove assembly while working as assistant production
manager, J. Hilton Whitcomb Sporting Goods, Inc., P. O. Box 316, Plymouth,
KS 66013   1979-present

Adjusted work assignments required by rush orders and absences, counseled
workers, and inspected work of fourteen operatives while working as line
supervisor, Haney Manufacturing Co., P. O. Box 1121, Portland, VA 22110
1977-1979

Originated plans for the "Teacher-of-the-Month" award sponsored by the
local Parent Teacher Association since 1980

As one of two delegates, attended the national convention of the Rotary
Club in Clear Springs, Colorado, in 1982

As president of a social fraternity in college, drew the plans for a
fraternity house that was built in 1979

During junior year in college, helped write the procedures for the annual
faculty evaluation program sponsored by the Faculty Senate

Won $1,500 scholarship on the basis of leadership and a cumulative B+
(3.81 on a 4.00 grading scale) scholastic average at the end of the first
semester of my senior year in college

**Figure 8-6 Continued:**

KELLY WILLIAM McKINNEY                                                    2

### Professional Education

Earned M.B.A. degree with emphasis in communication and personnel management, Highlands State University, Geneva, NC 28112  1976-1977

Completed requirements for B.S. degree with major in communications,
Biltmore State College, Littleton, NC 28111  1972-1976

### Personal Characteristics

Earned 100 percent of expenses for undergraduate and graduate degrees by
spending a minimum of twenty hours a week--and full time during summers--
loading merchandise onto trucks, helping maintain accurate inventory records, and preparing brochures and other mailing pieces for Raydnor Wholesalers, Inc., P. O. Box 17, Greenfield, NC 28032  1972-1976  College of
Business Administration, Highlands State University, Geneva, NC 28112
1976-1977

Have not missed a day of class or work since 1971.  Finished nineteenth
in a group of seventy-seven in my age group in the six-mile "Dogwood Run"
in 1985

Read six of the one hundred "Great Books" in 1985

### References

References supplied when requested

writing style and background. Examples are *professional educa-tion, academic preparation, practical experience, related work experience, personal traits,* and *personal details.* Use your originality in choosing headings for these traditional categories.

## Education

The background in formal education is often the most impressive part of the data sheet for a college student or a recent graduate. This section—when it appears to be the applicant's strongest attribute—should precede the sections for work experience and references.

Include in this well-organized record of education the name and the address of your college or university, years of attendance, academic major, and extracurricular activities. If your overall scholastic average, the average in your major field, or the average for your final two years of study is a B or higher, including it is probably advantageous.

You can strengthen this section of the data sheet by listing courses you have taken that apply specifically to the job you are applying for. As you will observe when studying the sample data sheets in this chapter, you can list courses in addition to those in your major field of study. Studying the job requirements will help you to decide which courses to list and how to list them.

Extracurricular activities can be an important part of your education and can make a favorable impression on employers. Rather than attempt to list all extra-class activities, select only those you believe will impress the prospective employer. Your record of activities may indicate that you have a well-rounded background or that your out-of-class experiences would contribute to your competence in a particular job.

The record of your educational background should go back as far as high school graduation. Show the school name and location and dates of attendance. If you apply for a job within a few years after graduation from high school, including data on high school academic achievements and outstanding extracurricular activities may be worthwhile. Ordinarily, however, the name and location and dates of attendance cover sufficiently the high school background for a college graduate.

Present the information in this section in the order of dates, with the most recent date first.

## Work Experience

An applicant who has work experience that would probably be more beneficial than formal education for a particular job should present the work experience section first on the data sheet. Applicants who have worked several years since attending college, graduate school, or a professional school usually present their record of work experience before that for formal education.

Under work experience show the dates of employment, the nature of the work you did, the names and addresses of employers, and possibly the names of your immediate superiors. Make specific statements about your work. For example, rather than say *clerical work*, give the title of your job and list specific duties such as typing letters, memos, and reports; filing correspondence; and calculating discounts for early payments of accounts.

Which should you list first—the title of your job or the name of the employer? If you believe the prospective employer will be more favorably impressed by a job title accompanied by a list of specific duties than by the name of the employer, list the job title first. On the other hand, if the prospective employer knows that your present or former employer hired only outstanding workers, you may list the name of the employer before the job title. Use parallel structure. For example, when you show the job title first for a present or a former job, list the job title first for all other work records on your data sheet.

When you give the name of your immediate superior, the prospective employer can reach that person by telephone or by letter to obtain information about you. Your immediate superior can supply more specific, helpful information than can the personnel director or others who have only a general knowledge of your performance. A former supervisor's statements about a specific task you performed or about a special trait you possess means much to a prospective employer. And remember that more and more employers are using the telephone to obtain recommendations for applicants.

If you have had limited work experience, include a record of part-time and summer jobs. If you have had no work experience for which you were paid a wage or a salary, include an account of work for which you received no pay. You may very well mention activities such as helping carry out a project for a civic club or serving as an officer for a club, a fraternity, or a sorority.

As a young applicant who has had little opportunity to work, include such experiences as delivering newspapers or baby-sitting, even as a child. This type of listing may make the prospective employer realize you have been accepting responsibility a long time.

The work experience does not have to be related directly to the job you are seeking. If you have worked as a laborer after school, on Saturdays, or during summers, include this experience on your data sheet. Referring to these jobs may help convince the prospective employer you are willing to work. Willingness to work and to perform some of the less desirable tasks as well as those you enjoy is a characteristic employers like. A young man who worked in a fast-food restaurant during his high school years studied electrical engineering in college. He was fortunate to obtain summer jobs that provided worthwhile experience for an electrical engineer. He thought the several prospective employers who interviewed him shortly before graduation from college would be especially interested in his practical experience as a student engineer. Much to his surprise, however, all of them spent more time talking with him about his restaurant work than about the jobs he actually enjoyed. Those executives were impressed by the young applicant's willingness to perform unpleasant tasks in order to achieve his goal, as well as by his excellent academic record in college.

Experience as a laborer is helpful for a person who aspires to advance to a management position. Because laborers look at a situation from a vantage point different from that of management personnel, people who have worked as laborers can better understand the thinking of the employees at that level of the organization structure. They can, therefore, manage more effectively than they could without this understanding.

You may be wise to omit some of the many short-term jobs you may have held if including them would clutter your data sheet. Do not, though, omit a job solely because it seems to have little or no relationship to the job you are seeking.

Make your data sheet interesting. Include any item that would help you to convince the prospective employer you are well qualified for the job for which you are applying, and omit any item that does not help you make a favorable impression. Active verbs contribute to the interest quality of a data sheet. Use active verbs, therefore, and use parallel structure. Instead of saying "*Was* responsible for closing the warehouse on Friday evenings," say, "*Accepted* responsibility for closing the warehouse on Friday evenings." Among the numerous active, interest-creating verbs or these:

| | |
|---|---|
| accepted | increased |
| conducted | installed |
| coordinated | maintained |
| designed | prepared |
| established | supervised |
| helped | verified |

Give specific information, and use parallel structure throughout your data sheet. Present the experience record in chronological order with the most recent data first, as you do with the items in the education section of your data sheet.

## Personal

The types of personal information to place on the data sheet vary among applicants. Be sure to include your full name, address, and telephone number. If you are living away from home temporarily, you may show two addresses and telephone numbers—temporary and permanent. Many successful applicants limit personal information to these items.

Including the maiden name for a middle name is a wise practice for a married woman. Knowing the maiden name can help former employers and teachers identify an applicant when they are asked to recommend her.

Marital status, number and ages of children, and hobbies are often given. An employer who is seeking someone to do strenuous physical work would probably like to know the height, weight, and general health of applicants. If you refer to health, state a fact such as "Have not missed a day of school or work since 1978" rather than say *good* or *excellent*.

The best step to take in choosing items of personal information to include is to study the requirements for the job and then ask yourself, "If I were an employer, what information would help me to decide whether I would like to interview this applicant?"

Omit any information that would not help the prospective employer in determining your qualifications for the job for which you are applying. Also, be sure to omit information that could be used advantageously by a disgruntled person who may wish to accuse the employer of hiring you on the basis of one or more factors against which a person must not be discriminated: race, sex, age, religion, or national origin. In most instances, of course, the prospective employer can determine your sex by your first or your middle name.

### References

Many prospective employers write, telephone, or converse in face-to-face situations with an applicant's references—people who know a good deal about the applicant's work experience, education, or personal traits. Prepare, therefore, a list of three to five people who can and are willing to give prospective employers an accurate evaluation of your qualifications for a job. Give the names (as they sign them), job titles, business addresses, and telephone numbers. Also, give them courtesy titles (Mr., Mrs., Ms., Professor, and so on).

You may include this information on your data sheet, or you may say you will send this information when the prospective employer requests it. More and more applicants today—especially those for jobs other than those at the entry level—state that the references will be supplied when requested. A reason for including the names on the data sheet is that it saves time for employers who want to contact those people. Prospective employers contact only the references for the applicants who are being considered seriously for a job. If you omit the names from your data sheet, have them ready to mail the day you receive a request for them.

One appropriate way to arrange a reference sheet is shown in Figure 8-8. Transmit this sheet, of course, by letter, which may be similar to the one in Figure 8-7.

Your list of references depends somewhat on your background. If you have had a considerable amount of work experience, include the names of two or more employers—present or former. If

**Figure 8-7**

P. O. Box 1576
Walker State University
Walker, NJ 07011
April 9, 1985


Mr. John B. Harmon
Personnel Manager
Reynolds Company, Inc.
P. O. Box 3145
Concord, DE 19121

Dear Mr. Harmon

The five people whose names, addresses, and telephone numbers
are on the enclosed sheet said they will be glad to tell you
about my qualifications for work as an accountant.

I look forward to hearing from you again.

Cordially

*Richard H. Krabbendam*
Richard H. Krabbendam

Enclosure

**Figure 8-8**

RICHARD HARRY KRABBENDAM

References

Dr. Walter M. Hutson
Professor of Accounting
Walker State University
Walker, NJ 07011
(609) 852-7877

Ms. Carole M. Littleton
Manager, Production Department
Billings Manufacturing Company
P. O. Box 8123
Havord, PA 19011
(814) 762-8011

Dr. Preston L. Switzer
Associate Professor of Accounting
Walker State University
Walker, NJ 07011
(609) 852-1126

Mr. James T. Hartley
Manager, Furniture Department
Clem's Department Store
1126 Broad Street
Miles, NJ 07011
(609) 615-2424

Ms. Lillian W. Waldrop
Administrative Assistant
Office of the Provost
Walker State University
Walker, NJ 07011
(609) 852-2157

you have had limited work experience, consider including the names of two or more professors. Ordinarily as a recent college graduate, you should list the name of your major professor or faculty advisor. Employers usually expect this listing because your major professor or faculty advisor probably knows a good deal about you.

By all means, list the names of people who will give you a good recommendation. When choosing between two people who are about equally well prepared to give you a good recommendation, choose the one who you believe can write the better letter and will write promptly. Receiving recommendations early gives an applicant an "edge" over another applicant whose letters of recommendation arrive later.

When a reference's job title does not indicate the reason you gave that name, add (possibly in parentheses) a note explaining your relationship with the person. If you should not indicate the person's relationship with you, the reader may conceivably think the reference is one of your relatives or one of your personal friends (roommate, boyfriend or girlfriend, sorority sister or fraternity brother).

List the name of a relative only when that person has been your teacher or employer. Even then, listing the names of nonrelatives is usually a better practice.

## Other

The four divisions—*education*, *work experience*, *personal*, and *references*—that have been discussed are somewhat basic to data sheets for job applicants. They are given as a guide in helping you organize the information an employer would like to know about you. People who have been out of school several years probably need to include additional divisions. Divisions they would include are those that show the community activities (memberships; offices held; or special work in civic clubs, church, or other organizations). They could also include a section indicating consulting services, professional activities, or honors received. An educator could very well include a section for publications (books, articles in professional journals, and so on).

A statement of the job objective may be a part of a data sheet. Make this statement specific enough to help the employer realize you know what you want, and make it general enough to cover a variety of jobs you are prepared to handle and would be willing to accept. In Figures 8-2, 8-5, and 8-6, the objective is preceded by a heading; in Figures 8-3 and 8-4, it follows the applicant's name.

Because employers look for applicants who can produce, tell the percentage of your college expenses you earned if you earned a significant percentage of them. You can present this information in a variety of places: under personal information, under experience, or elsewhere.

Some applicants prefer a functional data sheet form (see Figure 8-6) rather than the traditional form. For this form choose headings under which you group your personal characteristics and your experiences according to function. These headings may be *communication skills*, *organizing ability*, *management skills*, and so on.

The functional form is especially useful because it helps the applicants to analyze their personal traits and their past activities to see how they coincide with the kinds of jobs the applicants are seeking. A data sheet of this type helps many employers to see quickly how the applicant's qualifications fit the job requirements. Many people who have had limited work experience for which they were paid—but have had valuable experience in extracurricular activities in college, and so on—have used this form advantageously.

Whether you use a functional form or a traditional form, arrange the information attractively so that it is easy to read and is not crowded on the page. Use plain white 20-pound bond paper of 25 percent rag content. The size should be 8½ by 11 inches. Use a typewriter with clean type keys and a dark ribbon. An attractive data sheet helps you to make a favorable impression on the recipient. Even though your data sheet should be concise, do not limit it to one page if you need to use more pages. Include your name and the page number on the second and succeeding pages and staple the pages together. Place the staple diagonally in the upper left-hand corner.

## REQUESTS FOR PERMISSION TO
## USE NAMES AS REFERENCES

Even after professors, former employers, and others have given you permission to use their names as references, your letting them know the specific job you are applying for gives them helpful information for writing a letter about you. By your telling the references the type of job you are applying for, they have an opportunity to give adequate thought to the way they believe your qualifications fit the job you are seeking. They can refer to records in the personnel office if they are former employers. Or if they are former teachers, they can refer to their own records.

If a few years have passed since you have seen those people, tell them about your activities during that time. Mention something that will help them to remember you. You can usually do this incidentally.

An incidental reference to some particular thing such as, "Your comments on my letter refusing an adjustment to the woman whose bedspread had faded have helped me on several occasions when customers have returned merchandise," may be sufficient to jog a teacher's memory. On the other hand, a straightforward reference such as, "I am the man who dropped the screwdriver in the air-conditioning unit we sold Mr. Charles," could be just the remark that is needed to enable a former employer to remember you.

The content of this letter, like that of all others, depends on the situation. Ask yourself such questions as these:

1.  How well does the person know me?

2.  How long has it been since we were closely associated with each other?

3.  Is there a special incident that I can refer to that will help this person to remember a good deal about me?

4.  Is there another member of my family that this person may confuse me with?

5.   Is there someone else whose name is similar (or even identical) to mine that this person may confuse me with?

People recommending you for a job can write better letters if they know about your activities during the years since they were closely associated with you. Tell them, therefore, the names and addresses of your present and former employers and the nature of the work you have done. You may send them copies of your updated data sheet.

Certainly, let them know you will appreciate their recommending you. Make it clear when the letters of recommendation are to be written. Even though you use names as references, the prospective employer may not ask those people to recommend you. If the people are to wait until they are asked for recommendations, state that condition clearly. If you want them to write letters before the employer requests them, make that point clear and give the exact name, job title, and business address of the person who should receive the letters.

The letter in Figure 8-9 was written by a young man who had been given permission to use a name as a reference. The letter was written to bring the former employer up to date on the writer's activities.

## APPLICATION LETTER

Having studied the organization to which you plan to apply for employment and having prepared a data sheet, you are ready to write the application letter. Restrict the length to one page. Three to five paragraphs are enough. Attract favorable attention in the first paragraph.

If you know a vacancy exists, one way to attract favorable attention is to say who told you about the job. Many employers like to receive applications from friends, relatives, or acquaintances of present or former employees. An employer who advertises through journals, newspapers, and radio likes to know the advertisement has received responses.

If you do not know a vacancy exists, use another type of beginning to gain favorable attention. These opening sentences have been used in successful application letters:

**Figure 8-9**

517 South Cherry Street
Jacksboro, AL 35411
May 21, 1988

Mr. Clyde R. Armstrong
Armstrong Appliance Store
1146 Main Street
Macon, AL 35876

Dear Mr. Armstrong:

When I apply for the job of salesman with J. Watson Company in
Macon next month, I will again use your name as a reference.

As I mentioned to you just before my graduation from college in
1982, the recommendations you wrote then helped me to get favorable responses from prospective employers. Although going into
the Army prevented my going to work as a salesman then, I am
pleased to be completing a tour of military duty on June 12.

I am eager to return to Macon. The four years there as a student
at Denton College and as a part-time salesman for you during two
of those years—1980-1982—were enjoyable. Fortunately, though,
not all the work experiences were quite so wild as my dropping
the screwdriver into the air-conditioning unit we sold to Mr. Cox.
Sometimes I doubted that you and Mr. Reed would let me live that
episode down.

I hear your business has grown very rapidly during the past six
years. I congratulate you and wish you continued success. I
will come by your store to visit with you a few minutes sometime
next month.

If you are asked to recommend me for employment with J. Watson
Company, I will certainly appreciate your doing that.

                                Cordially,

                                *Derek Dodson*

                                Derek Dodson

Does an executive in your organization need a secretary who can type 110 words a minute and has had five years' experience in handling delicate problems in human relations?

\* \* \* \*

Mr. Russell M. Wagner, your sales representative for this area, told me you usually hire several extra salesmen for the summer months.

Make it clear in the first paragraph that you are applying for a *specific* job. Statements such as "Please consider my qualifications for the job of accountant" are much better than such statements as "I should like to apply for a position in your office," "Please consider my application for employment," or "I am interested in the vacancy you advertised." Use active verbs. *Work* is an excellent verb to use in this letter; for example, "I would like to work as an accountant for you."

In the middle section (between the first and the last paragraphs) convince the prospective employer that you understand the job requirements and that your qualifications fit those requirements. As you state this understanding, be careful that you do not appear to be *telling* the reader what the company needs. Contrast these examples that refer to job requirements.

| *Poor* | *Good* |
|---|---|
| That position is a responsible one. | The people whose names are listed as references on the enclosed data sheet can certify that I readily accept responsibility. |

| Poor | Good |
|---|---|
| You need a person in that position who can type accurately. | The legal documents I prepared during the past three years had to be typed without error. |
| An assistant manager has to be able to work well with others. | The other employees and I had no problems in cooperating when as a college student I managed a gasoline station at night. |

Even though your background has been outlined on the data sheet, use the middle paragraphs of the letter to emphasize your best qualifications. In addition to convincing the personnel officer that you have skills and knowledge that will enable you to contribute to the employer's objectives, let the personnel officer know you are energetic and eager to work.

Do not give the impression you are conceited, but do not sell yourself short. Remember, no one thinks more highly of you than you think of yourself. Do all you can to show you have the proper blend of self-confidence and modesty to succeed. What is the blend that suits *your* personality and the job you are seeking?

Although there is no need to highlight the fact that you are enclosing a data sheet, do mention in an incidental way that you are enclosing it. These ways have been used:

As is indicated on the enclosed data sheet, I have made the types of calculations required by the clerks in your office.

\* \* \* \*

Mr. Robert B. Haney and the other men whose names are on the enclosed data sheet can verify these statements.

\* \* \* \*

May I talk with you after you have studied the enclosed data sheet?

In the last paragraph ask confidently—not presumptuously or pleadingly—for an interview. If you can go for an interview at the convenience of the prospective employer, say so when you ask for an opportunity to discuss your qualifications for the job. If you know that examinations in school or peak-load periods in your present work schedule would preclude your going for an interview on certain dates, say you can go any time except those dates. The reader will understand your need to make this statement and will appreciate your forethought and conscientiousness. Possibly, you will be in the vicinity of the interviewer's office during certain dates and would like to have an interview then. Mention this arrangement. If that office is far away, you may suggest the possibility of an interview when a representative is in your region. Sometimes an arrangement such as this is advantageous to the prospective employer, especially if the company is paying your travel expenses.

Study the first draft of your letter and make any needed revisions. The prospective employer knows your application letter represents your best efforts in writing. In other words, the reader knows no other letter you would write would be better than the one you write to apply for a job.

Choose words that fit the occasion, and write in a style that reveals *your* personality. *Do not copy someone else's letter.* The reader wants to know about you. You have to use the pronoun *I* often to tell about yourself, but do not use it unnecessarily. You can use *I* and still maintain the *you* attitude by emphasizing the high-quality work you can do for the employer.

Your grammar should be impeccable. Strive for a good command of the English language when speaking; but even those minor errors that creep in occasionally in everyone's speech because of chance, changing thoughts before finishing a sentence, or for any other reason should be eliminated from the application letter. Including a misspelled word is inexcusable.

By all means, type your return address above the date. The reader will know that a letter sent to that address will reach you. Therefore, do not use the trite expression "write to the address given above." If you believe you will be at another address when the reader replies, specify the address to be used.

Try to learn the name and the job title of the officer in charge of employing someone for the job you are seeking. If you cannot learn from a friend or from printed materials the employing officer's name, call the organization. Ask the person who answers the telephone to give you the name and the title of the person to whom you should send your application. Verify the spelling of the name. Address your letter to that person. If you cannot learn the name, however, address the letter to the organization and use an attention line for the "Personnel Director."

Center the letter on the page. An attractive, well-written letter less than one full page in length helps to command favorable attention.

Use plain white 20-pound bond paper of 25 percent rag content for the letter *and* the data sheet. The size should be 8½ by 11 inches. *Do not use letterhead*. Make sure the typewriter keys are clean and the ribbon is dark. Correct all typing errors so carefully that they can be detected only through extremely close examination.

After you have proofread the letter and the data sheet as carefully as you can by reading them aloud, ask someone else to read them and to search for errors you may have overlooked.

Mail the letter and the data sheet in a plain white No. 10 envelope or in a large manila envelope. By using a manila envelope, the application papers do not have to be folded. They therefore make a better appearance. Neatness is important, but is not enough. Neat appearance must be accompanied by good, well-organized, easy-to-read content.

You can apply the suggestions in this chapter and still use originality in your letters. Sample application letters are shown in Figures 8-10 through 8-13.

Once you have typed, proofread, *signed with blue or black ink*, sealed, and mailed the application letter, you can give additional thought to the interview you requested in the final paragraph. If you are invited to go for an interview, you have been successful in your first step—writing the letter and the data sheet—in the application process. Prepare to confirm plans for an interview.

## INTERVIEW CONFIRMATION

When inviting you for an interview, the prospective employer either designates a specific date or gives you alternative dates. Acknowledge the letter *promptly*—within twenty-four hours. Use

**Figure 8-10**

P. O. Box 1162
Greeley State College
McMinnville, OR 97001
April 17, 1986

Mr. George M. Hatmaker
Director of Personnel
First National Bank
Caryton, ID 83001

Dear Mr. Hatmaker

Please accept this letter as the first step in my application
for a management trainee job. Mr. Wayne R. Goodwin, placement
director at our college, told me about the job opportunities
you announced yesterday.

As night manager of a busy service station for the past two
years, I have continued to accept responsibility, which I began
accepting as a newspaper carrier when I was fifteen years old.
My experiences on those two jobs combined with a special interest in banking and eagerness to work hard would help me to excel
in the work you would expect me to do.

On June 4 I will be graduated with a B. S. Degree from Greeley
State College. I have a business management major and a finance
minor. As is indicated on the enclosed data sheet, I have par-
ticipated in a number of extracurricular activities in college.

May I talk with you personally about ways I could contribute to
the progress your bank is making? I can come to your office at
any time, except final examinations week--May 28 through June 1.

Cordially

David W. Olive

David W. Olive

Enclosure

**Figure 8-11**

P. O. Box 1715
Northern Indiana State College
Denton, IN 41706
May 1, 1985

Mr. Harold E. Hiten
Personnel Director
Phillips Manufacturing Co.
2108 Walnut Ridge Road
Aaron, OH 44309

Dear Mr. Hiten

Can you use another stenographer whose basic skills have been highly
polished by hard work in the capstone course for secretarial students in our college?  I am taking that course this term, which ends
on June 1.  Please consider my application for a stenographic job.

I can transcribe rapidly and accurately the shorthand notes I take
from dictation at 130 words a minute.  Our teacher dictates scientifi-
cally constructed letters, memorandums, speeches, and reports that
require us students to determine the proper punctuation marks to use,
to verify mathematical computations, and to spell correctly.  We also
correct the errors in grammar she purposely makes.

Each day she includes a few hard-to-spell words that are not familiar
to us so that we will be well prepared to take dictation from almost
any executive.  Because only perfect copy is accepted for credit, I
have learned to be a better-than-average proofreader.  Additional
information about my background and preparation for stenographic work
is on the enclosed data sheet.

My fiance, who last week accepted a job as chemical engineer for
Scientific Industries, Inc., in Aaron, will begin working on July 1,
two weeks after our wedding date.  Aaron is obviously the city of
my choice for employment.

Please call or write me and suggest a time when we can discuss the
ways my sharpened skills can be used effectively in your company.

Cordially

*Linda K. Stokes*

Miss Linda K. Stokes

Enclosure

**Figure 8-12**

P. O. Box 1146
Morrison University
Morrison, KY 40506
October 2, 1988


Mr. Edward M. Hunt
Hunt and Oliver Accounting Firm
1126 Meadow Lake Road
Haleyville, KY 40201

Dear Mr. Hunt

I want to help you complete accurately and speedily that big stack
of income tax returns you will face early next year.  Mr. Joseph H.
Hale, my faculty advisor, told me this morning you plan to employ a
junior accountant to begin working on January 2, 1989.  Please consider my application for that job.

For the past three years I have worked part time for Aaron and Long
Accountants in Morrison.  This work fascinates me; and I am challenged by the demands that are made, especially during the rush
season for income tax returns.

Although this part-time work has forced me to sacrifice some of the
leisure time I enjoyed as a freshman, I have continued to participate
in a social fraternity, as well as in a service fraternity, and have
maintained a 3.32 scholastic average on a 4.00 scale.  As you can
well imagine, I have learned to budget my time.  I would like to
continue with a full-time schedule by redirecting my efforts to performing the tasks that are required in your accounting office.

Mr. Hale and the three other men whose names are listed as references
on the enclosed data sheet said they will be glad to give you an evaluation of my qualifications for accounting work.

Will you discuss with me the possibilities of working for you?  I
could come to your office at almost any time that would be convenient
for you.

                              Cordially

                              John E. Howser

                              John E. Howser


Enclosure

**Figure 8-13**

P. O. Box 134
James State College
Miller, CO 80477
May 7, 1988

Ms. Joy T. O'Hara, Vice-President
Springdale Bank and Trust Co.
P. O. Box 1124
Springdale, CO 81076

Dear Ms. O'Hara

Because of my college degree in management and three years' work
for a growing investment company, I can easily picture myself as
one of the management trainees you advertised for in the Daily
Herald this morning. Please accept my application.

My ability to supervise as well as to take directions from management personnel was applied during the past sixteen months when I
supervised two other students who worked part time for The Wheeler
Investment Company. Helping the executives adjust to a word processing center that was established a year ago was a challenge I
liked. Contributing to the continued progress of your bank while
developing my potential management abilities is an opportunity I
would accept enthusiastically.

The enclosed data sheet includes the names, addresses, and telephone numbers of four people who will be glad to tell you about
my qualifications for a management trainee position.

May I come to your office soon at a time that is convenient for
you to discuss the possibilities of my going to work for you in
June?

Cordially

*Stacey J. Smith*

Stacey J. Smith

Enclosure

the same type of plain paper you used for the application letter and the data sheet.

Be specific in your reply. Repeat the date and the time of day you will meet the prospective employer. Also, confirm the place. Confirming these points in writing impresses the interviewer and avoids some possible misunderstandings. The office of the personnel manager is often the place for the beginning of an interview, but sometimes arrangements are made for the interviewer (the employer) and the interviewee (the applicant) to meet elsewhere. Interviews are frequently conducted at conventions and sometimes even at airports. Repeat the title of the job for which you are applying. Repeating the job title is especially helpful for personnel managers who conduct numerous daily interviews for a variety of jobs.

When the prospective employer gets in touch with you by telephone to invite you for an interview, the telephone conversation may be sufficient confirmation for all these points. Even then, however, writing a confirming letter that afternoon or the next day would be a smart thing to do if at least a week is to pass before the interview date.

The letter in Figure 8-14 was written to confirm an interview.

## INTERVIEW

Ordinarily, an employer does not offer employment without talking with the applicant. Seldom would an applicant accept employment without talking with the employer. When you are invited to come for an interview, you can logically assume the employer has been impressed by your letter and your data sheet and probably by recommendations from the people whose names you listed as references.

Now, you must continue to sell yourself. The impression you make in the interview carries a great deal of weight in determining whether you obtain the job. No two job interviews are identical, yet all of them have similar characteristics. Here are suggestions for *before*, *during*, and *after* your talk with a prospective employer.

**Figure 8-14**

P. O. Box 451
Cutbank State College
Cutbank, WY 82512
May 5, 1988


Mr. George C. Spears
Vice-President
Boise Central Bank
1128 Market Street
Boise, MT 59632

Dear Mr. Spears

You can expect me to arrive at your office at 9 a.m. on Friday,
May 17, as you suggested.  Thank you for sending the map.

I look forward to talking with you about my qualifications for
the management trainee job.

Cordially

Frank O. Zanardi

**Before**

Take these steps before the interview:

1.  Review the information you collected about the organization before you wrote the application letter. The knowledge you gain from this review will help you to relax and to develop self-confidence as well as to answer some of the questions you will be asked.

2.  Prepare a list of questions you want to ask such as "What are the possibilities for further education?" and "What challenges could the job lead to?"

3.  Prepare answers to questions the interviewer will probably ask such as:

    a.  Why do you want to work for us?
    b.  What kind of work do you expect to be doing five or ten years from now?
    c.  What benefits besides money do you expect to receive?
    d.  What beginning salary do you expect to receive?
    e.  How would you describe yourself (use five adjectives)?
    f.  What are your strongest three attributes?
    g.  What are your weakest three traits?

Do not mention salary before the employer does. Study local conditions so that you know what to expect for various expenses and thus the salary you would need. Also, learn as much as you can about salaries paid by other employers for the kind of work you would do, and learn as much as you can about local salaries for jobs comparable to the one for which you are applying. If asked what salary you expect, do not give the impression that salary is the factor of greatest interest to you; emphasize your interest in the work and opportunities for growth. If, however, you are pressured to state a salary, the study of other jobs and local conditions provides the background required for stating an approximate amount.

4. Learn the name (the correct pronunciation) and the job title of the person who is to interview you.

5. Take a pen with you so that you can fill out forms if asked to.

6. If you expect to take a test, take with you the materials you will need. For example, an applicant for a stenographic or a secretarial job should take a pen, a notebook, and a pocket dictionary.

7. Dress well. A man should wear a suit and tie. A suit with a white or a light blue shirt and a "lively" tie that is not too colorful make a fine combination. A woman's attire should be appropriate for work in an office. Her jewelry should be simple. Some young women enhance their professional appearance by carrying a small attractive briefcase instead of a purse. Be sure your clothes are clean and well pressed and the heels of your shoes are in good condition. Good grooming is important for a successful job interview.

8. Go alone to the interview unless you are requested to bring your wife or husband with you. Many prospective employers ask applicants to bring their spouses with them. The spouse is not expected to remain throughout the interview; activities are planned for her or him while the applicant continues with the interview.

9. Arrive at the interviewer's office about five or ten minutes before the designated time. Arriving more than ten minutes early tends to make the interviewer believe you are nervous; arriving late certainly creates a poor impression.

10. When introducing yourself to the receptionist, give the name of the person you have come to see and identify the job for which you are to be interviewed.

11. As you wait in the reception area, read the literature provided; or write on note sheets you have taken with you. This type of activity will help you to appear to be relaxed. Applicants are often observed while they wait in the reception area.

## During

Here are points to keep in mind during the interview:

1.  Shake hands with the interviewer. A firm handshake is impressive. You can shake hands firmly without squeezing so hard you make the interviewer believe you are excessively nervous.

2.  Stand until the interviewer invites you to sit. The interviewer usually indicates the place for the applicant to sit if there are more than two chairs in the room.

3.  Do not chew gum.

4.  Wait about smoking until the interviewer invites you to smoke. If you smoke, use the ashtray rather than let ashes fall elsewhere.

5.  Do not place any item on the interviewer's desk unless you are invited to do so.

6.  Relax and show self-confidence without appearing to be over-confident. Some anxious feeling is expected. To relax so that your anxiousness is not obvious, take a few deep breaths before entering the interviewer's office.

7.  Maintain good posture. Good posture helps you to feel at ease and to create a favorable impression.

8.  Look at the interviewer. Although you are not expected to look directly into the interviewer's eyes throughout the interview, your doing so part of the time indicates good character.

9.  Let the interviewer guide the interview, but do more talking than giving simple "yes" and "no" answers to questions. The interviewer wants to hear you talk.

10.  Remain calm about any controversial points that are mentioned.

11. Omit negative comments about former employers, teachers, or colleagues.

12. Do not take notes. To be sure to remember details, jot them on note sheets immediately after leaving the interviewer's office.

13. If you are asked to fill out an application form, do it accurately. Be sure to give the proper date of birth. Many applicants inadvertently give the current year instead of the year of birth. Know your social security number.

14. If you have questions that have not been answered, ask them near the end of the interview. Usually, the interviewer asks whether there are questions.

15. Leave when the interviewer indicates through comments or gestures that the interview is ending. Shake hands and thank the interviewer for discussing your qualifications for the job.

### After

Regardless of the outcome of the interview, follow up by writing a letter to thank the interviewer for discussing with you your qualifications for the job. Write this letter promptly—usually within twenty-four hours after you return to your home. The exact time that you write, as well as the content of the letter, is governed by the results of the interview.

If you were offered the job and you accepted the offer, write immediately and after thanking the interviewer for the enjoyable visit, state the exact title of the job you have accepted, the starting salary, and the date you will report for duty. Say you look forward to working in that position. Of course, you would not accept an offer if you did not look forward to the job; but saying so provides a courteous, goodwill ending for the letter.

If you were asked to sign a contract that specifies the job title, the terms of payment, and the beginning date of employment, do not restate all these points in a letter. Usually, you need to restate the job title as an immediate reminder if the employer has hired persons for several job classifications within the past few days. Too, you could hardly express genuine enthusiasm for working without stating the title of the job you have accepted.

If you were offered the job and you promised to let the interviewer know by a specified date whether you will accept the offer, confirm your promise to give your decision by that date (and specify the date). State the job title. The letter in Figure 8-15 is an example.

If you were given forms (job application, expense statement, and so on) to complete, return them with the letter. (Remember that ordinarily when something is worth enclosing, it is worth mentioning in the letter.) If you have to wait three or four days to obtain all the information necessary for completing the forms, delay writing the letter to thank the interviewer until you can enclose the forms. If you must wait *several* days to obtain the information, write the thank-you letter immediately and mention the date on which you expect to return the completed forms.

If the interviewer is to let you know by a specific date whether you will be offered the job, say that you look forward to hearing the decision by the date that was mentioned (and specify the date). Try to add something about your qualifications that will help to convince the prospective employer you are the person for the job. Of course, use discretion to keep the reader from thinking that you are overzealous or that you are trying to exert pressure for an offer of employment.

The letter in Figure 8-16 was written by an applicant who was eager to get the job for which she had been interviewed.

Suppose that even though you are quite interested in the job, it was not offered to you. Write immediately and thank the interviewer for discussing your qualifications with you. The courtesy you display in this letter may impress the reader so that you will be considered for a future vacancy you are qualified to fill. Also, the interviewer may be inclined to recommend you to someone else who has a vacancy for which you are well suited.

Personnel directors try to employ persons who they think will be happy in their jobs. Sometimes an applicant is rejected because the interviewer realizes the applicant would not be challenged by the job. An employer's rejecting you for this reason is doing you a favor, so always be courteous and make that good businesslike impression that will help you succeed in business.

**Figure 8-15**

1216--21 Street
Salem, TN 38915
May 17, 1988


Mr. Duane E. Fisher
Personnel Director
Sterrett Aircraft Corporation
1144 Ridgewood Parkway
Salem, TN 38915

Dear Mr. Fisher

Thank you for interviewing me yesterday for the secretarial job
in your purchasing office.  I am convinced I would be challenged
by the work you and Mr. Atkins, the chief purchasing officer,
described; and I am favorably impressed by all the employees I
met.

As I mentioned to you, though, I am committed to go out of town
next Monday for another interview.  I appreciate your offering
me the job; and I will certainly let you know my decision by
Thursday, May 23.

Sincerely

Mary Ann O'Donnell
Mary Ann O'Donnell

**Figure 8-16**

P. O. Box 1715
Northern Indiana State College
Denton, IN 41706
May 29, 1985

Mrs. Opal M. Rhyne
Personnel Director
Randle Manufacturing Company
2445 Walnut Ridge Road
Aaron, OH 44309

Dear Mrs. Rhyne:

Thank you for giving me an opportunity yesterday to discuss with
you my qualifications for a stenographic job.  I enjoyed the entire visit, including lunch in the company cafeteria with the
two executive secretaries.

The tour of the office building was impressive; and I am excited
about the possibilities of working in such a pleasant and stimulating environment.  I am confident that my preparation and the
four months' experience you require in the training program will
qualify me to do top-level work as an executive secretary.

I look forward to hearing from you by June 20.

Cordially,

*Linda K. Stokes*

Miss Linda K. Stokes

Most employers write to the applicants by the dates they promised to give their decisions. If, though, you do not hear from the employer by the date that was specified, you may call long distance to inquire about the decision. Your calm, businesslike tone of voice and well-chosen comments can portray your interest in the job and continue the favorable impression you have made.

## JOB-OFFER ACCEPTANCE

Promptness is important in accepting an offer of employment. When you accept by letter, address it to the person who made the offer unless you are instructed to send it to someone else. Be sure that in the letter you state definitely and cheerfully that you accept the offer. State the job title, the salary, and the date on which you are to begin working. Existing circumstances may, of course, require your including additional information.

The essential points of a job acceptance letter are in the example in Figure 8-17.

What should you do if you believe you have a good chance of being offered another job that would be better? This question, of course, has no specific answer. Some applicants have requested permission to delay acceptance, and their requests were approved. If you choose this alternative, be fair. Request permission to delay only a short time, and do this only when you are sincerely interested in the two jobs—the one offered to you and the one you believe will be offered to you.

Employers want their employees to be well satisfied with their jobs, and many are willing to wait a reasonable length of time for a decision if they do not have to fill a vacancy immediately. Some college seniors who wrote letters similar to the one in Figure 8-18 were granted the request. You will observe that the letter has a positive, cordial tone.

If you should make a request such as this one and receive approval to delay acceptance, be sure to give your decision by the specified date.

**Figure 8-17**

P. O. Box 1146
Morrison University
Morrison, KY 40506
May 16, 1985


Mr. Charles M. Kline, President
Kline and Hatcher Accounting Firm
1126 Meadow Lake Road
Haynesville, KY 40201

Dear Mr. Kline

I accept your offer of employment as a junior accountant
in your Haynesville office at a salary of $21,000 a year.

Thank you for sending the information on apartments.  This
afternoon I wrote to the manager of the Terrace Apartment
Building and sent the required deposit.  I will move to
Haynesville on June 12 and will be ready to go to work in
your office at eight o'clock on Monday morning, June 17.

I look forward to working for you.

Cordially

Kirby J. Davis

Kirby J. Davis

**Figure 8-18**

Box 396, Walton College
Gainesville, TN 38181
July 5, 1985


Mr. Walter T. Hansard
Personnel Manager
Wycliff Wholesale Co.
1234 Second Avenue
Livingston, PA 19111

Dear Mr. Hansard

Working as a junior accountant for you still appeals to me,
and I appreciate your offering me the job.  Could I wait,
however, until August 1 to give you my decision?  I have an
interview scheduled with another company on July 26 and
would like to keep that appointment.

Will you please write soon to approve my letting you know
on August 1 whether I accept your employment offer.

Cordially

*David M. Eakins*

David M. Eakins

## JOB-OFFER REJECTION

In many instances a job is offered to an applicant a few days after an interview. If you receive a letter containing a job offer you wish to decline, reply immediately (within twenty-four hours) and say you decline the offer. You may give the reason for your decision, but you do not have to. If the reason is a pleasant one, you may very well state it. Do not mention unpleasantness when rejecting an offer.

By declining promptly, you make a favorable impression on the "would-be" employer. That person will appreciate your thoughtfulness and fair-mindedness in declining quickly so that someone else can be employed soon. Probably, the interviewer has considered another person who also has good qualifications for the job; and your promptness in declining the offer may enable the interviewer to hire the other well-qualified applicant. Observe the promptness with which the letter in Figure 8-19 was written.

Employers discuss among themselves good applicants they have interviewed, and favorable comments about you could lead to your receiving special attention by another employer who could offer you a job. But if for no other reason, decline offers promptly and courteously simply for the sake of fair play.

## RESIGNATIONS

Most people change jobs at least one time during their lives. You hope, of course, that you will change jobs only because you have an opportunity to go into a better situation. The situation may be better because you are going to a job that pays a higher immediate salary, offers a better chance for advancement in salary or prestige, provides an opportunity to use your skills and knowledge to greater advantage, or provides an opportunity to do the kind of work that is most satisfying to you. Or you may be going to a geographic area that is especially appealing to you.

Some women resign their positions because they get married and no longer work for pay. Others leave their jobs to rear children. These reasons for resigning are only a few of the many reasons a person may resign a position under pleasant circumstances. You

**Figure 8-19**

123 White Avenue
Jasper, VA 22031
May 17, 1988

Mr. Ernest J. Miles
Personnel Manager
Riggs Manufacturing Company
1426 Longview Road
Anchorage, MS 39614

Dear Mr. Miles

Yesterday afternoon, before I received your letter offering me
employment in your management training program, I accepted a
similar job with a company in Louisiana.  That company pays a
higher salary than you offered, and the working conditions and
the opportunities for advancement are somewhat the same.

Thank you for the offer.  I feel confident the person you employ
will enjoy working for you.

Sincerely

Steve A. Myers

have very little difficulty in writing a letter of resignation when leaving a pleasant situation.

State specifically the last day you are to work on the job you are leaving and state the title of your job. Ordinarily, address the letter of resignation to your immediate superior. In some organizations, however, all such letters are addressed to the personnel director. Studying the way the group for which you work is organized helps you to determine the officer who should receive the letter.

Possibly, it would be desirable for you to state your willingness to help orient the person who will replace you. You may, conceivably, feel it is appropriate to suggest the name of a person to replace you. The conditions existing at the time you resign help you to determine just what to include in the letter. Write a letter that leaves a good impression on the people who will read the letter. The letter will be filed in your personnel folder and may be read by several people at various times.

The letter in Figure 8-20 was written under pleasant circumstances, and it left a good impression of the writer.

Ethical, capable, hard-working persons sometimes face unpleasant conditions that cannot be remedied. They must, therefore, resign under unpleasant circumstances. The resignation letter is about as important as the application letter because it is often the last document that goes into the writer's personnel file in that organization.

If you ever resign because of unpleasantness, make the tone of your letter of resignation as pleasant as it would be if you were leaving under pleasant conditions.

When you have a grievance (and some grievances occur in the best-run organizations), you owe yourself and the other person involved an opportunity to discuss the problem. Often, the person who you feel is responsible for the conditions does not realize they are unpleasant for you. When this is the case, the other person involved will gladly make whatever adjustments are needed to correct the situation and will appreciate your bringing the problem up for discussion.

Sometimes a situation seems unpleasant because you do not fully understand the conditions that exist. The fair thing to do is to discuss the grievance with the person involved so that it can be explained. The person involved will appreciate an opportunity to ex-

**Figure 8-20**

## BRADLEY MANUFACTURING COMPANY
### WATERFORD, NJ 08099

October 23, 1985

Mr. Joe D. Scott
Personnel Manager
Bradley Manufacturing Company
2455 Handley Road
Waterford, NJ 08099

Dear Mr. Scott

Because the Westfield Manufacturing Company has offered me a
job that affords especially good opportunities for advancement
as well as a starting salary that is considerably higher than
I am earning here, I am submitting this resignation from my
present job.  Friday, November 22, will be my last working day
here.

I have certainly enjoyed working as assistant manager of the
production department; and I appreciate the courtesies that
have been shown me since I joined this company on July 2, 1979.
The experiences I have had here are invaluable, and I will always value highly the friendships with the other employees.

I will be glad to assist in any way you suggest in orienting
my successor to the job.

Cordially

*Gary L. Harr*

Gary L. Harr
Assistant Manager

plain the situation so that pleasantness can be restored. Dismiss the grievance when you understand it is something that should not offend you. If you feel you should apologize for a misunderstanding, do so simply and then forget about it. Remember, a simple apology (when an apology is due) exemplifies strong character. Repeating the apologetic remarks, however, can lead the listener to think that you are weak-kneed or that you were unfair in asking for an explanation.

If you should have difficulty with a superior who is unethical or who will not attempt to correct a situation that imposes undue hardship on you, you certainly have a right to object to the refusal. You owe it to yourself and to your subordinates (if you have subordinates on the job) to stand up for your rights. Intelligent people of strong character control their temper, but they should fight the case and when necessary take the grievance to personnel further up the organization chart if they want to continue working in their present positions.

Any disagreeable situation should be discussed only with those persons who can do something to remedy the inequity.

The point to be stressed is that regardless of the degree of unpleasantness that exists and regardless of what you say or *do* about it, do not include any reference to unpleasantness in your letter of resignation.

## QUESTIONS FOR DISCUSSION

1. Why should a letter of application be written on plain paper rather than on letterhead?

2. Why should you send a data sheet along with a letter of application even though you know you will be asked to complete an application form?

3. What are appropriate ways of reproducing copies of a data sheet?

4. Why is it important that you list your experience as a laborer (if you have had such experience) when you prepare a data sheet as a part of an application for a job in management?

5. What action should you take if you do not receive a reply within thirty days to your application letter?

6. If you resign because of unpleasant working conditions, why should you not mention the unpleasantness when you write a letter of resignation?

## EXERCISES

Improve the following sentences.

1. Please send your letter of acceptance as soon as possible.

2. A survey of my college work can be found on the enclosed data sheet.

3. I should like to thank you for recommending me for the job of assistant buyer for the Hamilton Department Store in Knoxville.

4. You can get in touch with me by writing to the address given above.

5. You asked me to return the enclosed form before June 25.

6. Please inform Mr. Hanson that I appreciate his writing the recommendation letter for me.

7. I should like to express my appreciation for your help.

8. Please inform me of the exact time of the interview.

9. The forms you asked me to complete are being mailed under separate cover.

10. Enclosed is the form you asked me to sign and return to you.

## PROBLEMS

1. Libraries have valuable information about each of the twenty organizations in the following list. Do extensive research on one of these organizations, apply for the job of your choice even though you do not know whether a vacancy exists, and prepare for an employment interview. Prepare an effective data sheet to send with your application letter.

> The Dow Chemical Company
> Eastman Kodak Company
> Elgin National Watch Company
> Gerber Products Company
> The B.F. Goodrich Company
> Gulf Oil Corporation
> International Harvester Company
> The National Cash Register Company
> Phillips Petroleum Company
> Republic Steel Corporation
> Reynolds Metals Company
> Scott Paper Company
> Sears Roebuck and Company
> Swift & Company
> United States Rubber Company
> Colgate-Palmolive Company
> Corning Glass Works
> The Curtis Publishing Company
> E.I. Du Pont de Nemours & Company Incorporated
> Kimberly-Clark Corporation

2. The following advertisement was in the *Charlotte Times* yesterday.

*WANTED*

> Secretary, salesman, management trainee by June 1, Charlotte Office Equipment Company, 1104 Pinehurst Road, Charlotte, NC 28101

Write a letter of application for one of these three jobs. Enclose a data sheet.

3. Assume that the letter you wrote for Problem 1 or Problem 2 was successful. You received a letter today inviting you to come for an interview. The date and the time of day for the interview were specified in the letter. Reply to the letter.

4.    You had an interview this morning. As another applicant is to be interviewed next week, you are to be notified within two weeks as to whether you will be offered the job. Write a letter thanking the person for the interview and let the interviewer know you are still very much interested in obtaining the job. Having had an interview, you know the name of the person to whom you are writing.

5.    At the conclusion of the interview you had last Friday, the personnel director (and of course you remember his name) told you he would let you know within two weeks whether he would offer you the job. You received his letter today offering you the job. Accept the offer.

6.    During your interview (see Problem 1 or Problem 2) you were offered the job for which you applied. You promised to let the interviewer know your decision within two weeks. Yesterday (one week later) another company offered you a job that you prefer. Write a letter to decline the offer of employment with the company you corresponded with in Problem 1 or Problem 2.

7.    Assume that for the past two years you have been working for the Thomas Manufacturing Company. You will need to make some reference to the kind of work you have been doing. You have an opportunity to take a better job with another company. Use your imagination! Why is the job better? When will you resign? What is the name of the other company? Have you profited by working two years for the Thomas Manufacturing Company? Add anything that is appropriate. Write a letter of resignation. Remember that this letter will be placed in your personnel file. Perhaps this letter will be the *final* good impression that you will make on the people who work for Thomas Manufacturing Company.

8.    You have been working as assistant manager of the production department of the Whaley Manufacturing Company since September 15, 1978. Things went along nicely until three months ago. Since that time many annoyances have hindered your work. You have discussed these legitimate grievances with your immediate superior and with the personnel director. Each person agreed with you that your requests for adjustments are in order. You're fed up! and you have a right to be! Resign. Write a letter of resignation.

# Chapter 9

# Disappointing News

Business activities involve frequent requests for both products and services. Requests may be for free assistance of some type or for products or services for which the person making the request expects to pay. Successful business executives realize the importance of helping others, and they are eager to help at appropriate times. When a person can help by complying with a request, there is no problem in writing the response. Letters of this type— complying with requests—were discussed in Chapter 5. Review that chapter for writing affirmative responses.

Regardless of how efficiently your organization is run or how much you are interested in helping other people, you will occasionally receive requests with which you cannot comply; or it may be possible to comply though you think you should not. Your responses to these requests are more difficult to write than they would be if you were complying, but you can reply in a way that will still maintain the goodwill of the people who made the requests. Letters of this type are discussed in this chapter.

Good public relations is important in any business endeavor or in any activity involving associations with other people. A good reputation for you and a good reputation for the organization you represent are established and maintained by handling all transactions efficiently and tactfully. Your attitude is reflected in your well-written letters. When you believe in yourself, others tend to believe in you also, provided of course you have reason to believe in yourself because you are honest, competent, tactful, and genuinely interested in the welfare of others. When your possession of these qualities is apparent, it is possible for you to decline a request and at the same time maintain the goodwill and friendship of the person who made the request.

A high percentage of the requests that business executives receive are made by fair-minded people who ask for only those products or services they believe the executives can provide. Some people, however, make unreasonable requests that the receiver cannot afford to respond to affirmatively. The requests made by fair-minded individuals are the ones you should treat with care. They are the ones you should decline in a way that will make the persons making the requests feel just as good toward you and your organization as they would feel if you complied.

Telling a reader you have declined a request is disappointing news. As you prepare to write disappointing news, remember to tell *first* what you *can* do when you cannot do what the reader requests.

Some of the letters that have an element of disappointing news are those that:

1. Offer substitutes or other alternatives

2. Promise to comply later

3. State the need for additional information in order to comply

4. Recommend another source of supply

5. Express outright refusals to comply


## SUBSTITUTES OR ALTERNATIVES

Suppose you are working for a department store, a wholesale house, or another supplier of merchandise that receives orders by mail. You know that the people who order items from you hope to receive them promptly; and you know that when those people receive letters from your organization, they hope the letters state that the items have been sent or will be sent soon. Any information other than this is disappointing news.

As a competent communicator, you understand the purpose of your response; and you write promptly. Decide specifically what you should say to the reader. By anticipating the reader's mood, you *begin with good news* and tell what you *can* do *before* telling what you cannot do. Write a letter that has a positive, pleasant beginning and ending and subordinates any necessary disappointing news within the body of the letter. (Remember, the beginning is the most important part of a letter and the ending is second in importance.)

When receiving an order for merchandise you cannot ship by the specified date, study the situation thoroughly to determine the best action to take. You may send a substitute item, tell when you can supply the particular item that was requested, ask another supplier to ship the item, or suggest that the customer order from another source. The more you know about the situation and the person ordering the merchandise, the better you can choose the right step to take.

## Substitutes

If the customer writes that an item must be received by a specific early date, you can suggest a substitute item if you believe the substitute is satisfactory. You may need to give a sales pitch for this product. Give *specific* reasons why you believe the substitute will be satisfactory. Merely telling the reader that the substitute should be satisfactory is not sufficient unless that person is already familiar with the substitute or already has a great deal of confidence in your judgment.

Even when suggesting a substitute, you can offer various choices. If the product is needed soon, you may send the substitute at the same time you write the letter explaining the reason for sending a substitute. Give the recipient an opportunity to return the product at your expense if it is not satisfactory. Because you believe the substitute will be a good one, encourage the ricipient to keep it. Since negative wording may prompt the recipient to return the merchandise, write in a positive, confident, courteous tone. The writer of the letter in Figure 9-1 offered what he believed was a good substitute.

Remember, sales are successful as long as the purchaser is satisfied with the product.

If the item requested is not needed soon, you may give a sales pitch on the suggested substitute and allow the reader to decide that you send it. Anyone who has an opportunity to contribute to a decision tends to be happy with that decision. Writing a letter *before* shipping the product may be extremely important if the product is heavy or difficult to ship.

A number of reasons exist for the need to suggest substitutes. Among the reasons are these:

1.   Inadequate inventory

2.   Discontinued item

3.   Lost franchise

4.   Better item available

**Inadequate inventory.**   Your inventory may be low because of a strike in the plant of the manufacturer or a strike in the railroad, truckline, airline, or other carrier groups responsible for delivering merchandise to you. Your inventory may be low because of an oversight in your organization (occasionally an error is made in the most efficiently run organizations), or it may be low because of inaccurate estimates of requirements. The inventory may be low because the manufacturer's production is behind schedule. Various other factors could cause your inventory to be inadequate.

**Discontinued item.**   The manufacturer of an item may have stopped producing the product or may have started producing a different model. If a new model is being produced, chances are good it is superior to the earlier model; but you often have to *convince* the reader that the later model is superior.

If a product has been discontinued without being replaced by another model, you have to *sell* an entirely new product as a substitute when you believe such a substitution is advisable.

### Figure 9-1

# The Farm and Garden Shop
**MONROE, AL 35470**

July 2, 1985

Mr. Randall N. Gray
1151 Rosemount Drive
Macon, AL 36267

Dear Mr. Gray:

We have a Model 8 riding lawn mower that is more popular this
year than the Model 6 because it has a two-inch wider cutting
area and has a quieter motor.  The new model has all the other
features the Model 6 has and sells for only $15 more, which is
a small sum when applied to a purchase of this amount.

We can send the Model 8 to you immediately.  August 17 is the
earliest date on which we can send a Model 6.  A strike in the
manufacturer's plant last month has prevented our obtaining a
supply of that model.

Considering the size of your lawn and the rate at which the
grass grows in your area, you are wise indeed to replace your
old mower with a riding model.  After mowing the whole lawn in
one afternoon, you will still feel up to eighteen holes of golf;
and by the way, one recent purchaser of a Model 8 is using it
as a golf cart.  Only one nut has to be removed to detach the
cutting blade.

A Model 8 riding mower will be on its way to you the day we
receive your approval to send it.

Cordially,

*Ronnie E. Pratt*

Ronnie E. Pratt
Sales Manager

grm

**Lost franchise.**   If you no longer have the franchise for a product, you obviously cannot supply it. Because you want to continue supplying other merchandise to the customer, you may suggest a substitute item and give the facts that would convince the customer that your product is as good as and possibly even better than the one ordered. After giving your sales pitch, tell why you are not sending the specific item that was ordered. You cannot afford to give the impression that you are ignoring the original request. The explanation would, of course, be followed by a pleasant, specific ending.

**Better item available.**   You may have, in addition to the specific item that was ordered, a similar product you believe would better suit the needs of the purchaser. The similar item may be more durable; it may sell for a lower price; it may have a longer guarantee; it may have a better appearance; or it may be superior because of some other characteristic. Suggesting that the purchaser accept this substitute would be doing that person a favor. The purchaser may appreciate your thoughtfulness in telling about the proposed substitute.

Any time you suggest a substitute, *begin* your letter with the good news of *what you can do for the reader*. Add enough sales talk to convince the reader that the substitute is a good one. Even though you write well enough to convince the reader that the substitute is as good as *or* is better than the item ordered, give a reason for suggesting an alternative. To appear to be ignoring the request for a specific item would be a poor business practice. *Present your explanation positively!*

Almost always this explanation can be presented without using a single negative word or negative connotation. Omit such negative terms as *unfortunately, regret, sorry, cannot, not, will not be able,* and *unable.* Contrast the negative expressions with the positive expressions in the two columns that follow:

| Negative | Positive |
|---|---|
| The raincoats cannot be shipped until November 3. | The raincoats can be shipped on November 3. |
| Why not consider this substitute. | By considering this item, you . . . . |
| . . . will not be available until . . . . | . . . will be ready to mail on . . . . |

Sales talk for other merchandise or services as well as other types of pleasant information may be included in the letter. In any case, end the letter with something that is pleasant, positive, and specific. Many otherwise well-written letters suggesting a substitute are spoiled by using such words as *hope*, *trust*, or *if* in the last paragraph in a way that makes the reader doubt the substitute will be satisfactory. Contrast the negative and the positive ending paragraphs in the two columns that follow:

| Negative | Positive |
|---|---|
| I hope you will be pleased with the Model 22, which we believe is superior to the model you ordered. | Mr. Ray Adams, who serves your area, will bring a supply of revised order forms when he comes to your office next Thursday morning. |
| We trust you will be pleased with this substitute. | A fall edition of our catalog will be mailed to you on June 4. |
| If you like this new model as much as the one you requested, we will be happy to fill orders for it. | We look forward to receiving your next order. |

Note that in each of these positive endings the next step to be taken is implied or is explained in detail.

## Alternatives

Requests for services or materials other than products you sell sometimes have to be declined. The technique for declining these requests is the same as for declining the requests for products: tell *first* what you *can* do when you cannot do what the reader wants you to do.

Among the requests for which business people sometimes suggest alternatives are those for speeches, contributions, and credit.

**Speeches.**   When asked to speak to a group, to participate in another way in a program, or to perform any other service, remember that the person making the request wants your reply to begin by accepting that responsibility. Obviously, you will sometimes be faced with invitations or requests you cannot comply with even though you would like to. When you can offer an alternative (and usually you can), present the alternative first and then subordinate the refusal of the request. You may suggest one or more alternatives. Any alternative you suggest should be one you sincerely believe would be satisfactory. Of course, in order to suggest acceptable alternatives, you have to have adequate background information about the request.

Suppose you are asked to speak on a selected topic to a group on a specified date. If you have another commitment for that date, you may logically agree to speak at another time, provided the meeting could be rescheduled. In this case offering to speak at a later time may be a good alternative.

If you know the group is especially interested in having a particular topic discussed on the date you have been invited to speak, you may suggest an alternate speaker if you know someone who you believe could present a good speech on the topic. Under some circumstances you may want to consult the person you plan to recommend before making the recommendation. Be sure, though, to exercise special care in handling the situation so that the suggested alternate will not be embarrassed or offended if not invited. Also, make your suggestion in a way that the reader of your letter would not feel obligated to invite the person you recommend. Often, program planners have more than one speaker in mind so that they can choose an alternate if the first person they invite declines.

When you suggest an alternate speaker, make it easy to invite the person by sending the full name, mailing address, and telephone number. You also may offer to get in touch with the person you suggest.

Do give reasons for recommending the alternate. Tell some of the characteristics—knowledge of the subject, ability to speak, and so forth—of the person you say you believe would present a good speech.

When offering to speak on another date (see Figure 9-2), be as considerate of the reader as you are when recommending another speaker. The reader may have already made plans for the future meetings and would not want you to speak on any other date. To avoid an embarrassing situation, make it easy for the reader to proceed with any plan without feeling obligated to accept your offer to speak at a later meeting. You can make suggestions diplomatically without putting pressure on the reader to accept any alternative you suggest.

Study the situation thoroughly to determine whether to suggest one or more *appropriate* alternatives *before* declining a request of any kind.

**Contributions.** Organizations are frequently asked to contribute money, services, or materials to various groups—schools, civic clubs, and charitable organizations. They are also asked to help professional groups by advertising in convention programs and other publications or by renting space to exhibit their products at conventions. You may be asked to participate in these ways, and you may welcome that opportunity. If, however, you do not choose to participate, you are under no obligation to do so; and you can decline without hesitating. As an effective communicator, tell what you *can* do *before* you tell what you cannot do.

One alternative would be to offer (provided you are sincere in making this offer) to comply the next time a drive is sponsored. You may recommend that others participate. For example, you may place a note on the company bulletin board inviting the employees to contribute individually to a fund drive if company funds allocated for such purposes have been depleted. A thorough understanding of the existing conditions will enable you to suggest

**Figure 9-2**

## HASTINGS COMMUNITY COLLEGE
Hastings, CO 81041

January 8, 1988

Mr. Edwin A. Rogers, President
Administrative Management Society
Haynes Wholesalers, Inc.
P. O. Box 1234
Norfolk, CO 81422

SPEECH FOR CHAPTER MEETING

Could your chapter of the Administrative Management Society meet
at some time other than Thursday evening, May 9?  I would be
glad to speak to your group on the topic you suggested, "Let's
Maximize Efficiency," at any time I am free.

I have agreed to represent the Association of Colorado Community
Colleges at a national meeting in Houston, Texas, on May 9, 10,
and 11.

I realize that for any one of various possible reasons you may
have to stick to the May 9 date for your meeting.  If so, you
will no doubt have ample time to find another speaker for that
occasion.

*John J. Sharp*

JOHN J. SHARP, PROFESSOR

jfc

an alternative before *stating in a positive, cordial manner* the reason for declining the original request. Follow this reason with a pleasant, positive ending for the letter. Contrast the negative and the positive endings in the two columns that follow:

| Negative | Positive |
|---|---|
| We sincerely regret that we must decline your invitation. | We wish you the best of luck in your fund-raising campaign. |
| We are sorry that we cannot exhibit our machines at your convention this year. | Please give us an opportunity to exhibit our machines at your next annual convention. |
| We apologize for any inconvenience this may have caused you. | We heartily endorse the work your organization does. |

Negative statements such as these at the end of an otherwise good letter cause the reader to concentrate more on your declining a request than on your willingness (and possibly even eagerness) to help in whatever way you mentioned in the beginning of the letter.

**Credit.**   Persons who seek credit obviously believe they or the organizations they represent would benefit by having the credit privilege. When you must decline this request, present the disappointing news as tactfully and cordially as you can. Naturally, you would want to receive the orders because increased sales volume can result in increased profits. You therefore have a selfish interest as well as an interest in the prospective customers in adding their names to your list of current customers.

A good beginning for a letter declining credit is the explanation of special consideration you can give to customers who pay cash. When you can offer a cash discount, for example, make this arrangement sound as attractive as you can by including some specifics. Perhaps doing arithmetic involved in an order would help convince the reader that a cash discount is worthy of consideration. The writer of the letter in Figure 9-3 stressed the advan-

**Figure 9-3**

## WILLIAMSON WHOLESALE CO.
Muncie, OH 43262

July 8, 1985

Mr. Reginald R. Chambliss
Manager, Scott Clothiers, Inc.
Lakeview, GA 30635

Dear Mr. Chambliss

Our 3 percent discount on purchases of $300 or more is somewhat
larger than that offered by any other clothing supplier in this
region.  We encourage you to take advantage of this liberal discount.

We can--except for very rare occasions--ship merchandise within
twenty-four hours after receiving an order.  This prompt shipping
would enable you to borrow money from a bank at the beginning of
a month and then sell the merchandise before that money has to
be repaid.

By borrowing $350, the amount you mentioned in your letter of
July 5, you would have to pay only the minimum that is charged
for one month; and by paying cash for the clothing you order from
us, you would save $10.50.  The markup on the merchandise would
afford you a sizable profit without having to use any of your own
money.  I urge you to take advantage of our cash discount plan
until the ratio of your assets to liabilities is 2 to 1.

The people whose names you gave as references for our routine
investigation of your credit application were very complimentary
of your selling ability, as well as your personal character.  I
am confident, therefore, that your assets-to-liabilities ratio
will be in fine condition soon.

Until then, Mr. Chambliss, let us supply your clothing requirements through our 3 percent cash discount plan.  Please remember
that we can almost always ship any of the merchandise described
in the enclosed catalog within twenty-four hours after we receive
an order.

Cordially

*Pamela S. Rodgers*

Mrs. Pamela S. Rodgers
Credit Manager

dlb

Enclosure

tages of cash purchases until the customer could attain a satisfactory ratio of assets to liabilities.

Present the figures in a way that makes the readers think about the saving you are pointing out rather than think you are simply doing arithmetic for them. Giving *specific* figures such as $4.39 as a saving on an order of $219.43 worth of merchandise is more meaningful than a statement that the reader qualifies for a 2 percent discount. Use specific, positive, cordial statements to "sell" the alternative to credit.

Certainly, most applicants for credit realize their backgrounds will be investigated before their applications are approved or disapproved. Even though this procedure is generally understood, referring to your investigation as *routine* may be good psychology to use.

In declining a request for credit, you have to obey the law and give the reason. If the reason is based on information from a credit reporting agency, you must tell in your refusal the name and address of the agency. If the information on which the refusal is based came from another third-person source, your obligation is to inform the applicant of the right to learn the *nature* of the information within 60 days if the applicant chooses to exercise that right. The following sentence would satisfy this legal requirement: "You have a 60-day right to learn the nature of the information they gave us."

You may promote goodwill by making whatever complimentary statements you can about the applicant. Personal habits or selling ability may be qualities you can compliment sincerely.

If you decline to grant credit because of financial conditions of the applicant, you may invite another request when financial conditions improve to a specified level. Whether or not you encourage the reader to reapply for credit later, end with a positive statement. Contrast the negative and the positive endings in the following columns:

| Negative | Positive |
|---|---|
| We regret that we cannot approve your application for credit at this time. | Any item listed in the catalog can be shipped to you the day we receive your order. |
| If you would like to send another credit application when . . . . | Feel free to send another credit application when . . . . |

## Delayed Compliance

When you cannot provide the requested product or service and have no suitable substitute to recommend, you may be wise to encourage the customer to wait until you can comply with the request. Begin the letter by telling *when* you can comply and then explain in a positive, tactful manner the reason for the delay. A positive explanation omits *delay, inconvenience, failure,* and other negative words.

A sales pitch on an additional item may be included in letters explaining delays. Resale information on the product that was ordered may also be desirable. The specific situation would, of course, enable you to decide whether to include a sales pitch or resale information.

Since the ending of a letter is second in importance only to the beginning, write an appropriate ending to any letter you send to explain a delay in compliance. Notice the positive tone in the final paragraph of the letter in Figure 9-4.

## NEED FOR MORE INFORMATION

If you need more information in order to comply with a request, begin by telling the reader you can comply when you receive the additional details. Be specific in asking for the additional data. Always write tactfully and positively and minimize the use of negative words, phrases, or ideas.

**Figure 9-4**

*Ranchland Department Store*

**Spring City, Kansas 66012**

February 15, 1985

Mrs. Kenneth E. Odlund
247 East Walnut Street
Lawrence, UT 84730

Dear Mrs. Odlund:

A supply of the best seller <u>Cascade Adventures</u> by Walter E.
McMillan is scheduled to arrive at our store on February 28.
We can, therefore, send a copy to you that day so that it will
reach you before your nephew's birthday on March 5.

I am confident he will be pleased with your gift. This book
has received some of the best reviews of any publication within
the past eight years. Because it has been enjoyed by so many
adults as well as by teenaged boys, I suspect that you, too,
would enjoy reading it.

The demand for this book has been so great that our first supply, which we received on February 5, was exhausted before the
end of the week.

We will gift wrap your copy of <u>Cascade Adventures</u> with a paper
that appeals to many young men so that it will be ready for
you to present to your nephew before March 5.

Sincerely,

Christopher E. Ward

Christopher E. Ward
Manager, Book Department

btb

244 | Communicating in Business:   Key to Success

Contrast the negative and the positive statements in the two columns that follow:

| Negative | Positive |
|---|---|
| You neglected to specify the model you prefer. | Which of the two models do you prefer? |
| You did not specify your color preference. | Please specify your color preference. |
| You failed to complete the column for model numbers. | Please complete the column for model numbers. |

One or more sentences assuring the reader you will grant the request promptly upon receipt of the additional information will lessen the impact of the disappointing news that there is a delay.

Resale information is on some occasions quite suitable for this type of letter. A few sound, courteous statements reassuring the readers they will be pleased with the products that were ordered may help motivate them to send the needed information quickly so that you can fill the orders. If the readers' interest in the product has waned since placing the orders, resale information may provide the stimulus they need to send the data you must have to send the products.


## ANOTHER SOURCE

Perhaps you will at some time be asked to supply a product you do not carry in stock and you do not have a suitable substitute to offer. In this case, it is wise to suggest another source.

By suggesting another source, you make a more favorable impression on the customer than you would make by suggesting a mediocre substitute. Two alternatives from which you can choose are: (1) to request another supplier to send the item to the purchaser (2) to tell the purchaser the name and address of a supplier who can furnish the item.

The alternative you choose should depend on such factors as the urgency of obtaining the item, your relationship with the customer, your relationship with the other supplier, and the location of the other supplier. If the person who orders is one of your regular customers and needs the product soon, you would probably do that customer a favor by asking another supplier to send the product by the date specified in the customer's letter. This procedure seems to be the proper action to take if the other supplier is in your city or a nearby city.

Under certain conditions you may ask the other supplier to send the requested item and charge it to your account. You would then charge that amount to the account of the customer who requested the product. Begin the letter to the customer by saying you have asked another supplier (identify the supplier by name and address) to send the product by the time it is needed. An explanation, stated in positive terms, of why you asked someone else to send the product should follow the explanation of the action you have taken. Having done as much as you feel you should do, there is no need to offer any kind of apology. End this letter, like all others, with something pleasant and specific. Study the letter in Figure 9-5.

Promptness in writing a letter of this type is extremely important. To have the merchandise arrive from the other source before your letter of explanation arrives would be embarrassing to you and the organization you represent.

When you send the name and address of another supplier so that the customer can place the order, begin the letter by giving this information. Follow this information with a cordial, positive explanation of your action. End with something pleasant and specific. Except for the first paragraph, this letter could be identical to the one telling the customer you have asked another supplier to send the desired product.

The importance of maintaining good public relations can hardly be overemphasized. Your taking the action necessary to enable a person to obtain a needed product or service is as important as your supplying that product or service.

When writing a letter that contains an element of disappointing news, resist the temptation to begin with a trite "Thank you for . . . ."; and, of course, omit any variation of the trite ending "If I can be of further assistance to you, please do not hesitate to contact me."

## Figure 9-5

### WILLIAMSON WHOLESALE CO.
Muncie, OH 43262

May 15, 1985

Mr. Guenther H. von Braun
Manager, Byland Department Store
122 South Main Street
Oxford, GA 30367

Dear Mr. von Braun

This morning I called Mr. William R. Chadwell, manager of the
Stevens Wholesale Company in Muncie, and asked him to send you
three dozen 52-inch plastic wading pools in assorted colors.
He said he will ship them to you by truck tomorrow afternoon.
The price is the same as ours.

The last one in our warehouse was sold on Monday.  Since our
next supply is scheduled to arrive on June 6, two days after
your sale will begin, we called the Stevens Wholesalers immediately after receiving your order so that you would have the
wading pools for the sale.

After June 6 we will have an ample supply of wading pools, and
of course we still have our usual large variety of merchandise
ready to ship when we receive your next order.  I will send you
one of our fall catalogs when they come from the printer next
week.

We wish you the best of luck with your special sale, and we look
forward to hearing from you again soon.

Cordially

*Regina M. Parker*

Regina M. Parker
Sales Manager

wjl

By telling *first* what you *can* do, you can minimize the effect the disappointing news has on the reader.


## OUTRIGHT REFUSALS

Most requests are legitimate, yet there are those that you cannot grant or that you choose to decline without offering a substitute or another alternative. For example, you may be asked to contribute to a fund you do not care to support because you do not agree with the objectives of the group conducting the fund-raising campaign. You may be requested to grant credit to a person whose reputation is such that you do not want to transact business with that person even on a cash basis. You may receive an employment application from someone you cannot employ. (Rejecting applicants for employment is discussed in Chapter 10.) You may receive still other requests you do not wish to grant.

The letter in Figure 9-6 was written to decline a request to contribute to a charitable organization.

Remember always that as a person of strong character you uphold your convictions. People respect you for this strength of character. When you receive a request with which you do not choose to comply, you can decline in a firm, clear, tactful, straightforward manner. Tact is an important trait of successful business people.

Whether you comply with a request, offer a substitute or other alternative, or make an outright refusal, apply the letter-writing guidelines in this book.

## Figure 9-6

### WILLIAMS MANUFACTURING COMPANY
Pinehurst, TN 37094

October 8, 1985

Mr. Bob O. Zin, Chairman
Regional Help Fund
P. O. Box 265
Lancaster, TN 38569

Dear Mr. Zin

We have heard some complimentary statements about the work your
organization does, especially in the Upper Cumberland Area.

For the past five years, we have contributed to another group,
"Joined Forces," the entire amount of the money that was budgeted
for charitable organizations.  Because our employees support so
enthusiastically the plan we adopted, we expect to continue with
it indefinitely.

We appreciate your inviting us to participate in your campaign,
and we wish you much success.

Cordially

*Karen S. Smith*

Karen S. Smith
Public Relations Director

dlm

## QUESTIONS FOR DISCUSSION

1. Suppose you do not have the materials someone ordered from you and you do not have anything that seems to be an acceptable substitute. You do not know where the materials can be obtained. What should you tell the person when you acknowledge the order?

2. What are some of the requests business people may likely receive that they would have to refuse to grant?

3. What are some disadvantages of referring a customer to another source when you cannot supply the merchandise that was ordered from you?

4. Sometimes customers request adjustments you feel they are not entitled to, yet you grant the adjustments anyway. What are some advantages to granting these requests?

## EXERCISES

Improve the following sentences.

1. The books you ordered cannot be sent until May 30.

2. I hope you will be pleased with the substitute, which is superior to the product you ordered yesterday.

3. Any of our salesclerks will be glad to be of assistance to you in the selection of the furniture for your new office.

4. You will find that brochure is full of many ideas for shortcuts.

5. Due to the fact that the schedule was changed, we will be unable to attend the meeting.

6. I have received your invitation, and I regret to inform you that I shall be unable to accept.

7. We hope this arrangement will not be inconvenient for you.

8. You will find a self-addressed envelope enclosed.

*For your convenience, a self addressed envelope is enclosed.*

9.   The pamphlet you mentioned in your inquiry of October 8 will not
     be off the press until November 15.

10.  In the event that we receive a shipment earlier than June 5, we will
     send the books you ordered immediately.

## PROBLEMS

1.   You are the owner and manager of a large motel in a popular resort
     area. Mr. Donald E. Chapman and his family have come to your
     motel for a two-week vacation each summer for the past five years.
     Year after year they have written to you in February to reserve the
     same efficiency apartment. Because your motel is perhaps the best
     in the area, all space for the summer months is reserved by May 1
     each year.

     The Chapmans wrote to you in February, but discovered on
     April 16 that the letter had not been mailed. They called your office
     that day while you were on a business trip. When you returned to
     the office this morning, your assistant told you that the Chapmans
     had called and that all space for the entire summer had been reserved
     by April 10.

     You would like to help the Chapmans, and you would like for
     them to return to your motel next summer. Write to them.

2.   You are director of customer relations for Hager Jewelers, makers
     of expensive watches. You received two days ago a watch from Ms.
     Margaret H. Shaw, 1151 Long View Road, Rachel, TX 76010. Ms.
     Shaw's parents gave her the watch for a Christmas present when
     she was a college student in 1944.

     The watch has given excellent service throughout the years with
     only minor occasional repairs. Beginning five weeks ago, the watch
     would stop within a short time after Ms. Shaw would wind it. A
     local jeweler examined the watch and found that its years of service
     have brought about so much wear that the winding stem could no
     longer function and that stems of that type were no longer
     available. Another jeweler gave her the same report.

     The watch has much sentimental value for Ms. Shaw, especially
     since her parents have died since giving it to her. Your  experts ex-
     amined the watch and determined that, although it looks almost as
     good as it looked when it was new, it is so badly worn it cannot be
     repaired. Write to Ms. Shaw.

3.  Joseph A. Albright purchased a ceiling fan from you thirteen months ago. The motor has burned out. Mr. Albright realizes that the fan had only a twelve-month warranty, but he returned the fan by UPS with the request that you replace it. Write to him.

4.  Edward M. Latham, chairman of the United Way fund-raising campaign in your city wrote to you and asked you to help with the campaign by soliciting contributions from twenty-five small businesses in a somewhat economically depressed section of your city. You helped in this way last year and the year before, but you received very few contributions. Some of those little organizations appeared to be struggling so much to exist that you felt that perhaps they should be seeking help instead of being asked to contribute.

    Because of the financial condition of the organizations, you are actually glad you will be out of town on an extended business trip during the fund-raising drive. You cannot, therefore, contact the twenty-five small businesses to ask for contributions; but you would like for Mr. Latham to receive help with his worthwhile endeavor. What can you do to help him? Write to him. His address is 1176 Washington Drive, Hopewell, WS 53110.

5.  As the manager of a hardware and paint store in a town of some 15,000 people, you received a request from a group of former local residents to donate paint to repaint an old rural church building that is no longer used. Several former residents acquired the building and plan to renovate it and to maintain it for purely sentimental reasons. Those former residents, who as youngsters attended church services in the old building, have arranged to have the restoration work done without charge. They are asking local businesses to provide the materials. Although you appreciate their interest in restoring the old building that has much sentimental value for them, you cannot donate the paint. Write a courteous reply promptly.

6. Today you received a letter from Charles E. Ramsay. The letter was an order for thirty copies of a book entitled WRITING BUSINESS LETTERS by Harold O. Richards. You cannot fill the order immediately. You have sold all your copies of the book, and you will not receive another supply until the end of two more weeks. You regret this unfortunate circumstance because Mr. Ramsay is one of your best customers. You want to continue to serve him well because you want to keep him as a good customer. His book sales are usually very good during this season. He works for the Longfellow Department Store in Dayton, Ohio. He is the manager of the book department. The store is located at 122 South Jefferson Avenue, and the ZIP number is 43221. Write to him.

7. The principal of a high school 60 miles from your college has asked you to speak to the forty-two seniors in that school who are interested in majoring in business in college. The occasion for your speech is the annual high school career-day program, which is scheduled for 9 a.m. You would like to speak to that group; but you will be at home, which is 250 miles away, for a one-week vacation at that time. Write to the principal.

8. On December 1 James E. Riley sent you an order for three dozen Model 27 Recordex tape recorders. These small tape recorders were good sellers in his store last year during the holiday shopping season. Your wholesale price was $33.75 each. No Model 27 tape recorders are available anywhere since that particular model is no longer manufactured. You now supply a Model 33 Recordex that is superior to the Model 27 (use your imagination to determine the specific characteristics that make it superior to the old model) and wholesales for $34.50. Write to Mr. Riley. You want him to handle the new Model 33, and you want him to receive the three dozen tape recorders in plenty of time for sale during the holiday season. The address of his store is The Gift Shoppe, 2206 Broadway, Hartford, Kentucky 40475.

9.  You are the credit manager of a wholesale house in St. Louis, Missouri. Three weeks ago Keith L. Sharp opened an appliance store in Xenia, Illinois. This is his first business venture. You received a letter from him today asking you to sell small appliances to him on credit. You would like to have him as a customer, but you grant credit to only those businesses that are already well established. You have added several new appliances to your line of merchandise this fall. Among them are a new electric drill, an especially attractive hair dryer, and a polishing machine. Reply to his letter.

10. You are the manager of Stockdale Wholesalers, Inc., in Midland, Illinois. Today you received from the Ratcliff Sewing Center in Phoenix, New Mexico, an order for twelve Model 9 Whistler Sewing Machines. You do not have any sewing machines in stock and do not expect to receive another shipment until the end of six more weeks. Mr. Bradley F. Bush, manager of the Ratcliff Sewing Center, wants the machines for a special sale that will begin in four weeks. You know that the Swathmore Wholesale Company in Lake Charles, Minnesota, handles the Whistler machines and probably has them in stock at a price that is comparable to yours. Write to Mr. Bush and suggest that he order the machines from Swathmore.

11. You cannot fill order No. 57W2110 from Mrs. Omar W. Childers until you receive some essential information. The infant's snowsuit she ordered comes in two styles. One style has elastic stirrups on the pants and has a separate hat. The hat has a leather-look vinyl trim on the earflaps and peak and matches the coat. The second style has knit ankles and an attached drawstring hood edged in the pile which trims the coat. Make it easy for Mrs. Childers to send you the information you need and assure her the snowsuit will be sent as soon as you receive her reply. Remind her that these plush pile snowsuits are easy to care for, warm, and long wearing. Mrs. Childers' address is 55 North Shore Drive, Alma, New Hampshire 03411.

**12.** You are the assistant manager of Lee Walls, Inc., a mail-order needle art and creative crafts center. Mrs. Althea Bond sent in her first order for No. NN33-40, a decoupage purse kit that was featured in your spring, 1985, catalog. In July, 1985, this purse kit was discontinued; and a similar one, No. NN33-44, was added. A double-catch lock was added to the new purse. The same charming prints depicting the world of children are used; and, of course, the kit includes the prints, decoupage finish, and all hardware and materials needed to complete the purse. The new purse kit is, however, 50 cents higher. You would expect to pay at least $13.99 for this unique accessory kit, which is now only $8.33. Write Mrs. Bond at 2399 South Maple, Cranston, Rhode Island 02856, and suggest the substitute purse. Make it easy for her to order by enclosing a card and any other literature you think would be appropriate.

# Chapter 10

# Letters From Employers

Effective personnel administration is a major factor in the efficiency of an organization. Effective administration can provide an atmosphere for high morale, which leads to goodwill. Goodwill depends on good communication—oral and written—with prospective, present, and former employees.

Some of the situations encountered in personnel administration are pleasant; others are not. All must be handled firmly, yet tactfully. Frequently, these situations are handled by means of well-written messages. Among the numerous messages employers write are those to:

1. Seek information about prospective employees

2. Invite prospective employees for interviews

3. Make offers of employment

4. Welcome new employees

5. Reject applicants

6.   Accept resignations

7.   Dismiss employees

8.   Recommend employees

## SEEKING INFORMATION ABOUT APPLICANTS

Employers usually gather information about applicants before they interview them, or they gather it after the interview but before offering employment. Most interviewees who do not voluntarily supply names of references are asked to do so.

The best way to collect information from references is through a face-to-face conversation, provided it can be arranged conveniently for the employer and the references. Ordinarily, people supply pertinent information more freely in this way than in telephone conversations or correspondence.

When face-to-face interviews are not practical, the employer may attempt to collect the desired information by telephone. Although people are more hesitant to make pertinent negative comments on the telephone than in personal conversations, they usually make those comments more freely in telephone calls than in writing.

If neither face-to-face conversations nor telephone calls can be arranged conveniently, the employer has to write letters to collect information about applicants. When you write a letter of this type, do all you can to make it easy for the addressee to reply. Here are some pointers:

1.   Give proper identification of the applicant; for example, "Mr. Michael L. Lyons, who worked in your shipping department from 1979 through 1984 . . . ."

2.   Tell the addressee the applicant has given the addressee's name as a reference.

3.   Identify the specific job for which the applicant is being considered.

4.  Request specific types of information. Ask for an evaluation of such factors as tact, accuracy, and punctuality instead of asking such general questions as "What kind of employee is this person?"

A few years ago employers could treat replies confidentially. Today, however, a federal law requires that this information be revealed to the applicants. Do not, therefore, promise to treat the information as confidential even though you should not reveal it unless you are required to do so.

The letter in Figure 10-1 was written to a former employer of an applicant for a salesclerk's job.

## INVITING TO AN INTERVIEW

An interview is a significant part of the employment process. Rarely do applicants accept a permanent job without first visiting the job location. The applicants want to see the specific place (office, store, factory, and so forth) in which they will spend the workday; and when the geographic area is not familiar to them, they most likely want to see enough of the city to become acquainted with some of its characteristics such as residential areas, schools, shops, and recreational facilities.

Prospective employers, too, usually want applicants to be aware of the environment in which the work is to be done. Both the applicants and the prospective employers realize that regardless of how much workers like their jobs, they continue to be happy and to do their best work only when satisfied with their surroundings. Prospective employers realize that the applicants, the employers and their staffs, the job to be filled, and the local environment are under close study during a job interview. Employers put their best foot forward, therefore, when talking with applicants and of course expect applicants to do the same.

Because inviting an applicant for an interview is good news, the letter is easy to write. *Begin with the good news.* Include—in addition to an invitation—the date, the time, and the exact location for the interview. In most instances mention the job title under consideration. Whether you should include other information de-

**Figure 10-1**

## BORDERS DEPARTMENT STORE
Littlefield, Mississippi 39440

November 1, 1985

Ms. Juanita Y. Murphy, Manager
Children's Clothing Department
Hall-Marx Department Store
1224 Church Street
Cain Creek, AR 86020

Dear Ms. Murphy

Ms. Betty E. Wilkinson, who worked in your department from 1980
through 1983, has applied for a salesclerk's job in our Ladies'
Wear Department and has given your name as a reference.   Will
you please answer the following questions:

1.  Did she quickly establish a good rapport with most of her
    customers?

2.  Was she well informed about the quality of the merchandise
    she sold and about its availability?

3.  Did she arrive at her work station at the proper time each
    day?

4.  Would you rehire her if you had a vacancy in that department?

I will appreciate your answering these questions as soon as you
can.  Any other information you wish to supply about Ms. Wilkinson
will be welcomed.

Cordially

*Jeffery Ryans*

Jeffery Ryans
Personnel Director

wtn

pends on the particular situation. The examples in Figures 10-2 and 10-3 include items that seem appropriate for the situations involved.

When your schedule is tight, you may have to ask the applicant to confirm plans to come for an interview. Under some circumstances, however, you may omit a request for a confirmation so that on the basis of whether the applicant confirms the arrangements at an appropriate time you can learn more about the applicant's thoughtfulness, promptness, and acceptance of responsibility.

## OFFERING EMPLOYMENT

Because a letter offering employment bears good news, it is easy to write. Ordinarily, this letter should specify the:

1. Title of the job that is being offered

2. Salary

3. Date on which the new employee is to begin working

When a formal contract is enclosed for the new employee's signature, most of these details can, of course, be omitted.

The information that has already been exchanged during the interview and through correspondence helps you to choose other appropriate statements to include in the letter offering employment. The plans such as locating housing and arranging for a physical examination you know the new employee will have to make may also be mentioned.

Since you offer employment to only those persons you believe will be assets to the organization, you look forward to having them join the group. Telling them so in this letter is good psychology. Most people do their best work when motivated through *positive* action. Letting new employees know you are favorably impressed by their abilities and personal attributes can pay rich dividends. Compliments in the letter offering employment can be beneficial to your organization and to the new employee. The new employee can sense the difference between sincere compliments and flattery.

**Figure 10-2**

# Jackson Manufacturing Company, Inc.
### P.O. Box 4783 • Colliersville, TN 38211

October 15, 1985

Miss Margaret Anne Kyle
P. O. Box 1714
Fairview Junior College
Colliersville, TN 38211

Dear Miss Kyle

You are one of four applicants we are inviting to come to our
plant for an interview for the job of secretary to the production manager.  We would like you to come to my office at
10:30 a.m. on Thursday, October 24.

After you complete the Wonderlic Personnel Test and our usual
dictation and transcription exercise, you will have an opportunity to discuss the job requirements with Mr. H. B. Chandler,
the production manager.  Please come prepared to stay until
about 2 p.m.

We look forward to your visit on October 24.

Sincerely

*Mary W. Edwards*

Mrs. Mary W. Edwards
Personnel Director

dbf

**Figure 10-3**

# Jackson Manufacturing Company, Inc.
### P. O. Box 4783 • Colliersville, TN 38211

May 24, 1985

Mr. Stephen J. O'Mary
P. O. Box 1428
Randolph Community College
Randolph, AR 72359

Dear Mr. O'Mary

We would like you to come to my office at 9 a.m. on June 6 to
discuss your qualifications for one of the four management
training jobs that are open. The three men whose names you gave
as references have recommended you highly.

A room has been reserved for you for Wednesday night, June 5,
at the Holladay Hills Motel, which is only seven blocks from my
office. The interviews with the training supervisor and me and
the tours of our factory and the city can be completed by 4 p.m.

May we expect you that day? We will reimburse you for your room,
meals, and traveling expenses.

Sincerely

*Mary W. Edwards*

Mrs. Mary W. Edwards
Personnel Director

dbf

Confine your comments to those that are sincere and will likely be accepted as sincere compliments instead of attempts to flatter. This easy-to-write letter helps to establish early a good rapport between the new employee and others who work there.

The letter in Figure 10-4 was written to a young man who was completing the requirements for a college degree.

## WELCOMING A NEW EMPLOYEE

In a small organization the officer who writes the letter offering employment is probably someone who will work closely with the new employee. In such a case a sentence or two in the letter offering employment is enough to welcome the new person to the organization. In some large organizations, however, the letter offering employment is written by a personnel officer who may seldom see the new employee. Or at least the personnel officer may not be closely associated with the new employee. In a situation of this type, the immediate supervisor or someone else who expects to work closely with the new employee may write a short letter welcoming the newcomer to the group. That letter can be effective in helping the newcomer get off to a good start.

The letter should contain the same type of good-will information that is sent by a personnel officer offering employment. While the size and the nature of the organization and the existing conditions help you to decide what to write when welcoming a new employee, remember to make only those comments that are sincere.

The letters in Figures 10-5 and 10-6 were used by a first-line supervisor. Notice that the second letter contains some items that are not appropriate for the person to whom the first letter is addressed.

## REJECTING AN APPLICANT

Unless existing jobs exceed the number of available personnel, at least two—and frequently more than two—applicants are interviewed to fill a vacancy. Applicants realize that probably more

**Figure 10-4**

ARNOLD AND WILLIAMS ACCOUNTING FIRM

MADISON, MICHIGAN

May 22, 1985

Mr. Donald H. Robinson
Terrace View Apartments, No. 257
2114 Lake View Drive
Canton, MI 49231

Dear Mr. Robinson

We invite you to join our staff as a junior accountant on June 17
at a salary of $14,800 a year.  Insurance provisions, vacations,
and other fringe benefits are described in the enclosed booklet.

All of us who had an opportunity to talk with you on May 10 are
very favorably impressed by you as a candidate for this job, and
we look forward to receiving your acceptance of our offer.

Good luck with your final examinations next week.

                         Sincerely

                         *Cheryl L. Qualls*

                         Cheryl L. Qualls
                         Senior Accountant

lar

Enclosure

**Figure 10-5**

# Rutgers Manufacturing Company, Inc.
P.O. Box 1714
Creekmore, OK 73639

July 2, 1985

Miss Clair Richards
225 Whitehall Avenue
Amherst, OK 73014

WELCOME TO THE WORD PROCESSING CENTER

You will certainly be a welcome member of our staff when you
join our word processing center on September 1.  I congratulate you on your excellent performance on the dictation and
transcription test.

I am confident you will enjoy working with the three other
stenographers.  They, too, are highly skilled; and we appreciate their efficiency.

*Michael L. Wombwell*

MICHAEL L. WOMBWELL, ADMINISTRATIVE ASSISTANT

srf

**Figure 10-6**

# Rutgers Manufacturing Company, Inc.
P.O. Box 1714
Creekmore, OK 73639

August 3, 1985

Miss Jane N. Harrison
Box 1112
Watterson Community College
Watterson, CO 80082

Dear Miss Harrison

We look forward to your joining our staff on September 2.  As
secretary to the purchasing officer, Mr. Joseph H. Wellington,
you will have an opportunity to meet many people and also to
use the skills you have developed during the past two years of
college.

Since Mr. Wellington will be on vacation from August 25 to September 8, you will begin working at an ideal time.  Miss Rainey,
who is working for him now, will continue to work until September 12.  She will have ample time to help you become acquainted
with the tasks to be performed in that office.

I hope the vacation you have planned for the last two weeks in
August will be especially pleasant.

Sincerely

*Michael L. Wombwell*
Michael L. Wombwell
Administrative Assistant

srf

than one person will be interviewed for a job, and they know only one will be employed. Each person who is genuinely interested in obtaining the job hopes, of course, to be the one selected for it.

A letter telling an applicant that another person has been selected is obviously a disappointing letter. Begin this letter by telling *what you can do* for the reader. You can say you will keep the application in an active file so you can consider the applicant for another vacancy that is to occur, or you may take some other positive action. Make only those offers that are sincere and appropriate. Whether you can help in finding employment, you want to maintain good public relations with the applicant and the applicant's associates. Be courteous, therefore, and never write a letter that sounds curt or rude.

The letter in Figure 10-7 was written to a young woman who was well qualified for a typist's job, but she could not take dictation.

Do not discourage applicants unduly. They most likely possess good qualities for jobs that are open elsewhere. A courteous letter can help an applicant to develop or to maintain self-confidence when applying for employment with another organization.

Try to soften the blow as much as you can when rejecting an applicant, but in all fairness make it clear that you have decided to employ someone else. Do not give the reader false hope of obtaining the job. As a skillful writer, you can reject an applicant and still maintain goodwill.

## ACCEPTING A RESIGNATION

When a letter of resignation is received, a member of management should in most instances reply to the employee by letter accepting the resignation. A cordial tone should characterize this letter. Pleasantness can permeate the message regardless of the circumstances under which the resignation is submitted. You are probably sorry to lose satisfactory employees from the group, but you are pleased they have better opportunities elsewhere. Rather than exemplify a selfish attitude by emphasizing your regrets that employees have decided to resign, let them know you are pleased they have opportunities to move to better jobs. Let the employees know, of course, that you are sorry they are leaving. Omitting any

**Figure 10-7**

# Hathaway Wholesale Company
MINOT, MN 55571

April 28, 1985

Mrs. Ruth Taylor Moore
305 West Seventh Street
Blue Lake, MN 56341

Dear Mrs. Moore

We are keeping your application in our active files so we can
get in touch with you when we need another typist, which will
probably be about September 1. Your 70-words-a-minute typing
speed is impressive indeed, and so are your general clerical
scores and your courteous manner.

Yesterday we employed a young woman for the receptionist job
for which you were interviewed. She can take dictation rapidly;
and as we told you during your interview, the receptionist in
our office will be given some dictation almost every day.

I am glad you plan to study shorthand this summer. The ability
to take dictation combined with your typing skill will help
you to land a challenging, higher-paying job.

Cordially

*Sharon E. Buckner*

Sharon E. Buckner
General Manager

awb

reference to your regrets could lead the employees to believe you are pleased by their resignations.

Acknowledge the resignation from the specific job that is held, and make it clear that you understand the date of the last workday for your organization. You may need to say something about the way in which the final paycheck is to be received. Mention other financial matters such as insurance and retirement benefits when applicable. Numerous other matters such as keys, tools, and uniforms that are to be turned in may also be mentioned. Such matters as these are determined by the policies and the practices of the organization.

The letter in Figure 10-8 was written to a valued employee who had decided to accept employment with another company.

If the persons resigning are not satisfactory employees, you are probably pleased they have decided to resign. Even then, your letters should carry a cordial tone. You are happy if the employees have obtained jobs they prefer over the present ones, and you can congratulate them on that achievement if you feel that a note of congratulations is in order. When congratulatory comments may not seem appropriate, you can at least wish an employee good luck.

Honesty is the best policy. Do not express regrets that employees have resigned if you are not pleased with their behavior or job performance, yet there is no need to express elation. The employer who wrote the letter in Figure 10-9 was completely honest, yet cordial, in accepting a resignation from an employee who would have been dismissed if he had not resigned within thirty days. The employee might have realized he would be dismissed soon; but no one had told him that such action had been planned. When you write a letter of this type, remember that good public relations is a genuine asset to an organization.

Under certain circumstances you would try to persuade the person who is resigning to reconsider the decision and to continue working for you. If you do this, do it *before* you write a letter accepting the resignation.

**Figure 10-8**

## *BRADLEY MANUFACTURING COMPANY*
### WATERFORD, NJ 08099

September 19, 1985

Mr. T. Martin Lambert
Assistant Manager
Bradley Manufacturing Company
Waterford, NJ 08099

Dear Martin

Congratulations on being chosen for the job with the Westfield
Manufacturing Company.  Through talking with one of my friends
there, I learned that they interviewed some high-calibre candi-
dates; and I agree with them that you were the best choice.

Their gain is our loss.  Although we do regret losing you, we
are pleased you have been offered a better situation than we can
afford now.  We appreciate the fine work you have done here.

You can leave your office keys at the payroll window when you
go by to pick up your November paycheck.  The payroll clerk is
glad to write the check three days early for you as you will
be leaving us on November 27.

We wish you the best of luck in your new job.

                              Cordially

                              Joe D. Scott

                              Joe D. Scott
                              Personnel Manager

msb

## Figure 10-9

**BRADLEY MANUFACTURING COMPANY**
WATERFORD, NJ 08099

July 17, 1985

Mr. George S. Folger
Department of Accounting
Bradley Manufacturing Company
Waterford, NJ 08099

Dear Mr. Folger

We accept your resignation from the job of junior accountant.
Since your last workday with us will be July 31, you will have
earned another week's vacation.  An extra week's pay, therefore,
will be added to your final salary check.

We wish you the best of luck in your new job and in all your
other future endeavors.

Cordially

Joe D. Scott

Joe D. Scott
Personnel Manager

msb

## DISMISSING AN EMPLOYEE

Dismissing an employee is an unpleasant task for both the employer and the employee. Frequently, the employer who has to dismiss persons the employer was responsible for hiring has to admit having made poor selections when offering employment to those persons. Sometimes, though, when there is a shortage of personnel available for screening, an employer has to hire workers whose abilities to perform assigned duties or to work well with associates are questionable. Even under circumstances such as these, the employer faces the problem and the financial burden of finding, employing, and training a replacement for the worker whose services are terminated. Also, other factors contribute to the unpleasantness of firing an employee. The employer is perhaps genuinely concerned about the personal welfare (financial, social, and psychological) of the employee and is concerned about the effect the action will have on the employee's family and friends and the other members of the employer's organization.

Employees who are dismissed stand to suffer financially and psychologically now and possibly for some time in the future. They realize this action becomes a part of their permanent record, and they know the dismissal will have to be explained to future employers. The employees' morale is affected, therefore, by being dismissed.

Because the task of dismissing employees is difficult, regardless of the way in which it is handled, the letters announcing dismissals or confirming this news that has already been released are difficult to write. Writing letters of this type requires much thought and finesse.

When personnel matters have been handled properly, employees are partially prepared to receive dismissal letters. Before the letters are written, the superiors will have discussed with the employees the fact that their work is substandard and the ways in which job performance should be improved. Employers are usually eager to help conscientious employees improve their skills and knowledge; and if the employees cannot become proficient in their present jobs, they are transferred to other jobs within the organization, provided their skills are needed elsewhere. In many instances employers are eager to retrain workers. When no other suitable jobs are available within the organization, employers will usually offer to help the workers obtain employment with another group.

In a letter terminating an employee's services, tell *first* what help you can give. Obviously, circumstances are such that you can offer to assist a deserving person in a specific way. Study the letter in Figure 10-10. Although the employee who received that letter seemed incapable of performing satisfactorily in her present position, she possessed the qualifications for another job within the organization.

The letter in Figure 10-11 was written to an employee who had a good attitude toward his work and his associates and had tried to raise his performance to the required level. He could not, however, acquire the skills necessary for acceptable performance on his present job; and no job for which he was qualified existed within the organization.

The letter in Figure 10-12 was written to an employee who had been convicted of stealing merchandise from the store in which he worked. The employer was happy to see the employee go, but in the letter she did not express her happiness.

Whether a person is dismissed from a job because of lack of ability, unwillingness to cooperate with others in the group, reduction in work force, or any other reason, the letter bearing the news of dismissal should contain certain items of information. In this letter state clearly, yet tactfully, that the addressee's employment is to be terminated. Specify the last day the employee is to work for you.

Other information that is appropriate depends on the existing conditions. You may need to mention the last paycheck the employee will receive as well as other financial matters. Much of the content of the dismissal letter should be similar, or even identical, to the content of the letter accepting a resignation.

Certainly, do not make any statement that could validly be interpreted as accusing or slanderous. Some employees who are dismissed attempt to take legal action against the employer. To protect yourself and your organization, be sure the reasons you give for dismissal are correct, precisely stated, and defensible. Write so carefully that if the employee contests the dismissal, no attorney, arbitrator, or union official can use the letter to your disadvantage.

**Figure 10-10**

# BRADLEY MANUFACTURING COMPANY
### WATERFORD, NJ 08099

June 12, 1985

Miss Yvonne E. Bowman
Planning Department
Bradley Manufacturing Company
Waterford, NJ 08099

Dear Miss Bowman

Perhaps you know Miss Sherry Moss is leaving us on August 1.
We would like you to replace her as receptionist in the
administration building.

With your pleasant disposition and ability to converse with
the company visitors, you would represent us well in that
job. Your salary would be the same as for the job you have
now as secretary to Mr. Wheatley.

Since Mr. Wheatley's added responsibilities require him to
have a secretary who can write shorthand, we must remove you
from your present job so that he can employ someone who has
that skill.

You may begin working as receptionist on July 25, a week before Miss Moss leaves. Please let me know by July 1 whether
you wish to accept the receptionist job. I believe you would
enjoy working in that office.

Sincerely

Joe D. Scott

Joe D. Scott
Personnel Manager

msb

**Figure 10-11**

# BRADLEY MANUFACTURING COMPANY
### WATERFORD, NJ 08099

January 15, 1985

Mr. Thomas C. Adfield
Auditing Clerk
Bradley Manufacturing Company
Waterford, NJ 08099

Dear Mr. Adfield

You are well liked by your associates, and your efforts to perform
the tasks that are assigned to you are appreciated.  I hope you will
return to college to acquire the knowledge necessary for you to realize your potentials in accounting or in whatever field you choose
to work.

As you know, the volume of our business has increased so much that
we must employ someone who can handle more work without supervision
than you are prepared to handle.  We have employed a young man who
has a college degree and a CPA certificate to do the jobs you are
doing plus others that require the high degree of training he possesses.  He will join us on March 1, which means we must terminate
your employment with us on February 28.

The paycheck you will receive that day will include an extra week's
pay for the vacation time you have earned since July 31.

I am glad you are interested in returning to college.  When you get
ready to go to work again, both Mr. Bradford, the senior auditor,
and I will be happy to recommend you for any job you are qualified
to perform.  Please feel free to use our names as references.

Sincerely

*Joe D. Scott*

Joe D. Scott
Personnel Manager

msb

**Figure 10-12**

# Jackson Manufacturing Company, Inc.
### P. O. Box 4783 • Colliersville, TN 38211

October 22, 1985

Mr. Leon J. Russell
126 High Street
Mayfield, MO 64051

Dear Mr. Russell

You can pick up your final paycheck at the payroll office
on October 31.  The check will include your earnings through
October 12, the last day you worked for us, and the vacation
time you earned but did not take.

We hope you secure satisfactory employment in a desirable
location.

Sincerely

*Mary W. Edwards*

Mrs. Mary W. Edwards
Personnel Director

dbf

Try to maintain the goodwill of all former employees. Much of the credit for success in business endeavors can be attributed to good public relations. Exhibiting your willingness to be fair and considerate of others helps you to maintain a good image with the general public.

## RECOMMENDING AN EMPLOYEE

Some people remain in their first job until they reach retirement age. These people, however, make up only a part of the work force. Most workers change jobs two or more times; some change jobs many times.

Managers are asked frequently to recommend their employees for promotions or for employment with other groups and to recommend former employees for employment. In some instances these recommendation letters carry much weight in determining whether the promotion or the job offer is granted. Promptness in writing these letters is important. When two people who seem to be equally well qualified for a job are being considered, the applicant whose recommendation letters are received first has an advantage over the one whose letters are received later. This advantage is, of course, more pronounced when the vacancy is to be filled within a short time. When you are asked to write a recommendation letter, write it as quickly as you can.

Some requests for a recommendation state specific qualities that are to be evaluated. You may be asked to evaluate the person's ability to perform the duties that will be assigned, or you may be asked to comment on personal traits. In many cases you will be asked to comment on both ability and personal factors. When the factors you are to cover are specified, the recommendation letter is easier to write than when you have to decide which types of information to give.

If specific types of information are requested, you have an opportunity to add comments. These comments can include further details, or they can serve as explanations for your remarks.

When you have to decide the kinds of information to include, study first the job for which the applicant is being considered. Consider the qualifications a person should possess to do the job well and then think about the applicant's preparation, experience, and personal traits in relation to the job.

If you are fair-minded and sincerely interested in the welfare of the persons you are recommending, you will try to help them obtain jobs for which they are well suited. Only when workers are satisfied with assignments they can handle well will they ordinarily do "a fair day's work for a fair day's pay." Proper adjustment on the job is important for both the employees and the employer.

Although you want to compliment the people you are recommending and to emphasize their best qualities, you cannot afford to exaggerate. Your writing style and the tone of your letters have a bearing on the effectiveness of the recommendations. A flowery style or insincere tone tends to lead the readers to believe you have overrated the applicants. Specific, positive statements are as important in these letters as in any other. Choose your words carefully. Well-chosen adjectives that describe the applicants can be quite helpful to those persons. Among the almost limitless number of adjectives used to describe people are these:

| | | |
|---|---|---|
| amiable | fair-minded | receptive |
| candid | frank | resourceful |
| capable | honest | self-confident |
| competent | imaginative | skilled |
| congenial | industrious | skillful |
| courteous | intelligent | strong |
| creative | modest | tactful |
| dependable | neat | trustworthy |
| diplomatic | perceptive | versatile |
| energetic | polished | vivacious |
| enthusiastic | polite | well-mannered |
| even-tempered | punctual | witty |

Certainly, only a few of these adjectives should be used to describe one person.

While appropriate use of adjectives helps the reader to know about the nature of the person you are recommending, references to specific incidents help convince the reader that the applicant has the qualities you mentioned. When recommending his secretary for another job for which she had applied, a college professor gave the following comments to support his statement that she was competent and that she had initiative.

> When a long-distance telephone call delayed my going to class yesterday, she went to the classroom and told the students why I had been detained and that they could expect me within the next few minutes. Thoughtful acts such as this combined with her skill, courteous manner, and genuine pride in her work make her a valued assistant.

The writer of the letter in Figure 10-13 pointed out the good traits of punctuality and dependability by stating that Mike Hanson was always at work on time and had not missed a day. He supported the statement that Mike was energetic by saying he completes his assignments cheerfully and promptly. These specific references helped to sell the young man's capabilities.

When you are asked to comment on specific factors, your omitting a reference to any one of them would probably make the reader believe you rate the person low on that factor.

To be honest with the reader and with the person you are asked to recommend, you must in some situations mention negative traits that exist. Mention them if you believe the prospective employer should know about them. Those traits can be referred to discreetly and can be subordinated so the reader becomes aware of them but is not overly concerned.

Under special circumstances you may write a recommendation letter and give it to the person whom you have recommended so that it can be presented at an interview. This practice is followed very rarely, however. Letters presented in this way usually contain no reference to negative traits the prospective employer would like you to evaluate. If a person requests a recommendation letter to be delivered personally, explain that the letter is more beneficial if you mail it directly to the interviewer.

## WRITING OTHER MESSAGES

In addition to the letters discussed in this chapter, other messages have to be written by employers. Among them are those that pertain to vacations, appointments, grievances, anniversaries, promotions, and announcements. Memorandums are used for many of these intraorganization messages. The content and the writing style for memorandums are the same as for letters addressed

**Figure 10-13**

## MONTGOMERY CREDIT ASSOCIATION
MONTGOMERY, GA 31365

July 8, 1988

Mr. Lee J. Carter
Regional Manager
McConnell Publishing Co., Inc.
1242 Palmetto Road
Athens, SC 29821

RECOMMENDATION FOR MICHAEL E. HANSON

Mr. Michael E. Hanson, about whom you inquired, seems to possess
the qualities needed by a representative for a publishing company.
He is a clean-cut, well-dressed, well-mannered young man who gets
along well with his associates.

Perhaps he told you that next month he will complete a one-year
appointment with us as a replacement for a clerk who asked for a
year's leave. We are pleased with Mike's work. He is always at
work on time; he has not missed a day. He completes his assignments cheerfully and promptly. Not only is he energetic, but he
also has the proper blend of self-confidence and modesty to sell
himself, and I believe, McConnell publications.

I have no reservation in recommending Mike Hanson for the job of
sales representative.

*Scott A. Barkalow*
SCOTT A. BARKALOW, MANAGER

bks

to employees. The main difference between letters and memorandums is format. Format and the uses of intraoffice memorandums are discussed in Chapter 15.

## QUESTIONS FOR DISCUSSION

1. What specific types of information would you like to receive from an applicant's references before you interview the person for a job as an accountant?

2. Assume you are asked to recommend a former secretary who did excellent work for you and you are not given specific factors to evaluate. What factors would you include in the recommendation?

3. If you should receive a letter asking you to recommend a former employee who was an unsatisfactory worker and who is poorly qualified for the job the person is seeking, how would you reply?

## EXERCISES

Improve the following sentences.

1. I should like to welcome you to our staff.

2. Please return the completed form as soon as possible.

3. My secretary will be more than glad to be of assistance to you.

4. Enclosed you will find a copy of the letter that I mailed to Mr. Ralph Ralston under the date of October 1.

5. You will be enrolled in a training program for a period of one year.

6. I am happy to send this information in reply to your inquiry.

7. Why not come in to talk with us about those plans before October 1.

8. When you decide whether or not you will accept the job offer with us, please advise me.

9. Please inform us of your plans within ten days' time.

10. A copy of our agreement is attached hereto.

## PROBLEMS

1. Randle W. Swain has been working as a salesclerk in your department store for the past twenty-two months. He was an excellent salesman and had a good rapport with his customers until about three months ago. Several customers have indicated to the department manager that Mr. Swain had been rude to them on more than one occasion. He was late arriving for work several mornings, and he took longer lunch breaks than were allotted. After the department manager talked with him, he performed better until two weeks ago. Because he did not improve his performance after the department manager talked with him again, you talked with him. Because he still is doing a very poor job, you must terminate his employment at the end of this month—two weeks from now. Write a firm yet courteous letter to him and tell him that his employment with your store is being terminated. You are the personnel manager for the store.

2. You are the administrative services manager of the Wakefield Wholesale Company in Tacoma, South Dakota. During the past several weeks, four of your customers who frequently get in touch with your office by telephone have complimented your receptionist who answers the telephone. They say that she is courteous and very efficient. Write a short letter to her and tell her you appreciate her helping to project a good image for your company.

3. For the past year you have had the best secretary you have ever had. She arrived from 30 to 45 minutes before the 8:30 opening time, and she often stayed late to finish dictation you had not been able to give her until after 3 p.m. She was thorough in her work and had taken over one third of your work load. She is now resigning for personal reasons. Accept her resignation with a letter detailing her superb qualities.

4.   As personnel director of the Morrison Wholesale Company in Waterford, Iowa, reply to Jon L. Reese's letter applying for the job of junior accountant that was filled last week. Mr. Reese, who will be graduated from the Joelton Community College in Joelton, Iowa, next June, sent a well-written letter and an impressive data sheet.

5.   Terry L. Hicks, who is to be graduated from Biltmore University, Cummings Falls, Ohio, next June, has applied for the job of junior accountant in your bank. He has listed four names as references on his data sheet. Write to one of those four persons, Dr. Julian B. Harris, Associate Professor of Accounting, Biltmore University, and ask him to recommend Mr. Hicks. So far you are favorably impressed by the applicant.

6.   Mary Ellen Rice, who worked as your secretary from June 1, 1981, until May 31, 1985, has applied for a job as secretary to the personnel manager of the St. Louis Manufacturing Company, St. Louis, Missouri—an organization similar to yours. She was an outstanding secretary for you. As personnel manager of your organization, write a letter recommending her.

7.   Once each year your company evaluates your employees by filling out an appraisal form. The supervisors complete a form for each employee, and the employee fills out the same form. A week or so later, the supervisor and the employee have an interview to discuss their individual evaluations. These appraisals are usually beneficial to the employee and the company and tend to keep employee morale fairly high. Yesterday, however, you received a letter from Sara Proctor, a word processing secretary, who—although she signed the appraisal form during her interview with you—now thinks she has been misjudged. Sara is a shy person who expresses herself better in writing than in speaking.

    Send her another appraisal form and ask her to explain her answers with specific examples of her work. Although Sara may be shy with her supervisor, she is not with her peers; and you do not want her complaint to grow into a formal grievance. You will, therefore, have to use tact and persuasiveness.

8. Harold L. Gray, an accounting clerk in your office, has asked for permission to take a two-week vacation the last two weeks of March. He has an opportunity to travel to the West Coast then with his parents and his brother and sister. Because that period is an unusually busy time for your firm, decline his request. In January you and he had scheduled his vacation for the first two weeks of July. As chief accountant for Hobart and Sams Accountants, write to Harold and decline his request.

9. A serious illness required you to be hospitalized for three weeks and then to spend a fourth week at home. Your administrative assistant, Jan C. Borek, made several trips to the hospital and also to your home. The first two visits to the hospital were to cheer you, and later visits were to bring papers to be signed and to discuss business transactions at the office. Jan's handling the work at the office and assisting the other employees with their decisions as well as visiting you in the evenings and on weekends on her own time deserve more than an oral "Thank you." Write her a letter and be specific in thanking her for the tasks she performed. She will welcome your letter and will appreciate having this record in her file.

# PART THREE

# REPORTS

# Chapter 11

# Report-Writing Guidelines

For an organization to operate effectively, the personnel must decide on numerous courses of action. Sound decisions are based on adequate pertinent information. In some cases the decision makers collect information and add it to the information they already possess. Often, they require information from other people so that sound decisions can be made. This information is frequently presented as a written report to the decision makers.

College graduates who know how to collect the right information and how to present it so that it is easy to interpret have excellent opportunities to advance to responsible positions that pay high salaries. Routine reports, which are rather easy to prepare, are adequate for some situations. For many complex situations in business, industry, and government, the reports that are needed require much thought, time, and effort for collecting information and writing various drafts.

While there is no formula for writing business reports, using the following guidelines will help you to write reports of high quality:

1.   Understand why the report is needed.

2.   Keep the reader(s) in mind.

3.   Outline the report.

4.   Collect enough relevant information.

5.   Document information sources.

6.   Construct and interpret appropriate graphic aids.

7.   Write objectively.

8.   Write accurately, concisely, interestingly, and simply.

9.   Add headings.

**Understand why the report is needed.**   You may decide that a report is needed, or someone may assign you the task of writing one. Before you begin planning the report, be sure you understand how the information is to be used. Will it give instructions for doing a job? Will it bring the reader(s) up to date on the status of a project? Will it enable someone to make a decision? The information you present may serve one of these functions or another one; but before you can write an effective report, you have to know why it is needed and how it is to be used.

When you are assigned a report, you may need to communicate face to face, on the telephone, or by written words with the person who assigned it to determine the specific purpose. Are you to present information only? Are you to draw conclusions? Are you to make recommendations? When you determine the specific use, write a statement of the purpose or the objective to be achieved and refer to this statement often as you prepare the report.

Some good writers write this statement as a question to guide them in their work and then restate it as a declarative sentence in the finished report. Here are examples for a report to be written to enable a group to decide whether to build a series of mini-warehouses:

> Is there sufficient need for a series of mini-warehouses in Chattanooga, Tennessee, to justify our building them?
>
> This study was made to determine the need for a series of mini-warehouses in Chattanooga, Tennessee.

For an analytical report, you may follow the statement of the objective or purpose with the main questions to be answered:

> *Factors of the Problem*
>
> To determine the need for mini-warehouses, these questions had to be answered:
>
> 1. Who will use them?
>
> 2. What will be stored in them?
>
> 3. Is a suitable site available?

These analytical questions, which are asked in the introductory section, are answered in the body of the report. Make certain that you answer adequately any question you ask in a report.

Understanding the need for the report will help you to collect the right information and to present it well.

**Keep the reader(s) in mind.**   You may prepare a report for one reader or for a group. In most instances formal reports are read by several persons; and you may assume that more than one person will read your letters, memorandums, and other informal reports. To make a report most effective, try to answer these questions that you ask yourself about the readers:

1. How much do they know about the topic on which I am writing?

2. What do they know about the situation that led to the need for this report?

3. What official positions (job titles) do they hold, and what is their role in the action to be taken on the information I present?

4. Are they familiar with the terms I may need to use?

The more you know about the readers, the better you can write so that they grasp quickly and easily the information you give them.

**Outline the report.**    Before you begin to write, think about the most important points you need to cover. Jot down notes so that you will remember these points, and then arrange them in the order in which you will present them in the finished report.

For simple memorandums and letter reports, notes on a slip of paper provide an adequate outline. For more complex reports—especially formal analytical reports—you can work better from a formal outline. A good outline not only helps to present the information in proper order, but it also helps make the writing task easy. The alphanumeric style that follows is only one of several correct styles. This style is popular and easy to follow:

```
I.     ——
    A.    ——
    B.    ——
II.    ——
    A.     ——
        1.    ——
            a.    ——
                (1)   ——
                (2)   ——
            b.   ——
            c.   ——
        2.   ——
        3.   ——
    B.   ——
    C.   ——
III.   ——
```

When constructing outlines, writers sometimes overlook the fact that at least two parts are created when an item is divided. For example, when the information for a Roman numeral is divided, at least two letters (A and B) must follow. The information for either letter may then be divided further into two or more parts. Dividing one part does not require dividing any other part of equal rank.

You may use this alphanumeric style for either a topic outline or a sentence outline. The topic outline, which includes only a word or a short phrase for each division, is usually sufficient for a simple report. And experienced writers may prefer a topic outline for complex reports. Here is a topic outline:

    I.   Problem orientation
         A.  Purpose
         B.  Factors
             1.   Users
                  a.   Company
                  b.   Outside
             2.   Volume
             3.   Times
         C.  Procedures
    II.  Facilities
         A.  Space
         B.  Equipment
    III. Personnel
    IV.  Conclusion
         A.  Summary
         B.  Conclusions
         C.  Recommendations

A topic outline can be made into a sentence outline, which is a step nearer the completed report. A sentence outline such as the one that follows is especially helpful for inexperienced report writers and for experienced writers of some types of reports that are new to them. A portion of the preceding topic outline was made into the sentence outline that follows:

    I.   Problem orientation
         A.  The purpose is to determine whether to open a word
             processing business.
         B.  These factors will be studied:
             1.   Who will use it?
                  a.   Company executives will dictate letters.
                  b.   Executives outside the Company will dictate
                       special reports.
             2.   The volume of dictation will keep three
                  transcribers busy most of the time.
             3.   Company dictation will be even; most dictation
                  from outside will come at two periods each
                  month.
         C.  The information was collected by mail questionnaires
             and telephone interviews.
    II.  Facilities
         A.  Two large rooms are available.
         B.  Equipment can be obtained immediately.

A well-planned outline directs the flow of thoughts and helps the writer to arrange the information into a clear, logical order. Also, the sentence outline provides a brief summary of the report.

**Collect enough relevant information.**   Even though you have top-notch writing skills, you can write an effective report only when you have adequate pertinent information. Begin with the knowledge you possess, and remember that other personnel of your organization can provide worthwhile facts and suggestions for the study you are undertaking. Your organization records and library holdings are valuable sources of information. Some of the most frequently used publications and methods of collecting data from people are described in the chapter on information sources.

To become a better writer, support your writing skills with knowledge of sources of business information.

**Document information sources.**   Use your originality and creativity, of course; and when appropriate, add strength and authority to your reports by including information you take from other sources—publications, interviews, and so on. Collecting again the data other people have already collected and made available for use would be a waste of your time, effort, and money. Use this secondary information and give due credit to the people who provide it. You can give the credit that is due—and oftentimes make your report more convincing—by using footnotes properly. Current ways of arranging footnotes, constructing bibliographies, and quoting from publications and interviews are presented in the chapter on documentation.

**Construct and interpret appropriate graphic aids.**   Much of the information in business reports is presented in sentence and paragraph form. In many reports, though, you should use graphics to present part of the data. When a well-chosen, properly constructed graphic can make a body of data easy for the readers to understand, use it because your chief objective is to present adequate relevant information in a concise form so that readers grasp it quickly and easily.

Because graphics play an important role in business reports, an entire chapter of this book is devoted to choosing, constructing, and interpreting graphics.

**Write objectively.**   Give your readers facts, which may be supported by examples or clarified by analogies. Choose words that state facts precisely. When you draw conclusions from the facts in an analytical report, make clear to the readers that your conclusions are not only logical but also valid—based on the facts you present.

When you believe readers will welcome your opinions, express them in the letter with which you transmit the report.

**Write accurately, concisely, interestingly, and simply.**   The readers of your report are busy people. Your job, therefore, is to give them accurately, concisely, interestingly, and simply the information they need. How can you accomplish this task? Here are some steps to take:

a.   Expand your knowledge of the English language. Continue developing your vocabulary, and pay special attention to terms that apply specifically to your field of work. In your reports, use only the words you feel confident the readers know.

b.   Pay close attention to sentence structure so that you have no misplaced modifiers, incorrect punctuation, or other faults that create inaccuracies or ambiguities.

c.   Make all mathematical computations carefully and record them accurately. Put decimal points in the proper places, align numbers correctly in columns and in graphics, and express numbers correctly in sentences.

Align dollar marks and percent signs, and include one for the first and the total entries only, as in these illustrations:

| | |
|---|---|
| $   16.72 | 8.4% |
| 876.20 | 71.2 |
| 9.00 | 13.0 |
| 1,843.57 | 7.4 |
| $2,745.49 | 100.0% |

d.   Spell words correctly and divide them correctly at the ends of lines. (Rules for word division are in the reference section of this book.)

e.  Although you need to vary your expressions, especially in reports that are longer than one page, use as many short words, phrases, and clauses as you can and still maintain an interesting, smooth-flowing writing style. Here are examples:

| Instead of saying | Say |
|---|---|
| in an easy manner | easily |
| subsequent to | after |
| arduously | hard |
| by the use of electricity | by using electricity |
| in the state of Nebraska | in Nebraska |
| for the purpose of | for |
| The graphic that is on the next page . . . . | The graphic on the next page . . . . |
| Words that are to be emphasized . . . . | Words to be emphasized . . . . |
| The marketing director, whose name is George Long, . . . . | The marketing director, George Long, . . . . |

Do not eliminate so many words that your message sounds like a telegram, but use only those words the readers need to grasp quickly the essential facts.

f.  Add interest to your reports by using verbs in the active voice, as in these examples:

| Instead of saying | Say |
|---|---|
| The report was written by the supervisor. | The supervisor wrote the report. |
| The merchandise was sent by the clerk. | The clerk sent the merchandise. |

g.   Eliminate hidden verbs to contribute to interest and conciseness, as in these examples:

| _Instead of saying_ | _Say_ |
|---|---|
| the elimination of hidden verbs | eliminating hidden verbs |
| the accomplishment of the objective | accomplishing the objective |

h.   Add interest and clarity by choosing words with precise meanings, as in these examples:

| _Instead of saying_ | _Say_ |
|---|---|
| a car | a Buick |
| person | vice-president |
| went by | sprinted by |

i.   Eliminate clutter. Do not punctuate page numbers:

| _Instead of this_ | _This_ |
|---|---|
| 1. | 1 |
| (1) | 1 |
| -1- | 1 |

Follow these examples when numbering items in a tabulation:

| Instead of this | This |
|---|---|
| (1.) | 1. |
| 1) | 1. |

When including numbers within a division labelled with a letter of the alphabet, however, you need parentheses, as in "j," which follows:

j.  You may emphasize a point in a number of ways. Here are some:

   (1)  Present in the first paragraph of a report a point to be emphasized. Also, use the last paragraph for emphasis.
   (2)  Emphasize ideas by placing them at the beginning or at the end of a sentence.
   (3)  Underline some words or phrases that you want to stand out.
   (4)  Indent and single space a paragraph for emphasis even though the rest of the report is double spaced.
   (5)  Emphasize some items by numbering them.
   (6)  Use a short sentence for emphasis when you have long preceding sentences.
   (7)  Use a longer-than-average sentence when short sentences precede the point to be emphasized.

k.  Help the readers by dividing material into paragraphs of various lengths. Which of the following two illustrations would you rather read?

## Illustration 1

As was stated in the preceding chapter, a business report may be defined as a presentation of information that pertains to some element of business. That information can be presented orally or in writing. Written reports play a vital role in the conduct of business affairs. Some of the reports are written for individuals or groups outside the organization in which they are written; others are written for internal use. Intraorganizational reports flow in upward, downward, or lateral fashion and affect personnel in all levels of the organizational structure. So that the objective of a report can be reached readily, the report must be written clearly, accurately, and in an appropriate style. Some reports should be presented in an informal manner, though others should be presented formally. Informal business reports are discussed in this chapter; formal business reports are discussed in Chapters 15, 16, and 17. The objective of the report, the circumstances surrounding it, the intended readers, and the characteristics of the writer are among the most important factors that determine the way information should be presented.

## Illustration 2

As was stated in the preceding chapter, a business report may be defined as a presentation of information that pertains to some element of business. That information can be presented orally or in writing. Written reports play a vital role in the conduct of business affairs. Some of the reports are written for individuals or groups outside the organization in which they are written; others are written for internal use. Intraorganizational reports flow in upward, downward, or lateral fashion and affect personnel in all levels of the organizational structure.

So that the objective of a report can be reached readily, the report must be written clearly, accurately, and in an appropriate style. Some reports should be presented in an informal manner, though others should be presented formally. Informal reports are discussed in this chapter; formal business reports are discussed in Chapters 15, 16, and 17.

The objective of the report, the circumstances surrounding it, the intended readers, and the characteristics of the writer are among the most important factors that determine the way information should be presented.

1. Make smooth transition from sentence to sentence and from paragraph to paragraph. Here are a few of the many frequently used transitional words and phrases:

> To signify similarities, use *similarly, likewise, in the same way,* and others.
>
> Such words and phrases as *on the contrary, however,* and *on the other hand* show contrasts.
>
> *Consequently, therefore, as a result,* and *thus* are among the words and phrases that show cause-and-effect relationships.

**Add headings.**  Adding headings at appropriate places in a report contributes to interest and easy reading. Headings also help the readers to follow the information flow and to locate specific information they want to reread.

Usually, more than one paragraph follows a heading; but sometimes one paragraph contains all the information that needs to be highlighted by the heading. Determining the places for headings in a short informal report is usually easy. For the complex report, use a topic outline or a sentence outline as a guide in choosing headings.

Observe the relationship between the outline and the headings in Illustrations 1 and 2.

**Illustration 1**

```
I.     ——
   A.    ——
   B.    ——
II.    ——
   A.    ——
         1.   ——
         2.   ——
   B .   ——
III.   ——
```

**Illustration 2**

*First-Degree*

_ _ _ _ _ _ _ _ _ _ _ _ _ _
_ _ _ _ _ _ _ _ _ _ _ _ _ _

*Second-Degree*

_ _ _ _ _ _ _ _ _ _ _ _ _
_ _ _ _ _ _ _ _ _ _ _ _ _

*Second-Degree*

_ _ _ _ _ _ _ _ _ _ _ _ _
_ _ _ _ _ _ _ _ _ _ _ _ _

*First-Degree*

_ _ _ _ _ _ _ _ _ _ _ _ _
_ _ _ _ _ _ _ _ _ _ _ _ _

*Second-Degree*

_ _ _ _ _ _ _ _ _ _ _ _
_ _ _ _ _ _ _ _ _ _ _ _ _

*Third-Degree.* _ _ _ _ _ _

_ _ _ _ _ _ _ _ _ _ _ _ _

*Third-Degree.* _ _ _ _ _ _

*Second-Degree*

_ _ _ _ _ _ _ _ _ _ _ _ _
_ _ _ _ _ _ _ _ _ _ _ _ _

*First-Degree*

_ _ _ _ _ _ _ _ _ _ _ _
_ _ _ _ _ _ _ _ _ _ _ _ _

In this plan you would underline a key word in the first line of the paragraph to indicate a *fourth-degree* heading.

## QUESTIONS FOR DISCUSSION

1. How are report outlines and road maps similar?

2. What are some reader characteristics not mentioned in this chapter that you may consider when preparing a report?

3. Identify ways in which headings contribute to the effectiveness of a report.

## EXERCISES

Improve the following sentences.

1. Only 89 percent of the members were in attendance at the annual convention.

2. It is the purpose of this report to recommend a site for the new office building.

3. A clerk can be of assistance to you in tabulating the data.

4. The arbitrator attempted to be of assistance in reaching a settlement of the dispute.

5. The assistant made an effort to help the researcher collect the data.

6. Outline the report prior to your collecting information.

7. The writer will try to find a solution to the problem.

8. Because of the fact that the computer was broken, they could not tabulate the responses.

9. The graphic that can be found on page 8 contains the information you need.

10. This company will open a branch in the state of Illinois next summer.

## PROBLEMS

1. The president of Local Services, Inc., is considering the possibility of building an automatic car-wash facility near the Forest Hills subdivision. He asked you to study the feasibility of establishing this business.

   a. Write a statement of the problem in question form that you will refer to often as you prepare the report for the president.
   b. Write the statement in declarative sentence form for the completed report.
   c. Write the factors of the problem to be studied.
   d. Prepare a topic outline for the report.
   e. Make the topic outline into a sentence outline.

2. The manager of an office in which thirty people work is disturbed because there has been excessive absenteeism during the past three months. She has asked you to study the problem and to give her a report on your findings.

   a. Write a statement of the problem in question form that you will refer to often as you prepare the report for the office manager.
   b. Write the statement in declarative sentence form for the completed report.
   c. Write the factors of the problem to be studied.
   d. Prepare a topic outline for the report.
   e. Make the topic outline into a sentence outline.

3. For more than fifteen years, J.L. Magura has operated successfully a high-quality restaurant in a city of some 365,000 population. During the past four months, however, he has been disturbed by a significant decrease in the number of people who dine in his restaurant. He has asked you to study the situation and to give him a written report on what you learn.

   a. Write a statement of the problem in question form that you will refer to often as you prepare the report for Mr. Magura.
   b. Write the statement in declarative sentence form for the completed report.
   c. Write the factors of the problem to be studied.
   d. Prepare a topic outline for the report.
   e. Make the topic outline into a sentence outline.

   Use fictitious information for this problem.

# Chapter 12

# Information Sources

Once you have determined the purpose or objective of a report you are to write, you are ready to develop a tentative outline and collect needed information. You will, in most instances, possess some of the required information because the reports you choose to write or those assigned to you will be related to your work. You can write many letters, memorandums, and other short informal reports on the basis of what you already know. For some informal reports and most formal reports, you will have to collect more information.

You may collect *primary* data or *secondary* data, or you may collect both types.

## PRIMARY

Primary data are those data that have not been collected previously. Often you need primary data in addition to—or instead of—the available secondary data. Primary data are collected by experimenting, by observing, by interrogating, or by combining two or all of these methods.

## Experimenting

Experimenting is used extensively as an effective method of research in the physical sciences, but it is used much less frequently in business. Some business situations in which experiments are sometimes conducted involve marketing research, systems and procedures studies, and communication effectiveness.

Products may be marketed in small areas as a trial; procedures are tried on a few cases or are simulated to test their efficiency before a complete reorganization of the current system is made; and various sales and collection letters are tested for comparative effectiveness.

Experimenting requires a good deal of time. An experiment may be conducted by using two groups at one time: one is the control group and performs in the usual way the activities being tested, while the other group uses a new way to perform the activities. Another arrangement is to have one group perform in the usual way a set of activities at one time and then have the same group perform in a new way those same activities. As a result of the experiment, one of the ways is proved to be better; or both ways are proved to be equal. Always in an experiment all factors except the variable to be tested are held constant.

Although experimenting is used much less frequently in business than in the physical sciences, it is used sometimes; and when done properly, it produces results with a high degree of accuracy.

## Observing

Much valuable data can be obtained by observing certain activities. Office personnel or consultants may observe the work of office employees when a systems and procedures study is under way. Marketing analysts sometimes study the traffic flows inside a specific store, among stores within a specified section of a city, or along the sidewalks. City traffic departments observe the amount of traffic on certain streets to determine whether a traffic light is needed. Helpful data can be collected by observing numerous other activities. The examples mentioned here are only representative of the types of studies that may include data that are collected by this means of research.

One person may make all the observations, observers may work in pairs or in larger groups, or they may alternate so that some work during certain hours or days and others work at other times. The observers may use a prepared checklist for recording the data they collect, or they may just jot down notes about the activities they see. Using a checklist helps the researchers to observe objectively and reduce personal bias. During the observations, photographs can be taken and sketches can be made to support statements you make in the report.

The objective of the study, the types of activities to be observed, and the work habits of the researchers are some of the factors that help you to determine the procedures to follow when collecting information by observing.

## Interrogating

Interrogating is a popular method of collecting data for some types of business reports. Questions are asked orally during personal interviews or telephone interviews, or they are submitted in writing.

**Personal interviews.** Some advantages of asking questions during personal interviews are these:

1.  You have an opportunity to discuss any concerns the interviewees have about your reason for asking the questions. Usually, therefore, you can obtain full cooperation from the interviewees and get more information than by presenting the questions any other way. Also, many people feel complimented by being interviewed.

2.  You have an opportunity to explain the meaning of any question that seems ambiguous to an interviewee.

3.  You get immediate responses to your questions.

4.  Because the interviewees may suggest items you had not thought about, you frequently obtain valuable data you are not actively seeking.

5.  You may get answers people will not put in writing.

A major disadvantage of collecting information through personal interviews is the expense involved. The time required for conducting interviews (time for both the interviewer and the interviewee) and the time required for traveling make this method too expensive for use when a large number of people are to be interrogated and when they are scattered over a wide geographic area.

As a matter of courtesy and to ensure that the interviewees will be available, make appointments when you collect information through personal interviews. Appointments give the interviewees time to prepare for the interviews and to have more information ready than would be possible in impromptu visits. Prepare a list of questions to take with you. This list will enable you to ask the same questions of all interviewees. Arrange the questions in a logical order for recording the answers rapidly and accurately.

Answers to questions such as the following can be recorded easily:

1. How many office employees do you have?
   _____ Women
   _____ Men

2. What factors do you consider in selecting office employees?
   _____ Appearance
   _____ Attitude
   _____ Letter of application
   _____ Personal recommendations
   _____ Scholastic average
   _____ Verbal fluency
   _____ Voice qualities
   _____ Work experience
   _____ Other _____

Other arrangements for prepared questions and answers are also appropriate for the interview method of collecting information.

By all means, be a good listener because the interviewees will want to talk about topics of interest to them. Keep the interviews friendly and informal. Formality makes people reserved and less willing to share their knowledge and feelings.

You may use a tape recorder if the interviewees approve. At times it is not wise to make many notes. You may not be able to write and listen intently at the same time and also observe the nonverbal cues that are quite important to understanding. Whether or not you make notes, immediately after each interview write down what you remember. When obtaining conflicting opinions, be sure to include them in your report to show the readers that the report is as bias-free as possible.

**Telephone interviews.**   Some interviews can be conducted by telephone. Use the same type of questions for telephone interviews as you use for personal interviews. Although you can obtain some types of information more readily when talking with the interviewees in person than on the telephone, you can interview more people and cover a larger geographic area by telephone than through personal interviews. When these two methods of interviewing are compared, the telephone method obviously is less expensive.

**Postal card.**   A major portion of the business information collected through interrogating is obtained by mailing lists of questions. When only a few questions (one to five or six) are asked, a return postal card or a letter in which the questions are numbered is the best way to present them. The following illustration contains questions that were typed on a postal card.

---

1.   How many people five years old or older reside in your home?   _____

2.   What type TV set do you own?

_____ Color                    _____ Black and white

3.   What style TV set do you own?

_____ Console                  _____ Portable

4.   How old is your TV set?

____ 0-2.9 yrs.     ____ 3-5.9 yrs.     ____ 6 yrs. or older

5.   Have you ever had TV cable service?

____ Yes            ____ No

---

The return portion of a postal card has adequate postage. Add the name and address of whoever is to receive the answers.

**Letters.**   When you send a letter to request data, address the letter to an individual—not to an organization; and enclose an addressed, stamped envelope for the addressee to use in returning the answers.

The letter in Figure 12-1 contains questions that require more than check marks for answers.

**Questionnaires.**   To obtain answers to several questions, prepare a questionnaire to be mailed with a cover letter. To collect a sufficient quantity of reliable data with a questionnaire, construct it carefully by following these important points:

1. State each question clearly—*so clearly that it cannot be misunderstood*! To write clearly, use only the words that are familiar to the readers. Each word in the questionnaire must convey precisely the same meaning to all readers so that they interpret the question the way you intended.

2. Ask only those questions the respondents are willing to answer. Omit those questions they hesitate to answer because of their religious, political, or personal views. Many people will not answer questions pertaining to age, income, or financial status.

3. Arrange the questions in a logical order with the easy-to-answer questions first. This arrangement encourages respondents to complete the questionnaire. After they have answered most of the questions, they are more likely to answer a few hard-to-answer questions than if these questions appeared earlier. Hard-to-answer questions near the beginning lead the respondents to believe that many of the questions are difficult. They are, therefore, inclined to discard the questionnaire instead of completing it and returning it to you. Many questionnaire respondents have to refer to their records for answers to some of the questions on a list. They usually are unwilling to do this extra work unless they have already answered most of the questions.

**Figure 12-1**

# Watkins Manufacturing Company
## Hastings, IN 47010

August 10, 1984

Ms. Janice R. Haskins
Manager, Production Department
Bedford Manufacturing Company
P. O. Box 137B
Wheeling, IN 47001

Dear Ms. Haskins

Will you please help us decide whether to enter into a contract
with the Wiley Cleaning Service to maintain our assembly-line
area? We are asking you and fourteen other managers to answer
these questions:

1. Is your assembly-line area cleaned while the production
   lines are operating?

2. How often are your floors swept?

3. How long have you used the Wiley group to clean your
   assembly-line area?

4. How many square feet does your assembly-line area cover?

5. What are the advantages of using the Wiley Cleaning Service instead of hiring a staff to clean your plant?

Your answering these questions will be very much appreciated,
and any other information you send will be welcomed.

Cordially

Tom Schaffhauser
Plant Manager

mbs

4.  Place the most important questions early in the questionnaire since the respondents may become tired of reading and thinking and become careless in answering.

5.  When you can, supply several possible answers so that the respondent can merely make a check mark beside the answer. Provide a space for other answers, as in this example:

What was your job title on your most recent full-time job?

____ Accountant      ____ Programmer
____ Analyst      ____ Word Processor
____ Executive Aide      ____ Other (specify)_____

When a check mark can be placed by a range such as those in the next example, people are more inclined to supply the desired information than if you ask for a specific figure.

What is your age?

____ 16-18 (years)      ____ 39-48
____ 19-28      ____ 49 or older
____ 29-38

When a question cannot be answered by using a simple check mark, ask for other short answers. People hesitate to write long answers. Some respondents ignore questions of this kind, or they give incomplete answers. Other respondents decline to complete any part of a questionnaire if some of the questions require long answers.

6.  After you have listed all the questions, end with an item such as *Other?* that permits the respondents to write comments. Although these answers are difficult to tabulate, they supply valuable information; besides, respondents like to have an opportunity to express their opinions.

Limit the questionnaire to one page if you can include all the needed questions and still maintain an attractive and easy-to-read arrangement. Material arranged neatly and with plenty of white space on the page looks shorter and easier to answer.

Prepare the questionnaire with clean, legible type and have it duplicated on good-quality paper. Expensive bond paper is not necessary, but the paper must be a kind on which the respondent can write easily and clearly.

Clear, concise instructions for answering should precede the list of questions. Also tell the respondents that no personal identification is needed unless they desire a summary of the survey findings. Assure them no names or other identification will be used in the study. Instructions for returning the completed questionnaire may be on the same sheet as the questions, or they may be in the transmittal letter.

Send a letter with the questionnaire to get the readers interested in the survey and to tell them the benefits they can receive by participating in it. A promise to send a summary of the findings may be the best thing to offer them to show you appreciate their help. Sometimes, however, small amounts of money or small gifts are offered for the return of the completed questionnaire. The conditions that apply to the survey and the respondents' interest will help you determine an appropriate offer for their assistance.

Assure the respondents that all answers will be treated confidentially. Enclose an addressed, postage-paid envelope and, of course, mention it in the letter. To get more and quicker replies, make the need for the information sound vital and the reply urgent.

Study the transmittal letter and the questionnaire in Figures 12-2 and 12-3.

### Sampling

Seldom is it possible to collect information from 100 percent of a large group of people to be surveyed. You, therefore, collect from only a sample; and you want it to represent the entire group. You may choose a random sample, a stratified sample, or a systematic random sample.

**Random.** In a random sample, all individuals in the universe (the entire population from which a sample is taken) have equal chances for inclusion. Let's say we want to select a sample of the

**Figure 12-2**

## *Carter Manufacturing Company*
### *Wellington, TN 37010*

_____

_____
_____
_____

_____

To complete the information we must have to decide whether to
open a branch in San Carrollton, will you please fill out the
enclosed questionnaire?

We were pleased to learn from your local employment office that
you are available for office work.  If we decide to open a
branch in San Carrollton, we will send you an application form
by June 15.

The addressed, stamped envelope that is enclosed is for you to
use in returning the questionnaire, which will require only a
few minutes to complete.  Your returning the completed questionnaire by March 10 will be very much appreciated.

Cordially

Clay Kearley
Personnel Manager

tra

Enclosures

**Figure 12-3**

# Carter Manufacturing Company
### Wellington, TN 37010

AVAILABILITY OF OFFICE WORKERS IN SAN CARROLLTON

Please answer the following nine questions by placing check marks in the
appropriate spaces and by writing the answer to Question 2.  You <u>may</u> need
to write answers to Questions 5 and 6.

1.  How many years have you worked full time?
  _____0-2.9   _____9-11.9   _____18-20.9
  _____3-5.9   _____12-14.9  _____21 or more
  _____6-8.9   _____15-17.9

2.  What was the most recent year you worked full time?_____

3.  What was your job title on your most recent full-time job?
  _____Accountant     _____Programmer
  _____Administrative Assistant _____Typist
  _____Analyst      _____Word Processor
  _____Clerk       _____Other (specify)_____

4.  What was your monthly salary the last year you worked full time?
  _____800 (dollars) or less _____1001-1100
  _____801-900     _____1101-1200
  _____901-1000    _____1201 or more

5.  For what type(s) of organization(s) have you worked full time?
  _____Banking     _____Retailing
  _____Educational    _____Service
  _____Manufacturing   _____Other (specify)_____

6.  What is the highest level of formal education you have attained?
  _____High School Diploma _____Bachelor's Degree
  _____Business College  _____Graduate Study
  _____Two Years of College _____Other (specify)_____

7.  Which shifts would you be willing to work?
  _____8 a.m. to 4 p.m.
  _____4 p.m. to 12 midnight
  _____12 midnight to 8 a.m.

8.  Would you accept part-time employment?
  _____Yes
  _____No
  _____Undecided

9.  Specify the type of office work in which you are most interested,
and make any comments you wish to make about possible employment
with us.

people whose names are in a telephone directory. One possible—though impractical—way to take this sample is to write each name on a slip of paper and drop it into a container. Shake the container thoroughly and without looking at the slips of paper draw the number of names you wish to include in the sample.

Generally, we tend to believe that the larger the sample, the better it represents the entire universe. In many instances, though, a small random sample represents the universe quite well.

**Stratified.**    To take a stratified sample, divide the names of the universe into categories. For example, divide the names according to employment groups such as bankers, teachers, and government workers. Then draw names until you have the same percentage of bankers, teachers, and government workers as in the total universe.

Choose categories that have significance for the study you are conducting. Grouping by the three professions mentioned here would have little, if any, significance when studying the brands of paint preferred for the respondents' houses.

**Systematic Random.**    For a systematic sample, draw every tenth name in the list for the entire group. First of all, shuffle ten slips of paper bearing the numbers 1 through 10 and draw one of them. If you draw the number 6, for example, draw the 16th, the 26th, the 36th, and so on through the list. With this technique all names that make up the universe have equal probability of being drawn for the sample.

The systematic random sample is usually used when randomness is desired.

## Processing Information

Once the information needed for a business report has been collected, it has to be tabulated and analyzed for appropriate presentation.

**Tabulating.**    Tabulating may be required for some secondary data. The major tabulating task, however, is in the processing of primary data. With the widespread use of computers, the tabulating task can usually be performed in a computing center. This facility saves a tremendous amount of time and provides for a high degree of accuracy. Even with this help, the report writer is sometimes responsible for coding the information that was recorded on a checklist or was received in answer to the questions asked in a letter, on a postal card, or in a questionnaire. The report writer may even be required to transfer the coded data from the original source document (letter, questionnaire, and others) to the input medium (tape, punched card, or other) for the computer. The report writer who must perform these tabulating tasks should consult an operator in the particular computing center in which the data will be processed for specific instructions for performing the coding function.

The report writer, who is usually responsible for tabulating small quantities of data, may actually perform this detailed task or may instruct clerical workers to do the tabulating. A quick and easy tabulation of the small quantity of data obtained from fifteen responses to a postal card questionnaire follows the postal card, which is repeated here for easy reference.

---

1. How many people five years old or older reside in your home?  \_\_\_\_\_

2. What type TV set do you own?

   \_\_\_\_\_ Color            \_\_\_\_\_ Black and white

3. What style TV set do you own?

   \_\_\_\_\_ Console          \_\_\_\_\_ Portable

4. How old is your TV set?

   \_\_\_\_ 0-2.9 yrs.     \_\_\_\_ 3-5.9 yrs.     \_\_\_\_ 6 yrs. or older

5. Have you ever had TV cable service?

   \_\_\_\_ Yes          \_\_\_\_ No

---

Answers to postal card questionnaire (fifteen responses)

| | Question Number | | | | | | | Question Number | | | | |
|---|---|---|---|---|---|---|---|---|---|---|---|---|
| | 1 | 2 | 3 | 4 | 5 | | | 1 | 2 | 3 | 4 | 5 |
| 1. | 5 | c | c | 0 | n | | 9. | 3 | c | p | 3 | n |
| 2. | 3 | c | c | 3 | n | | 10. | 3 | c | p | 3 | n |
| 3. | 2 | c | p | 3 | n | | 11. | 4 | b | c | 6 | y |
| 4. | 2 | c | p | 3 | n | | 12. | 6 | c | c | 3 | y |
| 5. | 3 | c | c | 3 | y | | 13. | 2 | c | p | 3 | n |
| 6. | 2 | c | c | 3 | n | | 14. | 3 | c | p | 3 | y |
| 7. | 5 | b | c | 6 | n | | 15. | 4 | c | p | 6 | n |
| 8. | 4 | b | c | 6 | y | | | | | | | |

Key to Answers to Questions:

1. actual number given
2. c = color; b = black and white
3. c = console; p = portable
4. 0 = 0 − 2.9 yrs.; 3 = 3 − 5.9 yrs.; 6 = 6 yrs. or older
5. y = yes; n = no

By studying this tabulation, you can see that respondent No. 8, for example, had four people five years old or older residing in the home; the respondent had a black and white TV; the TV was a console model; the TV was six years old or older; and the respondent has had TV cable service.

From this type of tabulation, you can make whatever cross tabulations you wish to make. For example, you may like to show how many people who had color TV have had TV cable service. To obtain that information, cross tabulate the "c" answers to Question 2 with the "y" answers to Question 5.

**Analyzing.** By cross tabulating the answers to the questions you have asked, you can see relationships that exist between answers to any two questions. By studying an analysis of this type, you can see that some relationships are *meaningful* while others are *meaningless*. Those relationships of no value can usually be omitted from the report. Because some readers would believe that such an analysis would reveal significant findings, however, some of them should be presented.

Present the significant findings in the report body and include in the appendix the detailed analyses that seem to be of little significance. (Further discussion of the appendix section of a report is in Chapter 16.)

## SECONDARY

Information that has already been collected, but in another form from what you intend to use it, is secondary data. Some of the most frequently used sources of secondary data for business reports are the files of your organization, the files of other organizations, and publications—periodicals and books.

### Organization Files

The files of your organization may include letters, memorandums, manuals, contracts, ledgers, journals, drawings, minutes of meetings, photographs, notes from conversations, and reports that contain information that pertains to your report. Do not overlook this sometimes valuable storehouse.

Other organizations may also have these various types of records that contain information you need. Possibly, someone in another organization has written a report similar to the one you are writing and would gladly share the report and other records with you. Collecting information someone else has already collected is usually a waste of time, money, and effort when you can work cooperatively with the people who can make the information available to you. Sharing information with other groups is one of the many benefits of maintaining good public relations with other organizations.

### Publications

The more you know about business publications the more efficiently you can find information you need. Both periodicals and reference books contain valuable information.

**Periodicals.** Most newspapers contain business information worth your reading. Even the advertisements are helpful in making some business decisions. *The Wall Street Journal*, which is published daily, is an exceptionally good source of current, reliable information pertaining to business. *Fortune, Business Week, Nation's Business*, and *Changing Times* are among the popular magazines that specialize in business information. Journals that are published for particular fields such as accounting, marketing, and management contain a wealth of valuable information. Many magazines that are written for the general public and that cover a wide variety of topics often include items that may very well be useful in business reports.

You may consult various indexes to locate information in periodicals. For popular magazines of a general nature, refer to the *Reader's Guide to Periodical Literature*. For items in business, industrial, and trade periodicals, consult the *Business Periodicals Index*.

**Encyclopedias.** Encyclopedias are some of the published works most familiar to many writers of business reports, perhaps because some children's editions are used as early as grade school. Among this group of publications are the *Encyclopedia Americana, Encyclopaedia Britannica, World Book, Exporter's Encyclopedia*, and *Encyclopedia of Banking and Finance*. These volumes are well organized and indexed. Therefore, locating the information that applies to the topic on which you are writing is rather easy.

**Almanacs.** The various almanacs are concise and well organized. *The World Almanac and Book of Facts*, an annual publication, *Information Please Almanac, The Economic Alamanac*, and *Reader's Digest Almanac* are among those available.

**Dictionaries.** Desk-size dictionaries such as *Webster's New Collegiate Dictionary* and *The American Heritage Dictionary of the English Language* contain information that is helpful to writers of business reports.

Libraries have a number of specialized dictionaries, including *A Dictionary of Business and Finance, Dictionary of Insurance, A Dictionary of Statistical Terms, Dictionary of Economics, Management Dictionary*, and *Dictionary of Occupational Titles*.

**Biographies.** Among the biographies are *Who's Who in Commerce and Industry, Who's Who in America, Who's Who in Education, Who's Who in American Women, Who's Who in Labor*, and *Who's Who in Railroading*.

**Directories.**   A number of directories give the names of organizations, officers of the organizations, products and services provided, and other data. Some of these are *Rand-McNally Bankers' Directory, Corporation, Directors and Executives, Thomas' Register of American Manufacturers, Guide to American Directories, Trade Directories of the World, Dun and Bradstreet's Million Dollar Directory, Middle Market Directory*, and *Hotel and Motel Red Book*.

Checking with libraries to find other directories and becoming acquainted with the types of information they provide is worthwhile.

**Government publications.**   Local, state, and federal governments disseminate much information through reports, leaflets, and larger volumes. Some of these documents are presented only once; others are published regularly. Some of the monthly publications are the *Federal Reserve Bulletin, Monthly Labor Review*, and *Survey of Current Business*. The *Statistical Abstract of the United States* is a special help to writers of business reports.

The *United States Government Publications: Monthly Catalog* lists federal publications, and so does the *Guide to U.S. Government Publications*. You can obtain additional information about government publications by writing, calling, or visiting government offices.

**Other Reference Books.**   Among other frequently used reference books are the *Accountants' Index* and numerous handbooks such as the *Handbook for Business Writers*.

**Card catalog.**   To determine the published materials in a particular library, consult the card catalog. Traditionally, this file contained three cards for each volume of the library holdings. These cards were filed alphabetically by author, title, and subject.

More and more libraries have transferred the card entries to computers. The techniques for using the computerized catalog are different, but the general procedures are the same: you search by author, title, or subject. If you cannot find a book and question whether it exists, consult *Cumulative Book Index: A World List of Books in the English Language* for any book that has been published in the English language.

**Subscription services.**   The services that businesses may subscribe to have become numerous in recent years and are the most up-to-date sources of business information. Two of the well-established services are *Moody's Manuals* and Standard and Poor's *Corporation Records*. Kiplinger's *Newsletter* has also been in circulation for many years.

## Data Bases

In addition to the printed sources of secondary data mentioned in the preceding paragraphs, data bases provide a wealth of business information. A data base is an accumulation of bibliographic and/or nonbibliographic computer-processible data.

As the name implies, bibliographic data bases provide the information needed to find publications on various subjects; and some of them include an abstract of each item in the bank of information. Nonbibliographic data bases are of two kinds: (1) numeric and statistical data and (2) textual information equivalent to that in frequently used publications such as encyclopedias and directories.

Here are examples of the many data bases that apply specifically to business: *Trade and Industry Index*, *Standard and Poor's News*, *Harfax Industry Information Sources*, *Economics Abstracts International*, *Foundation Grants Index*, *Trade Opportunities*, *Nonmanufacturing Establishments*, *Consumer Price Index*, *Labor Force*, *International Forecasts*, and *U.S. Exports*. Producers of data bases include Economic Information Systems, U.S. Department of Commerce, Imprint Editions, and Learned Information, Ltd., as well as others.

Anyone who has a computer compatible with those in a system that provides data base information can arrange with a supplier to receive available information. Most users, however, who need such information infrequently prefer to request it from a local library. The library can then make the search to find the desired information and can ask the supplier to transmit the data immediately by computer or to send it by mail. Sending the data by mail is, of course, much less expensive than is sending it by computer.

## Note Taking

Because taking notes as you read is time-consuming, use a method that enables you to work efficiently. For each printed source, use a 3 by 5-inch or a 5 by 8-inch index card and record the information you will need for a footnote. (Footnotes are discussed in the next chapter.) Then record the information you expect to use in your report. If you expect to quote verbatim, be sure to quote the exact words, numbers, punctuation, and capitalization. If the quoted material contains an error of any type, insert [sic] beside the error to signify that you recognize it. If the error would mislead a reader (1982 may be shown instead of the correct year 1892), include the correction [1892].

Number—starting with 1—the first index card for a source. When you fill the card, record that number plus a 2 to indicate your second page of notes from Source 1. Continue this way, as in the following illustration.

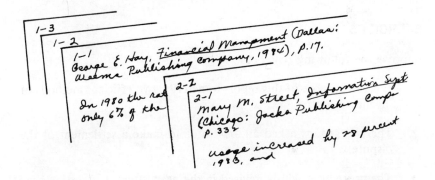

By following this procedure, you can save the time that would be required for labeling each card with footnote information.

When you do not expect to quote verbatim, copy only the gist of the material and thus save time. Make sure, however, that you make adequate notes so that you will not need to consult the source again for this particular report.

After you record all the information you intend to record, you can easily shuffle the cards to get the data in the order in which you will use them in the final report. Store all cards until the final report has been typed, proofread, and submitted to the main reader.

Documenting sources of information, an important factor in preparing the final copy of a report, is discussed in the next chapter.

## QUESTIONS FOR DISCUSSION

1. What are some types of business data that can be gathered by experimenting?

2. Identify some reports for which you would gather data by observing.

3. Identify some reports for which you would gather data by sending a questionnaire.

4. What steps can you take to eliminate ambiguity from the questions you include in a questionnaire?

5. What factors should you consider when determining the format to use for a questionnaire you will prepare?

## EXERCISES

Improve the following sentences.

1. It is the purpose of this report to describe two efficient methods of inventory control.

2. The two groups asked an arbitrator to make a settlement of the dispute.

3. The procedures will be revised in the near future.

4. There are several copies of that reference book in the library.

5. In the event that the copier cannot be repaired today, we will have to postpone the mailing of the questionnaire.

6. The new trainee would like to be of assistance to you in the collection of the data.

7. Charles R. Jackson, who is the business manager's assistant, made a revision of the reporting procedures.

8. You can collect the data in an easy manner.

9. This report was requested by the vice-president.

10. You will be able to present these data in a pie chart.

## PROBLEMS

1.   The president of Office Machines, Inc., is studying the feasibility of establishing an office machines service center in Dunlap, Kentucky. Dunlap has a population of 65,000; and six other towns, with populations ranging from 13,000 to 39,000, are within a 70-mile radius of Dunlap.

Within the past two years, a community college and two factories have opened in Dunlap. Other small factories and other businesses are well established in Dunlap and the six other towns nearby. You do not know how the machines in that region are maintained.

Your company vice-president sent you a list of the names and addresses of the area organizations that probably use several office machines. Prepare a questionnaire you can mail to those organizations to collect data that will help you to decide whether to open a service center in Dunlap.

2.   You are the director of student employment on your campus. During the past six years, your students have worked during the summer vacations for a large number of organizations throughout your region. So that you can learn more about the way the students have performed and so that you will be better prepared to help students obtain summer jobs in the future, prepare a postal card questionnaire for mailing.

3.   You want to know the favorite soft drinks in your city, and you want to know why these drinks are favorites. You also want to know about the people who prefer the various drinks. Prepare a questionnaire you can mail to the residents.

4.   You are the assistant manager of a men's clothing store in a college town. A limited number of college students have bought clothing at your store. You want to increase the volume of sales to the students, so you decide to observe them on campus for a week to determine the types of clothing they wear. Prepare a checklist you will use.

5.   You are the director of student employment on your campus. So that you will be better prepared to help students secure part-time jobs, you will interview the personnel managers of several large local organizations. Prepare the checklist you will duplicate and use during these interviews.

6.  You have been asked to study the kinds of foods the students eat for lunch in your school cafeteria. Prepare a checklist to be used in collecting this information as the students go by the cash register or as they reach another designated place in the cafeteria.

7.  Find the names of the chief executive officer or the president of five banks in different states. Give the source of your information.

8.  Find the number of rooms in five Holiday Inn motels in different states. Give the source of your information.

9.  Find the number of rooms in five Hyatt Regency hotels in different states. Give the source of your information.

10. Find the office address and the types of items produced or services provided by each of these organizations: Evans Products Co.; General Datacomm Industries, Inc.; IPCO Corporation; Olla Industries, Inc.; Upjohn Company. Give the source of your information.

11. Use the *Reader's Guide to Periodical Literature* to find three articles on diet or weight control in the *Good Housekeeping* magazine.

12. Locate three articles on decks or patios in the *Southern Living* magazine or three articles on golf in the *New Yorker*.

13. Describe a stratified sample to be taken from your class, which is the universe.

14. Describe a systematic random sample to be taken from the first two pages of your student directory or the first two pages of your telephone directory.

15. Using the fifteen responses to the postal card questionnaire given in this chapter, (a) determine how many respondents with TVs 3-6 years old had had TV cable service and (b) determine how many respondents with three residents in their homes had portable TVs.

# Chapter 13

# Documentation

Information collected from secondary sources can be presented in a variety of ways. Some should be paraphrased; some should be quoted verbatim; and some should be presented graphically. When writing paragraphs, you should in most cases present in your own words (paraphrase) the information you take from another source. By using your own writing style, you enhance the readability of the report. Also, this practice requires you to study thoroughly the information you include and is evidence that you have done so. Quote verbatim when the quotation adds strength to your report and when it is especially well stated for your particular writing style.

Whether you paraphrase, quote verbatim, or use a graphic aid, make sure to give credit to the source of the information. Give this credit by presenting the information appropriately in the text and by including footnotes in proper form. Examples of paraphrasing and of leading in to quotations are shown next. The first paragraph was paraphrased from a duplicated report.

Because the average number of letters written each day by junior executives in the Southeast has risen from seven to eleven, an increase of slightly more than 57 percent, greater emphasis should be placed on dictating efficiency.[1]

[1] Talmadge A. Holtzman, "Increasing Correspondence Costs" (Athens: AMS Committee on Reducing Office Expenditures, 1984), p. 14. (Duplicated.)

You can weave short quotations into your sentences. One way to do this is shown in the next illustration.

When reporting on the effects of heat and humidity on the operating efficiency of electronic computers, Hayes and Ryan said, "Your computer will not operate well where the temperature is higher than 80° Fahrenheit or where the humidity is higher than 70 percent."[2]

[2] Arthur T. Hayes and Leonard P. Ryan, "Housing the Computer Installation," *Machine Accountants' Journal*, April 1984, p. 27.

The quotation in the preceding illustration could be paraphrased. A verbatim quotation may, though, add strength to the point you wish to make if the readers of your report consider the authors of the quotation to be experts in the subject.

For quotations four lines or longer, single space and indent four spaces from the left margin when using eight spaces to indent the first line of a paragraph of text. Use no quotation marks. Introduce each quotation and use variety in the introductions. Here are examples:

When discussing the need for a systems study, Potter said:

The employees of the administrative services department of our organization are well trained. They are also intelligent, industrious, and cooperative; but they have been so closely related to their tasks so long they tend to think of the current systems and procedures as being the best that can be used.[1]

Yet, according to Raleigh:

The ideal systems and procedures are yet to be established. In some offices the routine paperwork can be handled efficiently by hand. In other offices the volume of routine work is so great that the use of electronic computers is obviously a *must*.[2]

Ramsey, author of one of the most widely used textbooks in office management, commented on the desirability of systems studies as follows:

> Regardless of how intelligent, open-minded, and progressive employees may be, they cannot possibly keep abreast of all the technological changes that are taking place today. Employing experts to study the conditions is often necessary.[3]

---

[1] Hobart N. Potter, *Office Systems and Procedures* (New Orleans: Wate Publishing Company, Inc., 1982), p. 87.

[2] Dwight O. Raleigh, *Information Handling Systems* (New York: Wilson Publishers, Inc., 1983), p. 281.

[3] John S. Ramsey, *Paperwork Simplification* (New York: Wilson Publishers, Inc., 1981), p. 196.

When you indicate that a statement is a direct quotation, use the exact wording and punctuation the author used.

## FOOTNOTES

Footnote arrangements vary slightly among widely recognized authorities. Many good writers use the arrangements illustrated in this chapter. Unless you are instructed to use a specific arrangement that is slightly different from the illustrations given here, you can use these confidently.

### First Reference

Here are footnote illustrations for the first reference to various types of information sources.

#### Book—One Author

[1] Ralph Edward Poe, *Executive Communication* (New York: Williams Publishing Company, Inc., 1983) , p. 38.

#### Book—Two or Three Authors

[2] Ruby L. Bates and Marie S. Peters, *Today's Clerical Workers*, 2d ed. (Hastings: The Western Press, 1983), pp. 37-38.

### Book—More Than Three Authors

[3] Charles E. Yates and others, *Communicating in the Office*, 3d ed. (Chicago: The MacDonald Press, 1983), p. 219.

### Book—Edition

[4] Mary Ellen Holt, *Writing Effective Reports*, 2d ed. (Boston: McKinley Press, 1983), pp. 68-70.

### Editor of a Collection

[5] John W. Hanson (ed.), *Intraorganizational Communication* (New York: Alton Publishing Company, Inc., 1981), p. 416.

### Chapter in a Yearbook

[6] William Harold Bolton, "Communication Mediums Before 1900," *History of Communication in American Business Enterprises*, Twenty-first Yearbook of the National Business Communication Association (Knoxville: Knoxville Press, 1984), pp. 311-317.

### General Encyclopedia

[7] Reaumur S. Donnally, "Writers' Cramp," *Encyclopedia Americana* (1979), XXIX, 558.

### General Encyclopedia—Unsigned Article

[8] "Writing," *Encyclopaedia Britannica* (1973), XXIII, 817.

### Report—No Author Given

[9] *Annual Report of the Planning Committee of the Accountants' Association for the Year Ending June 30, 1982* (St. Louis: St. Louis Publishing Company, 1983), p. 19.

### Report—Author Given

[10] Walter E. Sloan, *Communicating with Computers*, A Report to the Second National Conference of the Accountants' Association, Kansas City, April 29 to May 1, 1982, Prepared by the Committee on Improving Communication Effectiveness (Kansas City: The Conference, 1982), p. 4.

### Government Publication

[11] U.S. Bureau of the Census. *Census of Population: 1970.* Vol. 1. Characteristics of the Population. Part 1, United States Summary—Section 1.

### Article in a Periodical—No Author Given

[12] "Maintenance of Electronic Equipment." *Equipment Journal*, July 14, 1983, p. 15.

### Article in a Journal—Author Given

[13] Lynn D. Smith, "Communication Effectiveness," *National Communication Journal*, (June, 1982) pp. 27-29.

### Article in a Newspaper—No Author Given

[14] News item in the *Chattanooga Daily*, June 3, 1982, p. 3.

### Duplicated Article

[15] Howard E. Hines, "Communicating with Peers" (Bruswick: AMS Committee on Communication Effectiveness, 1983), p. 11. (Duplicated.)

### Dissertation

[16] Alex M. Mason, "Annual Report Readability" (Ph.D. dissertation, Wheaton University, 1984), p. 23.

### Interview

[17] Statement by Edward M. Watson, management consultant, personal interview, Burlington, Georgia, July 9, 1984.

### Letter

[18] Letter from Charles M. Johnston, Director of the Tims Communication Center, October 12, 1984.

The preceding illustrations represent the footnotes used most frequently in business reports. If you should need examples of sources not illustrated here, you may refer to a publication that includes more extensive examples of footnotes. Some of the publications used widely for footnote construction are these:

*A Manual of Style*, 12th ed. (Chicago: University of Chicago Press, 1969)

William Giles Campbell and Stephen Vaughan Ballou, *Form and Style*, 6th ed. (Boston: Houghton Mifflin Company, 1982)

*The MLA Handbook* (Washington: Modern Language Association of America, 1977)

*U.S. Government Printing Office Style Manual*, rev. ed. (Washington: U.S. Government Printing Office, 1973)

Kate L. Turabian, *A Manual for Writers of Term Papers, Theses, and Dissertations*, 4th ed. (Chicago: University of Chicago Press, 1973)

You may have a source for which no example is given in the reference books you examine. If you have that experience, arrange the footnote the best way you can by studying the examples for the sources that are similar to the source to which you wish to give credit.

## Second Reference

Although some writers still use Latin abbreviations in second references to sources, the trend is away from this usage. Before presenting the simpler, more popular way of making second references, the Latin forms are shown so that they can be used for the readers who prefer them.

**Ibid.** is used for a second reference to the same volume and page when there is no intervening reference. Example:

[1] Mary Ellen Holt, *Writing Effective Reports*, 2d ed. (Boston: McKinley Press, 1983), p. 68.

[2] Ibid.

Add the page number to *Ibid.* when referring to a different page of the same source, as in this example:

[3] Ibid., p. 73.

With at least one intervening reference, a second reference to the same volume that has been cited (in this case Poe's), give the surname and the page number:

[4] Poe, p. 78.

**Op. cit.** is used when references to the same work follow each other closely but not consecutively and when they refer to different pages. This Latin term and the page number follow the author's name, as in this example:

[5] Poe, op. cit., p. 91.

**Loc. cit.** follows the author's surname to signify that the reference is to the same page of a previously cited work—but not the source immediately preceding this one. Example:

[6] Holt, loc. cit.

The people who work with formal reports often are the only ones who remember the meanings of the Latin terms. Most readers of business reports, therefore, probably prefer that you use the informal style. This reference style includes the author's name, the page numbers, and any other information that may be required for positive identification of the source. For example, when quoting from two or more authors who have the same surname, you need to include the first name of the author you are referring to, as in this example:

[7] John N. Whitmire, p. 87.

## Placement

You can place footnotes at the bottom of the page, at the end of the report, or on the page near the material you cite. (See Chapter 14 for footnotes for graphic aids.)

**Bottom of page.**  Footnotes are usually typed at the bottom of the page on which the quoted or paraphrased material is presented. This traditional placement has this advantage in addition to being familiar to many readers: the readers can quickly note the source without having to turn pages. To use this plan, type a 1½-inch line to separate the footnotes from the text. Indent each footnote and use single spacing with double spacing between footnotes. Arrange them so that the last one ends about an inch from the bottom of a full page, as in this illustration:

temperature is higher than 80° Fahrenheit or where the humidity is higher than 70 percent."[2]

[2] Arthur T. Hayes and Leonard P. Ryan, "Housing the Computer Installation," *Machine Accountants' Journal*, 1984, p. 27.

A footnote on a partial page begins a double space after the last line of the text, as in this illustration:

---

temperature is higher than 80° Fahrenheit or where the humidity is higher than 70 percent."[2]

---

[2] Arthur T. Hayes and Leonard P. Ryan, "Housing the Computer Installation," *Machine Accountants' Journal*, April, 1984, p. 27.

---

Other examples of this traditional placement are in the formal report at the end of Chapter 16.

**End of report.**   Some writers of business reports prefer to present all the footnotes at the end of the report. This arrangement is easy for the typist, but it is difficult for the readers because they have to turn pages to refer to the footnotes. A point to remember is that formal reports are usually prepared for readers who are above you on the organization chart. Their salaries, therefore, are higher than yours and the typist's. Ordinarily, it is more economical, therefore, for the typist to spend the time required to type the footnotes at the bottom of the page than for the readers to spend the time required to turn pages to refer to the footnotes.

When footnotes are typed at the end of the report, they are typed on a separate page and in the order in which they are used in the text. Here is an illustration:

### Footnotes

[1] Charles Y. Gilbert, *How Reports Are Written*, (Houston: Cummings Press, 1984), p. 31.

[2] Marie V. Anderson, *Effective Oral Communication*, (Louisville: Hartman Publishing Company, 1984), p. 68.

[3] Gilbert, p. 57.

**Near the material.**    Typing the footnotes immediately after the quoted or paraphrased material is perhaps the least frequently used placement. In this arrangement, a line is typed before and a line is typed after each footnote to separate the footnote from the text, as in this illustration:

temperature is higher than 80° Fahrenheit or where the humidity is higher than 70 percent."[2]

---

[2] Arthur T. Hayes and Leonard P. Ryan, "Housing the Computer Installation," *Machine Accountants' Journal*, April, 1984, p. 27.

---

Adequate space must be provided for the computer operators and for the service representatives, but the. . . .

For the typist this arrangement is easier than the traditional placement, but it is more difficult than placing the footnotes at the end of the report. Also, this arrangement detracts from the appearance of the page and the readability of the text, especially for the footnotes the readers will not refer to. And in many reports not all footnotes are referred to by the readers.

## BIBLIOGRAPHY

If you do not list the footnotes at the end of the report, prepare a bibliography to follow the last page of the report body. In business reports the word *references* is often used instead of *bibliography*. In this listing, present in alphabetic order the printed and the unpublished works cited by footnotes in the body of the report. Alphabetize by the last name of the author. When you do not know the author's name, alphabetize by the first word in the title (excluding the articles—*A*, *An*, and *The*). Also, document interviews, lectures, and other oral sources.

Include the page numbers for an article, but omit the page numbers for a book.

The next illustration contains a variety of information sources.

**References**

*2 spaces* →  Bates, Ruby L. and Marie S. Peters. *Today's Clerical Workers.* Hastings: The Western Press, 1983.

*Chattanooga Daily*, June 3, 1982.

Donnally, Reaumur S. "Writers' Cramp." *Encyclopedia Americana*, 1979, XXIX, 558.

Hanson, John W., ed. *Intraorganizational Communication*. New York: Alton Publishing Company, Inc., 1981.

Hines, Howard E. "Communicating with Peers." Bruswick: AMS Committee on Communication Effectiveness, 1983. (Duplicated.)

National Business Communication Association. *History of Communication in American Business Enterprises*. Twenty-first Yearbook. Knoxville: Knoxville Press, 1984.

Holt, Mary Ellen. *Writing Effective Reports*. 2d ed. Boston: McKinley Press, 1983.

"Maintenance of Electronic Equipment." *Equipment Journal*, July, 1983, p. 15.

Mason, Alex M. "Annual Report Readability." Ph.D. dissertation, Wheaton University, 1984.

Poe, Ralph Edward. *Executive Communication*. New York: Williams Publishing Company, Inc., 1983.

Smith, Lynn D. "Communication Effectiveness." *National Communication Journal*, (June, 1982), pp. 27-29.

Tims Communication Center. Personal correspondence between Charles M. Jonston, Director, and the writer. October 12, 1984.

Watson, Edward M. Personal interview. Burlington, Georgia, July 19, 1984.

"Writing." *Encyclopaedia Britannica*. 1973. XXIII, 817.

Yates, Charles E., and others. *Communicating in the Office*. Chicago: The MacDonald Press, 1983.

If the bibliography is extensive, you may divide it into books, articles, and unpublished materials. Because the bibliography for a business report is seldom extensive enough to make this division helpful, however, no example is given here.

## QUESTIONS FOR DISCUSSION

1.  What are ways of obtaining information from published books that are not in your local library?

2.  Assume that you have used in your business report material from a source not included among the illustrations for footnotes. You cannot find a footnote for that type of source in any other publication. How would you arrange a footnote for that source?

## EXERCISES

Improve the following sentences.

1.  Will Leland make a revision of this draft?

2.  Please ask the vice-president to give you an explanation of the changes.

3.  Samuel L. Richardson, who is a new trainee, will help you move the chairs.

4.  The manager's office is located in the next building.

5.  Eight accountants worked a total of eighty-four hours; seven clerks worked a total of seventy-seven hours; and eleven administrative assistants worked a total of fifty-one hours.

6.  Due to the fact that the duplicator is broken, the questionnaire cannot be duplicated today.

7.  How many people were in attendance at the meeting?

8.  It is a chore making a production schedule for two weeks.

9.  How many cars were sold during the month of July?

10. Janice said that she would like to be of assistance to you in writing the new procedures.

## PROBLEMS

1.  Prepare a bibliography that includes two books, one newspaper article, an encyclopedia, two journal articles, and a personal interview. These references can pertain to the topic of your choice.

2.  Prepare a bibliography that includes a book with two authors, a book with three or more authors, a U.S. Government publication, and a doctoral dissertation. These references can pertain to the topic of your choice.

3.  Prepare footnotes for the sources in Problem 2. You may supply the page numbers.

4.  Prepare footnotes for a personal interview, a book with one author, a chapter in a yearbook, and a newspaper article. You may supply the page numbers.

# Chapter 14

# Graphics

A young man who grew up in a warm region of India had not seen snow before he moved to the United States. One of his memorable sights during his first year in America, therefore, was a beautiful snowstorm that left snow clinging to the trees and an accumulation of some five inches on the ground. The young man was eager to share this exciting experience with his family in India; but because none of his family members spoke English and because their language contained no word to represent snow, he could not describe snow adequately to make his experience interesting for them. So, after he spent some time trying to describe the snowfall, he gave up the effort.

What could the young man from India have done to enable his relatives to appreciate his excitement about the snowfall? He could have sent them a color photograph, for often a picture is worth a thousand words.

If he had sent a photograph, do you suppose he would have enclosed it without mentioning it in his letter? No, he would have introduced the enclosure by telling the readers he had photographed snow. Not only would he have introduced the photograph, but also he would have discussed it. He could have related the whiteness of the snow to that of milk, white fluffy clouds, or other white objects familiar to his family to help them to understand what snow looks like. He would have probably given further interpretation by mentioning the depth of the snow, the time required for the accumulation, the temperature during that time, and the effects the snow had on the people. He probably would have referred to the gaiety of sledding and snowball fighting as well as to the traffic problems the snow created.

Often, photographs can be used more effectively than words not only in personal letters, but also in business reports. Since, as a writer of business reports, your goal is to present accurate pertinent information so that it is easy to read and understand, use photographs and other graphics when using them to supplement the paragraphs in your messages contributes to clarity, interest, and readability.

To use graphics effectively, construct them well and interpret them for the readers.

## CONSTRUCTING GRAPHICS

Various formats can be used for graphics. Whether you use one format or another, you want your graphics to be accurate, attractive, and easy to read. By following the suggestions in this chapter, you can construct informal tables, formal tables, and other graphics that your report readers will appreciate.

### Informal Table

An informal table (often called a *text table*) is a useful device for presenting simple data. Like all other graphics, an informal table must have at least three items to justify its use: fewer than three items can be presented better in sentence form. An informal table may consist of a simple list of items, or it may have two or three columns. While this table may have column headings and totals, it has no table number or title and is not ruled. An informal table is preceded by a lead-in sentence that is usually followed by a colon, as in these four examples:

The agent handles these four types of insurance policies:

Collision
Fire
Life
Medical

The brands studied and the number of employees who preferred each brand follow:

Essex . . . . .    27
Shear . . . . .    16
Gold . . . . . .    11

Here is a list of last month's transportation expenditures:

| | |
|---|---:|
| Gasoline . . . . . . . . . . . . | $ 976.32 |
| Oil . . . . . . . . . . . . . . . . . . | 82.98 |
| Parts . . . . . . . . . . . . . . . | 49.27 |
| Tires . . . . . . . . . . . . . . . . | 1,987.00 |
| Total . . . . . . . . . . . . . . | $3,095.57 |

These employees gave the following responses:

| Employee | Yes | No |
|---|---|---|
| Typist . . . . . . . . . . . . . . . . . . . . . . . | 26 | 17 |
| File Clerk . . . . . . . . . . . . . . . . . . . . | 21 | 11 |
| Word Processor . . . . . . . . . . . . . . | 12 | 23 |
| Administrative Assistant . . . . . . . . | 5 | 8 |
| Totals . . . . . . . . . . . . . . . . . . . . | 64 | 59 |

Seldom do you need to interpret an informal table. Sometimes, though, you may help the readers by commenting on some of the items that are included.

## Formal Table

A formal table, one of the most frequently used graphics, is the only practical device for presenting a large quantity of precise information. You can use a formal table to compare or classify a small number of related items as well as a large number. Although you should restrict the length to only the number required to achieve the purpose for which you construct the table, the length can be more than a page.

Here are suggestions to help you prepare effective formal tables such as those in Figures 14-1, 14-2, and 14-3.

1.  When a report is to have more than one table, use Arabic numerals to number the tables consecutively. Center the word "Table" and the number two lines above the table title.

2.  Identify each table by placing the title two lines below the table number and two lines above the double line that precedes the column headings. When possible, include in the concise, descriptive title the answers to *What? When? Where?* and *How classified?*

    If the title is long, make two or more lines. The thought units in the title help you to determine whether to use an inverted pyramid, an alternating long and short line, or a pyramid arrangement, as in these examples:

Average Number of Customers Served
By Waitresses 9 and 12
Clarkston Restaurant
October 6-11, 1985

Hours Worked by Welders
Clemson Manufacturing Company
April 15-30, 1985

Seals Weekly Sales
January 1—March 31, 1985

Do not end a line with a preposition.
Do not use abbreviations in the title.
Capitalize the first letter in the main words in the title.

3.  Put a double line between the title and the column headings.

4.  Use column headings that tell accurately the kind of information in the columns. Use singular forms of nouns.

5. Use a spanner heading to connect columns, as in this example:

| Gasoline | | |
|---|---|---|
| Texaco | Phillips 66 | Sinclair |

Use a single line between the column headings and the body of the table.

6. Single space or double space (see Figure 14-1) the items in the table. Also, you may single space groups (three or five) and double space between the groups (see Figures 14-2 and 14-3).

7. When you show column totals, put a single line between the column entries and the totals.

8. Use a double line to signify the end of the table. A single line at the bottom of a table indicates that the table is continued on the following page (see Figure 14-3).

9. Use standard symbols and abbreviations. (Remember, however, not to use abbreviations in titles.)

10. To indicate notes in a table, use asterisks or slightly raised letters next to figures or slightly raised figures next to letters and explain these asterisks, letters, or figures about two lines below the double line at the end of the table.

11. Omit needless vertical lines.

12. When no figure or item is available, use *n/a* for not available or use a dash. Do not use a zero. Zero could be misleading by indicating *nothing* when that might not be true.

13. If a table is too wide for the page, present it sideways; place the page so that the top of the table is near the binding (left side) of the report. Figure 14-3 is an example.

14. Put the source notation two lines below the final item—double line or explanatory notes.

15. Space columns for easy reading and attractiveness.

**Figure 14-1**

Table 1

Expenditures for Advertising for Rains Company
By Media, 1986--1987

| Medium | Dollars | | Percent | |
|--------|------|------|------|------|
| | 1986 | 1987 | 1986 | 1987 |
| Newspapers | 11,000 | 11,980 | 23.0 | 23.6 |
| Radio | 10,560 | 10,980 | 22.0 | 21.7 |
| Television | 9,965 | 9,990 | 20.8 | 19.7 |
| Magazines | 7,150 | 8,176 | 15.0 | 16.1 |
| Direct Mail | 6,575 | 6,550 | 13.8 | 12.9 |
| Miscellaneous | 2,560 | 3,000 | 5.4 | 5.9 |
| Totals | 47,810 | 50,676 | 100.0 | 99.9 |

Source:   Company Accounting Records

**Figure 14-2**

Table 2

Sales of Jones-Hampton Appliances
in Eleven Southern States
in July, 1985

| State | Appliance | | | Total |
| | Dryer | Range | Washer | |
|---|---|---|---|---|
| Alabama | 479 | 296 | 14 | 789 |
| Arkansas | 182 | 404 | 416 | 1,002 |
| Florida | 86 | 492 | 89 | 667 |
| Georgia | 719 | 385 | 492 | 1,596 |
| Kentucky | 742 | 846 | 224 | 1,812 |
| Louisiana | 97 | 299 | 924 | 1,320 |
| Mississippi* | 204 | 77 | 114 | 395 |
| North Carolina | 774 | 54 | 246 | 1,074 |
| South Carolina | 658 | 406 | 571 | 1,635 |
| Tennessee | 720 | 314 | 92 | 1,126 |
| Virginia | 863 | 67 | 492 | 1,422 |
| Totals | 5,524 | 3,640 | 3,674 | 12,838 |

*No authorized dealer until July 16

Source:  Sales Manager's Files

**Figure 14-3**

Table 2

Sales Income from Fruits and Vegetables in Five Southern States
Johnston-Campbell Produce Company
June—August, 1985

|  |  |  | State |  |  |  |
| Product | Alabama | Arkansas | Florida | Georgia | Louisiana | Total |
|---|---|---|---|---|---|---|
| Apples | $ 10,177 | $ 11,080 | $ 9,987 | $ 11,012 | $ 10,101 | $ 52,357 |
| Apricots | 876 | 1,021 | 1,000 | 816 | 767 | 4,540 |
| Artichokes | 697 | 874 | 902 | 921 | 821 | 4,215 |
| Asparagus | 2,012 | 1,998 | 3,012 | 1,121 | 2,087 | 10,230 |
| Bananas | 8,764 | 9,762 | 7,872 | 9,921 | 8,224 | 44,543 |
| Beans | 11,021 | 11,009 | 11,212 | 11,998 | 12,002 | 57,242 |
| Broccoli | 8,772 | 9,012 | 9,992 | 8,828 | 7,092 | 43,696 |
| Cabbage | 982 | 1,002 | 727 | 829 | 1,020 | 4,560 |
| Cantaloupes | 9,002 | 7,008 | 8,028 | 7,098 | 8,971 | 40,107 |
| Carrots | 6,981 | 7,082 | 6,112 | 5,088 | 4,087 | 29,350 |
| Cauliflower | 5,081 | 6,082 | 4,992 | 7,072 | 3,087 | 26,314 |
| Cucumbers | 916 | 938 | 912 | 894 | 927 | 4,587 |
| Grapefruits | 10,012 | 9,916 | 8,912 | 8,076 | 10,120 | 47,036 |
| Grapes | 698 | 796 | 514 | 916 | 419 | 3,343 |
| Lettuce | 2,119 | 1,987 | 2,914 | 1,112 | 2,788 | 10,920 |
| Oranges | 12,012 | 11,191 | 11,101 | 10,916 | 12,010 | 57,230 |
| Peaches | 976 | 1,998 | 910 | 1,912 | 1,001 | 6,797 |
| Pears | 1,276 | 2,919 | 2,002 | 1,862 | 2,912 | 10,971 |

**Figure 14-3 Continued:**

Table 2 (continued)

| Product | Alabama | Arkansas | State Florida | Georgia | Louisiana | Total |
|---|---|---|---|---|---|---|
| Peas | $ 11,058 | $ 12,973 | $ 10,006 | $ 10,551 | $ 13,117 | $ 57,705 |
| Peppers | 487 | 912 | 1,001 | 916 | 717 | 4,033 |
| Plums | 1,012 | 876 | 1,069 | 1,012 | 2,017 | 5,986 |
| Squash | 4,076 | 3,917 | 4,917 | 5,102 | 6,002 | 24,014 |
| Tangerines | 7,017 | 8,972 | 6,071 | 3,012 | 7,072 | 32,144 |
| Tomatoes | 12,001 | 9,072 | 10,012 | 11,012 | 12,011 | 54,108 |
| Watermelons | 3,012 | 1,016 | 5,016 | 4,022 | 5,912 | 18,978 |
| Other | 4,012 | 3,076 | 2,012 | 1,017 | 3,054 | 13,171 |
| Totals | $135,049 | $136,489 | $131,205 | $127,096 | $138,338 | $668,177 |

Source: Monthly Sales Reports

## Other Graphics

In addition to informal tables and formal tables, many types of graphics can be used effectively in business reports. Only those used most frequently, however, are described in this chapter. So that graphics are effective, make them simple and attractive. Do not try to show too much information in any one device. Choose the types that help the readers to grasp the particular points you want them to grasp.

Here are suggestions to help you design effective graphics such as those illustrated throughout this chapter:

1. When a report is to have more than one graphic besides tables, use Arabic numerals to number them consecutively. (Use only one number sequence for bar charts, line charts, maps, pie charts, and so on; use a separate number sequence for formal tables.) Center the word "Figure" and the number two lines above the graphic title, or place it below the graphic.

2. Identify each graphic by placing the title two lines below the figure number, which is above the graphic (see Figure 14-8) or below the graphic (see Figure 14-4). When possible, include in the concise, descriptive title the answers to *What? When? Where?* and *How classified?*

   If the title is long, make two or more lines. The thought units in the title help you to determine whether to use an inverted pyramid, an alternating long and short line, or a pyramid arrangement, as in the examples that were shown for formal tables. The title may also appear in the form shown in Figure 14-7.

   Do not end a line with a preposition.

   Do not use abbreviations in titles.

   Capitalize the first letter in the main words in the title, or use all capitals.

3. Enclose graphics with lines on all four sides.

4. Use a black felt-point pen or India ink to draw borders and guide lines. You may use these items to draw the entry lines, or you may use other colors of felt-point pens to draw the entry lines.

**Figure 14-4**
*Bilateral Bar Chart*

**Figure 4**

*GROSS PROFIT (LOSS) FOR APPLIANCE DIVISION*
*Babcoc Manufacturing Company*
*1981—1985*

**Source:**   Records of Vice-President for Finance

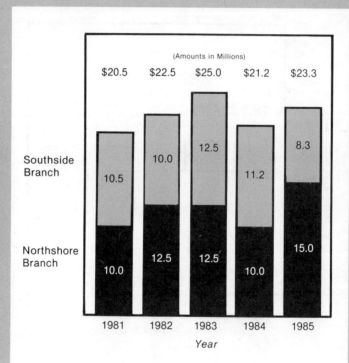

**Figure 14-5**
Compound Bar Chart

(Amounts in Millions)

$20.5   $22.5   $25.0   $21.2   $23.3

Southside Branch

10.5   10.0   12.5   11.2   8.3

Northshore Branch

10.0   12.5   12.5   10.0   15.0

1981   1982   1983   1984   1985

Year

**Figure 5.** *Deposits in Savings Accounts, Southside Branch and Northshore Branch, Huntington State Bank, 1981—1985*

**Source:** *Bank Audit Records*

5. Present items systematically such as according to age, size, alphabet, or location.

6. Include the zero line to avoid giving a misleading impression. Start the vertical scale at zero. Use accurate and appropriate scales. Show breaks in scales clearly, as in this example, where the differences are between 100 and 180. Including 20 to 100 would result in excess blank space.

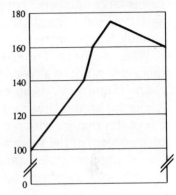

7. Show on the graphic itself the figures (amounts, percentages, and so forth) from which the graphic is made.

8. Choose a scale that gives the effect you want. Larger scales are needed to show minor changes. A scale suitable for representing weather temperature changes, for example, would be virtually useless for body temperature changes.

9. Do not put more than five curves (lines) on the same graph.

10. Place explanatory notes, if any, and a source notation about two lines below the chart.

Preparing attractive, well-designed graphics is time-consuming; but an effective graphic is well worth the time and effort required to complete it for some reports. You will need these supplies to prepare graphics:

| | |
|---|---|
| ruler | colored pencils |
| pencil | compass |
| India ink or black | protractor |
| felt-point pen | T square |

In the following paragraphs, specific instructions are given for preparing bar charts, pictograms, line charts, pie charts, maps, flowcharts, and organization charts.

**Bar chart.** Use a bar chart when you want the readers to observe relative quantities more quickly than is possible by comparing large numbers. You can use bar charts also to show percentages. Make the length of each bar proportional to the quantity or amount it represents.

When showing figures such as profits and losses for a certain time, use a bilateral bar chart (see Figure 14-4). Compound bar charts (Figure 14-5 is an example) have a number of components for each bar and thus need shaded or colored segments. Multiple bar charts require within the border lines a legend or key made up of short bars of the same width and color or shading pattern as the bars themselves (see Figure 14-6).

Here are suggestions for preparing bar charts:

1.  Start all bars at zero.

2.  Represent the variables with bars of the same width.

3.  Separate the bars with about half as much space between them as the width of the bars, except when multiple bars are used. Then leave about half the space of a bar between the sets (Figure 14-6).

4.  When a legend is needed, place it within the boundary lines of the chart.

5.  If plus and minus quantities are to be shown, use a bilateral bar chart with the zero base drawn across the middle of the graph. (Figure 14-4 is an example.)

6.  If time is not involved, use a logical arrangement such as descending order.

Observe in Figure 14-6 that no corn was produced in Clayton County in 1983. Space was left for the bar. No entry in the space indicates to the readers that nothing was to be depicted here for corn production.

Other types of bar charts are in Figures 14-7 and 14-8.

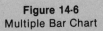

**Figure 14-6**
Multiple Bar Chart

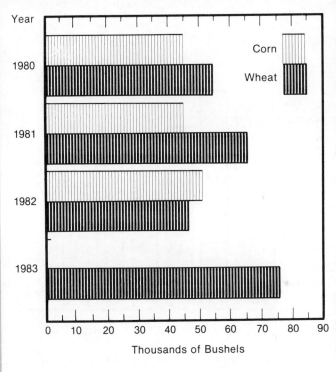

**Figure 6.** *Grain Produced in Clayton County*
*1980—1983*

**Source:** *County Agent's Files*

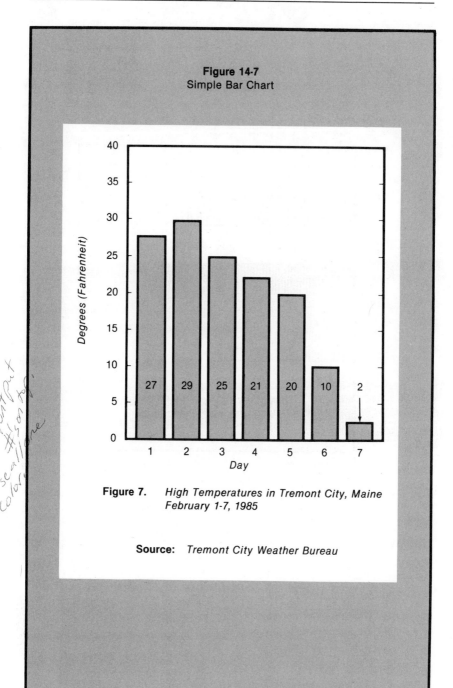

**Figure 14-7**
Simple Bar Chart

**Figure 7.** *High Temperatures in Tremont City, Maine February 1-7, 1985*

**Source:** *Tremont City Weather Bureau*

**Figure 14-8**
One Hundred Percent Bar Chart

**Figure 8**

*DISTRIBUTION OF VEHICLE PRODUCTION*
*BY ALTON AUTOMOBILE MANUFACTURERS, INC.*
*1985*

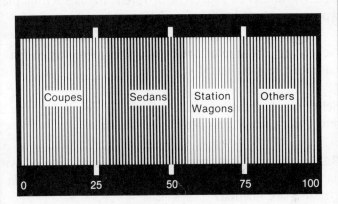

**Source:**  *Records of Vice-President for Production*

**Pictogram.** A pictogram (Figure 14-9) is a bar chart with pictorial symbols instead of bars. A pictogram, which quickly gains the attention of the readers and leads to the paragraphs of discussion that follow it, is often used in reports that go to the general public. Often a degree of preciseness can well be sacrificed and offset by the interest this graphic generates.

Helpful suggestions for making pictograms follow:

1. Choose symbols that are easy to identify. They must be self-explanatory.

2. Use interesting symbols that give a clear picture. Use different symbols to represent different items such as men and women, cars and trucks, and houses and factories.

3. Never vary the size of the symbols; show comparison on the basis of the *number* of symbols.

4. Select the number of symbols to represent clearly the largest and the smallest quantities.

5. Rather than have more than one horizontal line of symbols, let each represent a larger number or amount so that fewer symbols are needed.

6. Avoid using a half symbol at the beginning. In fact, some chart makers portray a whole symbol for over 50 percent of a fractional value and no symbol if the fractional value is less than 50 perent. After all, pictograms are not meant to give precise information.

7. If a quantity is not large enough to have even a part of a symbol, use a dot and explain it in a legend.

8. Leave enough space between the lines to enable the readers to see the rows clearly.

**Figure 14-9**
Pictogram

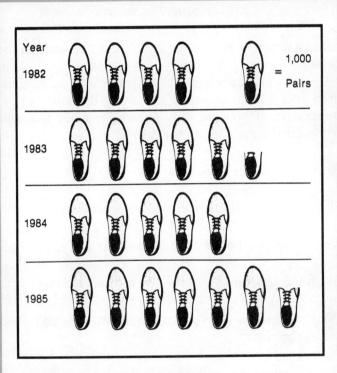

**Figure 9.**   *Men's Shoes Produced*
*By Hansen Shoe Manufacturers*
*1982—1985*

**Source:**   *Files of Production Manager*

**Line Chart.** A line chart is the best graphic for showing changes in a value for a time span. This chart is made by drawing lines between points in a series (see Figure 14-10). The horizontal scale is read from left to right; the vertical scale, from bottom to top. You can show two or more values on one chart (see Figure 14-11).

Here are suggestions for designing line charts:

1.  Make a different pattern for each line on the chart. Lines can be solid (———), broken (———), dotted (........), hollow (═══) , and combinations of patterns. You may use colored lines instead of varied patterns if the chart is not to be duplicated. If you use only one color, make the solid line represent the most important item.

2.  Show time on the horizontal scale.

3.  Show variation of quantity on the vertical scale.

4.  Keep spaces on both horizontal and vertical scales equal.

5.  Begin the vertical axis at zero or with a base year.

6.  When a time period is omitted, draw two parallel jagged lines across the chart.

7.  Draw the lines that represent the data heavier than those that form the squares of the chart.

8.  Use surface charts as variations of line charts. This type of chart emphasizes data that may not look as significant in a line chart. Instead of just a line or lines on the chart, the space from the base of the chart to the line (and between the lines if more than one value is represented) is filled in with color or a pattern such as solid black, lines, crosshatching, or dots. Figure 14-12 is an example of a surface chart.

**Figure 14-10**
Line Chart

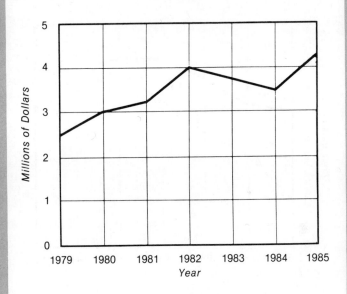

**Figure 10**

*Gross Sales
Reynolds Retail Outlet
1979-1985*

**Source:**   *Vice-President in Charge of Marketing*

**Figure 14-11**
Line Chart

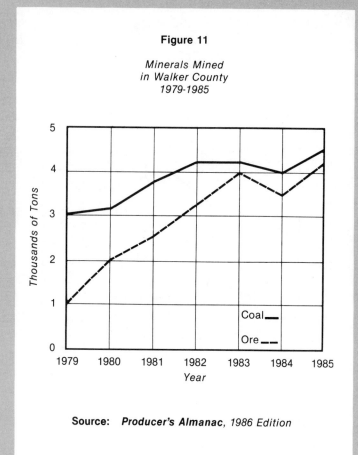

**Figure 11**

*Minerals Mined
in Walker County
1979-1985*

**Source:** *Producer's Almanac, 1986 Edition*

**Figure 14-12**
Surface Chart

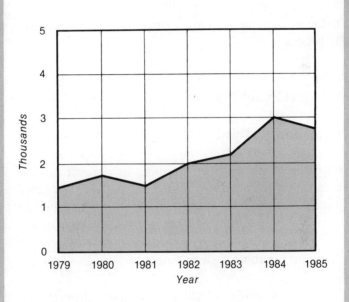

**Figure 12.**   *Bicycles Produced*
*By Preston Manufacturing Company*
*1979-1985*

**Source:**   *Records of Production Manager*

**Pie Chart.**   A pie chart is a circle divided into segments (called slices) to show comparison of parts to one another and to the whole. Data are presented less accurately in this chart than in some other types, but the generalizations are easy to see. You have, no doubt, observed in newspapers pie charts showing the sources and the distribution of the revenue for the federal, the state, or the county government.

Whether you use a pie chart to show the breakdown of a dollar or to show percentages for other items, the numbers in the chart must total one hundred, as shown in Figure 14-13.

Suggestions for designing a pie chart follow:

1.   Divide a circle into twenty 5 percent divisions and then make the proportions you need.

2.   Arrange the slices clockwise in descending order of size with the largest section beginning at the "twelve o'clock" position.

3.   If a portion is labeled "Other," place it last regardless of size.

4.   Place the labels and the amounts or percentages inside the slices unless they are too large for the space. If a label cannot fit inside a slice, place it outside the circle with an arrow pointing to the appropriate section (see Figure 14-13).

5.   Limit the number of slices to six.

6.   Use colors, shading, stippling, or crosshatching to distinguish the portions. Use a different color or pattern for each slice of the pie.

You can prepare a pie chart by drawing a circle with a compass or a round object.

**Map.**   Any time geographic distribution needs to be visualized, no better graphic can be used than a map. A map can be drawn for an area as large as the world or as small as a part of a city.

**Figure 14-13**
Pie Chart

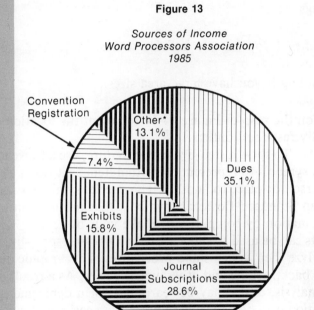

**Figure 13**

*Sources of Income*
*Word Processors Association*
*1985*

Convention
Registration

Other*
13.1%

7.4%

Dues
35.1%

Exhibits
15.8%

Journal
Subscriptions
28.6%

*No item in this classification amounted to more than 3.0 percent.

**Source:**   *Annual Report of Word Processors Association*

Use these suggestions for drawing maps:

1.  Draw a plain outline map leaving out rivers and mountains unless they are pertinent to your message.

2.  Select bars, dots, circles, or other shapes to show sites at geographic points. You can even use symbols such as trees or buildings.

3.  Draw lines if you want to indicate routes.

4.  Use shading if you have large area sizes.

The dots on the map in Figure 14-14 represent the locations of the McCreedy fast-food outlets.

**Flowchart.**   To show a step-by-step procedure, use a flowchart. You can use symbols to represent the actual item as it flows along from one person or place to another. Use special symbols such as the American Standard flowchart symbols that are used in processing information by computer, or make your own.

Flowcharts can be used to show analysis. Offices, especially, use them to analyze their systems and procedures. This graphic helps to point out backtracking and other inefficiencies. As a result of a flowchart analysis, desks may be rearranged or a department of the organization may be relocated to provide an easier and quicker flow of work.

The steps taken to produce a letter or a memorandum are shown in the flowchart in Figure 14-15.

**Organization chart.**   An organization chart is an effective device for showing lines of authority and span of control. To make an organization chart, follow these suggestions:

1.  Place the box for the chief office at the top.

2.  Place below the level of the chief office the boxes for the other positions that are on the same organizational level.

3.  Continue with the remaining levels.

**Figure 14-14**

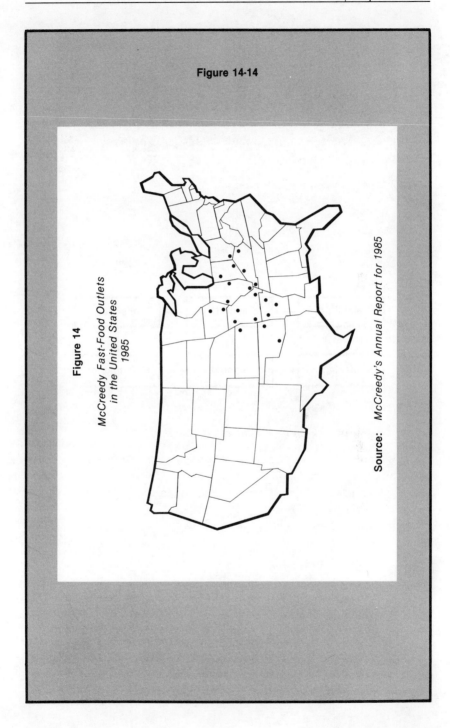

**Figure 14**

*McCreedy Fast-Food Outlets
in the United States
1985*

**Source:** *McCreedy's Annual Report for 1985*

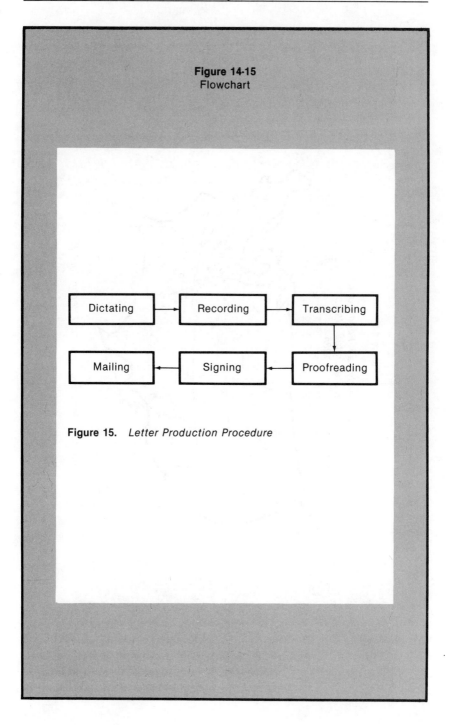

**Figure 14-15**
Flowchart

**Figure 15.** *Letter Production Procedure*

4.   Join the boxes with solid lines to show lines of authority; draw broken lines to show staff or functional authority.

5.   Include the names of people as well as the names of positions unless the turnover is so great that including the names of people would be impractical.

Figure 14-16 is an organization chart for Eakins Electronics Sales. Because frequent turnover exists among the salesclerks, the names of the individuals who hold those positions are omitted.

**Photographs and drawings.**   In addition to the graphics you have seen in this chapter, photographs and drawings sometimes serve as means of presenting data in a report. Photographs and drawings can help readers to see locations and processes that cannot be described well in words. Annual reports are made clear, attractive, and interesting through the use of numerous colored photographs of products and people.

## USING COMPUTERS

Today numerous software packages are available for making charts on computers. Computer users save much time by using these packages rather than preparing charts by hand. Some of the software packages, though, do not provide for some of the fine points that make the charts clear and easy to read. For example, while the proportions of pie chart segments (slices) are accurate, they do not begin at the "twelve o'clock" position; and the slices may not appear in largest-to-least order. And for bar charts, the spaces between the bars are as wide as or are wider than the bars themselves. Also, no provision is made for including in the title the answers to the four questions *What? When? Where?* and *How classified?* when these answers apply to the graphic being constructed.

Some software packages may be designed to include these fine points. Until they are available to you, however, you may use the current packages to prepare the drafts of your graphics and then use a black felt-point pen or India ink and colored pencils to draw the final copy. By following this procedure, you still save time by not having to prepare both the draft and the final copy by hand.

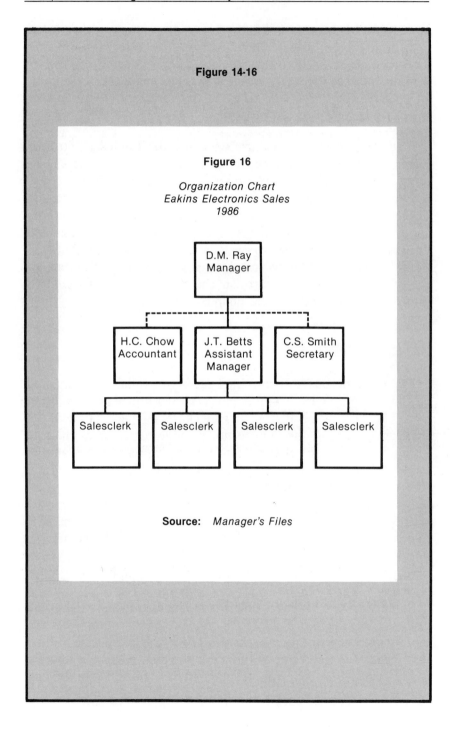

**Figure 14-16**

**Figure 16**

*Organization Chart*
*Eakins Electronics Sales*
*1986*

**Source:**   *Manager's Files*

## INTERPRETING GRAPHICS

Even though most readers understand easily the information in a well-constructed graphic, some need help in interpreting part of it. To ensure accurate interpretation, write statements to call attention to specific points. Without your comments, the readers may not recognize some significant meanings your information provides. Also, some readers may know so little about the particular data your report contains that you need to make interpretative comments so that they see the information in its true perspective. Write, therefore, an introduction and an interpretation of each chart, photograph, or formal table in your report.

Introduce each graphic before you present it. Use variety in the introductions, and emphasize the content rather than the graphic itself. Here are some of the effective ways to introduce graphics:

> The production totals varied greatly during the ten years, as shown in Table 1 on page 9.

> Six percent of the budget goes to education (see Figure 3).

> The brands of copiers purchased by libraries in 1985 are shown in Figure 4 on page 22.

When you cannot place a graphic on the page with the introduction, place it on the following page. Ideally, you would introduce the graphic, present it, and then interpret it. Because spacing often prevents this ideal sequence, part of the interpretation may precede the graphic, and part of it may follow the graphic.

No set of strict instructions can be given for interpreting the information in a graphic because no two graphics are identical and because the purpose for which reports are written differ. Always keep in mind the purpose of the report and point out significant meanings. You may need to point out or explain trends, forecasts, or exceptions. Also, you may consider pointing out any of these factors:

| | |
|---|---|
| similarities | high and low figures |
| patterns | second to high and second |
| peaks | to low figures |
| troughs | mean |
| incongruities | median |
| changes | mode |
| number of classifications | total number of items |
| in the graphic | |

You will not, of course, include all of these factors when interpreting any one graphic aid.

Although you show specific figures in graphics, avoid restating these specifics when interpreting nontechnical data. After all, unless a survey includes 100 percent of the population of the universe studied, the data can be only an approximation, anyway. Readers of nontechnical data are ordinarily more concerned with close approximations than with specifics, and they remember them longer. Therefore, instead of stating "This product was purchased by 31.2 percent of the residents," write such statements as "This product was purchased by slightly more than 30 percent of the residents." Or you may convert these percentages to fractions; thus "This product was purchased by almost one third of the residents."

Do not use approximations in some reports. For example, a packer is planning to ship frozen foods by refrigerated trucks or railway cars. The foods must be transported in compartments in which the temperature never exceeds 32°F. To tell report readers that the high temperature in a compartment is about 30° when the high is actually 33° could lead them to make a costly decision: the frozen foods would spoil. The readers may then lose faith in your reporting ability.

Eliminate bias from your report, but help to make the meaning of the data immediately apparent by including interpretative words. You may, as an example, write *"Only* eighteen copiers were sold in Knoxville in 1984" rather than merely state the fact, "Eighteen copiers were sold in Knoxville in 1984." By including the word *only*, you tell the readers that eighteen is a small figure in comparison to expectations, to other periods, to other items, or to other cities.

Instead of writing "Fifteen word processors were purchased by schools in May," you may write *"You may be surprised that* fifteen word processors were purchased by schools in May." The second statement helps to interpret, and it presents the fact interestingly.

Use interpretative words such as these judiciously. Remember that the purpose of your interpretation of a graphic is to help the readers to understand quickly the significance or proper meaning of the information you have collected and have studied carefully.

When you use graphics to simplify complex information or to add interest to a report, your readers will appreciate your using them.


## QUESTIONS FOR DISCUSSION

1.  What factors would you consider in deciding whether to use a table or some other graphic to present data?

2.  If a simple and clear graphic is presented, why may interpretation by the author be needed?

3.  Why are pictograms often misleading?

4.  What uses are made of organization charts?


## EXERCISES

Improve the following sentences.

1.  The report was accepted by the committee.

2.  The researcher learned that two programs are in existence.

3.  Report writers should make an analyzation of the data before they prepare graphics.

4.  In the event that the manager requests a copy, please send it by first-class mail.

5.  Installation of the computer will require only four days.

6.  The committee met for the purpose of making a revision of the proposal.

7. It was a pleasure working with you.

8. In the event that the computer cannot be repaired by tomorrow, the data cannot be analyzed this week.

9. The report can be typed in a short period of time.

10. Here is the sales report for the month of February.

## PROBLEMS

1. From an annual report dated 1982, you learned that the funds of the Southeastern Chapter of the Administrative Management Society were allocated as follows:

   Monthly meetings, 25.1%; Newsletter, 15.0%; Annual convention, 33.2%; Promotion, 16.9%; Other, 9.8%

   Present this information in a pie chart.

2. If you do not know how much money you spent for school expenses last year, estimate the amount. Estimate the percentage of that amount that you spent for each of these items: rent, books, clothing, recreation, transportation, and meals at school.

   Present this information (or the actual amounts if you know them) in a pie chart.

3. You learned from the treasurer of the Personnel Managers Association the sources of income for that organization in 1985. That information follows:

   | | |
   |---|---|
   | Journal subscriptions | 24.6% |
   | Convention registration | 9.3 |
   | Dues | 39.0 |
   | Other | 8.4 |
   | Exhibits | 18.7 |

   Present this information in a pie chart.

**4.** When you interviewed the husband and the wife of Family A, you learned that their income for January, 1985, was distributed this way:

```
Clothing ...........    19.3%
Food ..............    45.3
Insurance ..........     5.0
Rent ..............    20.0
Other.............    10.4    (No item in this classification
                              amounted to more than 3.0 percent)
```

Present this information in a pie chart.

**5.** Prepare a line chart to show the enrollment trends for three colleges of the Western State University, Omaha, Oregon, from 1979 to 1984. You received the following enrollment figures from the records in the admissions office:

College of Business Administration—700 students in 1979; 1000, 1980; 1300, 1981; 2800, 1982; 4000, 1983; 5000, 1984

College of Home Economics—200 students in 1979; 200, 1980; 1000, 1981; 1500, 1982; 1500, 1983; 1500, 1984

College of Liberal Arts—2100 students in 1979; 2200, 1980; 2600, 1981; 2600, 1982; 2600, 1983; 2000, 1984

**6.** Prepare a line chart to show the figures for grain production in White County, Indiana, for the years 1940, 1950, 1960, 1970, and 1980. The following figures were obtained from the White County Department of Statistics:

Corn—2800 bushels in 1940; 2800, 1950; 3200, 1960; 3600, 1970; 4000, 1980

Wheat—2000 bushels in 1940; 2500, 1950; 2500, 1960; 3000, 1970; 4000, 1980

Oats—1400 bushels in 1940; 1500, 1950; 1900, 1960; 1000, 1970; 700, 1980

**7.** Records of Pianos, Inc., reveal the types of customers who purchased pianos from 1982-1986. That information follows:

Churches . . . . . . .  15, 1982; 20, 1983;  2, 1984; 17, 1985; 22, 1986
Schools . . . . . . . . .  27, 1982; 25, 1983; 31, 1984; 19, 1985; 28, 1986
Individuals . . . . . .   3, 1982;  4, 1983;  4, 1984; 10, 1985;  8, 1986

Present this information in a line chart.

**8.** Gross sales figures for the Reynolds Retail Outlet for 1980 through 1986 follow:

1980 . . . . . . . . . . . . . . . . $2,500,000
1981 . . . . . . . . . . . . . . . . . 3,000,000
1982 . . . . . . . . . . . . . . . . . 3,000,000
1983 . . . . . . . . . . . . . . . . . 4,000,000
1984 . . . . . . . . . . . . . . . . . 3,750,000
1985 . . . . . . . . . . . . . . . . . 3,500,000
1986 . . . . . . . . . . . . . . . . . 4,250,000

Present this information, which you received from the sales manager's files, in a line chart.

**9.** According to the following figures that you obtained from records in the admissions office of your institution, the total enrollment has increased almost every year since 1977:

In 1977 the total enrollment was 1700; in 1978, 1850; in 1979, 1951; in 1980, 2250; in 1981, 2100; in 1982, 2300

Present this information in a bar chart.

**10.** You learned from the 1981 edition of *Producer's Almanac* that Xan County produced coal and steel in the following quantities for the period 1978 through 1982:

| Year | Coal | Steel |
|------|------|-------|
| 1978 | 5 tons | 10 tons |
| 1979 | 10 tons | 12 tons |
| 1980 | 12 tons | 12 tons |
| 1981 | 17 tons | 12 tons |
| 1982 | 19 tons | 25 tons |

Present this information in a bar chart.

11. Prepare a bilateral bar chart to show the low temperature readings for the last week of January, 1982, in Wolf Creek, Kentucky.

   Sunday, 33°; Monday, 28°; Tuesday, -5°; Wednesday, -12°; Thursday, -3°; Friday, 12°; Saturday, 18°

12. Show the information in Problem 6 in a multiple bar chart.

13. Show the information in Problem 9 in a line chart.

14. In 1985 Salesman B represented the Scofield Paper Company in Minnesota, Iowa, Wisconsin, and Illinois. Use a United States map to show this information from the files of the sales manager for Scofield Paper Company.

15. Draw a map of the United States and show the locations of your seven plants in four states. (Use fictitious data.)

16. Draw an organization chart to show the proper relationships and lines of authority for a small business that employs these people:

   President, vice-president, manager of the production department that has seven assembly-line workers, manager of the sales department that has three salespeople

17. When you studied the company files, you learned the figures for the number of three-bedroom houses the Flanagan Construction Company built from 1980-1984. Present this information in a pictogram.

   | | |
   |---|---|
   | 1980 . . . . . . . . . . . . . | 12 houses |
   | 1981 . . . . . . . . . . . . . | 28   " |
   | 1982 . . . . . . . . . . . . . | 20   " |
   | 1983 . . . . . . . . . . . . . | 27   " |
   | 1984 . . . . . . . . . . . . . | 38   " |

18. Prepare a pictogram to show the number of television sets sold by the Appliance Store from 1982 through 1984. Those figures follow:

   | | |
   |---|---|
   | 1982 . . . . . . . . . . . . . | 150 sets |
   | 1983 . . . . . . . . . . . . . | 175   " |
   | 1984 . . . . . . . . . . . . . | 165   " |

**19.** Write an introduction and an interpretation for the line chart you prepared for Problem 5.

**20.** From the records of campus automobile registration offices in nine northwestern universities, you learned how many students owned foreign automobiles in the summer of 1982. Present that information, which follows, in a formal table. Show not only the *number* of men and women owning each type of car but also the *percentages* of men and women owning each type.

> Marc, 187 men and 176 women; MacKelsy, 67 men and 58 women; Super-A, 185 men and 161 women; Le Oui, 98 men and 76 women; Jaurez, 165 men and 159 women; Toyette, 153 men and 139 women; Karato, 157 men and 150 women; Other, 23 men and 19 women (No more than six people owned any one of the eight makes included in the classification *Other*).

**21.** Write an introduction and an interpretation for the formal table you prepared for Problem 20.

# Chapter 15

# Informal Reports and Proposals

After you have determined the purpose of a report, have studied the situation leading to the need for the report, have considered carefully the readers, and have collected the needed information, you are ready to write the report. Will it be informal? Or will it be formal? These two types of reports differ in writing style as well as in format. The writing style for most informal reports parallels that described in Chapters 2 and 11. The writing style for formal reports is discussed in Chapter 16.

Informal reports and proposals, which may be informal or formal, are discussed in this chapter.

## INFORMAL REPORTS

Among the informal reports are memorandums, letters, and fill-in forms.

## Memorandums

Memorandums are the most frequently used reports by many groups. Because memorandums are for use inside the organization, they are quite informal in both format and writing style. Large organizations usually have stationery prepared on which these reports are written. The name and the address of the organization are not needed since memorandums are for internal use; but the word *memorandum* or *memo* and the guide words *to*, *from*, *date*, and *subject* are printed. These memorandum forms save a considerable amount of time that is required for typing. As is true for business letters, the second and succeeding pages of multiple-page memorandums are written on plain paper.

Plain paper is appropriate for the first page of a memorandum. When you write on plain paper, choose a format that contributes to easy reading. Numerous formats are good; but to minimize mechanical details in this chapter, only one format is illustrated. Begin by writing *memorandum* at the left margin and about one inch from the top of the page. Type *memorandum* and the guide words *to*, *from*, *date*, and *subject* in capitals at the left margin to make them stand out. Triple space between the word *memorandum* and the guide words, which are double spaced, and then triple space between *subject* and the first line of the message. Single spacing is usually preferred for the message, though double spacing is acceptable.

Beginning the names, the date, and the subject line two spaces beyond the colon that follows *subject* makes these items easy to read and simplifies the mechanics of typing. Starting this informal report about one inch from the top of the page is appropriate and makes typing easier than if you center it vertically on the page. Study the illustration in Figure 15-1.

Additional headings for long memorandum reports can be inserted (see Figure 15-2).

Including a courtesy title such as *Mr.* or *Ms.* is not necessary. Include the addressee's position title, though, after or below the name since more than one person by the same name may be employed by an organization. Include the writer's position title after the name so that if the memorandum is referred to much later, the position the writer held at the time the memorandum was

**Figure 15-1**

```
MEMORANDUM


TO:       Ada M. Adfield
          Thomas E. Farnsworth
          Marie T. Hollingsworth

FROM:     James W. Hatcher, Production Manager

DATE:     April 3, 1985

SUBJECT:  Planning Vacation Schedules


Please come to Room 126A at 10 a.m. next Monday to discuss the vacation
schedules for assembly-line employees.  We will need to meet for about
an hour.


hrw
```

## Figure 15-2

MEMORANDUM

TO:      Walter L. McKnight, Marketing Research Analyst

FROM:    Terry M. Compton, *gmc,* Vice-President for Marketing

DATE:    September 3, 1985

SUBJECT: Duties of the Assistant to the Vice-President for Marketing

I look forward to working with you as assistant to the vice-president for marketing, and I congratulate you on the fine work you have done in this department during the past four years. Promoting those who are capable and industrious--as in your case--is a practice I am confident our company will continue.

Even though you already have a good understanding of the work that is done in this department, no doubt you are eager to know more about the specific duties you will assume on October 1. Your primary duties will involve budgets, motivation, and research.

Budgets

As you know, it is important that we prepare a budget for each new product. We must pay special attention to these factors:

1.  The cost of creating the product

2.  Advertising the product in newspapers and magazines, on the radio, and on the television

3.  The time and the expenses involved in helping our salespeople to know the product thoroughly

Motivation

A continuing activity, of course, is that of motivating the sales force. I want you to assume the primary responsibility of keeping the morale high and of detecting problems to be solved. You have already convinced me that you have a special knack for this kind of work.

Research

To compete with other companies and to continue to make a fair profit, we must increase our level of research. Your innovations and your ability to work well with the other analysts will enable you to excel in this area.

**Figure 15-2 Continued:**

Walter L. McKnight
Page 2
September 3, 1985

When I return on September 10, we can talk about the computer we plan to
buy.  In the meantime, be thinking about the furniture we should order for
your new office, which will be in Room 407.

ktl

written will be evident even though that person may have left the organization or may have been promoted.

Use a short, specific subject for your memorandum to help the reader immediately identify the purpose. The subject line later serves for filing identification. Capitalize the first letter in each word in the subject line except articles, conjunctions, and short prepositions.

If more than one page is needed, type the addressee's name, the page number, and the date on plain paper. Triple space and continue the message, as in the next illustration.

```
        Steve M. Rader
        Page 2
        August 23, 1984


        only four days a week.  Eight of the employees who were
        affected by the change were enthusiastic about it, and
        they were glad to express their feelings.
```

Since no closing lines are used on a memorandum, write your initials or name beside your typed name in the heading or sign your name at the end of the message. If other people are to receive copies, type their names at the bottom or after the guide word *to*.

The message must be independent: no part of it can depend on the subject line. For example, if you should have this subject line *SUBJECT: Meeting for First-Line Supervisors*, you could not mention merely the meeting in the message. You would have to identify the meeting as that for first-line supervisors. This practice is followed for all headings in any kind of report.

Accuracy, completeness, conciseness, and courtesy are as important for internal messages as for those that go outside the organization. The conversational style and tone discussed in Chapter 2 apply to memorandums.

## Letter Reports

Letters—not memorandums—are often written to report small amounts of information to people outside the organization. The format for these reports, which always include a subject line, is the same as for other business letters. (See Chapter 4 for letter format.) As in the case with memorandums, no part of the body of the letter can depend on the subject line; that is, the message has to be complete without the reader's having to pay attention to the subject line. The subject line is used to help the reader immediately identify the purpose and to serve for filing identification.

The guidelines in Chapter 3 apply to letter reports as much as to other types of business letters. Use the conversational style of writing that you use for other letters and memorandums. Do not use special abbreviations and other in-house terms that may confuse people outside your organization. Include simple graphics that help make the report effective.

Letter reports are shown in Figures 15-3 and 15-4.

Often, letters are used for short recommendation reports. The recommendation is given first and is followed by an explanation or the reasons for the recommendation.

## Fill-in Forms

Government and other external agencies require numerous reports from most types of organizations. Constant internal reporting is also taking place among departments, branches, and subsidiaries. Even though the preparation of many of these reports has been simplified by using printed forms, much time and energy must be spent to furnish the vast amount of information that is called for. Although perhaps you can do little to reduce the amount of work required in reporting to some outside agencies, continue to simplify internal reporting.

In many instances certain items of information are required for two or more reports. When you design the report forms for recording information, arrange them so that the person who receives your report can easily transfer the information from your form to the others that must be completed. For example, if three items on one page of a report can be transferred to one page, rather than to two or three pages of another report, the efficiency in reporting can be increased. The information can be transferred faster and more accurately.

Forms A and B that follow were used for reporting to two offices within the same university. After Form A was revised so that

**Figure 15-3**

## Watertown Interior Decorators
*Watertown, ME 04131*

March 19, 1985

Mr. George L. Maxwell, Manager
Ranch and Farm Insurance Company
1182 Main Street
Lawrenceburg, ME 04453

Dear Mr. Maxwell:

Subject: Office Interior Decorating

Here is the report you requested on the work we have contracted
to do for you:

1. The lighting fixtures are in our warehouse and
   can be installed the day your electrical contractor finishes rewiring your building.

2. The carpets you selected are being shipped from
   the supplier in Kansas City on March 29. We can
   lay the carpets on the 31st.

3. All the draperies have been completed and are
   ready to be installed as soon as the carpets have
   been laid. Installing them will require only
   about three hours.

When I drove by your office building yesterday afternoon, I was
very much impressed by the work your contractor has done to the
exterior of the building; and I am glad we have an opportunity
to contribute to the good appearance of the interior.

Please call me when the electrical contractor finishes rewiring
your building.

Cordially,

*Linda J. White*

Mrs. Linda J. White
Assistant Manager

wyc

## Figure 15-4

# Ryan Wholesale Company
## P.O. Box 286
## Bedford, MN 56110

July 8, 1985

Miss Marjorie J. Metcalf
Assistant Sales Manager
Ryan Wholesale Company
P. O. Box 286
Bedford, MN 56110

JUNE SALES FIGURES FOR CLOTHING

The figures for our gross sales of clothing in June follow:

| | |
|---|---|
| Boys' | $ 7,876.21 |
| Girls' | 9,206.27 |
| Men's | 8,111.84 |
| Women's | 11,202.00 |
| Total | $36,396.32 |

The information on colors and styles that you requested in your
letter of July 3 will be sent to you on July 20, the day the
tabulating will be completed.

*Brenda S. Mayberry*
BRENDA S. MAYBERRY, ANALYST

chr

the sequence of the items was the same as that for Form B, the person who completed Form B each quarter by transferring information from the other form could complete the task in less time, with less effort, and with a higher degree of accuracy than that which was possible before the form was revised.

---

Form A

SCHEDULE OF CLASSES

_____Quarter, 19___

College of _____

List courses according to the course number (lowest number first)

| Dept. | Course No. | Code No. | Course Title | Hrs. Cr. | Instructor | Room No. |
|---|---|---|---|---|---|---|
|  |  |  |  |  |  |  |
|  |  |  |  |  |  |  |
|  |  |  |  |  |  |  |

---

Form B

SCHEDULE OF CLASSES

_____Quarter, 19____

List courses according to departments within each college (alphabetical order for departments).

| Code No. | Dept. | Course No. | Course Title | Hrs. Cr. | Room No. | Instructor |
|---|---|---|---|---|---|---|
|  |  |  |  |  |  |  |
|  |  |  |  |  |  |  |
|  |  |  |  |  |  |  |

## Other Multiple-Page Reports

Any of the reports described in this chapter may be more than one page, though most memorandums and letters are only one page. In many instances an informal report that is longer than two pages should be written in a format similar to the one in Figure 15-5 and should be sent with a transmittal letter to the readers.

As a general rule, busy executives and others will, with very little hesitation, spend the time necessary to read a well-written short letter or memorandum. No persuasion is generally required to get them to read a routine form report. Persuasion is required, however, to get some of the intended readers to read a long report. Neatness, correctness, and interesting writing style are of utmost importance in encouraging people to read business reports. In addition to these features, which have already been discussed, the following features help to encourage people to read multiple-page reports: organization, headings, spacing, and illustrations.

**Organization.**   Good organization is especially important for business reports several pages long. The ideas should be presented in a logical order so that the readers can grasp them quickly and easily. These three steps, which have been recommended for many years, still apply:

1.   Tell what you are going to tell.

2.   Tell.

3.   Tell what you have told.

The *tell what you are going to tell* section should follow the report title, which should be typed in all capitals and centered horizontally about one and a half inches from the top of the page. Make a few statements to get the readers' attention and to introduce the topics to be covered. Introduce the topics in a way that will create reader interest and help you to present the message in a logical, well-organized way.

In some reports you may ask questions that will be answered in the body of the report, you may make statements that will surprise the readers, or you may simply make statements that you feel con-

**Figure 15-5**

CARTER HOTEL CONVENTION FACILITIES

for

Chairmen, Convention Planning Committees

by

Milford L. Ross, Administrative Assistant
Carter Hotel

October 16, 1985

**Figure 15-5 Continued:**

CARTER HOTEL CONVENTION FACILITIES

Since our hotel was opened on November 15, 1978, we have hosted
an average of two and one half conventions a month.  The attendance for
these meetings has ranged from 73 to 546.  In addition to our almost
ideal location, carefully planned and efficiently operated facilities
contribute to the unusual appeal our hotel has for many groups.

### Rooms and Furnishings

Some of our specially planned convention facilities are meeting
rooms, exhibit areas, and bedrooms and suites.

#### Meeting Rooms

All the meeting rooms are on the first floor of the east wing and
have easy access to the corridors, the rest rooms, the exhibit area, the
parking lot, and the registration area.  Each of the nine meeting rooms
is fully carpeted, well lighted, and expertly decorated.  The electrical
outlets are spaced so that any ordinary appliance or piece of equipment
can be used in any section of the room.

Each room is equipped with a temperature control switch and a
switch that permits the occupants to adjust the brightness of the lights
to produce the desired effect for whatever activity is under way.  The
seating can be arranged for dining, and it can be arranged in theatre
style or in conference style.  Some rooms are designed to be used individually; others can be combined.

Individual.  Five meeting rooms are used individually.  Each room
will seat twenty-four persons in a conference room arrangement or forty

1

**Figure 15-5 Continued:**

2

persons when the chairs are arranged in theatre style.  Meals are served
in only one of these small rooms; twenty persons can be served there.

      Combinations.  Four meeting rooms can be used individually, or any
of them can be combined by opening the folding doors that separate them.
Each room will seat 75 persons for dining or 150 persons by arranging the
chairs in theatre style.

Exhibit Area

      A large exhibit area that is 120 by 130 feet is between the group
of five small meeting rooms and the group of four large meeting rooms.
This location is ideal for organizations meeting in any of these nine
rooms.  The electrical outlets are spaced 10 feet apart across the entire
exhibit area.

      Our sales manager will instruct Jason Decorators, a local organiza-
tion, to provide any special items you need for exhibits.

Bedrooms and Suites

      The 600 spacious guest rooms and suites have shag carpets and
Mediterranean-style furnishings.  Each room is equipped with a color
television, a radio, and a direct-dial telephone.  Standard-size beds
are in the 300 rooms that have two beds.  Queen-size beds are in the 290
rooms that have one bed each.

      The ten suites--each of which consists of a large parlor, a bed-
room, two bathrooms, and two dressing rooms--have queen-size beds.

Services

      Outstanding catering service, recreational activities, and expert
handling of room reservations and registration activities enhance the
appeal of our hotel as a convention site for a group of any size.

**Figure 15-5 Continued:**

3

Catering

      Banquets, luncheons, breakfasts, receptions, and so on, at our
hotel are catered by the Lacy Catering Service, a nationally known organization. Our sales manager can arrange an appointment for any group representative to discuss menus. For any menu that you choose, the food will
be excellent; and the price will be reasonable.

Recreation

      The recreation manager will reserve tickets for you to take the
regularly scheduled tours of the city, and she will arrange special tours
for groups of four or more. She will also reserve tickets for you to any
local theatre. We are within five blocks of the three leading theatres
in the city.

      High-calibre music and floor shows are provided nightly in our
main dining room.

Reservations

      All you have to do to reserve bedrooms for your conventioneers is
send us a list of their names and addresses. Or if you prefer that they
make their own room reservations, we will send you a supply of forms they
can use. We will confirm each reservation within one week from the time
we receive it.

Registration

      We provide tables, typewriters, and any other equipment you may
need to register those who attend your convention. An area in the main
lobby is set aside for registration.

      You may deposit the money you collect for registration fees in our
safe for overnight protection.

**Figure 15-5 Continued:**

4

Summary

The five small meeting rooms, the four large meeting rooms, the 600 bedrooms and suites--along with the ideally situated exhibit area-- accommodate large conventions as well as small ones.  These physical features; the recreation we provide; and such services as catering, handling the reservations, and handling the registration activities account for the fact that we have hosted an average of two and one half conventions a month since we opened our hotel on November 15, 1978.

fident the readers will be interested in. Choose the strategy you believe is best for the particular report and for the intended readers.

The *tell* section is the body of the report. In this section discuss the topics in the order in which you introduced them. The degree of thoroughness with which you cover the topics should, of course, be determined by the purpose of the report, the characteristics of the readers, and the other factors involved.

To *tell what you have told*, summarize the key points you presented in the body. A short summary of the topics you have discussed serves as a quick review and as a desirable reinforcement for the ideas. This type of ending also helps the readers to perceive the proper relationships that exist among the major points.

The four-page report in Figure 15-5 contains the features discussed in this chapter.

**Headings.** For a multiple-page report, you are wise to remember the principle that length breeds length; that is, features such as headings should be added to long reports to contribute to easy reading and comprehension. Such features encourage busy executives to read these long reports immediately rather than to defer reading them until they have completed their shorter tasks.

Headings help readers to see at a glance that the information is organized. Headings provide stopping places if the readers must interrupt their reading of the report, and they help them to locate the point at which they are to resume reading after the interruption. Headings also help readers to find specific sections they wish to reread. By organizing your reports well, you will probably have two or more paragraphs to follow each heading. In some cases, however, you may need a heading for only one paragraph.

Use headings to highlight key points, but the content of a division must always be independent of the heading it follows. People who read the report text but skip the headings should obtain as thorough an understanding of the report content as they would if they read the headings too. The headings, therefore, must be restated or paraphrased in the text that follows the headings. The key word or phrase in a heading should be included in the topic sentence, which ordinarily comes early in the first paragraph, for that division. Although the topic sentence is often the first sentence of a paragraph, you can vary this arrangement to help provide variety in writing style and thus make the report more interesting.

Use short headings that indicate the key ideas for the sections that follow. Use consistent, parallel style; that is, if you use a word or a phrase once, use a word or a short phrase for each heading in that section of the report. Or if you use a question for one heading, use a question for each heading in that section of the report. Observe the headings in the following illustration.

*New Products*

————————————————————
————————————————————

*Brooms*

————————————————————
————————————————————

*Nylon Brushes*

————————————————————
————————————————————

*Mops*

————————————————————
————————————————————

*Strategy*

————————————————————
————————————————————

*Shall We Distribute Samples?*

————————————————————
————————————————————

*What Is the Expected Sales Volume?*

————————————————————
————————————————————

Type the headings so that they stand out from the text and are easy to read. A good plan to follow is to type the headings in upper- and lower-case letters and underline them. Center horizontally the headings for divisions, and type flush with the left margin the headings for subdivisions. For a sub-subdivision, indent the heading like the paragraphs and add a period and two spaces. To indicate further divisions, merely underline the key word or phrase in the first sentence of the paragraph. Triple space before a heading; double space after it.

**Spacing.**    You may single space or double space a report. With single spacing you get more information on a page, of course, and thus save stationery and possibly postage for long reports when the the report is to be mailed. Sometimes several copies are mailed. Parts of a report can be spaced so that specific points are emphasized. For example, the information in one section can be highlighted by single spacing that part if the rest of the report is double spaced. Also, that special part can be typed with shorter lines than those used for the major portion of the report.

When you double space a report, indent the first line of each paragraph seven or eight spaces. You do not need to indent paragraphs of single-spaced reports.

Leave ample margins—one to one and a fourth inches. This spacing produces a good appearance that does not seem crowded, and it leaves space for the readers to make notes in the margins if they care to. Avoid a crowded appearance. Alternating text and graphic illustrations helps to keep the pages open and easy to read.

**Illustrations.**    Illustrations contribute to the clarity, interest, and readability of some reports. Use illustrations that will help the readers to understand and appreciate the ideas you wish to convey. You can use such illustrations as analogies, stories, and actual cases; and you can use such graphics as maps, tables, charts, graphs, drawings, and photographs.

The instructions in the preceding paragraphs apply also to leaflets, pamphlets, brochures, and similar publications. If the report is printed, you can use color to enhance the appearance and to encourage people to read it. You can use colored headings, stationery, and illustrations of various types. Appropriately used color contributes to wide readership of long business reports prepared for a large audience.

For some multiple-page informal reports, you may include a title page, as described in the next chapter. You may transmit these reports by letters or by memorandums for internal use. Transmittal letters are described in the next chapter.

## PROPOSALS

Proposals, which may be informal or formal, are reports submitted to other organizations or to government agencies to convince them you or your company can provide a product or a service for them. Proposals are especially important to some groups because their future depends on successful proposals to get business.

Individuals or teams of writers submit proposals for doing research or for providing a service. As an employee, you may someday want to make suggestions for changes in your organization. You can make those suggestions by writing your superior a proposal describing what you want to do and how you plan to do it.

Proposals, which may be solicited or unsolicited, vary in length from one page to several volumes. Proposals for such highly complex products as airplanes have exceeded fifty volumes. A solicited proposal is submitted in response to a request for a proposal (RFP), which generally is accompanied by a guide or a set of instructions for preparation. Specifying the form of a proposal allows the agency or organization that issued the RFP to compare easily the proposals submitted in response.

When preparing an unsolicited proposal, include these parts in the order given here: introduction, proposed solution, qualifications for providing the products or services, and appendix.

### Introduction

You may call the first part of the proposal an introduction or a statement of the problem. In either case, you need to begin by demonstrating that you have a clear understanding of the job to be done. Sometimes background information or a discussion of how the problem developed is useful to the readers. The readers of an unsolicited proposal may not know that a need exists.

**Proposed Solution**

Possibly, a clear solution to the problem may not exist. In that case, describe the method or approach you think is best for solving the problem. Sometimes you will want to suggest more than one approach. Discuss the advantages and the disadvantages of the various methods and then explain why you think your solution is the best. Make sure your information is accurate; otherwise you may find yourself committed, as the result of an error, to do something you do not want to do.

In proposing a solution, think of any objections or questions your readers may have. Here are some usual questions:

Is the proposal practical?
Would the results justify the expense?
Would the solution create other problems?
Is there a precedent for the method or approach suggested?

**Qualifications**

Proposals are accepted or rejected on the basis of any or all of these factors:

1.  Abilities of the personnel

2.  Facilities of the submitter

3.  Time required to provide the service or product

4.  Costs

5.  Method of reporting

**Personnel.**  Include in the personnel section the background and experience of the people who will carry out the proposal, and describe convincingly your expertise and that of others who will work with you.

**Facilities.**  In the facilities section, list or describe briefly any materials or equipment you will use to do a good job. You can include pictures or samples to provide concrete evidence.

**Time requirements.**   The time requirements section is your work schedule, which tells the time you will need to complete the project. If you will complete the project in segments, give the dates for completing each segment.

**Costs.**   Itemize the estimated costs for necessary materials, personnel, travel, and other factors.

**Reports.**   You may write one report when the proposed activity is completed, or you may make several progress reports if the time extends beyond a short period. Whichever procedure you follow, include a description of this activity in your planning and in the proposal.

### Appendix

Detailed descriptions, drawings, photographs, samples, and testimonial letters from previous clients are usually placed in the appendix, which follows the body of the report, and are referred to in the body of the proposal.

### Writing Style

Proposal writing is persuasive writing. The proposal may be your only opportunity to do a job or to get your ideas accepted. Before you begin to write, ask yourself these questions:

1.   Will the readers be open-minded? Will they be skeptical? Will they be critical of what I am offering?

2.   What do the readers already know about the situation?

3.   How much detail should I include? (When in doubt, include more rather than less detail than is necessary.)

Write directly to your readers even when you know they may have to consult with others before approval can be given. Stress the advantages of accepting the proposal, but do not overlook the disadvantages. If you should overlook them, your readers would probably become suspicious. Emphasize the primary appeal and the secondary appeals as you would in a sales letter. Such appeals could be convenience, efficiency, comfort, utility, flexibility, service, availability, economy, or a combination of two or more.

To make the ending effective, you can summarize the primary appeal or make a direct suggestion for action. Make sure to state clearly the action you want the readers to take. A proposal attracts more attention when extra space is left before the action section. You can indent or single space this part to make it stand out.

A brief proposal is shown in Figure 15-6.

**Figure 15-6**

PROPOSAL FOR GROUNDS MAINTENANCE

Problem

The heavy clay soil on which your three new apartment buildings stand will require special care for grass, shrubs, trees, and other plants to grow satisfactorily.  Without a good turf and large plants, the area will erode rapidly.

Grass and appropriate shrubs and trees are needed to display the attractiveness of your beautifully designed, well-constructed apartment buildings.

Proposed Solution

The builders have brought some topsoil to the site, and they have sowed ample grass seed.  For the grass to grow, it will have to be fertilized, watered, mowed, and thatched.  Shrubs and trees of your choice can be set out and fertilized, watered, sprayed, and trimmed for the finest appearance.  My two partners and I can provide these services when they are needed, and we can provide them for a fair price.

If you want help in planning the landscaping of your facilities, we will be glad to help you.  You can purchase the shrubs and the trees wherever you wish, or we will purchase them for you.  Whether or not we purchase them, we will set them out and give them expert care.

Personnel

My two partners and I are juniors in college.  One partner is majoring in industrial arts; the other one and I are majoring in horticulture. We started our business when we were twelve years old.  Our first jobs were

1

**Figure 15-6 Continued:**

2

mowing lawns for neighbors.  For the past three years, we have had complete charge of maintaining the city park grounds, and we have maintained a privately owned golf course--Leisure Acres.  Letters from the city manager and the golf pro expressing appreciation for our work are appended to this proposal.

In addition to our practical experience and college courses, my father, who has a master's degree in horticulture and who owns a landscaping business in a nearby city, has taught us a great deal about planning and maintaining lawns.

The partner who is an industrial arts major keeps our equipment in top-notch condition.

### Facilities

Our two riding mowers, one self-propelled push mower, weed eater, sprayer, electric shears, and two sprinklers are in excellent condition.  My father lends us the other items we need from time to time.

### Duration

With a one-year contract, we will begin working on your property this fall.  We will set out the shrubs and the trees and water them as needed throughout the winter.  Early in March we will fertilize the lawn; mow once a week throughout the growing season; water and spray the grass, the trees, and the shrubs as needed; and trim the shrubs in the fall.

A second-year contract would include thatching the lawn in addition to the first-year services.

### Costs

The original landscaping cost will depend on the number, the size, and the types of shrubs and trees you choose and on whether you furnish them.

**Figure 15-6 Continued:**

3

The cost for the other services will be $1200.  Because thatching and additional trimming will be required the second year, the cost will be slightly more for the second and succeeding years.

Report

At the end of March, June, September, and December, we will send you a written report on the condition of your grounds and will recommend action for problems that arise.

Because shrubs and trees that are set out in the fall in this region almost always grow well, we recommend that you write to us soon and suggest a time for us to discuss plans for maintaining the grounds on which your beautiful new apartment buildings stand.

## QUESTIONS FOR DISCUSSION

1. How are headings in informal reports related to captions on file folders?

2. What are some examples of informal reports that were not mentioned in this chapter?

3. How can you apply the word processing concept to recurring types of informal reports.

4. What are the advantages of using memorandums instead of letters for internal communication?

5. Why is a study of forms important for making your communication mediums more effective?

## EXERCISES

Improve the following sentences.

1. I make the recommendation that the audit be made before December 31.

2. The schedule was approved by the production manager.

3. The desk that is in the next office cost more than $300.

4. Sharon tabulates large quantities of data in an easy manner.

5. They have two refineries in the state of Louisiana.

6. The consultant will conduct a study of the procedures before he recommends changes.

7. The assistant manager, whose name is Jeffery Span, wrote to them on September 1.

8. In the event that the plane is late, call me when you arrive at the airport.

9. In order to improve the situation, they appointed a committee to study it.

10. At the present time only four production lines are in operation.

## PROBLEMS

1.  A local contractor is planning to build a ten-story office building and to lease space to both short-term and long-term tenants. To get a good idea of the needs of the professionals who would lease small suites for a short time, he has asked several prospective leasors to give him a description of what they need.

    Kenneth R. Poston, one of your friends who is an attorney, will move to your city within two years to begin a private practice. Kenneth believes that for the first five years of his practice a four-room suite plus a rest room would be ideal for him. He will employ one para-legal and one administrative assistant. He will combine a storage room and a library; he will need a reception room, a room for his two assistants, and of course a private office for himself.

    Prepare a scaled drawing of the space (include doors, windows, electrical outlets, and heating vents). Give dimensions.

    Draw a layout for the furniture, filing cabinets, shelves, and so on. Keep these items in mind as you draw the layout:

    1.  Lighting
    2.  Work flow
    3.  Privacy for conversations
    4.  Confidentiality of records
    5.  Attractiveness
    6.  Convenience
    7.  Efficiency

    Write a short informal report to accompny this layout. Explain the desirable features of your layout. Also, prepare a transmittal letter and address it to Mr. Brady E. Whitman, Manager, Millington Contractors, Inc., P.O. Box 719, Bakertown, IL 61011.

2.  Within the next six months, Knapp, Toriano, and Downey—a large accounting firm that has offices in several cities across the country—will open an office in St. Thomas, a city of some 600,000 population. The new office will be on the sixth floor of a new bank building. The office will be staffed with twenty-two men and women who are well qualified to provide high-quality service; and it will be equipped with up-to-date furniture, computers, and word processors.

    Ms. Anita J. Toriano, one of the partners of the accounting firm, has asked you to write rules and regulations for the personnel in the new office in St. Thomas. Your rules and regulations should cover standards of dress as well as office conduct. The people in the St. Thomas office will have frequent telephone conversations with clients and prospective clients. Many clients will visit the office. You do not want your personnel to use such expressions as "Hang on" when asking a telephone caller to wait; neither do you want an employee to greet a visitor with "Yes?" or a similar inappropriate expression.

    Write positively: give more suggestions for what *to* do than for what *not* to do. You can write these rules on a sheet of paper and transmit them by memorandum to Ms. Toriano, or you can include them as part of a memorandum to her.

3.  You are an assistant personnel director in a company that awards 10-, 20-, and 30-year service pins. The company president wants to know the names of the employees who will receive service pins next month. He wants to know also how many 10-year, how many 20-year, and how many 30-year pins have been awarded since the practice was begun in 1942. Give him this information in a memorandum.

4.  A club, of which you are the treasurer, has carried out several fund-raising projects this year and has contributed to several worthwhile causes. To let the other officers and the committee chairpersons know how much the club has accomplished, write a memorandum and include specific figures and statements about the year's work. The club secretary can make a copy for each interested person.

5.   Your company office employees have expressed dissatisfaction
     with the acoustics in the new five-story office building you moved
     into four weeks ago. The office workers for the five other groups
     that are leasing office space in the building have expressed the same
     concern. Your company owns the building. Study the situation
     carefully and write a letter to the president to describe the situation
     and to recommend corrective action. (The president needs to know
     the types of jobs that have to be performed so that he can explain
     them to the builder.)

6.   The president of the large organization for whom you do con-
     sulting work is considering the possibility of investing a large sum
     of money in word processing equipment. He has asked you to col-
     lect, as a preliminary part of a feasibility study, the following infor-
     mation: the number of employees who dictate at least ten letters a
     week, the number of people who transcribe at least ten letters a
     week, the number of typewriters in the offices, the number of in-
     dividual dictating and transcribing machines in the offices, and the
     number of pages (letters, memorandums, reports, and others) that
     were typewritten last month.

     Write a letter to the president and give him this information. His
     name is T. Carroll Heilman; his address is Southeast Insurance
     Company, P.O. Box 1722, Kingsville, TN 37006.

7.   Homes, Inc., has been building houses since 1964. The company
     draws plans, acquires the materials, builds the houses, decorates
     them, and landscapes the lot. All the homeowner is required to do
     is provide the lot and choose a plan from among the many that
     Homes, Inc., has on hand. If the owner wishes to have an existing
     plan modified, Homes, Inc., will make any modification that is
     sound. The owner can choose the colors and the shrubbery and the
     trees used in landscaping.

     If the owner prefers to do the decorating and/or the landscaping,
     Homes, Inc., will do the rest of the work and specify in the contract
     that these functions are to be performed by someone other than the
     builder.

     On April 16 Homes, Inc., signed a contract to build a house on a
     wooded lot for the Donald L. Kittrell family now living in Athens,
     Nebraska, about 400 miles away. The house was to be completed so
     that the family could move into it on September 1. Because of
     unusual weather conditions throughout most of the construction
     period, building progress has been slow. The Kittrells have sold
     their house in which they are residing and must move out of it by
     September 1.

To give the Kittrell family as much assurance as you can that the house will be ready for them on September 1 and to continue good public relations practices, Homes, Inc., sends the Kittrells periodic reports on the progress that is being made.

You learned yesterday, August 8, that enough carpeting has been shipped to carpet all the floors except two bedrooms. Carpeting for those rooms will be shipped to you so that you can lay it on August 29. Some of the wallpaper has been hung, and you have enough paper to finish the rest of the house except for the teenaged daughter's bedroom. The paper for her room is to arrive at your warehouse on September 6. You can hang it on September 7. The electrical wiring will be completed on August 22. The concrete walks have been poured. Some lighting fixtures have been installed; the others will be installed by August 27. The painting will be completed before August 26.

Before signing the contract, the Kittrells decided to do the landscaping themselves after they move into the house.

If you could receive the wallpaper for the one bedroom, you could have the house ready for occupancy on September 1. The Kittrells may prefer to choose another paper; yet they may prefer to have the paper hung in that room after they move into the house.

Write a letter report to Mr. Kittrell and bring him up to date on the situation. His address is 249 Woodland Drive, Athens, Nebraska 68001. As vice-president of Homes, Inc., sign the letter report.

8. Write a complete, clear set of instructions for the operation, care, and maintenance of some type of appliance or piece of equipment (an office machine, a household appliance, a lawn mower, or another item). Use headings and possibly some type of graphic that would help the user to follow your instructions.

9.   The manager of each department of the organization for which you work has been asked to prepare a procedures manual for his or her department. Assume you work in the personnel office, the purchasing office, the printing office, or the mailing department. Write a detailed description of a procedure you follow regularly to complete a particular task. Write the description so clearly that a new employee could follow the procedure without further instructions.

     This report will be combined with the others that are being prepared for the department manual.

10.  As assistant personnel director of your company, write a description of the fringe benefits your company provides to the 300 assembly-line employees and other factory workers. Use headings, examples, illustrations, and so on so that the information can be easily understood by each employee. Submit this well-organized, well-written report to the personnel director for approval before a brochure will be printed for distribution to the employees.

     Prepare a title page for your report and transmit it with a letter to the personnel director.

11.  Within fifteen months the Edenfield Insurance Company will move its headquarters to Farmingham, Illinois, a city of 3,500,000 residents. You know, of course, that the company has many office machines—typewriters, calculators, word processors, small computers, and so on. Also, you know the company has not yet contracted for maintenance service for its machines. As the owner of an efficient, reputable office machines service company, send a proposal to the president of the Edenfield Insurance Company and try to convince him to let you service his office machines. Describe the services you can provide, the frequency of service, the costs, and so on.

     Write a letter to transmit your proposal. The president's name is E. Carl Jarman. His address is 854 Euclaire Avenue, Copperfield, MN 55001.

12. James E. Preston has been city manager of Remington Falls, North Carolina—a city of some 100,000 residents—for three years. Since assuming this position, Mr. Preston, a forward-looking executive, has brought about numerous changes that have helped the people of Remington Falls. Under his leadership Remington Falls has experienced cultural, economic, and environmental improvements. Among the improvements have been the construction of a new drama center, the influx of several manufacturing organizations, and the installation of measures to minimize pollution.

Remington Falls has no city bus transportation system. Residents work in all parts of the city. A large number work in the industrial park, where seven factories are located; in the four major shopping districts; and in the downtown area, which has several office buildings, two hospitals, and several banks. The downtown area has a critical shortage of parking space, and the available space is expensive.

You have had much experience with bus transportation systems and could finance an efficient system for Remington Falls. Send a proposal to Mr. Preston and try to convince him to let you provide city bus service for Remington Falls. Write a letter to transmit your proposal. Mr. Preston's address is Municipal Building, Remington Falls, NC 28101.

# Chapter 16

# Formal Reports

Whether you write an informal report or a formal report is determined primarily by the occasion for which you are writing. Formal reports, like informal ones, may be written for people inside the organization or for those outside. Usually, your formal reports for internal use will go to your superiors in the organizational structure. These reports may likely provide your best opportunity to show your superiors how well you can perform. By writing high-quality reports, you have the satisfaction that comes from excellence in the performance of your duties; and continued good reporting helps win for you the confidence of your superiors. And remember, the business employees who write well have a distinct advantage over their peers who are equally well qualified except for the ability to write well. Put your best foot forward, therefore, and make your report thorough, concise, attractive, interesting, and easy to understand.

The writing style for formal reports is about the same as that for informal reports except that you do not use contractions and shortened forms such as *memo* for *memorandum*, *lab* for *laboratory*, and *steno* for *stenographer*. Also, first- and second-person pronouns such as *I, me*, and *you* are used sparingly in formal writing.

A thorough understanding of the conditions that led to the need for a report will help you to decide whether to write a formal report.

## ORGANIZATION

A formal business report consists of four major parts: preliminary pages, introductory section, presentation of data (body), and reference materials. These major parts may typically include the elements listed in the following outline:

I.   Preliminary pages*

    A.   Letter of transmittal
    B.   Title page
    C.   Table of contents
    D.   List of tables and/or illustrations**
    E.   Summary
    F.   Conclusions
    G.   Recommendations

II.  Introductory section

    A.   Statement of the purpose *or* Objective of the study
    B.   Description of the research method
    C.   Other introductory information

III. Presentation of the data***

    A.   Exposition
    B.   Graphics

IV.  Reference materials

    A.   Bibliography
    B.   Appendix

*May include a letter (or memorandum) of authorization for the report and a letter (or memorandum) of acceptance of the assignment.
**Frequently omitted.
***May be presented in one or more major divisions.

The elements of this outline are discussed in the order in which you would probably write them. Then at the end of this chapter a skeleton report is presented to illustrate the organization and the format of a formal analytical business report that contains these parts.

## Introduction

Write an introductory paragraph or so to attract the readers' attention and to encourage them to continue reading. Here is an example:

> The number of small businesses that use our computer services has increased rapidly since 1977. Even though we added two computers last year, our users keep the equipment operating twenty-four hours a day six days a week. Within the past three months, several of these computer users have inquired about word processing. They need word processing services, but they cannot justify purchasing the equipment required to produce letter-quality copy.
>
> Should we provide word processing services for these computer users?

If the readers are already familiar with the problem, include only a little background material. On the other hand, if many readers do not know about the problem, give a more detailed explanation; but keep the explanation short. Readers do not like to read a long introduction.

The introduction should lead naturally into the statement of the purpose *or* objective of the report.

**Statement of the purpose *or* Objective of the report.**   State the purpose *or* the objective of the report clearly so that the readers will easily understand what you are attempting to convey. One sentence is ordinarily best for this subdivision. In a few instances, however, additional sentences may be needed. Example:

> This study was made in 1984 to determine the feasibility of establishing a word processing center in the Cumberland Area.

**Elements of the problem.**   Some statements of the problem may be followed by a list of elements or factors from analyzing the problem statement. Examples follow:

To determine the feasibility of establishing a word processing center, answers to these questions were needed:

1. How many businesses would use the center?

2. For what kinds of work would they use it?

3. Would the center be used more heavily at some times than at others?

4. Where are most of the potential users of word processing services?

5. How many more transcribers would need to be hired?

6. How much would the equipment cost?

7. (Other questions would follow here.)

Questions asked in this section should be answered in the body of the report in the order in which they are asked.

**Definitions of terms.** When you have to use terms that have special meanings in a particular report, define those terms. For only one to three terms, define each one in parentheses immediately after it appears the first time in the report or use footnotes. Here are illustrations:

Sales in the Cumberland Area (Henson, Jackson, Stonewall, and Winston counties) increased by 12 percent in June.

Sales in the Cumberland Area* increased by 12 percent in June.

———————

*Henson, Jackson, Stonewall, and Winston counties

When you have several terms with special meanings, include a list such as this one:

The following terms are defined as they are used in this report:

*Cumberland Area*—Henson, Jackson, Stonewall, and Winston counties.

*Full-time employee*—a person who works at least thirty-two hours a week.

*Late shift*—from 10 a.m. until 6 p.m.

*Small business*—a business that has no more than eight employees and that has gross sales below $100,000 a year.

Use parallel structure for the definitions; that is, if one definition is a fragment, the others should be fragments. If one definition is a complete sentence, the others should be complete sentences.

**Research Method.** The extent to which you cover the procedures used in collecting and analyzing information for a formal report should be based on the desires of the readers and the nature of the report. In some nonroutine reports, you should describe the research method so clearly that if readers should question the validity of your findings, they could redo the research if they wanted to.

Some readers who know the researchers well and who are convinced their methods are sound prefer to have only a brief description of the research method. In such a case they would consider a detailed description a waste of time for the writers and for the readers.

When you question the degree of coverage to present, you may be wise to present somewhat more information than is necessary rather than to present less than is needed.

The following description of the research method for a report was adequate because the readers knew the writer was well qualified and was trustworthy:

> Kelly S. Hartman, director of our computing center, prepared a questionnaire (see Appendix) and mailed it to each of the 227 small businesses that have used our computing center since it was established in 1977. Within ten days, 216, or 95.15 percent, of the users returned a completed questionnaire. Seven of the computer center users that did not complete a questionnaire have merged with other organizations.
>
> The questionnaire responses were tabulated by computer, and the results are shown in graphics and narrative in this report.

**Scope and limitations.** For some formal reports, a paragraph or so may be needed to define the scope and to identify limitations. The scope sets the boundaries and may tell what *is not* included in the report as well as what *is* included. Factors such as a short time, a small sum of money available, and a minimum of existing information should be mentioned sometimes to let the readers know why the report is less comprehensive than they otherwise would expect it to be.

For many reports, the statement of the purpose *or* objective of the report makes the discussion of the scope and the limitations unnecessary.

## Presentation of Data

Having prepared the readers by writing a concise, relevant, thorough introduction, you are ready to present the information you have gathered. As was stated earlier, you may present the information through expository writing entirely or through a combination of expository writing and graphic aids and other illustrations—analogies, and so on. The facts, analyses, and interpretations in this section (the report body) serve as evidence that the purpose or objective of the report has been achieved.

The body of the report may be only one major division of the report, or it may be divided into two or more sections. In typical business reports, the main body of material is presented in a logical, a psychological, or a chronological plan.

**Logical.**　In the logical plan, which is used most frequently, major ideas are presented first with the details following. The information of lesser importance follows in descending order of importance. Spatial (discussing certain parts of an organization) and geographical can be considered as logical.

**Psychological.**　For the psychological plan, the information is presented according to the effect the facts are expected to have on the readers. The facts that will interest the readers most are presented first, and the facts the readers are likely to disagree with are placed last.

**Chronological.**　The chronological plan is best when the readers need to know what happened in a time sequence or what events took place that resulted in certain effects (cause to effect). Because this plan is the least interesting and does not emphasize the most important elements, readers have to work harder to interpret and understand the significant points.

For any plan, proper transition is needed for coherence and smooth reading. One way to achieve coherence (to relate ideas) is to use reference pronouns by making a statement and referring to it in the next sentence.

Example:

The trucks are in good condition. They were purchased last year.

Numbering items, as in the next illustration, leads the readers through a series of steps or ideas.

Most of the funds were spent on these steps: (1) testing, (2) drilling, and (3) blasting.

Transitional words or phrases such as *however, moreover, further, in addition, as a result, for that reason*, and *on the other hand* help readers to relate thoughts. Transitional words are best placed after the beginning of a sentence, however, unless they are emphatic. Here are examples:

They were revised, however, on July 1.

They will, therefore, order the Model 9.

For this reason, she chose the second one.

Good transition, carefully written sentences, well-constructed paragraphs, precise wording, appropriate headings, accurate documentation, and other details of the mechanics of writing help to make the information you present meaningful to the readers.

### Preliminary Pages

After you write the report body, write a summary, draw conclusions (when applicable), and make recommendations (when appropriate). Then prepare a title page, a contents page, a list of illustrations (when applicable), and a letter of transmittal.

**Summary.** Most readers want to see a summary of a long formal report before they read the entire report; and some of the readers read the summary, conclusions, and recommendations only.

In the summary, restate or paraphrase the statement of the purpose or the objective of the report and mention—but do not describe in detail—the procedures used. Include only the highlights of the report; and integrate these concisely worded statements for smooth, easy-to-understand reading. Do not include any information in the summary that is not included elsewhere in the report.

Here is an example of a report summary:

> A questionnaire was used to collect data to determine the feasibility of establishing a word processing center in the Cumberland Area. The most significant findings of that study follow:
>
> 1.   Seventy-nine small businesses would use a word processing center if it were available.
>
> 2.   The businesses would use the center primarily for making multiple copies of letters and memorandums; for mailing invoices and monthly statements; and for sending advertising pieces.
>
> 3.   At least 40 percent of the respondents would use the center daily; more people would use it the last two weeks of each month than at other times.
>
> 4.   (Other findings would follow here.)

To make the short summary appear to be shorter and therefore to encourage people to read it, single space it even though you may have double spaced the rest of the report.

**Conclusions.**   A conclusion is a statement of what a finding or a combination of findings means. To draw a conclusion, ask yourself, "What does this finding (or these findings) mean in relation to the purpose of the report?" By summarizing all the most significant findings of your study, you can base your conclusions on the information in the summary. Analyze all findings thoroughly and study all possible relationships that exist among them. On the basis of this thorough study, draw conclusions that are not only logical but also valid.

The following conclusion was drawn from the three findings in the preceding summary example:

> 1.   A sufficient demand exists to justify establishing a word processing center.
>
> 2.   (Other conclusions would follow here.)

Number the conclusions and single space them with a double space between them. A good idea is to draw conclusions as you analyze and present the information in the report body. By recording these conclusions somewhere, they do not escape your memory when preparing the conclusions section. Some writers record conclusions in the body of the report and repeat them in the conclusions section.

**Recommendations.**  ⸱Base your recommendations on the conclusions—and obviously on the findings—drawn from your study. When you make alternative recommendations, present them in the order of feasibility according to your best judgment. You would not be asked to make recommendations if the person who assigned the report did not believe you are capable of making them.

The following recommendations were based on the preceding conclusions:

1.  Establish a word processing center.

2.  (Other recommendations would follow here.)

Number the recommendations.

Present the summary, the conclusions, and the recommendations on one page when space permits.

**Contents page and list of graphic aids.**    Prepare a contents page, which shows the page number for each organizational heading and each first-degree subject-matter heading, to precede the report summary. Third-degree headings are usually omitted from the table of contents.

For a long report that contains several graphics, a list should follow—on the same page if space permits—the table of contents. When several tables and several other graphic aids are used, show both a list of tables and a list of figures. All figures besides formal tables should be in numerical order in one list (see the lists on the contents page of the skeleton report at the end of this chapter).

**Title page.**    Prepare an attractive, well-arranged title page to include the report title, the name of the person or the organization for whom the report was written, your name, and the date. Make the title concise and descriptive of the report contents and type it in all capitals. The report title and the statement of the purpose *or* objective of the report should contain the same information, but the wording should be different. The title is, in most instances, a phrase; whereas the statement of the purpose is a complete sentence.

Figure 16-1 is a title page example.

**Transmittal letter.**    Write a letter (or a memorandum) to transmit the report to the person for whom it was written. Identify the report and tell who authorized you to write it. The reactions of

**Figure 16-1**

ESTABLISHING A WORD PROCESSING CENTER

for

Mr. Kermit M. McWilliams

Vice-President, Office Services Co.

by

Wanda M. Seal

Administrative Assistant

June 1, 1984

some readers are usually affected by knowing who authorized you to write the report. For example, if a top-ranking official in the organization authorized it, the readers tend to realize quickly the need for the report.

You may mention a few of the most significant, the most surprising, or the most interesting findings; but do not clutter the letter by including many of them.

Although you should omit your opinions from the report body, you may include them in the transmittal letter if you wish. Your specific assignment, your knowledge of the situation, and your relationship with the readers will enable you to determine the extent to which you include opinions.

Apply the letter-writing guidelines in Chapter 3.

Figure 16-2 is an example of a transmittal memorandum.

### Reference Materials

Reference materials, which may include a bibliography and an appendix, follow the body of a formal business report. Review Chapter 13 for bibliography preparation.

Place in the appendix copies of questionnaires, checklists, and other instruments used in collecting data for the report. You may also place in the appendix such details as formulas and illustrations not essential to the report text. When you include several items, you may letter them Appendix A, Appendix B, and so on.

## FORMAT AND APPEARANCE

A good format not only provides for an attractive appearance, but it also contributes to readability and reader acceptance. Pay careful attention to stationery, spacing, pagination, color, and duplicating and binding.

### Stationery

Type your report on a good quality 8½ by 11-inch white bond paper. Paper of 20-pound weight and 25 percent rag content is excellent.

**Figure 16-2**

MEMORANDUM

TO:      Kermit M. McWilliams, Vice-President

FROM:    Wanda M. Seal, Administrative Assistant

DATE:    June 1, 1984

SUBJECT: Establishing a Word Processing Center

As you requested in a memorandum of May 1, I have made a study to determine the feasibility of establishing a word processing center in the
Cumberland Area.

At least seventy-nine small businesses need word processing services
immediately. Other respondents made comments that led me to believe
that about ten other businesses would use the center if it were available. I believe the high-quality service we have provided in data
processing has had a positive effect on the users.

Because of the enthusiastic responses of the questionnaire recipients,
completing this study has been a real joy.

I would be glad to discuss the report at any time you wish.

bfk

Use a typewriter that has clean type keys and a dark ribbon. Make neat corrections. A well-written, carefully typed report represents you well.

## Spacing

Ordinarily, formal reports are double spaced; though they may be single spaced. Leave top, bottom, and right side margins of about one inch. Use a 1½-inch left margin so that when the report is bound there is a 1-inch left margin and the lines appear to be centered horizontally on the page.

Indent the first line of each paragraph seven or eight spaces.

## Pagination

While no page number should appear on the title page, assign a number to it. Use lower-case Roman numerals for preliminary pages. Center the number horizontally on the fifth line from the bottom of the page. Use Arabic numerals for other pages. Center the number for the first page horizontally on the fifth line from the bottom of the page. For each of the other pages, type the number in the upper right corner five spaces from the top and at the right margin. Double space to the first line of the text (see Figure 16-3).

## Color

You can use color to enhance the appearance of your report and to highlight some points. By coloring graphics, you can complete them in less time than is required if you shade them. If your report is to be duplicated, make certain that the duplicator will reproduce satisfactorily the colors you use. Otherwise, shade the areas instead of coloring them.

If your typewriter has a two-color ribbon, you can easily use a special color for headings or for underlining.

## Duplicating and Binding

Use a duplicating method that produces neat, clear copies on a high-quality paper, and place the completed report in paper or plastic covers. Spiral binding is preferred. A spiral-bound report

**Figure 16-3**

ESTABLISHING A WORD PROCESSING CENTER

for

Mr. Kermit M. McWilliams

Vice-President, Office Services Co.

by

Wanda M. Seal

Administrative Assistant

June 1, 1984

**Figure 16-3 Continued:**

MEMORANDUM

TO:       Kermit M. McWilliams, Vice-President

FROM:     Wanda M. Seal, Administrative Assistant

DATE:     June 1, 1984

SUBJECT:  Establishing a Word Processing Center

As you requested in a memorandum of May 1, I have made a study to determine the feasibility of establishing a word processing center in the
Cumberland Area.

At least seventy-nine small businesses need word processing services
immediately.  Other respondents made comments that led me to believe
that about ten other businesses would use the center if it were available.  I believe the high-quality service we have provided in data
processing has had a positive effect on the users.

Because of the enthusiastic responses of the questionnaire recipients,
completing this study has been a real joy.

I would be glad to discuss the report at any time you wish.

bfk

ii

**Figure 16-3 Continued:**

MEMORANDUM

TO:        Wanda M. Seal, Administrative Assistant

FROM:      Kermit M. McWilliams, Vice-President

DATE:      May 1, 1984

SUBJECT:   Need for a Word Processing Center

. . . . . . . . . . . . . . . . . . . . . . . . . . . . . . . . . . . . .
. . . . . . . . . In this memorandum, Mr. McWilliams authorized . . . . . . .
. . . . . . Ms. Seal to study the need for a word process- . . . . . . .
. . . . . . ing center and to write a report.       . . . . . . .
. . . . . . . . . . . . . . . . . . . . . . . . . . . . . . . . . . . . .
. . . . . . . . . . . . . . . . . . . . . . . . . . . . . . . . . . . . .

tec

iii

**Figure 16-3 Continued:**

CONTENTS

GRAPHICS

1. (Graphic titles would be typed in upper- and lower-case
   letters with the same words as in the graphic titles
   themselves.) . . . . . . . . . . . . . . . . . . . . . . . .

iv

**Figure 16-3 Continued:**

Summary

A questionnaire was used to collect data to determine the feasibility of establishing a word processing center in the Cumberland Area. The most significant findings of that study follow:

1. Seventy-nine small businesses would use a word processing center if it were available.

2. The businesses would use the center primarily for making multiple copies of letters and memorandums, for mailing invoices and monthly statements, and for sending advertising pieces.

3. At least 40 percent of the respondents would use the center daily; more people would use it the last two weeks of each month than at any other time.

4. (Other findings would follow here.)

Conclusions

These conclusions were drawn from the findings of this study:

1. A sufficient demand exists to justify establishing a word processing center.

2. (Other conclusions would follow here.)

Recommendations

The following recommendations are based on the conclusions drawn from this study:

1. Establish a word processing center.

2. (Other recommendations would follow here.)

v

**Figure 16-3 Continued:**

ESTABLISHING A WORD PROCESSING CENTER

<u>Orientation</u>

The number of small businesses that use our computer services has increased rapidly since 1977.  Even though we added two computers last year, our users keep the equipment operating twenty-four hours a day six days a week.  Within the past three months, several of these computer users have inquired about word processing.  They need word processing services, but they cannot justify purchasing the equipment required to produce letter-quality copy.

Should we provide word processing services for those computer users?

<u>Statement of the Problem</u>

This study was made in 1984 to determine the feasibility of establishing a word processing center in the Cumberland Area.

<u>Factors of the Study</u>

To determine the feasibility of establishing a word processing center, answers to these questions were needed:

1.  How many businesses would use the center?

2.  For what kinds of work would they use it?

3.  Would the center be used more heavily at some times than at others?

4.  Where are most of the potential users of word processing services?

5.  How many more transcribers would have to be hired?

1

**Figure 16-3 Continued:**

2

6.  How much would the necessary equipment cost?

7.  (Other questions would follow here.)

Definitions of Terms

The following terms are defined as they are used in this report:

Cumberland Area--Henson, Jackson, Stonewall, and Winston counties

Full-time employee--a person who works at least thirty-two hours a week

Late shift--from 10 a.m. until 6 p.m.

Small business--a business that has no more than eight employees and has gross sales below $100,000 a year

Research Method

Kelly S. Hartman, Director of our computer center, prepared a questionnaire (see Appendix) and mailed it to each of the 227 small businesses that have used our computing center since it was established in 1977.  Within ten days 216, or 95.15 percent, of the users returned a completed questionnaire.  Seven of the computer center users that did not complete a questionnaire have merged with other organizations.

The questionnaire responses were tabulated by computer, and the results are shown in graphics and narrative in this report.

Word Processing Activities

. . . . . . . . . . . . . . . . . . . . . . . . . . . . . . . . . .

. . . . . .   The body of the report would begin here.  The    . . . . .
              information collected from potential users would
. . . . . .   be presented in this division of the report.     . . . . .

. . . . . .   The questions in the Factors of the Study section . . . . .
              would be answered in the order in which they were
. . . . . .   asked in the introductory section.                . . . . .

. . . . . . . . . . . . . . . . . . . . . . . . . . . . . . . . . .

. . . . . . . . . . . . . . . . . . . . . . . . . . . . . . . . . .

**Figure 16-3 Continued:**

                                                                      3

. . . . . . . . . . . . . . . . . . . . . . . . . . . . . . . . . . . .
. . . . . .   In the introductory paragraphs of this division,   . . . . .
              the second-degree headings would be introduced
. . . . . .   (possibly paraphrased).                            . . . . .

. . . . . . . . . . . . . . . . . . . . . . . . . . . . . . . . . . . . .
. . . . . . . . . . . . . . . . . . . . . . . . . the probable users, the
kinds of work they would do, the times they would use the center, and the
location of the users.

Probable Users

. . . . . . . . . . . . . . . . . . . . . . . . . . . . . . . . . . .
. . . . . .   Although you would not always see a graphic under   . . . . .
              each heading, one is shown under the first three
. . . . . .   headings in this skeleton report merely to show     . . . . .
              how they may likely be arranged on a page.
. . . . . . . . . . . . . . . . . . . . . . . . . . . . . . . . . . . . .
. . . . . . . . . . . . . . . . . . . . . .

. . . . . . . . . . . . . . . . . . . . . . . . . . . . . . . . . . . . .
. . . . . . .   Seventy-nine businesses, as shown in Figure 1 on the next
page, indicated a need for a word processing center.

. . . . . . . . . . . . . . . . . . . . . . . . . . . . . . . . . . . . .
. . . . . .   Because Figure 1 would require more space than is   . . . . .
              available on this page, it would appear at the
. . . . . .   top of the next page.  The interpretation of the   . . . . .
              graphic would begin here and would continue after
. . . . . .   the graphic is presented.                          . . . . .
. . . . . . . . . . . . . . . . . . . . . . . . . . . . . . . . . . . . .
. . . . . . . . . . . . . . . .[1]
. . . . . . . . . . . . . . . . . . . . . . . . . . . . . . . . . . . . .
. . . . . . . . . . . . . . . . . . . . . . . . . . . . . . . . . . . . .
. . . . . . . . . . . . . . . . . . . . . . .

_____

[1]Richard D. Grayson, Word Processing in the 1980's (Montgomery:
Stanford Publishing Company, 1984), p. 18.

**Figure 16-3 Continued:**

4

FIGURE 1

Figure 1 would be presented here.

. . . . . . . . . . . . . . . . . . . . . . . . . . . . . . . .
. . . . . . . . . . . . . . . . . . . . . . . . . . . . . . . .
. . . . . . . . . . . . . . . . . . . . . .

Kinds of Work

The kinds of work for which a word processing center would be used

are shown in Figure 2 on page 5.

. . . . . . . . . . . . . . . . . . . . . . . . . . . . . . .
. . . . . . Figure 2 would take up the whole next page.  The    . . . . .
. . . . . . interpretation of Figure 2 would be completed on
. . . . . . this page.                                          . . . . .
. . . . . . . . . . . . . . . . . . . . . . . . . . . . . . . .
. . . . . . . . . . . . . . . . . . . . . . . . . . . . . . . .
. . . . . . . . . . . . . . . . . . . . . . . . . . . . . . . .
. . . . . . . . . . . . . . . . . . . . . .
. . . . . . . . . . . . . . . . . . . . . . . . . . . . . . . .
. . . . . . . . . . . . . . . . . . . . . . . . . . . . . . . .
. . . . . . . . . . . . . . . . . . . . . . . . . . . . . . . .
. . . . . . . . . . . . . . . . . . . . . . . . . . . . . . . .
. . . . . . . . . . . . . . . . . . . . . . . . . . . . . . . .
. . . . . . . . . . . . . . . . . . . . .

**Figure 16-3 Continued:**

5

FIGURE 2

Figure 2 would take up the whole page.

**Figure 16-3 Continued:**

6

Time of Use

. . . . . . . . . . . . . . . . . . . . . . . . . . . . . . . . .
. . . . . . . The first ten days of each month would be the busiest time
for a word processing center (see Figure 3).

Figure 3 would be presented here.

. . . . . . . . . . . . . . . . . . . . . . . . . . . . . . . . .
. . . . . . Figure 3 would be interpreted here. . . . . . . . . . .
. . . . . . . . . . . . . . . . . . . . . . . . . . . . . . . . .
. . . . . . . . . . . . . . . . . . . . .[2]

User Location

. . . . . . . . . . . . . . . . . . . . . . . . . . . . . . . . .
. . . . . . No graphic is used under the heading User Location. . . . .
. . . . . . . . . . . . . . . . . . . . . . . . . . . . . . . . .
. . . . . . . . . . . . . . . . . . .
. . . . . . . . . . . . . . . . . . . . . . . . . . . . . . . . .
. . . . . . . . . . . . . . . . . . . . . . . . . . . . . . . . .
. . . . . . . . . . . . . . .[3]

---

[2]Jennifer A. Jones, Time-Sharing (Wellington: Harris Publishing
Company, 1983), p. 71.

[3]Robert E. McDonald, Artificial Intelligence (Harrisonville: Ray
Publishing Company, 1984), p. 364.

**Figure 16-3 Continued:**

Facility Requirements

. . . . . . . . . . . . . . . . . . . . . . . . . . . . . . . . . . . . . . . . .

. . . . . . The body of a report may be divided into parts.  . . . . . .
The second part of the body of this skeleton
. . . . . . report would begin here.           . . . . . .

. . . . . . In the introductory paragraphs of this division, . . . . . .
the second-degree headings would be introduced
. . . . . . (possibly paraphrased).           . . . . . .

. . . . . . . . . . . additional transcribers, cost of the equipment, and

(other headings).


Transcribers

    . . . . . . . . . . . . . . . . . . . . . . . . . . . . . . . . . . . . . .

. . . . . . . . . . . . . . . . . . . . . . . . . . . . . . . . . . . . . . .

. . . . . . . . . . . . . . . . . . . . . . . . . . . . . . . . . . . . . . .

. . . . . . . . . . . . . . . . . . . . . . . . . . . .

    . . . . . . . . . . . . . . . . . . . . . . . . . . . . . . . . . . . . . .

. . . . . . . . . . . . . . . .


Equipment Cost

    . . . . . . . . . . . . . . . . . . . . . . . . . . . . . . . . . . . . . .

. . . . . . . . . . . . . . . . . . . . . . . . . . . . . . . . . . . . . . .

. . . . Harbin, a nationally known expert said:

        . . . . . . . . . . . . . . . . . . . . . . . . . . . . . . .
    . . . . A verbatim quotation of four lines or more
    . . . . appears here single spaced and indented four   . . . . . . .
    . . . . spaces from the left margin.           . . . . . . .
. . . . . . . . . . . . . . . . . . . . . . . . . . . . . . . . . . . . .
. . . . . . . . . . . . . . . . .4

        . . . . . . . . . . . . . . . . . . . . . . . . . . . . . . . . . .

. . . . . . . . . . . . . . . . . . . . . . . . . . . . . . . . . . . . . . .

─────────────────
    4Walter T. Harbin, Equipment Economy (Billings:  Georgetown
Publishing Company, 1984), p. 276.

**Figure 16-3 Continued:**

8

. . . . . . . . . . . . . . . . . . . . . . . . . . . . . . . . . . . . .
. . . . . . . . . . . . . . . . . . . . . .

(Other Headings)

. . . . . . . . . . . . . . . . . . . . . . . . . . . . . . . . . . .
. . . . . . Note that the footnote on this partial page   . . . . . . .
       appears two lines below the last line of text.
. . . . . . . . . . . . . . . . . . . . . . . . . . . . . . . . . . . .
. . . . . . . . . . . . . . . . . .[5]

_____

[5]Thomas R. Moon, Information Retrieval in the Modern Office
(Lineville:  Hamilton Publishers, Inc., 1984), p. 74.

**Figure 16-3 Continued:**

9

References

*Dspace* → Grayson, Richard D. _Word Processing in the 1980's_. Montgomery: Stanford
Publishing Company, 1984.

Harbin, Walter T. _Equipment Economy_. Billings: Georgetown Publishing
Company, 1984.

Jones, Jennifer A. _Time-Sharing_. Wellington: Harris Publishing Company,
1983.

McDonald, Robert E. _Artificial Intelligence_. Harrisonville: Ray Publishing Company, 1984.

Moon, Thomas R. _Information Retrieval in the Modern Office_. Lineville:
Hamilton Publishers, Inc., 1984.

**Figure 16-3 Continued:**

10

Appendix

. . . . . . . . . . . . . . . . . . . . . . . . . . . . . . . . . . . . . . .

. . . . . .  This appendix would include a copy of the ques-   . . . . .
             tionnaire that was used and other helpful infor-
. . . . . .  mation such as statistical formulas that some of   . . . . .
             the readers may want to study.

. . . . . .                                                      . . . . .
             If several items are included in the appendix,
. . . . . .  they may be labeled Appendix A, Appendix B, and    . . . . .
             so on.

. . . . . . . . . . . . . . . . . . . . . . . . . . . . . . . . . . . . .

can be handled easily, and it can be opened so that minimum space is required for displaying any page. If facilities for spiral binding are not available, use a loose-leaf cover.

## SAMPLE REPORTS

To illustrate the format features described in this chapter, a skeleton report is shown in Figure 16-3.

## USAGE

In business, formal reports are written much less frequently than are informal ones. Your learning to write good formal reports can, however, prepare you to meet some needs and can enhance your chances for recognition that can lead to professional advancement.

## QUESTIONS FOR DISCUSSION

1.  Why should the summary section be placed *before* rather than *after* the body of a formal report?

2.  What are some other shortened forms of words such as *lab* for *laboratory* and *memo* for *memorandum*?

3.  What are some appropriate ways to include definitions of specialized terms in a formal business report?

## EXERCISES

Improve the follow sentences.

1.  The form was returned by Mrs. Strickland.

2.  It is the purpose of this report to show reasons for product changes.

3.  After making an analyzation of the data, the assistant manager decided to recommend a change.

4.   The plant manager, who is a well-known speaker, will conduct the seminar.

5.   The report was written by my assistant.

6.   We are looking forward to making the survey.

7.   She mailed you a check in the amount of $257.

8.   The shipment was accepted by the clerk.

9.   The computer was installed for the purpose of increasing efficiency.

10.   Please send me a copy of the book entitled *Management Concepts* that was written by H.R. Sloan.

## PROBLEMS

1.   Write a formal report on a problem in your major field of study or on a problem that affects you at school (library hours, parking facilities, or others). Use both primary and secondary data.

2.   A group of local businessmen operate several small businesses, and they hire many college students. Those men are considering the possibilities of establishing two more businesses—a janitorial service and a recreation area in a mall that is near your school. They have asked you to study the feasibility of opening one of these businesses (either one you choose). Assume you have conducted the study (use fictitious information) and write a good report. Write a letter to transmit this report to one of the men. You know his name and address.

3.   Study the reading habits of a sample of the students in your business school, college, or department and present your findings in a short formal report. Write a letter to transmit this report to your instructor.

4.   Study thoroughly the registration process used in your college or university. Then write a formal report in which you recommend ways to improve the registration process.

## CASES

### 1.    Association of Word Processors

The Association of Word Processors was organized seven years ago. The purpose of the organization is to help the members keep abreast of new developments in word processing—technological developments, applications of these developments, and the status of word processing systems—and to share problems encountered by members of word processing systems. Although membership is open to anyone who is interested in joining the organization, most of the members are managers of word processing systems. All regions of the country are represented by the current membership.

A twenty-member board of directors includes three members from each of the Eastern, Southern, Midwestern, and Western regions; three at-large members; and a president, a president-elect, a vice-president, a secretary, and a treasurer, who make up the executive board.

The organization publishes a quarterly newsletter and holds an annual three-day convention. The conventions are held in various parts of the country. The committees who choose the convention sites try to accommodate the membership by varying the locations of the conventions and by choosing sites that have suitable, economical facilities.

As chairman of the Site Selection Committee for next year's convention, you have been asked to recommend to the president one of three hotels. The three other members of your committee collected the following information on these three hotels: Sheridan Hotel in Longview, Nevada; Winkler Hotel in Richmond, Colorado; and Broadacres Hotel in Princeton, Kansas.

#### Sheridan Hotel

400 bedrooms available. $49 single, $57 double, $63 triple. Three 3-room suites free for officers if 175 bedrooms are reserved. Two 3-room suites free if 150 bedrooms are reserved. One 3-room suite free if 125 bedrooms are reserved.

Eight meeting rooms available. Four seat fifty each conference style or seventy-five theater style. Four seat thirty each conference style or forty-five theater style. Two banquet rooms that seat 100 each. Exhibit area available for thirty to fifty exhibit booths between registration area and the entrance to two meeting rooms—one large meeting room and one small meeting room.

Three 8-foot tables, one electric typewriter, six chairs, cash box available without charge for registration.

Limousine service to and from airport $8 each way. Ample parking space in indoor parking area $2.75 a day.

Available for rental:   overhead projectors $5 a day; screens $2 a day; film projectors $11 a day; slide projectors $6 a day; tape recorders $4 a day.

Dining facilities include a coffee shop, two restaurants, two bars—live music—and several other restaurants and cafeterias within a few blocks of the hotel.

### Winkler Hotel

250 bedrooms available. $49 single, $53 double, $60 triple, $8 for rollaway bed. Three two-room suites free for officers if 200 bedrooms are reserved. One two-room suite free if 175 bedrooms are reserved.

Tours of city can be arranged if at least twenty people are interested for $12.50 for four-hour tour and $20 for six-hour tour to include lunch in a downtown restaurant.

Three 8-foot tables, six chairs, and a cash box available free for registration. Electric typewriter can be rented for $7.50 a day and calculator for $4.50 a day.

Limousine service to and from airport $8 each way. Ample parking space is available in nearby city-operated parking lots. Rates are from $1.75 to $3.25 a day.

Dining facilities include a coffee shop, one bar, two restaurants—and several other restaurants and cafeterias within a few blocks of the hotel.

Check-out time 12 noon.

Eight meeting rooms available. Three seat fifty each conference style or seventy-five theater style. Three seat forty each conference style or sixty theater style. Two seat thirty each conference style or forty-five theater style.

Hotel is only five blocks from the bus terminal.

### Broadacres Hotel

Six meeting rooms are available. Three seat forty each conference style or fifty-five theater style. One seats sixty conference style or eighty theater stye. Two seat eighty each conference style or one hundred theater style.

350 bedrooms available. $51 single, $57 double, $60 triple, $8 for rollaway bed. One three-room suite available for organization president if at least eighty bedrooms are reserved.

Check-out time is 12 noon.

Tours of the city can be arranged especially for the convention. Regularly scheduled tours are available. Three theaters are nearby for outstanding plays the year round.

Three 8-foot tables, six chairs, and a bulletin board are free for use in registering guests. An electric typewriter can be rented for $8 a day and a calculator for $7.50.

Limousine service to and from the airport is $8 each way. Ample parking space is available for $2.75 a day. This indoor parking is provided by the hotel.

Dining facilities include a coffee shop, three restaurants, a bar—live music—and several other restaurants and cafeterias within a few blocks of the hotel.

The exhibit area is available for twenty to forty exhibitors. This area is on the second floor. The registration area and the three small meeting rooms are on the third floor.

Projectors and screens are available. Screens, $2 a day; projectors, $6-$11 a day.

The banquet room seats seventy-eight people. Banquet meals from $15.00 to $17.50, lunch $6.25 to $9.00, and breakfast $4.95 to $7.50.

Hotel is within six blocks of the bus terminal.

For the past six annual meetings, the attendance has ranged from 160 to 214. The president of your organization has estimated that this year's attendance will be within that range. Because of the locations of these facilities, the air fare and the mileage would be about the same for all of them for most of the poeple who will attend.

Usually, only about a third of the people who attend this annual convention bring members of their families with them.

You can expect to have thirty exhibitors at the convention.

Organize the applicable data your three committee members have sent to you and send a well-written formal report to the association president. His address is P.O. Box 176, White Sands, UT 84085. Recommend one of the three hotels for the annual convention, which is scheduled for November 12-14. The president's name is Huland E. Harding.

Requirements for your formal report:

1. Title page.
2. Letter of transmittal
3. Contents page and list of figures (graphics)
4. Summary, conclusions, and recommendation—a single-spaced page (or pages) preceding the report body, which is double spaced.
5. Statement of purpose
6. Procedures (research method)
7. Body to include paragraphs supported by one or more of these graphics:

    a.    Text table
    b.    Formal table
    c.    Other graphic (map, pie chart, bar chart, or line chart)

## 2.   The McKinsey Company

The McKinsey Company has been manufacturing sporting goods—tennis rackets, nets, and balls; basketballs and uniforms; footballs; baseball bats, gloves, and uniforms; badminton rackets, nets, and shuttlecocks; and so on—in your city since 1946. The company began as a manufacturer of basketball and baseball uniforms and employed about eighty people. The production work and the administrative and clerical jobs were performed in a small two-story building. As the company increased the quantity and the variety of the items it produced, it grew so that this year 794 people are employed. Two hundred seventy-eight of the people are white-collar workers; 516 are blue-collar workers.

As the years have gone by, additions have been made to the original building, new buildings have been added, and up-to-date equipment and machines have been installed. Some degree of automation is evident in production and in paperwork. The production is accomplished in five separate buildings; and, of course, some paperwork and some administrative or managerial functions are accomplished in these buildings. Almost all the paperwork and the managerial or administrative functions are completed in a three-story, former factory building that was renovated eight years ago and is used exclusively by the 278 white-collar workers. This building houses the computers, the word processors, and other electrical and electronic office appliances. An electrical heating and air-conditioning unit is used for this building only. The two elevators are at the north and the south ends of the building.

Although the McKinsey Company has maintained a good record of safety throughout the years, several accidents (most were minor, but a few were major) have occurred in the factory and in the offices. To continue with this good record, the company makes a special study from time to time to assess the existing conditions, to study safety regulations, and to take steps desirable for employee protection.

The time has come for you to make this thorough study. Describe the existing conditions; relate them to government regulations; and recommend action to be taken to provide a safe, healthful, efficient environment for the white-collar workers. Write a letter to transmit your well-written report to Timothy E. Drake, your immediate superior.

# PART FOUR

# WORD PROCESSING

# Chapter 17

# Dictation and Word Processing

Because written messages play an important role in modern-day business transactions, management pays close attention to economy and efficiency in processing these messages. Up-to-date word processing systems have become widely used, therefore, within the past several years. Even so, written messages are expensive. The factor that contributes most to the high cost of written messages is the salary of the composer; next is the salary of the transcriber. These two people work as a team. As an executive, you can reduce costs, save yourself and the transcriber time and frustration, and increase the efficiency of your organization by dictating well.

Having studied the preceding chapters of this book, you are ready to learn to dictate. Among the messages you will dictate are letters, memorandums, reports, oral presentations, and instructions for employees.

## POINTERS FOR BEGINNERS

To dictate well, learn to write well. When you dictate a message, use the same guidelines and style of expression you would use if you were writing it. If you have had very little experience in writing business messages, prepare a rough draft and then revise it so that it is properly organized and properly worded. This process of writing and then rewriting helps you to become adept in preparing effective messages.

As a beginning dictator, you can benefit by reading to a stenographer or to a recording machine the messages you have written and revised. This exercise helps you to become accustomed to the dictating process and to become well acquainted with a recording machine if you use one. Reading your written message also helps you to develop the self-confidence needed to dictate well. If a machine is available, record the practice dictation so that you can play it back to hear how you sound. Listening to your recorded dictation helps you to improve your speaking ability and thus enhance your dictation skills.

## RECORDING MEDIUMS

You may dictate to a stenographer or to a machine. Each medium of recording has advantages the other does not have.

### Stenographer

Stenographers recorded dictation long before recording machines were invented, and they still record dictation for some people. Because some executives are accustomed to dictating to stenographers, they feel more at ease when talking to a person than to a machine. They, therefore, tend to relax and to compose messages that are conversational in tone and style. Here are other advantages to dictating to a stenographer:

1.    No dictation equipment has to be acquired and maintained.

2.    The dictation can be recorded at any location.

3.   The composer does not have to operate a machine.

4.   The composer and the transcriber can conveniently discuss the transactions to which the message applies.

## Machine

Using a machine for recording dictation has numerous advantages. Here are some:

1.   The machine can be used when the transcriber is not present (at night, on weekends, and so on).

2.   Only one person is tied up at one time.

3.   Dictation can be given at any speed.

4.   The message or any part of it can be played back instantly.

5.   The transcription is faster.

6.   Any typist can transcribe the dictation.

7.   More people are available who can transcribe efficiently from machine dictation than can write shorthand and transcribe it well.

You can use a machine efficiently for jobs other than recording messages to be transcribed. You can, for example, record instructions and work assignments to be listened to later by the transcriber. Executives frequently use machines for giving instructions at night and on weekends as well as during the usual workday.

A recording machine can be a part of a word processing center, a facility that is discussed later in this chapter and in Chapter 18.

## DICTATING EFFICIENCY

Learn to dictate efficiently. Schedule most, or possibly all, of the day's dictation for a particular time. Generally, the dictation period should begin as soon as you have collected the required information and have made the necessary decisions for replying to the correspondence received that day. Dictate the replies and other messages during the same period. Often, office work requires that another time during the day be scheduled for dictation; but the earlier the dictation can be given, the better the chances are of getting your messages in the mail that day.

Efficient dictating contributes to efficient transcribing. No matter how carefully a message has been organized and worded, it is of value only when it reaches the intended reader. As you dictate, therefore, do so in a way that makes transcription quick and easy. By dictating so that the message can be transcribed easily, you not only make the message more effective by getting it to the reader within a short time, but you also help reduce the cost.

Careful dictation increases the accuracy as well as the speed of transcription. Just as the message is of no value until it is delivered, it is of no value if it contains certain types of errors. In fact, some errors make the message a liability instead of an asset. Errors in amounts and dates often lead to confusion, embarrassment, and inconvenience. Incorrect spelling and improper choices of words that have similar sounds sometimes create comical situations. These situations could be tolerated and even appreciated, perhaps, if they did not require further correspondence, thus leading to delays and greater expense for both the sender and the receiver.

Here are suggestions, which are discussed in later paragraphs, for you to follow *before*, *during*, and *after* dictating so that you can produce good messages efficiently.

**Before.**   Before you begin to dictate:

1.   Collect the information needed for the message.

2.   Jot down notes in the margins or on slips of paper so that you will include all the information you intend to include.

3. Verify the accuracy of dates and other figures.

4. If you use a machine, make the necessary control adjustments for good recording.

5. Identify yourself when dictating to a word processing center or to any machine that is used by more than one transcriber.

6. Specify the type of message—letter, memo, formal report, and so on.

7. Tell how many copies to prepare and the kind of stationery to use.

8. Say whether to type a rough draft or a mailable copy.

**During.**   As you dictate:

1. Number the messages to which you reply; and after completing the dictation, give them to the transcriber so that names and addresses can be copied.

2. When dictating to a machine, hold the microphone about two or three inches from your lips and do not turn away from it.

3. Dictate in a conversational tone.

4. Pronounce *all* words—especially plural and past-tense sounds—*clearly* and *slowly* enough that the stenographer or the transcriber can hear them well.

5. Dictate numbers in groups rather than individually.

6. Spell proper names that cannot be copied from the messages you give to the transcriber.

7. Spell unusual or technical terms and words that sound alike.

8. Supply the punctuation marks for special or unusually difficult situations.

9.   Dictate simple tabulations, but hand a copy of complex tabulations to the transcriber so that they can be copied.

10.   When you need to give special instructions during the dictation, give a signal to let the stenographer or the transcriber know these instructions are not part of the message to be transcribed.

11.   Play back the dictation or ask the stenographer to read back when necessary.

12.   When using a machine, stop it when you pause.

13.   When using a machine, correct the errors you make; or indicate their presence so that the transcriber can correct them easily.

14.   At the end of a message, dictate the names of people to receive copies of the message.

15.   When using a machine, indicate the end of the message so that the transcriber can determine its length.

**After.**   After you dictate:

1.   Make the disc, tape, or other medium available to the transcriber when you use a machine.

2.   Supply any enclosures mentioned in the message.

3.   Proofread the typed copy.

4.   Sign the typed copy.

Careful preparation, dictation, and follow-up lead to dictating efficiency.

## Collection of Information

Before you begin dictating a message, collect whatever information you need for it. You may need to take one or more of these steps:

1.  Read correspondence in the files.

2.  Talk with fellow workers.

3.  Make one or more telephone calls.

4.  Secure information from a computing center or make calculations at your desk.

5.  Look at a calendar to verify dates (*very important*).

You may have to take still further steps to gather some of the information.

## Outlines

Enhance the effectiveness of your dictation by jotting down notes (dates, names, addresses, arithmetic computations, and other details) so that you will not have to stop dictating to find this information. You can easily record notes of these items on a scratch pad or in the margin of the letter you are answering. You may also record brief notes (one word may be enough to remind you of much data) about extraneous information such as a sales pitch or a special goodwill paragraph so that you will remember to include it in the letter.

The letter in Figure 17-1 was dictated from the following notes that were written on a scratch pad.

## Figure 17-1

**RONALD MANUFACTURING COMPANY, INC.**

P. O. BOX 748
RICHMOND, CO 81432

March 28, 1988

Mr. Harold M. Cunningham
Manager, Gold Office Supply Co.
1145 Grandview Road
Billings, UT 84512

DEMONSTRATION OF APPLIANCES

When could you demonstrate your copier, dictating machines, and
automatic typewriter for our office staff?  When Mr. Ed Reeves
was here last week, he said I should write you at least three
weeks before the demonstration is to be given.  Any Tuesday or
Thursday afternoon before June 1 would be a good time for us.

We expect to replace some office appliances late this summer and
would like to see your new models before we decide what to buy.

May we hear from you soon.

*Helen A. Turner*
HELEN A. TURNER, ASSISTANT MANAGER

trm

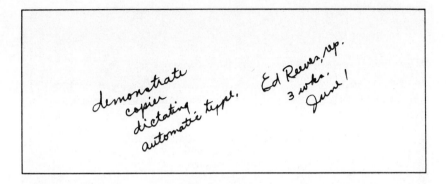

The notes in the margin of the letter in Figure 17-1 were suffi-cient for dictating the letter in Figure 17-2.

List your notes in the same order that you want to present them in the message. This informal outline not only serves as a reminder to include all the information you want to include, but it also helps you to organize it well. For simple routine letters, though, notes are not needed by an experienced dictator.

For the most difficult letters, you may need to prepare a detailed outline. As is true for other activities, a person's depending on a form of support is largely a habit. Use as your support for dic-tating whatever outline best suits the occasion for which you are composing the message, but cultivate the habit of dictating mostly from notes that serve only as a cue.

## Machine Requirements

Consult a manual or a manufacturer's representative for com-plete instructions for operating your machine. Before you dictate, make whatever adjustments are required for the particular machine you are using. These adjustments include turning the machine on; setting the controls for the desired tone and volume; and inserting the disc, tape, or other medium on which the dicta-tion is recorded. You also have to manipulate machine controls to: (1) play back any portion of the dictation you wish to hear, (2) make changes and corrections or to indicate corrections the transcriber is to make, and (3) mark the end of a message so that the transcriber can determine its length. To indicate accurate length, stop the machine when you pause during dictation.

**Figure 17-2**

*Gold Office Supply Co.*
1145 Grandview Road
Billings, VT 84512

March 30, 1987

Ms. Helen A. Turner, Assistant Manager
Ronald Manufacturing Company, Inc.
P. O. Box 748
Richmond, CO 81432

Bob Greene, one of our salesmen, will demonstrate our
copier, dictating machines, and automatic typewriter
for your staff at 2 p.m. on Thursday, April 23.  He
will come to your office at twelve o'clock to set up
the demonstration.

Thank you for inviting us to show you these machines.

*Bill Ford*
William E. Ford
Manager

hrt

If two or more persons use the same machine for dictation, identify yourself before dictating *anything*.

After recording the dictation, make the disc, tape, or other medium on which the dictation is recorded available to the transcriber. The way this step is taken depends on the procedure that is best for the particular situation in which you work.

## Names and Addresses

Although many people dislike their first or their middle name, most of us like our last name; and we like to hear it and see it fairly often provided it is pronounced properly and spelled correctly. Numerous names that have identical pronunciations are spelled differently. Here are examples:

| | |
|---|---|
| Boling | Bowling |
| Clark | Clarke |
| DeMent | Dement |
| Gray | Grey |
| Lee | Leigh |
| Lewis | Louis |
| Liles | Lyles |
| McDonald | MacDonald |
| Myer | Meyer |
| Noles | Knowles |
| Reese | Reece |
| Way | Wey |

Other names are similar although they are pronounced and spelled differently. Here are some:

| | |
|---|---|
| Daniel | Daniels |
| Herren | Herring |
| Johnson | Johnston |
| Moyer | Moyers |
| Roberson | Robertson |
| Woodard | Woodward |

Still other names such as *Elise* and *Elsie* are spelled similarly but do not sound alike. Take special care to see that the transcriber spells correctly each name you dictate.

When you dictate a reply to a letter, you can be certain the transcriber knows the correct spelling of the addressee's name if you hand the transcriber the letter you are answering. The name and the address can then be copied from that letter. This practice helps to reduce the time required for dictating replies.

To save time when replying to correspondence, number the messages (1, 2, 3, and so on) in the upper left-hand corner as in Figure 17-3; and as you begin a message, just dictate the number you have assigned and follow that number by the salutation and the message. After dictating all replies, give the transcriber the letters you have numbered so that the names and addresses can be copied.

When a typewritten copy of the name and address is not readily available for copying, dictate the information. Enunciate clearly and dictate slowly enough for a stenographer to write the names in longhand. Whether you dictate to a stenographer or to a machine, *spell* any name that is spelled differently from the way the transcriber is accustomed to spelling a name with an identical or a similar sound. For example, spell W-r-a-y if the transcriber is accustomed to spelling R-a-y; and spell J-o-n if the transcriber is accustomed to spelling J-o-h-n.

### Knowledge of Content

The way for you to dictate is affected specifically by the transcriber's understanding of the terms used and the content and background of the message. When the transcriber is familiar with these factors, you can afford to dictate rapidly. Even if you should enunciate less clearly than usual, the transcriber could probably transcribe accurately. When, on the other hand, the transcriber is not familiar with these factors, take special care to enunciate clearly and take the time to spell the more difficult, technical terms and those that sound alike.

One executive who was helping to eradicate mosquitoes from the region in which he lived dictated in one of his letters, "We have had *anopheles* mosquitoes in this area for a long time." The transcriber, who had little knowledge of the problem, transcribed, "We have had *enough of these* mosquitoes in this area for a long time." While the word *anopheles* seemed to be an ordinary word to the executive, his assuming it was familiar to the transcriber made retyping the letter necessary.

**Figure 17-3**

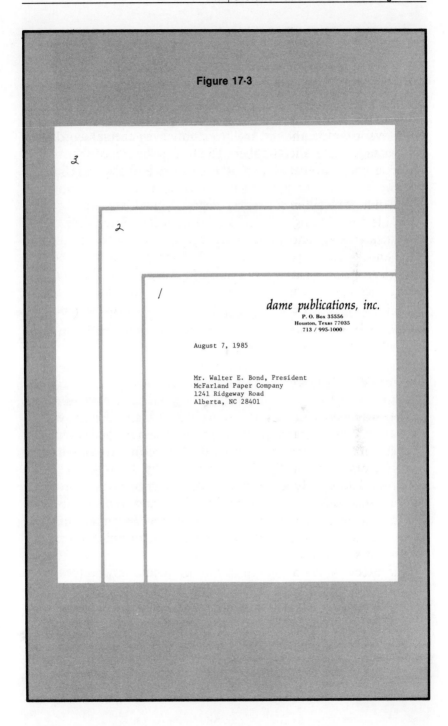

*3*

*2*

*1*

dame publications, inc.
P. O. Box 35556
Houston, Texas 77035
713 / 995-1000

August 7, 1985

Mr. Walter E. Bond, President
McFarland Paper Company
1241 Ridgeway Road
Alberta, NC 28401

A similar error was made when an executive dictated this sentence in a letter about a speaker for a special occasion, "Last year he won the *Pulitzer prize*." Because the word *Pulitzer* was not a part of the transcriber's vocabulary, she transcribed, "Last year he won the *pullet surprise*." Fortunately for everyone concerned, the error was found and then corrected before the letter was mailed.

Do enunciate clearly and spell (possibly even define) words you think are new to the transcriber. The transcriber is, of course, expected to use a dictionary and other reference books and to make the inquiries necessary for accurate transcription; but you are responsible for making dictation clear.

### Special Instructions

As you prepare to dictate, state to the stenographer or into the microphone the type of message (letter, memo, and so on) that is to follow. Tell how many copies to prepare and the kind of stationery to use. If there is a need for rush handling, mention that; and specify the method of mailing (special delivery, certified mail, or other) when it is anything other than first-class mail. Also, mention any other special notation such as *confidential* and *personal* that is to be typed on the message. Say whether to make a rough draft or a mailable copy. If, however, the transcriber knows the number of copies to make, the kind of stationery to use, and so on, you need not give these instructions except for special situations.

By your giving these instructions before dictating, the transcriber knows the steps to take before beginning to transcribe and the notations to type at the top of a page. Hearing these instructions first, the transcriber can save transcription time.

By preparing adequately for dictating, you seldom need to give special instructions during the dictation. When, however, you do need to interrupt the dictation for special instructions, give a signal so that the transcriber knows your instructions are not to be transcribed as part of the message. If you are dictating to a machine, you may say "operator"; or if you are dictating to a stenographer, you may call the stenographer's name to indicate instructions are to follow.

Even though the transcriber can be expected to punctuate most sentences, do indicate the punctuation marks for special or unusually difficult situations. Ordinarily, supply these marks during the dictating process. Also, designate the ends of paragraphs.

To ensure speed and a high degree of accuracy in transcribing, encourage the transcriber to ask questions for which answers cannot be found readily in the dictionary, handbooks, directories, and other sources a transcriber should use efficiently. Instruct the stenographer to ask any necessary questions *after* you have finished dictating the message. An interruption during the dictation can disrupt your trend of thought and affect adversely your dictating efficiency.

After you complete the message, give the transcriber the names and addresses of the people who are to receive copies.

### Style

When a stenographer records the dictation, the speed at which you dictate is obviously governed somewhat by the speed at which the person can write. Whether you dictate to a stenographer or to a machine, talk loudly enough to be heard easily. When you use a machine, hold the microphone about two or three inches from your lips and do not turn away from it. Remember, unusually loud dictation seems faster and more difficult to write than dictation given in a natural tone of voice. *Speak clearly* and vary the dictation speed, even within a sentence, *so that each word is easily understood.* Pause slightly after dictating a small group of words. The word grouping illustrated in the following paragraph is appropriate.

> Thank you,/Mr. Miller,/for writing to me on May 3/about your trip to Chicago./Sometime next week/I will talk with you again/about your plans for next year.

Other groupings could be just as effective.

Play back the dictation or ask the stenographer to read any part you wish to hear. The more carefully you have prepared for dictating the message, the fewer times you will need to review any part of it; but even the most careful dictators sometimes need to review.

Occasionally, hearing a faulty sentence you speak makes you recognize the need to reword it. There are other reasons, too—incoming telephone calls, other interruptions, and so on—for needing to listen to part or all of the message before it is transcribed.

Dictate as if you were talking with the person to whom you are sending the message. This style helps the transcriber to understand the content of the message as well as the individual words and thus leads to fast, accurate transcription.

## Numbers

Give special attention to the accuracy of numbers. An error in a ZIP code or in another part of an address almost always leads to a delay in the delivery of the letter. Errors of this type may make delivery impossible. A letter containing the date *Friday, April 27,* would certainly lead to confusion if the actual date is *Friday, April 26.* An error of this type usually requires further correspondence or a telephone call. *Verify all dates before dictating them,* and check them carefully when proofreading. Errors in amounts (money, time, supplies, and so on) can lead to loss of business or to a misunderstanding about a transaction.

When including complicated tabulations, let the transcriber copy them. Dictate simple tabulations and other numbers. Be especially careful to enunciate clearly, to read the numbers correctly, and to dictate them slowly enough for the stenographer to write them clearly. Dictate long numbers *in groups* rather than *individually.* For example, dictate the number 348672 this way:

three forty-eight, six seventy-two
or
thirty-four, eighty-six, seventy-two

Numbers dictated in groups can be understood easily and thus transcribed accurately.

## Follow-up

Proofread the typed copy of each message you dictate; be sure each enclosure mentioned is enclosed; and sign each letter and memo. Remember that when you sign a message, you accept responsibility for the completeness and accuracy whether it was typed by a public stenographer, your executive secretary, or a transcriber in a word processing center.

## WORD PROCESSING CENTER

A word processing center is a facility in which most, or possibly all, the dictation for an organization is recorded and transcribed in one place. The dictation may be given, however, at various locations. Many organizations that have two or more frequent dictators have established word processing centers. In these centers the dictation can be processed rapidly and economically.

One center that processes the dictation for about seventy dictators is equipped with a telephone and two of each of the following items:

> memory typewriters
> recording machines
> transcribing machines
> secretarial desks and chairs

The two recording machines are connected to telephone lines so that they can record the dictation of the seventy dictators who, by dialing the number for either machine, can dictate from any telephone. Dictation can be given in the office building or in any other place from which a telephone call can be made. The dictation can be recorded twenty-four hours a day seven days a week.

Two transcribers, who work eight hours a day five days a week, transfer the medium on which the transcription is recorded to one of the transcribing machines and use memory typewriters to transcribe the messages. Memory typewriters are used so that revisions can be made without having to retype the entire message. The transcribers are specialists in processing written messages. Their job does, however, include face-to-face and telephone communication in order to process written messages. Because of the work that is performed in the word processing center, the secretaries and the administrative assistants have more time for the countless required tasks besides recording dictation and transcribing.

No two word processing centers have to be identical. Each one should be arranged to suit the particular needs of the group it serves.

Word processing is discussed further in the next chapter.


## QUESTIONS FOR DISCUSSION

1.   What steps can executives take to improve their ability to dictate effectively?

2.   What steps can an administrative manager take to stimulate the other executives in the organization to improve their ability to dictate business messages?

3.   What are some of the modern technological developments that enable transcribers to transcribe dictated material faster than was possible earlier?


## PROBLEMS

1.   Assume you are Randy W. Long. If a dictating machine is available, use it to record the following script. Otherwise, dictate it to a stenographer. This script includes your identification, instructions, and a short letter:

> I am Randy W. Long. Please use department letterhead to transcribe this letter for my signature. Make two carbon copies. Use block style.
>
> Miss Mary L. Clarke C-l-a-r-k-e Manager, Williams Department Store, 715 Main Street, Athens A-t-h-e-n-s, MO 65432 Dear Miss Clarke: Linda H. Jones, who has applied for the bookkeeping job in your office, worked for us from June 15, 1980, through August 31, 1982. She understands accounting principles p-r-i-n-c-i-p-l-e-s *semicolon* and she operates office appliances *dash* calculators, posting machines, and transcribing machines *dash* skillfully. *paragraph*
>
> Miss Jones is neat and dependable. She works well with her associates. *paragraph*
>
> I am very glad to have this opportunity to recommend her for employment. Sincerely, Randy W. Long, Personnel Manager
>
> Send a carbon copy to Mr. George M. Miller
>
> (Mr. Miller supervised Linda's work the first year she worked for us.)

Play back the dictation or ask the stenographer to read it to you.

**2.**    Dictate the following letter. Supply the needed instructions.

Miss Catharine W. Smith
1126 Euclaire Avenue
Springville, KS 66762

Dear Miss Smith

The trade-in value of the freezer you mentioned in your letter of January 25 is $55. We would be glad to accept this appliance when you purchase either a Model 7 or a Model 10 refrigerator.

The serial number for the television set you asked about is 786445392. As you know, you bought that set in 1980 (perhaps you remember the month and the day) for only $679. A new television that has features identical to those on your set costs $739 today.

We are glad to know that you, as well as our many other customers, are pleased with the appliances you purchased here.

Cordially

**3.**    Dictate the following letter. Supply the needed instructions.

Mr. John W. Grey, Manager, West Office Equipment Co., Portland, FL 33616 Dear Mr. Grey: Thank you for offering to help us locate the Royal electric typewriter that was stolen from our accounting office on September 25. The serial number for that machine is HP-784752146.

Several office appliances (the exact number has not been determined) were taken from the local high school building the day our typewriter was stolen. I am confident the principal would appreciate any help you can give him in locating those machines. Cordially, Martha R. Thomas, Manager

**4.** Dictate a revision of the following rough draft.

> Mr. Walter T. Brown
> Building Maintenance, Inc.
> P.O. Box 314
> Plainview, OK 74560
>
> Dear Mr. Brown
>
> I should like to thank you for sending the serviceman to repair the chair in my office so promptly. The job they did is quite satisfactory. You asked me to let you know when it would be convenient for us for your staff to clean the carpets in our offices. Any Wednesday afternoon from 1 p.m. to 3 p.m. would be convenient for us.
>
> Sincerely

**5.** Dictate replies to the two letters that follow. Grant the requests.

> 243 East Seventh Street
> Delaware, IN 46923
> April 19, 1985
>
> Rodgers Book Store
> P.O. Box 1223
> San Mano, CA 95046
>
> Gentlemen:
>
> Please send a gift-wrapped copy of LITTLE PEOPLE by Scarlet Hale to my niece, Betty Starnes, whose address is 509 North White Oak Street, Dover, NM 88032. I would like her to receive it for her birthday, which is April 26. A check for $8.17 to cover the cost of the book and postage is enclosed.
>
> Please send me more information about the book TREES OF THE SOUTH, the title of which is included in the list that you mailed to me last week.
>
> Cordially,
>
> Elizabeth Whaley
>
> Enclosure

414 White Avenue
Knoxville, GA 30145
April 18, 1985

Rodgers Book Store
P.O. Box 1223
San Mano, CA 95046

Gentlemen:

Will you please suggest the names of three books that would
be appropriate gifts for two young boys who are very much interested in camping. One is twelve years old; the other, ten.

I would like to present three books to these boys before their
summer vacation begins next month.

Sincerely,

Mrs. James W. Driver

6.    You are the personnel manager of a large department store.
Thomas A. Armstrong has applied for a job as a salesman in your
furniture department. Dictate a letter to him inviting him to come
for an interview. His address is P.O. Box 1216, Southern State
University, Sparta, SC 29301.

7.    You are the manager of a large department store. This afternoon
you received a telephone call from a charge customer, Ms. Mario
M. MacDonald, who said that the day she received her statement a
month ago she paid the full amount of $437.91. Today, however,
she received a reminder that she still owes that amount.
      Dictate a memorandum to James E. Mathis, who handles your
customer accounts, and ask him to look into this situation and to
communicate with Ms. MacDonald.

8.    You are the vice-president in charge of marketing at your bank.
Dictate a memorandum to Dale E. Wright and Claire M. Haskins,
who have agreed to plan this year's Christmas party for your
employees and their families. Tell them the date that has been
chosen and give them instructions on the jobs you want them to
perform in order to complete the plans for the party.

9. The principal of a local high school has asked you to be one of several college students to talk to high school seniors who plan to enter college next year. He wants you to spend about three minutes telling them about your major. Tell them why you chose your major, the kinds of jobs you will be prepared for when you receive a college degree, and the kinds of jobs you can expect to advance to within a few years. You can include other relevant information.

   Dictate this presentation to a recording machine.

10. You are the personnel director of your company. You have invited William E. Barton to come to your office at 10 a.m. on Thursday to be interviewed for a management trainee job. Also, as treasurer of the local Civitan Club you expected to give a financial report at the luncheon meeting at 12:30 p.m. on Thursday.

    After your secretary left the office this afternoon (Monday), you learned that because of an emergency you will have to go out of town tonight and will return on Saturday morning. Dictate instructions for your secretary. Tell her to reschedule the interview for Mr. Barton sometime next week; and tell her to ask one of your employees, Jason L. Snyder, who is a member of the Civitan Club, to give the financial report for you. Ask your secretary to give the report to Mr. Snyder.

# Chapter 18

# Form Messages and Word Processors

Producing form messages is one of the common word processing activities in today's offices. Most organizations—small ones as well as large ones—have numerous occasions for distributing copies of one message to several people. Even though these copies can be individually handwritten or typewritten, either form of preparation would be excessively expensive and time consuming. Practical ways to produce multiple copies include duplicating (ditto, offset, and others); copying by such processes as Xerox; and making originals by using a memory typewriter or one of the more sophisticated word processors. The method used to produce copies should fit the existing situation.

Some frequently used form messages—letters, routing slips, and records of calls—and word processors are discussed in this chapter.

## LETTERS

Business letters are expensive. The average cost, which ranges from $5 to $10, includes both form messages and those messages dictated individually by high-salaried executives. When average costs are estimated, such items as stationery; postage; overhead expenses for energy, rent, furniture, and equipment; and salaries are included. Because of high costs, companies are making changes to keep these expenses from soaring higher along with the increased volume of written messages.

To save time and expense, some people write their responses at the bottom or on the back of letters and urge those to whom they write to reply that way. If a file copy is necessary, it can be made on a copying machine. The inquiry and the reply (at the bottom or on the back) can be copied on one sheet of paper. This practice saves paper and filing space.

Stationery suppliers sell forms that have multiple copies—for the sender, the receiver, and the file. Although these forms are used primarily for intraorganization messages, they are also sent to individuals outside the group. Most form messages, however, are letters that are reproduced through printing processes if thousands are needed; or they are typed on a word processor if from one to several hundred copies are needed. The messages are recorded, and more copies can be typed automatically when needed.

### Uses of Form Letters

Among the situations for which form letters can be used are these:

1. Inquiries and answers to inquiries

2. Order acknowledgements

3. Welcome to new customers

4. Adjustments

5. Collection and credit

6.    Sales and promotion

7.    Announcements to employees and stockholders

8.    Requests for information about job applicants and credit applicants

The form letters in Figures 18-1 through 18-3 have been used for some of these situations.

### Advantages of Form Letters

Although consumers do not always react positively to receiving form letters, here are some of the reasons form letters are good for the organizations that use them:

1.    Preparation time is saved for both the dictator and the transcriber.

2.    An expert can take the time to write the letters carefully and to revise them to suit different types of customers and changes in economic conditions.

3.    A large number of letters can be sent in one day so that all readers receive the message at about the same time.

4.    Acknowledgements of orders and replies to letters can be sent with little delay.

5.    Form letters are welcomed by customers who have forgotten to pay their accounts or who are late for some other good reason. Knowing this type of error is made by enough people to justify an organization's preparing a form letter helps the conscientious customers to be less disturbed than they would be if they received an individually dictated letter.

**Figure 18-1**

# Jayne's Mail-Order House
P. O. BOX 732
FREEWAY, ME 04112

March 11, 1985
Our 50th Year

Mrs. Lynne Williams
6101 Freeway Circle
Morgantown, ME 04037

Dear Mrs. Williams:

The transaction you inquired about has been adjusted.  A
corrected statement of your account is enclosed.

Thank you for bringing this transaction to our attention.

Sincerely,

*Joanne Williams*

Miss Joanne Williams
Accounts Receivable

stm

Enclosure

**Figure 18-2**

# Lee's Retailers

276 — 22 Street
Dover, CO 81212

Dear Customer

We welcome you as a charge customer.  Your credit card
is enclosed.  Complete details of the many advantages of
using your Lee's Credit Card are explained in the enclosed
brochure.

Our regular 30-day charge accounts are payable within 30
days of the closing date shown on your monthly statement.

At any Lee's store you will always receive the greatest
service and courteous treatment.  Giving you complete satisfaction with our merchandise and services is our aim.

Any time you have suggestions to make, we will welcome
them.

Cordially

*Jeff M Grissom*

Jeffrey M. Grissom
Customer Accounts Supervisor

trw

Enclosures 2

**Figure 18-3**

## Ranchland Department Store
### Spring City, Kansas 66012

July 5, 1985

Dear Charge Customer:

Our annual Mid-Summer Sale will begin on July 15 and will continue through July 20.

Prices on all our summer clothing will be reduced as much as
20 percent.  Greater price reductions will be made on picnic
and camping items and on yard and garden tools.

We will announce this sale in the local newspapers on July 12,
but we want you to know about it earlier.  We look forward to
seeing you in our store sometime during the week of July 15-20.

Cordially,

Maha Hejazi

Maha Hejazi
Assistant Manager

htr

### Disadvantages of Form Letters.

Nearly everyone realizes the need for form messages in business to keep expenses down and to speed up communication. For the following reasons, however, some people still resent receiving form letters.

1.  The wording is impersonal and too general.

2.  Some letters are not suitable for the situation; for example, a letter referring to a family is sent to a single person.

3.  Many form letters are not signed; and for some of those that are, the signature is a copy instead of an original.

4.  The appearance may be poor. Often, computer letters are mailed with incorrect word divisions, holes along the edges of the paper, and unattractive letterheads.

### Types of Form Letters

Some of the disadvantages can be overcome by using the right type of form letter. These types are common: (1) complete form letter, (2) form paragraphs, and (3) guide letter.

**Complete form letter.**   One complete form letter is not sufficient for all situations. Several letters should be prepared with specific wording to give the receivers the information they need. Many offices have word processors that can be programmed to stop, allowing an operator to insert such variable information as dates, names, or amounts of money. This feature gives the letter a personal touch and makes it apply to the specific situation. An example is in Figure 18-4.

**Form paragraphs.**   Paragraphs can be written to fit almost every situation an organization could have. These paragraphs can be coded with numbers and placed in a manual for the typist to copy as indicated by the dictator, or they can be put on tapes or disks and coded similarly. The dictator may write the code on the letter to be answered or dictate the code to a dictating machine or by telephone to a word processing center. Of course, the transcriber too has a copy of the manual or the word processor recording.

**Figure 18-4**

## Connor's Department Store
### 256 MAIN STREET
### BUTLER, TN 37121

Dear Customer

Because you always pay your account promptly, we suspect
that your check for $_____ for last month's pur-
chases has been misplaced in the mail or that through an
oversight you are waiting later than usual to mail your
payment.

If the check has been lost in the mail, perhaps you will
want to stop payment at the bank and send us a duplicate.

We are always glad to have you visit our store or to mail
your order to us.

Cordially

*Sallye Frith*
Ms. Sallye Frith
Accounting Department

jhn

One example of an office that receives many similar inquiries for which form paragraphs are used effectively is a university admissions office. Hundreds of prospective students write to that office each year, and many of them ask the same questions. They inquire about expenses, scholarships, part-time jobs, living accommodations, programs of study, and so on. Four benefits are realized from using a set of well-written form paragraphs.

1. The prospective students receive prompt responses to their inquiries. Because this routine information does not have to be dictated for each reply, a typist can copy a form paragraph that has been prepared for each question that was asked. No time has to be spent in dictating the reply, and the typist can type rapidly from typewritten copy or can produce copy from a word processor recording.

2. The prospective students receive well-written responses. Because each paragraph is used for many letters, the writer of form paragraphs can afford to spend the time required to cover every detail adequately and clearly. A person who is unduly pressed for time sometimes omits some details or does not write as clearly as when adequate time is available to devote to each letter.

3. The office sending the replies makes a real saving in time, and therefore in cost, in replying to these letters, which are quite important to the university as well as to the prospective students.

4. The writer creates a better impression for the university by sending carefully written replies promptly. Promptness in mailing these letters and the care with which they are prepared can have a significant bearing on prospective students' choice of the institution to attend. Often, prospective students send inquiries to more than one institution. The one that sends a good response quickly very likely has an edge over another that would like to recruit the prospect.

   For replies to inquiries, form paragraphs are more effective than complete form letters because the information in some of the paragraphs does not apply to all inquiries. The admissions officer knows, for example, that some students will live off campus. She therefore omits from her reply the paragraphs about on-campus housing. Some inquirers are not interested in part-time employment. In her replies to those persons, she obviously does not include the paragraph about part-time jobs. Including information the addressees are definitely not interested in may make them realize the letters they receive are form letters and would probably give them the impression they have been given little or no personal attention.

Well-constructed form paragraphs should not be used in an attempt to deceive the recipients of the letters. Actually, though, they can be used in a way that addressees benefit more from them than from a less carefully prepared paragraph that is dictated especially to reply to an inquiry.

When an office has a form paragraph for each question that is raised, the entire reply can be made from these paragraphs. The paragraphs can be presented in different sequences for various letters. A good practice to follow when sending information that has been requested is to reply to the questions in the order in which they were asked. This plan makes it easy for the writer to reply to each question, and it helps the addressee to see quickly that each question has been answered. Sometimes, too, the person requesting the information expects to use it in the order in which the questions were asked.

For the answers to inquiries from prospective students, the university admissions officer prepared these form paragraphs:

a.   **Programs of study**
Each of the five colleges of this university offers from three to seven programs of study that lead to a bachelor's degree. These programs, which are listed on page 7 of the enclosed catalog, are described in detail in that publication.

b.  **Expenses**
The expenses for a year in college vary, of course, among students. The average last year was $5,500 for those who lived in dormitories, $5,350 for those who lived off campus, and $5,100 for married students who lived in apartments. These figures include fees, tuition, clothing, recreation, transportation, etc.

c.  The expenses for fees, tuition, meals, and lodging are explained on page 67 of the catalog that is enclosed. Textbooks, which are available in the university bookstore, cost about $140 a quarter. You can obtain used books for some of your courses.

d.  **Living accommodations**
You can rent a single room in a dormitory for $425 a quarter or a double room for $350. We provide linens and maid service for all rooms.

e.  The dormitories, which are air conditioned, are maintained well. To reserve a room, complete the form on page 6 of the enclosed brochure and mail it with a $50 deposit to the address on the form.

f.  **Part-time employment**
Part-time jobs are available in the library, in the cafeteria, in the dormitories, in the gymnasium, and in various offices on the campus and downtown. Since Mrs. Vera G. Stamps is in charge of part-time employment, I suggest you write to her about your qualifications. Address your letter to Mrs. Vera G. Stamps, Placement Director, Central State University, Midtown, TX 75639.

g.  **Scholarships**
The scholarships we offer range from $1,000 to $2,000 a year. Miss Julia Ann Pryor, who processes the scholarship applications, will write to you within the next two days.

h.    **Courteous ending**
We would be glad to have you enroll in our university.

If a prospective student inquires about programs of study, expenses, and part-time work only and states that arrangements have been made to reside off campus, the reply may be only those paragraphs that answer the three questions, plus the ending paragraph.

Quite often form paragraphs are excellent for part of a reply; but more information is essential, or is at least desirable, for the reply. The additional information can be given in individually dictated paragraphs. Some letters begin with an individually dictated paragraph followed by form paragraphs. For some letters an individually dictated paragraph is placed between two form paragraphs or at the end of the letter. The content of the inquiry and the extent to which form paragraphs have been prepared help the letter writer determine how to intersperse the individually dictated paragraphs and the form paragraphs to produce an effective message.

The letter in Figure 18-5 is a reply to a prospective student who is to work in a downtown office while she studies marketing. She asked about expenses and whether she could enroll for only twelve quarter hours' credit each term. She will live on campus until the middle of the second quarter when she is to be married to a local resident. (Tuition is based on a load of twelve to twenty quarter hours a term; this plan is described on page 67 of the catalog, which is referred to in the paragraph on expenses.) Note that this reply consists of an individually dictated first paragraph followed by form paragraphs b, c, d, e, and h.

**Guide letter.**    A guide letter is complete, but is used only as a guide for the dictator. Certain words or phrases can be changed easily to make the message fit the situation.

## Preparation of Form Letters

To persuade the receiver of a form letter to read it, use the same guidelines for effective writing that you use in other letters. Date the letters and include a salutation and usually an inside address. Signing a letter with ink helps a great deal to personalize it. When a memory typewriter or a word processor is not available, you can

**Figure 18-5**

# *Central State University*
MIDTOWN, TX 75639

July 17, 1986

Miss Marie M. Welch
P. O. Box 348
Longhorn, TX 75138

Dear Miss Welch

You may enroll for only twelve hours.  Several others who work
part time take this minimum load for full-time students.

The expenses for fees, tuition, meals, and lodging are explained
on page 67 of the catalog that is enclosed.  Textbooks, which
are available in the university bookstore, cost about $140 a
quarter.  You can obtain used books for some of your courses.

The expenses for a year in college vary, of course, among students.  The average last year was $5,500 for those who lived in
dormitories, $5,350 for those who lived off campus, and $5,100
for married students who lived in apartments.  These figures
include meals, fees, tuition, clothing, transportation, etc.

You can rent a single room in a dormitory for $425 a quarter or
a double room for $350.  We provide linens and maid service for
all rooms.

The dormitories, which are air conditioned, are maintained well.
To reserve a room, complete the form on page 6 of the enclosed
brochure and mail it with a $50 deposit to the address on the
form.

We would be glad to have you enroll here.

Cordially

Andrea Lawson
Andrea Lawson
Director of Admissions

wen
Enclosures 2

have the letters prepared by the offset process. Take care, however, to see that the typewritten parts of the letter match the duplicated parts in color and type style and size. The object is not to disguise a form letter, but to show the reader you care enough to write a good letter and to make it neat and attractive.

## ROUTING SLIPS

Routing slips can be used effectively in many offices to speed up the circulation of letters, reports, memorandums, and other messages within the organization. Such a slip usually contains the names of people who are to receive these types of messages frequently, and it may contain short messages such as those in Figure 18-6.

To route a message to any group, merely place a check mark beside the name of each person who is to receive it. The first person who receives it reads it, initials the routing slip, and sends the message to the next person whose name is checked on the list. The person who attaches the routing slip to the message to be circulated can transmit a message by simply placing a check mark beside the message on the slip or by writing a note at the bottom.

## RECORDS OF CALLS

Using printed forms for recording messages from visitors or telephone calls can save time and effort for the person taking messages. The form also serves as a reminder to get all the information needed. The forms can be made or purchased from a stationery supply company (see Figure 18-7).

## WORD PROCESSORS

Word processors offer many advantages in preparing form messages. The greatest advantage, perhaps, is the speed with which a good system produces high-quality copies. Because errors can be corrected easily when preparing the first draft, keyboarding can be done at a considerably higher speed than is possible on a

**Figure 18-6**

# RONALD E. BEACH

### General Manager

| *To* | *Initials* | *Date* |
|------|-----------|--------|
| \_\_\_\_\_ Ms. Adams | _____ | _____ |
| \_\_\_\_\_ Mr. Clinton | _____ | _____ |
| \_\_\_\_\_ Mr. Colburn | _____ | _____ |
| \_\_\_\_\_ Ms. Hathaway | _____ | _____ |
| \_\_\_\_\_ Ms. Madison | _____ | _____ |
| ✔\_\_\_ Mr. Whitehall | _____ | _____ |
| \_\_\_\_\_ Mr. Woodworth | _____ | _____ |
| \_\_\_\_\_ Mr. Zane | _____ | _____ |

\_\_\_\_\_ please see me

\_\_\_\_\_ for your files

\_\_\_\_\_ for your signature

✔\_\_\_ please handle

\_\_\_\_\_ for your information

\_\_\_\_\_ for your suggestions

Comments:

*Please go to our Gadsden plant to negotiate with the contractor.*

**Figure 18-7**

WHILE YOU WERE OUT

M _____ of _____

Called _____   Date _____ Time _____

Was   in _____

_____

Message: _____

_____

_____

Message  Taken  By _____

typewriter. Then when the first draft is typed, the corrections and revisions can be made easily and quickly while the message is still displayed on a screen.

Once the draft is revised to suit the writer's wishes, a list of names and addresses can be merged with the recorded message to produce individually typed messages at a high speed (350 words a minute or faster) on any type of stationery. Envelopes for these messages can be addressed by inserting them and moving a switch. By the time a letter or a memorandum is signed, folded, and inserted into an envelope, the next copy is ready to be signed. The recorded message can be kept for more copies later, and it can be altered to fit future situations.

The names and addresses for these messages can be recalled easily for other mailings. The names can be arranged alphabetically or according to ZIP code, city, state, or other categories.

Many word processors serve also as computers for making mathematical computations and statistical analyses. Some executives have the small computers on their desks so that they themselves can prepare many of their messages efficiently, can communicate directly with other executives who have similar equipment on their desks, and can retrieve information from electronic files almost instantaneously. A popular prediction is that soon most executives' desks will be equipped with these up-to-date word processors.

## QUESTIONS FOR DISCUSSION

1. What are the major objections to receiving a form letter?

2. What are some specific situations for which form letters and form paragraphs can be used?

3. What are some ways to personalize form letters?

4. What are some of the form messages that the teacher of this course could use effectively to transmit information to the students?

5. What steps should you follow in developing form paragraphs or letters for the department in which you work?

## PROBLEMS

1. Write a letter that you as treasurer of an organization—fraternity or sorority, professional group, or college alumni—could mail to members to persuade them to pay their annual dues. They have already been notified that their dues should be paid, but you need to remind many of them and to persuade them to pay soon.

2. As personnel director of a large manufacturing company in a town that has a large business college and a state university, you receive many applications for secretarial jobs. Since you can employ only a small percentage of the well-qualified applicants, prepare a form letter that you can have produced in your word processing center for prompt mailing to each applicant that you cannot grant an interview.

3.  As placement director for student employees on your college campus, you receive inquiries about part-time work from many prospective students. You have a printed form that you ask students to complete for your files before you offer employment or place their names on a waiting list for a job. Prepare a form letter that can be typewritten for mailing to each prospective student who inquires about a part-time job. Send the printed form that each applicant is asked to complete.

4.  As editor of your college weekly newspaper, write a letter to the presidents of the clubs on your campus and request their reactions to a new format you are proposing for the college newspaper.

5.  As credit manager of a large department store, prepare a series of three form letters that you would write to collect an overdue account. Assume these letters would be mailed after you have mailed the monthly statement, a second copy of the monthly statement with a reminder notation attached, and an obvious form letter. This series that you will prepare will be used before you mention turning the account over to a collection agency or to an attorney for collection.

6.  You are the circulation manager for *Family's Best* magazine that has a very large circulation. Many subscribers neglect to renew their subscriptions at the proper time. You send them a card reminding them to renew and then mail another copy of that card if they do not renew their subscriptions before the expiration date. Prepare a form letter that you can use to encourage them to renew the subscription. Resell the magazine and perhaps tell them something about what to expect in forthcoming issues.

# PART FIVE

# ORAL COMMUNICATION

# Chapter 19

# Oral Communication

Recent studies reveal that top executives spend considerably more than 50 percent of their time in oral communication. Because oral communication plays such a significant role in executives' work, anyone aspiring to reach a management-level position would be wise to devote a good deal of time to sharpening oral communication skills. These skills are needed by everyone—not just management personnel—because everyone participates in oral communication.

For studying in order to improve oral communication skills, this chapter contains suggestions that pertain to these communication elements: listening, seeing, touching, and speaking.

## LISTENING

People spend more time listening than they spend writing, talking, or reading. Yet, listening is the element of oral communication that has been given least attention until recent years. Even though there are problems in listening, they can be overcome with awareness that they exist and with a conscious, organized effort.

An inherent problem in listening is that while a normal speaking rate is about 125 words a minute, an adult mind can assimulate 400 or more words a minute. And a person listening to easy or familiar information can assimulate considerably more than 400 words a minute. A problem in listening in typical situations is, therefore, evident. While receiving information presented well at about 125 words a minute, the listener's mind wanders and picks up thoughts in addition to those the speaker expresses. By picking up these other thoughts, the message receiver misses some of the information being spoken.

The capability of assimulating words faster than they are normally spoken is just one of the barriers to efficient listening.

### Barriers

In addition to the natural inclination to let the mind wander, other barriers that compete with the spoken words are sights, sounds, and feelings.

**Sights.** The appearance of the speaker, as well as the appearance of the surroundings, affects listeners. As a listener, try to arrange a time for studying appearance as thoroughly as you wish without breaking your concentration on the spoken message. If, for example, you enter an office to talk with someone, delay or at least minimize your study of the appearance of the person and the surroundings until after the conversation. Eliminating appearance awareness entirely is impossible, but knowing that you can delay that activity helps you to concentrate on the oral messages that are exchanged.

Moving sights such as flashing lights or automobiles and people passing by a window make strong distractions from oral communication. Conscious effort to ignore sight distractors helps listeners to listen effectively.

**Sounds.** Tone, volume, and other voice qualities of the speaker make efficient listening easy; or they make it difficult. A listener may need to ask the speaker to adjust the speech volume. Often, the listener has to adjust to tone and other voice qualities in order to listen efficiently.

Extraneous sounds such as the ringing of telephones, passing vehicles or people, and operating equipment or appliances compete strongly with spoken messages. Continued conscious effort to disregard these distractors is necessary for good listening.

**Feelings.**    Listeners' feelings—both physical and emotional— are often major barriers to effective listening.

For the listeners who have continuing seeing and hearing impairments, the use of eyeglasses or hearing aids usually alleviates these problems. In some instances, though, seating arrangements or poor graphics create difficulties that may or may not be adjusted satisfactorily. Fatigue or hunger are other *physical* conditions that sometimes distract listeners. Listeners may listen ineffectively because of discomfort caused by temperature that is too high or too low or by illness.

As you listen, anticipate as many of these conditions as you can and prepare to correct them or to compensate for them.

Anger, elation, and depression are among the *emotional* conditions that listeners may experience that would hamper their listening efficiency. Attitudes such as biases and prejudices and a tendency to judge or to criticize, as well as eagerness to talk, are other conditions that detract from effective listening. Listeners' awareness of these conditions can help them to overcome these distractions or to decide to postpone oral communication (when feasible) until conducive conditions exist.

### Tips for Effective Listening

Continued awareness of barriers to effective listening and conscious effort to overcome those barriers contribute to good listening skills. Here are other tips for further improvement of listening skills:

1.    Listen for ideas rather than facts. Associate these ideas with others you have so that you can apply them as you wish. This association helps to keep your mind productive instead of letting it wander because of the ability to assimilate words faster than they can be spoken.

2.    Judge the content instead of the delivery of the message. If you wish to think about the delivery, wait until you have listened carefully to the entire message.

3. Do not jump to conclusions. Listen to the whole message and then draw logical, valid conclusions.

4. Take enough notes to free your mind for further ideas, but do not take so many notes that writing them makes you miss some of the ideas that are presented. If you think of a question you want to ask, jot a note that will enable you to recall the question at the appropriate time to ask it.

5. Listen open-mindedly. Willingness to listen helps you to concentrate.

6. Hold emotions in check. Do not allow anger, fear, embarrassment, and so on to prevent your listening carefully to the ideas that are presented.

7. Remain quiet while ideas are being expressed. Wait until you have received the message and then make whatever statements you wish to make.

8. Help make the speaker feel comfortable by listening carefully and by using facial expressions and gestures that let the speaker know you are listening to what is said.

Good listening skills are closely related to seeing, touching, and speaking.

## SEEING

Seeing—a nonverbal communication medium—is closely related to oral communication and helps the listener to receive the oral message that is presented. Listeners usually want to see the speaker or the appliance that projects a recorded message. Seeing gestures, facial expressions, graphics, photographs, models, and other visual aids that a speaker uses helps the receiver to interpret accurately the ideas that are expressed orally.

## TOUCHING

Touching—like seeing—is a nonverbal communciation medium that is closely associated with oral communication. The way people shake hands, for example, helps to set the stage for the oral messages that follow. The way a person shakes hands with you will likely affect your interest in the words that person speaks. Other gestures such as a pat on the back have similar effects on oral communicators. In some situations a supervisor's giving an employee a pat on the back while communicating orally can transmit a message of approval more effectively than words can.

Touch in various forms affects people of all ages and in a great variety of situations. The effects can be positive, or they can be negative.

## SPEAKING

A major portion of business and social communication is oral. One of the most important attributes of speaking is clarity. Pronounce all words clearly, therefore, so that they can be heard easily. For words that have more than one correct pronunciation, use the pronunciation that seems natural for you. Generally, the pronunciation you use is the one that is used by the people with whom you associate. A speaker's using the most generally used pronunciation helps the listeners to concentrate on the message rather than on the delivery. Good grammar usage also helps listeners to concentrate on message content.

A well-modulated voice contributes to listening efficiency. The volume should be loud enough so that all words can be heard easily, but it should be soft enough to keep listeners from feeling uncomfortable or from believing that the speaker is uncomfortable. Voice inflection is important, too. Do not speak with a monotone. And vary your speaking speed to help make your statements interesting and easy to comprehend. Short pauses at various times are conducive to good listening, but long pauses tend to make the listeners lose interest or let their minds wander.

In addition to these general statements that apply to all oral communication situations, specific suggestions follow for informal conversations for groups of two or more, interviews, telephone calls, demonstrations, instructions, briefings, meetings, discussions, and speeches.

## Conversations

Good conversationalists are good listeners. They pay careful attention to what they hear, and they respond appropriately. They respond by looking into the eyes of the speaker part of the time—but usually not all the time—and by using facial expressions and gestures and by making oral comments.

Good conversationalists speak clearly and pleasantly, and they use voice inflection to make their statements interesting and easy to hear. Their statements, which are well worded, are concise: they are long enough to cover the topic adequately and interestingly, but they are not long enough to bore the listeners. As good conversationalists move from topic to topic, they use good transition and share participation with the others in the group. They reach a happy medium between the time they spend listening and the time they spend talking.

## Interviews

Interviews are carefully planned oral conversations. Before an interview the interviewer determines the kinds of questions to ask and the question sequence. Some of the questions may be written so they will be stated the same way for more than one interview. Other questions are suggested by the interviewee's responses. And, of course, the questions and the responses lead to discussion that is expected but is not planned specifically.

Interviewers ordinarily do most of the talking, but they want the interviewees to talk too. The amount of talking expected of an interviewee depends on the purpose of the interview. In an employment interview, for example, the interviewer wants to learn as much as can be learned about the interviewee in the time available. The interviewee may have questions to ask and should ask them at the appropriate times. Some of the questions come naturally in the discussion of various topics that are raised, and other questions should come near the end of the interview when the interviewer asks for questions. When preparing for an employment interview, review the suggestions that are given in Chapter 8. When preparing for an interview for research, review the suggestions in Chapter 12. The suggestions in Chapters 8 and 12 are helpful when preparing for interviews of other types, also.

Regardless of the type or the purpose of an interview, the interviewer and the interviewee should speak clearly, concisely, and interestingly.

### Telephone Calls

When you talk on the telephone, your voice and the words you use represent you. Facial expressions and gestures that help you to communicate effectively in face-to-face conversations help you in telephone conversations only to the extent that they enable you to project the proper tone of voice. A person who smiles while talking on the telephone is more likely to project a good image than is the person who frowns or holds a deadpan expression. Modulating your voice helps too to create a good impression on the listener.

An important tip for communicating effectively by telephone is to visualize the people with whom you are talking and to talk *with them* rather than *at the telephone transmitter.* Speak at a normal rate and with the same low-pitched tone that you use when conversing face to face. Use voice inflection to eliminate monotony.

Because you have immediate feedback or response to your comments, use the same words and sentence styles that are natural for face-to-face communication.

When mechanical interference makes the listener have difficulty in receiving your message, you may need to talk somewhat louder—and possibly a bit more deliberately—than usual, especially when you must use a word such as a proper name that is not familiar to the listener. For a word that is hard to understand (an example may be the proper name Luigs), spell the word this way: L for *Lincoln*, U for *United*, I for *Iceland*, G for *Gertrude*, S for *Samuel.* For each letter in a hard-to-hear word, use a word that is familiar to the listener.

Numbers, too, are sometimes hard to understand. When your listener has difficulty understanding a number, pronounce each digit rather slowly and enunciate as clearly as you can. A further suggestion for making clear the number you are pronuncing is to give the two or three numbers that normally precede it. For example, if the listener has difficulty understanding the number *nine*, you may say "seven, eight, *nine*" with emphasis on the last digit.

Always use a tone of voice that helps you to transmit the information and the feeling you want the listener to receive.

## Demonstrations

Oral communication situations include demonstrations of various kinds. Salespersons frequently demonstrate the uses or the operation of the products, appliances, or machines they sell. Employees give demonstrations for understudies, new employees, and visitors to their offices. Before you begin a demonstration of any type, make sure that you are thoroughly familiar with the items you are to handle and that you have all the necessary supplies, electrical outlets, and so on required for an efficient demonstration.

Move through the various steps quickly enough to make it obvious that you are well qualified for your task, but move slowly enough to permit the observers to understand each step. Even though you must spend a good portion of the time looking at the items you are demonstrating, look directly into the eyes of the observers during each pause and while you answer questions they ask.

Because you cannot face the audience all the time during a demonstration, be especially careful to enunciate clearly and to talk loudly enough to be heard easily.

You can enhance the effectiveness of a demonstration by telling the observers what to expect before you actually begin the demonstration. Then a quick review after you finish increases still further the effectiveness of the demonstration. Allowing an interested observer to go through each step under your guidance often pays rich dividends when you have finished a demonstration for the purpose of making a sale or of teaching an employee to perform a certain task.

As is true with all other situations involving oral communication, making it easy for the listeners to leave after completing your demonstration helps them to maintain a good attitude toward your work.

## Instructions

For a manager's instructions to be effective, the manager should tell the employees what the instructions will cover and should make the employees feel comfortable. Instructions are most effective when given when the employees realize a need to receive them.

As a manager, give instructions in a well-planned, step-by-step order and encourage the employees to ask questions that arise. Talk loudly enough to be heard easily, but not so loudly that you appear to be tense. Proceed slowly enough for the listeners to follow easily, yet rapidly enough to prevent boredom.

Give concise instructions. When you finish, leave, signal the employees to proceed with their work, or make a simple gesture to signify that you have finished.

## Briefings

Briefings are held usually to tell personnel about plans or about actions that have been taken. These sessions are sometimes held to convince people or to persuade them to accept or to approve plans or actions. Briefings should be short, yet long enough to accomplish the objective. While the personnel of any organization should always feel free to ask questions, the main purpose of a briefing session usually involves only the presentation of information for whatever reason is stated.

A good rapport and the other characteristics of good oral communication discussed earlier in this chapter apply to briefings.

## Meetings

As a business leader, you will have numerous occasions to preside over meetings. A meeting such as an interview may be for only two people. A meeting may be for a large group in a professional organization, for members of a civic club, or for members of management and union officials.

For any type of meeting, adequate preparation is a prerequisite for success in presiding. Make sure to know the purpose of the meeting, the organizational structure of the group, and the background of any anticipated business that will require action at the meeting. Knowing the purpose and the organizational structure will help you to determine the degree of formality by which to conduct the proceedings.

Your exhibiting self-confidence helps the participants to relax and to believe the leadership of the group is in capable hands. The points discussed in the sections on conversations, interviews, demonstrations, and so on in earlier sections of this chapter are equally important to the success of a presiding officer.

For a meeting in which formal parliamentary procedures are to be used, follow those in *Robert's Rules of Order Newly Revised* or those that have been adopted for your particular group. Know the rules that are to be followed. The ability to conduct a meeting according to the adopted rules without having to consult a printed source during the proceedings contributes much to the success of a presiding officer.

### Discussions

Whether or not you preside over the entire meeting, you may lead a discussion on a particular topic. Enticing people to discuss the matters that are to be handled can be a challenge. While no set of rules can be formulated for leading a discussion, some suggestions that are usually effective in stimulating participation are:

1.   Help the group members to relax.

2.   Ask for specific questions or comments.

3.   Avoid the trite "Are there any questions?"

**Relaxation.**   One way to help members of a group to relax is to direct questions to a few people who do not hesitate to talk when they have something worth saying. Ask questions that you know the participants can answer and that will require more than one or two short, simple sentences. Continue this procedure until several members of the group get involved in the discussion. Their participation will help to relax not only themselves but also the others present. All of them will then be more inclined to continue with comments that will bring out the needed discussion.

**Specific questions or comments.**　One way to get members of a group to ask questions for discussion or to make pertinent comments is to call on someone by name and say "What questions or comments do you have about . . . ?" A question such as this one tends to make the person you address believe you expect a question or a comment; and that person will, in most instances, feel free to say whatever comes to mind.

So that all the members of a group have an opportunity to ask questions, you may, after you have asked specific persons what questions or comments they have, say "What other questions or comments do you have about . . . ?" to the entire group rather than to an individual.

**Trite question.**　A poor way to stimulate discussion is to ask the trite question "Are there any questions?" This wording tends to inhibit the listeners. They believe the presider does not actually want them to participate, but merely asked this question to conform to a procedure that is followed by many other people. Only those who are somewhat outspoken or those who have a question they think is extremely important will respond to "Are there any questions?" *Do not ask this trite question when trying to stimulate discussion.*

Once the topic has been discussed to the extent you and the other participants think is desirable, end the discussion. Make a few cordial statements (perhaps express appreciation to the group for participating) to let them know the objective of the discussion has been reached. Do not, however, belabor the point. When members of a group realize the objective has been achieved, they are ready to leave the meeting. Allow them to leave promptly and gracefully.

## Speeches

When you are asked to speak to a group, you receive a compliment; for the people who ask you to speak believe that you have something appropriate to say for the occasion and that you can say it well. You can make the good presentation they expect by making sure you know the purpose of the presentation and then preparing adequately for it. The purpose may be to entertain, to inform, to persuade, or to inspire. The purpose and the audience guide your thoughts in preparing the presentation.

Do the needed research and organize the information to fit the occasion. Your thorough understanding of the information you present helps you to maintain the self-confidence necessary for an effective presentation. If you choose the topic, choose one you believe will appeal to most of the audience. If you are assigned a topic, simplify the information so that the audience can easily understand what you say. Do not, of course, oversimplify when talking to a group of people who know a great deal about the topic.

Prepare so well that you do not need to read your speech, but do not memorize it. Study your outline thoroughly so that you know what you are going to say and the order in which you will cover various points. Using note cards as cues is a helpful way to follow the outline, but excessive reading detracts from the effectiveness of an oral presentation.

For many oral presentations, you can use graphic aids advantageously. Choose those that are appropriate for the information you are to present and for the group. Flip charts, flannel boards, and chalkboards may be excellent graphic aids for small groups; but they are ineffective for large groups. Filmstrips and transparencies are effective for medium-sized groups when the room arrangement is appropriate. Whatever graphic aid you use, make it simple. Show only a few items on a graphic and also minimize the number of graphics. Make each item on a graphic large enough to be seen easily by each person in the audience. Practice using graphics so that you can present them easily and still maintain eye contact with the audience most of the time. Your spending much time looking at graphics or arranging them for showing would detract from the effectiveness of the presentation.

An outstanding quality of a speaker is the ability to make the listeners comfortable. A pleasant expression and enthusiasm for the topic contribute to achieving listener comfort.

An oral presentation should consist of an introduction, a body, and a summary. After you go to the front of the room, pause briefly and then introduce the topic. Introduce it in a way that will intrigue the audience. A startling fact, a question that will stimulate interest, or a humorous story relating to the topic are some of the appropriate ways to begin. Humor helps the listeners and the speaker to relax. In the introduction tell what you are going to talk about—the topics and the subtopics in the order in which you will discuss them. The body of the presentation is the well-organized information mentioned in the introduction. Analogies and examples can be used well to help explain the points you make and can entertain the audience. And regardless of the main objective of a speech, some entertainment is needed to maintain interest and a high degree of listening efficiency. Keep the oral presentation as short as you can make it and still cover the topic adequately and interestingly. At the end of the presentation, summarize the main points. Your using key words in the summary will help the listeners to recall the main points and to readily understand how they relate to one another. You hope, of course, that the relationships were clear as you presented them; but reinforcing those relationships is usually appropriate at the end of a speech. End the speech quickly enough to allow time for questions and answers (unless, of course, the speech is merely to entertain). Anticipate questions the audience will ask and be ready to answer them well.

Here are twelve suggestions all speakers can benefit from reviewing before each oral presentation:

1. Dress appropriately for the occasion.

2. Use good posture.

3. Exhibit self-confidence.

4. Show that you are enthusiastic about the topic.

5. Use gestures appropriately.

6. Modulate your voice so that it is pleasant and easy to listen to.

7. Choose words carefully.

8. Pronounce words correctly and naturally.

9.  Enunciate clearly.

10.  Use good grammar.

11.  Be perceptive to the reactions of the listeners.

12.  Look into the eyes of the listeners.

A good way to improve oral communication skills is to use a video recorder to record your practice sessions and then study the recording privately or with a friend and tutor so that good characteristics can be noted and continued and so that those characteristics that are ineffective can be minimized or eliminated through practice and conscious effort. If no video recorder is available, use a tape recorder. Some of your characteristics—good and bad—can be studied by listening to the recording. Practicing before a mirror is also worthwhile.

The best preparation for giving a speech is to continue to talk to groups. This type of practice is essential for raising speaking skills to the highest level.


## CONCLUSION

Complete coverage of all the points to consider in oral communication is obviously beyond the scope of any one chapter of a book. The suggestions offered in this chapter will, nevertheless, serve as a sound background for improving oral communication skills.

## QUESTIONS FOR DISCUSSION

1. Why should a speaker look at the people in the audience while delivering a speech?

2. What can inexperienced speakers do to help themselves relax before an audience.

3. What are some of the graphic or visual aids besides those mentioned in this chapter that a speaker can use advantageously?

4. What are some of the characteristics of a good speaker? And what are some of the characteristics of a poor speaker?

5. What are some of the factors people can use to improve the delivery of their well-prepared speeches?

## PROBLEMS

1. Give a short demonstration (perhaps five minutes) of the use of a small appliance such as a hair dryer, an electric drill, a food chopper, or a vacuum cleaner.

2. Give a short (three-minute) report on your first interview for a job. If you have had no job interview, report on the preparation you will make for the first interview you will have.

3. Give a three-minute report on the characteristics of a good manager of an office, a department store, a factory, or some other unit.

4. Give a three- to five-minute report on the qualifications required for a particular job (door-to-door salesperson, accountant, receptionist, grocer, or other).

# PART SIX

# REFERENCE
# SECTION

# Reference Section

Present your business message so effectively that the reader pays more attention to the content than to any other feature. Give due consideration to tone, format, appearance, style of expression, and mechanical details. The information in the preceding chapters is presented to help enhance the effectiveness of business messages. To supplement the information in the text and in the illustrations of this book, this reference section is appended.

The supplementary information in this reference section is presented under these topics:

1. Punctuation
2. Spacing with punctuation marks
3. End-of-line divisions
4. Capitalization
5. Numbers
6. Abbreviations
7. Sentence types
8. Addresses and salutations for special correspondence
9. Frequently misspelled words
10. Confusing terminology

509

## 1.   PUNCTUATION

### Period

**End of sentence.**   Use a period at the end of a declarative sentence (a statement), an imperative sentence (a command), a polite request, and an indirect question.

> The copier is described on page 4.
>
> Illustrate each principle you present.
>
> Will you please let us hear from you before March 10.
>
> He asked me when you would return.

**Abbreviations.**   Use a period to indicate that a letter or a group of letters represents a word or a group of words not spelled in full.

> Mr., Mrs., Ms., Dr., No., a.m., p.m., Ph.D., Co., C.O.D., f.o.b.

When several initial letters are used together as an abbreviation for a group of words, the abbreviation can be typewritten in all capitals without periods.

> ABC (The Association for Business Communication)
>
> AMS (Administrative Management Society)
>
> ROTC (Reserve Officers Training Corps)

**Decimal point.**   Use a period to separate dollars from cents in sums of money that are expressed in figures.

> $7.21, $8.05, $117.32

*Do not use* a decimal point with an even sum of money except in a series when at least one of the items includes cents.

> $7, $10, $23
> The books cost $11.75, $16.00, and $17.95.

**After a figure.**   Use a period after a figure that is used to enumerate tabulated items.

> The three letter styles illustrated in Chapter 4 are these:
>
> 1.   Modified block
>
> 2.   Block
>
> 3.   AMS simplified

## Exclamation Mark

Use an exclamation mark after a *strong* exclamatory word, phrase, clause, or sentence.

> Stop!          Run! The machine is afire!

## Comma

**Introductory subordinate clause.**   When a sentence begins with a subordinate clause, use a comma between the subordinate clause and the independent clause.

> If the price is low, I will purchase the land.

Ordinarily, *do not use* a comma between the clauses when the independent clause precedes the subordinate clause.

> I will purchase the land if the price is low.

**Direct address.**   Use a comma or commas to set off a word that is used as a direct address.

> Diane, will you type the letter for me?
>
> I believe, Mr. Salem, that the batteries can be shipped on August 26.
>
> You will like this report, Bob.

**Appositive.**   Use a comma or commas to set off a nonrestrictive (nonessential) appositive. A nonrestrictive appositive is not needed to identify the noun or the noun substitute to which the appositive refers.

> Please give your order to Mr. James H. Maze, our representative for your area.

> Mr. John C. Smith, the company auditor, will present the report.

*Do not use* commas to set off an appositive that is restrictive (essential) for identifying the noun or the noun substitute to which it refers.

> I believe your son Steve is heavier than his brother.

**Nonrestrictive (nonessential) clause.**   Use a comma or commas to set off a nonrestrictive (nonessential) clause. A nonrestrictive clause is not needed to identify the noun or the noun substitute it modifies.

> The president, who lives three blocks from the office, walks to work each day.

> The purchases journal, which is maintained by the assistant bookkeeper, has been misplaced.

*Do not use* commas to set off a clause that *is* needed to identify the noun or the noun substitute it modifies.

> The man who drove my tractor last year has accepted another job. (*The clause is needed to tell which man has accepted another job.*)

**Compound sentence.**   Ordinarily, use a comma before the coordinate conjunction that joins the independent clauses of a compound sentence when a subject is expressed in each clause.

> He has tried to state this principle simply, and he believes you can apply it easily.

> He stated this principle simply and gave you this sentence as an illustration.

*Note:*    When the independent clauses are *short*, the comma may be omitted.

> Harry dictated the letter and Judy transcribed it.

**Series.**    Use a comma between items (figures, words, or groups of words) in a series. A series consists of three or more items.

> We have shipped the paper, the books, and the typewriters you ordered last week.

> The business executive may spend the day writing letters, talking with customers, and supervising office workers.

**Parenthetical expression.**    Use commas to set off a parenthetical expression that tends to cause the reader to pause for that expression.

> The project will be supported, however, by several civic groups.

> A two-thirds majority of the residents, on the other hand, felt the tax rate was too high.

No comma is needed if the parenthetical expression would not tend to cause the reader to pause.

> The consultant is also of that opinion.

**Direct answer.**    Use a comma to set off the direct answers *yes* and *no*.

> Yes, I will serve on the committee.

> No, you will not be required to pay the special fee.

**Introductory phrase containing a verb form.**    Use a comma after an introductory phrase that contains a verb form.

> Having studied the assignment, he was ready to solve the problem.

> To get the most out of your courses, you must study every day.

**Long introductory phrase.** Use a comma after a *long* introductory phrase even though the phrase contains no verb.

> Within the next seven or eight weeks, they will make some major changes in their office procedures.

> Throughout Mr. Charles C. Hamilton's childhood, he was influenced by the writings of his parents.

**Introductory adverb.** Use a comma after an introductory adverb that is to be emphasized.

> Ordinarily, the receptionist screens incoming calls.

**Coordinate adjectives.** Use a comma between coordinate adjectives.

> She is a courteous, charming person.

> The brightly colored, loosely woven materials are very popular.

**Omission of common element.** Use commas to indicate the omission of a common element in the second and succeeding clauses of parallel structure.

> History had an enrollment of 76; English, 87.

> Mr. Harley coached baseball; Mr. Sams, football; and Mr. Holt, basketball.

**Short informal quotation.** Use commas to set off a short informal quotation.

> The speaker said, "You are good listeners."

> When the supervisor says, "I have news for you," we know what to expect.

**Abbreviation, *etc.*** Use a comma *before* the abbreviation *etc.* at the end of a sentence, and use a comma *before and after* that abbreviation within a sentence.

> The discussion of fringe benefits will include insurance, vacations, etc.

> They discussed insurance, vacations, etc., at the meeting on Tuesday afternoon.

**Addresses.**   Use a comma between parts of addresses that appear on the same line. When the city and the state are given in a sentence, use a comma after the state.

> Box 95, Route 2
> Minot, MN 56263

> The manager will meet you in Springfield, Wisconsin, on June 6.

**Dates.**   Use a comma between the day and the year when the month, the day, and the year are expressed. Also, use a comma after the year.

> On January 26, 1982, the company adopted the new policy.

*Do not use* a comma after the day or the year unless both are expressed except, of course, when the comma is needed because of some other punctuation principle.

> On January 26 the company adopted the new policy.

> In 1978 the company adopted the new policy.

> When you delivered the package to my home on January 26, I was attending a meeting in Philadelphia. (*The comma is needed because of the introductory subordinate clause.*)

**Large figures.**   Use commas to group digits in three's for large figures such as sums of money and items that can be counted.

> The estate is at least $2,800,000.

> Do you know that 17,891 people visited this site last summer?

**Two series of figures.**   Use a comma between two series of figures when each figure is so large it should be written as a figure rather than as a word.

> In 1978, 16,719 people visited this park.

> For a circulation of 5,255, 267 carriers will be needed.

**Special situations.** Sometimes you need to use a comma so that the meaning of the sentence can be grasped easily even though using the comma does not conform to any of the preceding principles.

> Outside, the fresh air is stimulating.
>
> Further, study of that problem will help the vice-president of your company. (*Meaning study of that problem will help the vice-president of your company in addition to accomplishing another goal.*)
>
> Further study of that problem will help the vice-president of your company. (*Meaning additional study of that problem will help the vice-president of your company.*)

## Semicolon

**Compound sentence containing a comma.** Many good writers use a semicolon before the conjunction that joins the independent clauses of a compound sentence when a comma is used at some other point in the sentence.

> When you learn punctuation principles, you will be prepared to punctuate accurately the sentences in your communication mediums; and you will be prepared to help other writers who seek help on this feature of effective writing.
>
> A thorough understanding of the rules of proper punctuation contributes to your self-confidence; and it enhances your ability to write interesting, easy-to-read messages.

**Compound sentence with no coordinating conjunction.** Use a semicolon to join the independent clauses of a compound sentence when no coordinating conjunction is used to join them.

> The writer applied the principles expertly; he had studied them thoroughly.
>
> They prepared these examples for you; use them advantageously.

**Compound sentence in which independent clauses are joined by a conjunctive adverb.**  Use a semicolon when the independent clauses of a compound sentence are joined by a conjunctive adverb.

> He learned the interest rate had been increased; consequently, he did not borrow the money.
>
> We received the contract for providing the maintenance services for the office machines; therefore, we must employ an additional serviceman.

**Series.**  Use a semicolon to separate the items of a series when a comma is used *within* one of the items.

> The manager ordered two dozen No. 2 pencils; eight reams of 20-pound, 25 percent rag content paper; and two quarts of blue ink.
>
> Within the next seven or eight weeks, the personnel manager will employ a receptionist; four file clerks; and six well-trained, experienced secretaries.

**Enumeration.**  Use a semicolon before such expressions as *namely, for example, i.e., e.g,* and *that is* when the expression introduces an enumeration.

> The interior decorator emphasized the use of the warm colors; namely, red, orange, and yellow.
>
> The speaker elaborated on the four management functions; that is, planning, organizing, coordinating, and controlling.

**Illustration.**  Use a semicolon to introduce an illustration that is a complete sentence and is preceded by such expressions as *that is, namely, e.g., i.e.,* and *for example.*

> Each executive must be a good dictator; that is, he must be skilled in dictating well-organized letters in a minimum of time.
>
> John's assistant works efficiently; for example, he takes the initiative to make decisions when his superior is out of the office.

## Colon

**Salutation.**   Use a colon after the salutation of a business letter. (The colon is not used after the salutation, however, when no comma follows the complimentary close.)

> Dear Ms. Gray:
>
> Dear Mr. Hartley:

**Time.**   Use a colon to separate the hour from the minutes when you express time in figures.

> 8:30 a.m.
>
> 4:45 p.m.

**Quotation.**   Use a colon to introduce a long formal quotation.

> The contract stated: "For all materials that are provided by the contractor, the owner will pay the purchase price plus 10 percent."

> According to Brown:

> Today's management trainee who can write clear, interesting, easy-to-read messages has an advantage over his peers who do not write well. The student who aspires to succeed in any business occupation must, therefore, spend sufficient time while in school to improve his writing ability.[1]

**Series of items.**   Use a colon to introduce formally a series of items.

> Please answer the three questions that follow:
>
> 1.   How many women do you employ?
>
> 2.   What is the average weekly income of the high school graduates you employ?
>
> 3.   How many men received a promotion in your organization last year?
>
> Some of the reasons are these:
>
> Too much time is required to train them.
>
> A limited number of people applied for the job.
>
> Only six of the people who applied came for an interview.

**Explanation or illustration.**   Use a colon to introduce an explanation or an illustration that is an independent clause.

> The reason for his great success is obvious: he works night and day.
>
> He is an industrious young man: he works from 8 a.m. until 5 p.m. six days a week.

## Question Mark

**Direct question.**   Use a question mark at the end of a question to which a verbal response is expected.

> How much did the machine cost?
>
> Have you completed the report?

*Note:*   *Do not use* a question mark after a courteous request that is stated as a question.

> Will you please reply before May 19.
>
> Would you kindly send me a copy of the brochure you advertised in the *Cookeville Times*.

**Within parentheses.**   A question enclosed with parentheses within a sentence is followed by a question mark, but it does not begin with a capital letter.

> I will bring the brochure (have you seen it?) to the meeting.

**Multiple questions.**   When several questions are abbreviated because they could be stated in the same way, use a question mark after each one.

> How many of your employees work on Monday? on Saturday? on Sunday?

## Hyphen

**Word division.**   Use a hyphen when dividing a word at the end of a line of writing.

work- ing

plan- ning

under- stand

**Compound adjective.**   Use a hypen to form a compound adjective before a noun that is modified by the compound adjective.

the past-due account

the easy-to-read sentences

a two-week vacation

*Note:*  *Do not use* a hyphen to join words that form a compound modifier that precedes the noun it modifies when one of the words is an adverb that ends with *ly*.

the widely recognized authority (*Widely* is an adverb ending with *ly*.)

a well-known speaker (*Well* is an adverb, but it does not end with *ly*.)

the assembly-line techniques (Assembly ends with *ly*, but it is not an adverb.)

*Note:*  *Do not use* a hyphen to join compound adjectives that appear *after* the noun they modify.

The account is past due.

The speaker is well known.

Use a hyphen with each term for which a common element normally follows.

two- and three-week vacations

six-, seven-, and eight-room houses

**Compound word.**   Use a hyphen to join words that are used as a unit. (Consult an up-to-date dictionary when you question the use of a hyphen for words of this type.)

sister-in-law

father-in-law

**Prefix.**   Use a hyphen with some prefixes such as *self-*, *ex-*, and *re-*. (Consult an up-to-date dictionary when you question the use of a hyphen for words of this type.)

self-confident

re-cover (meaning to cover again)

recover (meaning to regain)

**Compound numbers.**   Use a hyphen in compound numbers that are written as words.

forty-seven

ninety-four

**Fractions.**   Use a hyphen in a fraction that is a compound adjective preceding the noun it modifies.

a two-thirds majority

*Note:*   Many writers *do not use* a hyphen in fractions that do not serve as adjectives that modify a following noun unless some special construction indicates the need for such usage.

Two thirds of the members attended the meeting.

fifty one-thousandths

**Clarity.**   Use a hyphen when necessary to clarify the meaning you intend to convey.

> forty one-thousandths
>
> forty-one thousandths
>
> junior-college course
>
> junior college course

## Apostrophe

**Contraction.**   Use an apostrophe to form a contraction.

> can't for cannot
>
> won't for will not
>
> couldn't for could not

**Possession.**   To show possession, use an apostrophe and an *s* with nouns that do not end with *s*.

> man's car
>
> Mrs. Jackson's assistant
>
> children's clothing

Also use an apostrophe and an *s* with pronouns—except possessive pronouns—to show possession.

> someone's car
>
> anybody's guess

*Do not use* an apostrophe with possessive pronouns:

> *my, mine, our, ours, your, yours, their, theirs, his, her, hers, its.*

Show possession by adding an apostrophe to plural nouns that end with an *s* or a *z* sound.

> years' experience
>
> Joneses' property

Use only an apostrophe to show possession for words that end with an *s* or a *z* sound unless you expect the pronunciation of a second *s* or *z* sound.

> Mr. Childress' secretary *but* Lois's desk
>
> Vickers' check

**Joint possession.**    Use an apostrophe with the final name only to signify joint possession.

> Mary and Harry's home
>
> Childress and Wright's store

**Individual possession.**    Use an apostrophe with each name to signify individual or private possession.

> Mary's and Harry's homes
>
> Childress' and Wright's wives

**Compound nouns.**    For compound nouns show the possessive for the final word.

> father-in-law's office

## Parentheses

**Supplementary or parenthetical elements.**    Use parentheses to set off elements that are included as parenthetical or as supplementary information not to be emphasized.

> In many instances polysyllabic words (including those of a specialized, technical nature) should be used.

*Note:* When a complete sentence is enclosed with parentheses within a sentence, the parenthetical sentence does not begin with a capital letter; and it does not end with a period.

> He learned that one of the three vice-presidents (he does not know which one) will attend the convention in Omaha next week.

**Numbers or letters within a sentence.** Use parentheses to enclose numbers or letters that introduce items given in paragraph form.

> These three guidelines are emphasized: (1) Write promptly. (2) Determine the purpose of the letter. (3) Keep the reader in mind.

> My suggestions are these: *(a)* Choose your words carefully. *(b)* Pronounce words correctly and naturally. *(c)* Enunciate clearly. *(d)* Use good grammar.

## Dash

**Appositives, clauses, and parenthetical elements that contain a comma.** Use dashes to set off an appositive, a clause, or a parenthetical element that contains a comma.

> Miss Betsy Rayburn—frequently referred to as the most competent, most courteous, and most intelligent member of the staff—will represent us at the convention.

**Sudden break or abrupt element.** Use dashes to set off a sudden break in thought or an abrupt element.

> The owner, the officers, or all the employees of an organization—provided the total number is small—may sign the card.

> Dictation—whether it is to a stenographer or to a machine recorder—should be clear and well organized.

## Quotation marks

**Direct quotation.**   Use a quotation mark at the beginning and at the end of a direct (verbatim) quotation whether it was originally spoken or written.

> The personnel manager said, "We need a person who is well trained for this particular task."
>
> "You seem to be well qualified for the job," replied the correspondent.
>
> The personnel manager wrote, "On November 8 we interviewed four men for the job of assistant production manager. Two of them are well qualified for the job."

*Note:*   When you interrupt a quotation by inserting words, use quotation marks to enclose each part of the quotation.

> "We need a person," said the personnel manager, "who is well qualified for this particular task."

**Quotation within a quotation.**   Use apostrophes to set off a quotation within a quotation.

> Mr. Smallwood wrote, "When Mr. Haley replied to my request on April 6, he said, 'Yes, you may use my name as a reference when you apply for employment with the J.C. Burns Company.'"

**Multiple-paragraph quotation.**   When you quote more than one paragraph *in a letter or a memorandum*, use a quotation mark at the beginning of *each* paragraph and a quotation mark at the end of the *final* paragraph of the quotation.

> Mr. Smallwood had this to say in his letter of April 6:
>
> > "We have spent a great deal of time preparing for this program, and we believe the speakers we have chosen are the best that can be obtained.
> >
> > "Please encourage the employees in your department to send their reservations before May 15. Cards they may use to reserve rooms are enclosed."

Single space and indent quotations of three or more lines in a double-spaced *report*, but do not use quotation marks.

> According to Brown:
>
> Today's management trainee who can write clear, interesting, easy-to-read messages has an advantage over his peers who do not write well. The student who aspires to succeed in any business occupation should therefore spend sufficient time while in school to improve his writing ability.[1]

**Subdivisions of publications.**   Use quotation marks to enclose the titles of articles that appear in a newspaper or a magazine and to enclose other divisions such as chapters, units, sections, and parts of other publications.

> Did you read the article entitled "The Immediate Outlook" in the latest edition of *Newsmonth*?
>
> The June 8 edition of the *Cookeville Gazette* included a story entitled "Children's Outdoor Games."
>
> "The Form Message" is one of the shortest chapters of this book.

**Special meanings.**   Use quotation marks to enclose words that have special meanings in the context in which they are used.

> The "Other" sector of the pie chart includes a collection of classifications each of which contains insufficient data to justify individual designations. (*A sector of the pie chart was designated "Other."*)

## Ellipses

**Direct quotation.**   Use ellipses to indicate the omission of one or more words from the direct quotation. Ellipses can be used in these four ways:

> a.   *Three* periods at the beginning of a quotation signify that the beginning of the quotation has been omitted.
>
> > The writer said, ". . . he will gladly make the adjustment for you."

b.  *Three* periods within a quotation signify that the beginning
    and the end of the quotation are given but that some part of
    the statement is omitted.

> His letter stated, "October 28 was the announced
> deadline, but . . . we will accept the offer you made on
> October 30."

c.  *Four* periods at the end of the sentence signify that the final
    word or words of the quotation are omitted.

> He wrote, "Your check for $14 has been credited to your
> account. . . ."

d.  A full line of periods signifies that an entire paragraph or
    more has been omitted from a long quotation.

> When discussing the problems of moving, MacWilliams
> concluded:
>
> Houses that are much larger than the one you described
> have been moved great distances at apparently eco-
> nomical rates. Two firms would like to have the oppor-
> tunity to move the house.
>
> . . . . . . . . . . . . . . . . . . . . . . . . . . . . . . . . . . . . . . . . . . . . . .
>
> Further study of the hazards involved should be made
> before a final decision is reached.[1]

## Brackets

**Within parentheses.**   Use brackets to enclose parenthetical expressions within material that is already enclosed with parentheses.

> According to the representative, the message (we do not know what
> type of message [letter, telegram, or telephone call] he sent) contained
> an explanation of his plans.

**Within quotations.**   Use brackets to enclose statements within
quoted material when the statements that are enclosed were not
made by the person whose quotation is presented.

> Mr. Ramsey replied, "I refuse to give an explanation for my actions
> [we do not know the reason for his refusal] in regard to that particular
> matter."

**To mark an error.** Use brackets with *sic* or the correct information to show that an error appears in quoted material.

"The house was built in 1967 [*sic*] by the Hayes Construction Company."

"The house was built in 1967 [1976] by the Hayes Construction Company."

## 2. SPACING WITH PUNCTUATION MARKS

**Apostrophe.** Space once after an apostrophe that follows the last letter of a word. *Do not* space after an apostrophe that comes between two letters.

She has had three years' experience in this type of work.

She has had one year's experience in this type of work.

**Comma.** Space once after a comma that follows a word or a figure, but do not space after a comma that is used within a group of figures.

If you have completed a course in typewriting, you probably know these rules for spacing.

He mailed the check for $12,500 on May 16.

**Colon.** Space twice after a colon except when it is used within a group of figures.

The names of the most popular letter styles follow: modified block, block, and AMS simplified.

The plane will leave at 3:15 p.m.

**Dash.**   Space once *before* and once *after* a dash that is made by striking the hyphen once. *Do not* space before or after a dash that is made by striking the hyphen twice.

> The personnel director discussed the problem with his three assistants - Mr. Rains, Ms. Sloan, and Mr. Woods - on Thursday.

> The personnel director discussed the problem with his three assistants—Mr. Rains, Ms. Sloan, and Mr. Woods—on Thursday.

*Note:*   Do not use *both* styles within the same message or publication.

**Exclamation mark.**   Space twice after an exclamation mark.

> Help! The ladder is falling!

**Hyphen.**   Do not space before or after a hyphen.

> Miss Matmaker is a well-known writer.

**Period.**   Five rules apply to spacing after a period.

a.   *End of sentence.* Space twice after a period at the end of a sentence.

> They received the order on Monday. They shipped the merchandise that afternoon.

b.   *After abbreviation.*   Space once after a period that follows an abbreviation.

> Please send us four boxes of No. 2 pencils.

c.   *Within abbreviation.* Do not space after a period that is used within an abbreviation.

> He earned a Ph.D. degree at Iowa State University.

> They open the office at 8 a.m. each day.

d.   *After a figure.* Space twice after a period that follows a figure when numbering items.

> The speaker discussed these three topics:
>
> 1.   Profits
>
> 2.   Markups
>
> 3.   Discounts

e. *Within a figure.* Do not space after a period (decimal) within a group of figures.

Here is a check for $3.87.

## Question mark. Space twice after a question mark.

Do you have storage space in your warehouse? If so, the driver will deliver the lumber on July 8.

## Quotation mark. Three rules apply to spacing quotation marks.

a. *Comma and period.* When a comma or a period is used with an ending quotation mark, place the punctuation mark *inside* the quotation mark.

When the prospect said, "I would have to see it to believe it," the salesman gave him an impressive demonstration of the machine.

The secretary wrote, "My employer, will be in his office on Thursday morning."

b. *Colon and semicolon.* When a colon or a semicolon is used with an ending quotation mark, place the punctuation mark *outside* the quotation mark.

When my administrative assistant was asked to comment, he said, "The problem was solved by Jim, the chief engineer"; and he handed the representative the report that described a solution.

The names of the following senators were mentioned in the article "Today's Top Brass": Manning, Oliver, and White.

c. *Exclamation mark and question mark.* Place the exclamation mark or the question mark *outside* the quotation mark when the quotation is *not* a question or an exclamation. Place the punctuation mark *inside* the quotation mark when the quotation *is* a question or an exclamation.

Did the executive say, "I must have the report by May 1"?

The clerk asked, "Do you know his favorite letter style?"

**Semicolon.**   Space once after a semicolon.

He received the letter this morning; he will reply this afternoon.

## 3. END-OF-LINE DIVISIONS

**Between syllables.**   Divide words between syllables only.

prob- lems

sen- tence

*Note:*   Consult a dictionary when you need help to determine syllables. Words cannot be divided between some syllables, however, as is explained in the principles that follow.

**Between one-letter syllables.**   When 2 one-letter syllables come near the end of a line, divide between them.

situ- ation

**After single one-letter syllables.**   Generally, divide a word immediately after a single one-letter syllable.

cate- gories

situ- ate

*Exceptions:*   Divide immediately *before* the single one-letter syllable *a, i,* or *u* when it is followed by the syllable *ble, bly, cal,* or *cle.*

reli- able

prob- ably

cler- ical

mir- acle

**Hyphenated words.** When a word is already hyphenated, divide only at the existing hyphen.

> sister-in- law *or* sister- in-law *not* sis- ter-in-law
>
> self- confidence *not* self-con- fidence

**Between double consonants.** Divide between double con-sonants except when a suffix such as *ing* or *er* follows a double consonant in the root word.

> com- merce          call- ing
>
>              *but*
>
> plan- ning          tell- ing

**Sums of money.** Do not divide sums of money.

> $100,000     *not*     $100,- 000

**Minimum of two letters at end of line.** *Avoid* dividing a word so that only two letters are at the end of the line.

> in- crease
>
> re- ceived

**Minimum of three letters on following line.** Divide a word so that at least three letters are at the beginning of the next line.

> print- ing
>
> print- ers     *not*     print- er

**Dates.** *Avoid* dividing dates; but when a date must be divided, divide only between the day and the year.

> September 8,   1978   *not*   September   8, 1978
>
>                          Sep-  tember 8, 1978

**Proper names.** *Avoid* dividing a proper name; but when a name must be divided, divide immediately before the last name.

Mr. Leon J.  Henderson     *not*     Mr. Leon   J. Henderson

Mr.     Leon J. Henderson

**Contractions.**   Do not divide contractions.

don't     *not*     don- 't

**Excessive divisions.**   *Avoid* excessive word divisions at the line endings.

**Consecutive lines.**   *Avoid* dividing words at the ends of more than two consecutive lines.

**Last word on page.**   Do not divide the last word on a page.

## 4.   CAPITALIZATION

**Sentence beginnings.**   Capitalize the first word of a sentence.

Our representative will visit your store next week.

**Proper nouns.**   Capitalize proper nouns, except some foreign names.

Jones, Steinway, Brown, Paz, Dietz, de Haas, von Braun

Capitalize words that form a part of a proper name even though these words would not be capitalized when used in other contexts.

the Mississippi River     *but*     river

the Comer Building     *but*     building

Maple Avenue     *but*     avenue

*Do not* capitalize the plurals of such words.

the Tennessee and the Ohio *rivers*

the Blanton and the Hamilton *buildings*

Capitalize a word when it is understood that the word refers to a proper name.

> We toured the University campus while we were in Lexington. (*In this context the word* university *refers to a specific university, the University of Kentucky.*)
>
> He will enroll in a university next September. (*In this context no specific university is designated.*)

**Geographic area.**   Capitalize words that are used to designate a geographic area, but do not capitalize words that are used to designate directions.

> We will reside in the South.
>
> They will drive south on Interstate 65.
>
> His accent indicates that he is from the Middle East.
>
> The house faces east and is well shaded by several large trees.

**Specific course titles.**   Capitalize specific course titles, but do not capitalize course titles of a general nature.

> Thirty students are enrolled in Marketing 432 this term.
>
> Thirty students are enrolled in marketing this term.
>
> Mary teaches accounting and economics.
>
> Mildred's favorite course is Principles of Economics.

**Personal titles.**   Capitalize any title that immediately precedes the name of the person to whom the title refers.

> The letter was addressed to Mrs. Robert A. White.
>
> The article was written by Professor May.
>
> When Senator Ray spoke to our group on May 6, he outlined the plans for the project.

**Days and months.**    Capitalize the days of the week and the months of the year. Do not capitalize seasons of the year unless they are personified.

> They will meet on the first Thursday in October.
>
> The group will meet sometime during the spring.
>
> The winter snows were rather heavy.
>
> When Spring lifts her head for a look at her surroundings, she will see that Old Man Winter has buried his head in the ground.

**Titles of chapters, articles, books, and periodicals.**    Capitalize the principal words in titles of chapters, articles, books, magazines, newspapers, and other publications. Conjunctions, articles, and *short* prepositions are not usually capitalized. Long prepositions are usually capitalized.

> Did you read the chapter that is entitled "Safety in Investments"?
>
> I enjoyed reading your second newspaper article, "Organizational Controls."
>
> When I read the magazine story "Poise Throughout the Crisis," I was reminded of the book that is entitled *A Crisis at the Office.*

*Note:*    You may type the title of a book in upper- and lower-case letters and underline them, or you may type the book title in all capitals not underlined.

> J. Fred Rich wrote two books, *Investing in the Stock Market* and *The First Million.*
>
> I read the book A  CRISIS AT  THE  OFFICE last week.

*Note.*    Do not use *both* styles within one message or publication.

**Deity.**    Capitalize each noun or pronoun that refers to the Deity.

> He thanked the Lord for the many blessings.
>
> The minister said, "Trust in the Lord and ask Him for His guidance."

**Salutations.**   Capitalize the first word as well as titles and proper nouns in the salutation of a letter.

Dear Mr. Hayes:

Gentlemen

Dear Miss Roberts:

**Complimentary closings.**   Capitalize the first word—the first word only—in the complimentary close of a letter.

Sincerely yours,

Cordially yours

Very sincerely yours,

**Numbers in business papers and legal documents.** Capitalize numbers expressed in words in business papers and legal documents.

Three Hundred Sixty-three Dollars

One Thousand Four Hundred Ninety-two Dollars

**Quotations.**   Capitalize the first word of a quotation unless the beginning of the sentence is omitted from the quotation.

Mrs. Allen wrote, "The stationery will be shipped on the 26th of June."

Mr. Hunter said, ". . . the merchandise is ready to be shipped."

**Pronoun I.**   Capitalize the pronoun I in any context.

I will let you know whether I can attend the meeting.

**Parts of published works.**  Capitalize the major parts of books, volumes, documents, and plays.

Chapter 3

Volume II

Unit 6

Act III, Scene II

Article V

*Do not* capitalize *page* when referring to a page number.

The illustration is on page 6.

**Special abbreviations.**  Capitalize the abbreviation for the word *number* when it immediately precedes a figure, and capitalize the abbreviations for college degrees.

Do you like item No. 4?

He earned B.S. and M.A. degrees at an accredited college.

## 5. NUMBERS

**Sentence beginning.**  Always express a number as a word when it is used to begin a sentence.

Eight players reported for practice on Tuesday afternoon.

Forty-three members voted for the change.

Two hundred twenty executives subscribe to this publication.

**Large round numbers.**  Express large round numbers in words.

At least two thousand people attended the meeting.

Do you believe that property will sell for two million dollars?

or

Do you believe that property will sell for $2 million?

**Small general numbers.**   Use words to express numbers of a general nature one hundred and below.

> We ordered eighteen calculators last week.
>
> My secretary transcribed twenty-three letters yesterday afternoon.

**Streets and avenues.** Use words for street and avenue numbers that are ten or below.

> 259 East Ninth Street
>
> 286 West 22 Street
>
> 2911 Tenth Avenue

**House numbers, page numbers, model numbers, graphic numbers, and measures.**   Use figures for house numbers—except *one*—page numbers, model numbers, graphic numbers, and standard measures except time.

> 12 Market Street
>
> One Park Avenue
>
> page 3
>
> pages 22 and 23
>
> Model 8
>
> Figure 4
>
> 8 by 11 inches
>
> 6 feet
>
> 8 gallons
>
> 32°
>
> 32 degrees
>
> two weeks
>
> four hours

**Percentages and sums of money.**    Use figures as the preferred way to express numbers for percentages and for sums of money.

> At least 8 percent of the employees preferred the new model.
>
> Eight percent of the employees preferred the new model. (*Always express a number as a word at the beginning of a sentence.*)
>
> The pencils cost 10 cents each.
>
> You may spend as much as $32 a night for a single room. (*Omit the period and zeros in even sums of money except in a series when one sum includes cents.*)
>
> The prices of these desks are $350.00, $425.75, and $500.95.

**Time.**    Use figures to express time except when the word *o'clock* follows the hour that is specified. Use a colon and zeros only when minutes are expressed in the sentence.

> He will open the office at 8 a.m.
>
> They open the store at 9:00 a.m. and close it at 4:45 p.m.
>
> He will close the office at twelve o'clock on Saturday.
>
> He will close the office at 12 o'clock on Saturday. (*Also acceptable.*)

**Dates.**    Use figures to express the day when the month precedes the day.

> He will be graduated on June 8, 1988.

When the day precedes the month, use a figure with *st, d, nd, rd,* or *th*; or use words to express the day.

> 1st of May
>
> 2d of May *or* 2nd of May
>
> 3d of May *or* 3rd of May
>
> 4th of May
>
> twenty-second of May

**Separate series.**   When two small numbers appear together and represent different items, use a figure for one of the numbers and a word for the other.

4 eight-cent stamps

four 8-cent stamps

## 6.   ABREVIATIONS

Only a few abbreviations are acceptable for business messages. Those that are acceptable are preferred over spelling in full. Use these abbreviations:

Mr.          Mrs.

No. (when it precedes a figure)

I prefer style No. 16.     *not*     I prefer style number 16.

Co. and Inc. (*in an inside address when writing to an organization that abbreviates these words on its stationery*)

YMCA, TVA, and other abbreviations for long names (*when the abbreviations and the names they represent are well known by the recipient of the message*)

The state name in an address when the ZIP Code follows (*Only the two-letter abbreviations recommended by the post office are acceptable.*) A list of those abbreviations follows:

| | | | |
|---|---|---|---|
| Alabama | AL | Alaska | AK |
| Arizona | AZ | Arkansas | AR |
| California | CA | Colorado | CO |
| Connecticut | CT | Delaware | DE |
| District of Columbia | DC | Florida | FL |
| Georgia | GA | Hawaii | HI |
| Idaho | ID | Illinois | IL |
| Indiana | IN | Iowa | IA |
| Kansas | KS | Kentucky | KY |
| Louisiana | LA | Maine | ME |
| Maryland | MD | Massachusetts | MA |
| Michigan | MI | Minnesota | MN |
| Mississippi | MS | Missouri | MO |
| Montana | MT | Nebraska | NE |
| Nevada | NV | New Hampshire | NH |
| New Jersey | NJ | New Mexico | NM |
| New York | NY | North Carolina | NC |
| North Dakota | ND | Ohio | OH |
| Oklahoma | OK | Oregon | OR |
| Pennsylvania | PA | Puerto Rico | PR |
| Rhode Island | RI | South Carolina | SC |
| South Dakota | SD | Tennessee | TN |
| Texas | TX | Utah | UT |
| Vermont | VT | Virginia | VA |
| Washington | WA | West Virginia | WV |
| Wisconsin | WI | Wyoming | WY |

Spell in full the days of the week; the months of the year; and words in the inside address of a letter such as *avenue, street, road,* and one-syllable words that indicate direction:

126 *North* 18 Street      *but*      717 Fifth Avenue, S.E.

## 7. SENTENCE TYPES

Simple, compound, complex, and compound-complex sentences are discussed and illustrated in the next few paragraphs.

**Simple.** A simple sentence is the same as an independent clause: it is a word group that expresses a complete thought. Simple sentences are easy to construct, to punctuate, and to read. Use more simple sentences than any other kind, but do not bore the reader by using simple sentences excessively.

**Compound.** A compound sentence is made up of two or more independent clauses. When using a compound sentence, be sure that the ideas you express are related and that the clauses are joined by the appropriate conjunction or a semicolon. When the independent clauses of a compound sentence are parallel in meaning, use one of the coordinating conjunctions *or* or *and*. The choice between these two conjunctions should be based on the context of the sentence. When the independent clauses present possible alternatives, use *or*, as in these examples:

The sales manager will attend the meeting in St. Louis, or he will ask his assistant to go.

The two-page report will be mailed this afternoon, or it will be delivered by the salesman tomorrow morning.

Use *and* to connect the independent clauses that express parallel positive ideas, as in these examples:

The secretary took dictation from two executives this morning, and she transcribed all her notes before she left the office at four o'clock.

Mr. Green works hard, and he expects his employees to work as hard as he does.

Use *but* in a compound sentence in which you express contrasting ideas in the two independent clauses, as in the following sentences:

> The personnel director dictates very slowly, but he expects his secretary to be able to write very rapidly.
>
> Electronic computers are expensive, but they do much work rapidly and accurately.

You can use a semicolon instead of a coordinating conjunction to join the independent clauses of some compound sentences. In these cases the main ideas in the two clauses should be closely related, the clauses should be short, and the clauses should be in the same voice—active or passive. Here are examples:

> Mr. Thomas received the requisition for display cases on Thursday morning; he ordered them on Friday afternoon.
>
> The books were ordered on Tuesday; they were received on Friday.

Another way to join independent clauses in a compound sentence is to use conjunctive adverbs. Choose a conjunctive adverb that expresses the proper relationship between the ideas in the independent clauses. *Consequently* and *therefore* are two of the many conjunctive adverbs that show result. *Moreover* means additional, and *however* and *on the other hand* indicate contrasts. Here are examples:

> Their store will remain open until 7 p.m. each weekday until Christmas; consequently, they must employ additional salesclerks for that period.
>
> The assembly lines will close temporarily on July 16; therefore, the specifications for your automobile must reach us before July 5.
>
> Ms. Hargrove typed eight letters before 9 a.m.; moreover, she proofread them, signed them, and placed them in the mailbox.
>
> The manager has received a copy of the regulations; he cannot study them, however, until tomorrow afternoon.
>
> The personnel director liked the applicant's appearance; on the other hand, he questioned her ability to supervise subordinates.

**Complex.** A complex sentence is made up on one independent clause and at least one dependent clause. The sentence may begin with the dependent clause, or it may end with the dependent clause. The following sentences are examples:

> When you learn to write several types of sentences, you can write interesting letters and reports.
>
> You can write interesting letters and reports when you learn to write several types of sentences.
>
> After you study this textbook, you should write good letters and reports.
>
> You should write good letters and reports after you study this textbook.

**Compound-complex.** A compound-complex sentence is made up of two or more independent clauses and at least one dependent clause. Here are examples:

> If you return the card before October 8, I will send you our current catalog; and our representative will stop by your office before December 1.
>
> We have shipped the four electric drills you ordered on May 6; and because you are a preferred customer, the mailing department has placed your name on the list to receive copies of all brochures we produce.

Use variety in the types, as well as in the lengths, of the sentences in business messages.

## 8. ADDRESSES AND SALUTATIONS FOR SPECIAL CORRESPONDENCE

Although there is a trend toward informality in addressing government officials, military and naval personnel, and religious leaders, the forms of addresses and salutations used for those people are still somewhat different from those used for business personnel. Appropriate address forms and salutations for government officials, military and naval personnel, and religious leaders follow.

## President of the United States.

| | |
|---|---|
| The President<br>The White House<br>Washington, D.C. | Sir:<br>Mr. President: |
| The Honorable. . . (name in<br>    full)<br>President of the United States<br>Washington, D.C. | My dear Mr. President:<br>Dear Sir:<br>Dear Mr. President: |

## Vice-President of the United States.

| | |
|---|---|
| The Vice-President<br>Washington, D.C. | Sir:<br>Mr. Vice-President: |
| The Honorable. . . (name in<br>    full) | My dear Mr. Vice-President: |
| Vice-President of the United<br>    States<br>Washington, D.C. | Dear Sir:<br>Dear Mr. Vice-President: |

## Chief Justice of the United States.

| | |
|---|---|
| The Chief Justice of the United<br>    States<br>The Supreme Court<br>Washington, D.C. | Sir:<br>Mr. Chief Justice: |
| The Honorable . . . (name in<br>    full) | My dear Mr. Chief Justice: |
| Chief Justice of the United<br>    States<br>The Supreme Court<br>Washington, D.C. | Dear Sir:<br>Dear Mr. Chief Justice: |

**Other federal, state, or city officials.** For any of these officials, you may use The Honorable (name in full) followed by the title of the official.

a.  *Cabinet member.*

The Honorable . . . (name in
    full)
Secretary of . . . (office)
Washington, D.C.

Sir:
My dear Sir:
Dear Sir:
My dear Mr. Secretary:
Dear Mr. Secretary:

b.  *Congressman.*

The Honorable . . . (name in
    full)
House of Representatives
Washington, D.C.

Dear Sir:
Dear Mr. . . .: (last name)

c.  *Senator.*

The Honorable . . . (name in
    full)
The United States Senate
Washington, D.C.

Sir:
My dear Sir:
Dear Sir:
My dear Mr. Senator:
My dear Senator:
Dear Senator:
My dear Senator . . .: (last
    name)
Dear Senator . . .: (last name)

d.  *Governor.*

The Honorable . . . (name in
    full)
Governor of . . . (name of
    state)
Capital city, State

Sir:
My dear Sir:
Dear Sir:
My dear Governor . . .: (last
    name)
Dear Governor . . .: (last
    name)
Dear Governor: (informal)

e.  *Mayor*

The Honorable . . . (name in
    full)
Mayor of the City of . . . (name
    of city)
City, State

Sir:
My dear Sir:
Dear Sir:
My dear Mr. Mayor:
Dear Mr. Mayor:
My dear Mayor . . .: (last
    name)
Dear Mayor . . .: (last name)

**Military and Navy personnel.** Include the following items in the addresses for both officers and enlisted men of the armed forces:

1. Full title of rank or rating (Colonel, Commander, Sergeant, and so on)

2. Branch of the service (Ordnance Department, and so on)

3. An abbreviation for the branch of the service (U.S.C.G. for United States Coast Guard, and so on)

4. Mailing address

| | |
|---|---|
| Commander . . . (name in full)<br>Medical Corps, U.S.N.R.<br>(address) | Sir:<br>Dear Sir:<br>Dear . . .: (rank and last name)<br>My dear . . .: (rank and last name) |

**Pope.**

| | |
|---|---|
| His Holiness, the Pope<br>State of Vatican City, Italy | Your Holiness:<br>Most Holy Father: |
| His Holiness Pope . . . (name)<br>State of Vatican City, Italy | Your Holiness:<br>Most Holy Father: |

**Cardinal.**

| | |
|---|---|
| His Eminence (give name)<br>Cardinal (surname)<br>(address) | Your Eminence: |

**Archbishop or bishop.**

| | |
|---|---|
| The Most Reverend . . . (name in full)<br>Archbishop of . . . (or Bishop of . . .)<br>(address) | Your Excellency: |

## Monsignor.

The Right Reverend Monsignor . . . (name in full) (address)

My dear Monsignor:

## Priest.

The Reverend . . . (name in full) (address)

Reverend dear Father: (formal)
Dear Father: (informal)

## Mother Superior.

The Reverend Mother . . . (address)

Reverend Mother: (formal)
My dear Mother Superior: (informal)

## Sister.

Sister . . . (name) (address)

My dear Sister:
Dear Sister:
Dear Sister . . .: (name)

## Prostestant Episcopal Bishop.

The Right Reverend . . . (name in full)
Bishop of . . . (place)
(address)

Right Reverend: (formal)
Dear Sir: (formal)
My dear Bishop . . .: (last name) (informal)

## Protestant Episcopal Dean.

The Very Reverend (name in full)
Dean of . . . (place)
(address)

My dear Dean:

## Methodist Episcopal Bishop.

Bishop . . . (name in full)
Bishop of . . . (place)
(address)

My dear Bishop:

## Other Clergymen.

| | |
|---|---|
| The Reverend . . . (name in full) | Dear Mr. . . .: (last name) |
| *with a doctor's degree.* | |
| Dr. . . (name in full) (address) | Dear Doctor . . .: (last name) |

## Rabbi.

| | |
|---|---|
| Rabbi . . . (name in full) (address) | My dear Rabbi: |

For any salutation in this section, substitute *Madam* for *Sir* when writing to a woman.

## 9.  FREQUENTLY MISSPELLED WORDS

Many of the words in the following list are frequently misspelled in business messages.

| | | |
|---|---|---|
| accommodate | column | efficient |
| across | commensurate | eighth |
| aisle | commitment | electronics |
| allot | committee | eligible |
| allotment | competent | embarrass |
| among | competitive | emphasis |
| analyze | congratulate | emphasize |
| apparel | conscientious | enthusiastic |
| appearance | conspicuous | envelop |
| appropriate | contingent | envelope |
| attendance | convenience | environment |
| | conveyance | equipment |
| bankruptcy | corporation | exceed |
| basically | courteous | excessive |
| bibliography | | experience |
| birth date | damage | extension |
| birthplace | deficit | extracurricular |
| business | definite | extraordinary |
| | delinquent | |
| calendar | describe | familiar |
| candidate | dilemma | farther |
| category | dimension | fascinate |
| choose | discrepancy | feasible |
| chronological | dividend | February |
| collateral | | flexible |

fluorescent
foreclosure
forty
fourth
further
furthermore

gauge
genuine
gesture
government
grammar
grateful
grievance
guarantee

handling
height
hindrance
honorarium

illegal
illegible
incidentally
indispensable
inevitable
interfered
interpret
interrupt
itinerary

jeopardize

label
laboratory
letterhead
library
literature
loose
lose

maintenance
marital
mediocre
minimize
miscellaneous
misspell
morale
mortgage

necessitate
ninety
ninth
noticeable

occasion
occur
occurrence

pamphlet
parallel
parcel
partial
participate
particular
perseverance
persistent
personnel
precede
preferred
prerequisite
prestige
presumptuous
prevalent
privilege
probable
procedure
proceed
professor
promissory
proprietor

quantity
questionnaire

receive
reciprocate
recognize
recommend
recurrence
registration
reimbursement
remunerate
repetitive
representative
restaurant
retrieval
rotary

salesclerk
secretary
seize
separate
serviceable
similar
sincerely
sophomore
specific
statistics
studying
supersede
synthetic

tariff
temperament
temporary
tentative
traffic
twelfth

unanimous
undoubtedly
utmost

vacuum
variety
vein
verbatim
volume
voluntary

xerox

## 10. CONFUSING TERMINOLOGY

Some words are spelled or pronounced in a manner similar, and in some instances identical, to other words; yet they have entirely different meanings. The wrong word, therefore, is sometimes used. A careful study of the words in the following list will help you to use the proper word for the occasion for which you are communicating. The definitions given here are obviously limited. Only enough information has been provided to help you make distinctions in meaning. For a complete definition of any word in this list, consult a dictionary.

This list, although extensive, is by no means exhaustive.

*accede*—to adhere to an agreement, to give consent
*accept*—to receive, to approve
*access*—ability to enter, to approach
*ad*—advertisement

*addition*—the result of adding
*advise*—to give information
*affect*—to influence
*allowed*—permitted
*altar*—a place for worship
*any way*—any of several ways
*ask*—to call for
*assistance*—help that is given
*attendance*—the act of attending
*bare*—uncovered

*berth*—a bed, a place to rest
*billed*—charged
*board*—a piece of wood, a group of persons
*born*—brought into existence as if by birth
*brake*—to retard, to stop
*build*—to construct
*capital*—assets, upper-case letter, city
*ceiling*—overhead part of a room
*cereal*—a grain product
*choose*—to select
*cite*—to refer to

*exceed*—to go beyond, to be greater than
*except*—to exclude
*excess*—surpassing limits

*add*—to join, to unite so as to increase
*edition*—an issue of a publication
*advice*—information
*effect*—a result, to bring about
*aloud*—with the speaking voice
*alter*—to change
*anyway*—regardless
*asked*—past tense of ask
*assistants*—persons who help
*attendants*—persons who attend
*bear*—an animal, to support, to produce

*birth*—beginning of life
*build*—to construct
*bored*—affected by boredom, drilled
*borne*—past tense of bear (support)
*break*—to separate parts
*billed*—charged
*capitol*—a building

*sealing*—making secure
*serial*—arranged in a series
*chose*—past tense of choose

*sight*—something that is seen     *site*—a place

*coarse*—large, crude

*coma*—unconsciousness

*complementary*—serving to complete

*continual*—occurring often but with interruptions

*conscience*—sense of moral goodness of one's own conduct

*cooperation*—working with another or others

*correspondence*—letters

*council*—a group of persons

*course*—a path, a series of lectures

*device*—something formed by design

*die*—to stop living

*disburse*—to pay out

*discrete*—individually distinct

*disinterested*—not affected by

*disperse*—to scatter

*dye*—to color

*edition*—an issue of a publication

*effect*—a result, to bring about

*envelop*—to wrap

*exceed*—to go beyond, to be greater than

*except*—to exclude

*excess*—surpassing limits

*fair*—just, average, light in color

*farther*—a greater distance

*fiscal*—financial matters

*flew*—past tense of fly

*formally*—in a formal manner

*forth*—onward

*foul*—not favorable

*further*—additional

*gesture*—a motion as a means of expression

*hear*—to perceive by the ear

*course*—a path, a series of lectures

*comma*—a punctuation mark

*complimentary*—flattering

*continuous*—without stopping

*conscious*—mentally awake, active

*corporation*—an organization

*correspondents*—persons who write letters

*counsel*—advice, one who gives legal advice

*coarse*—large, crude

*devise*—to form in the mind

*dye*—to color

*disperse*—to scatter

*discreet*—showing good judgment in conduct

*uninterested*—not interested

*disburse*—to pay out

*die*—to stop living

*addition*—the result of adding

*affect*—to influence

*envelope*—a folded paper to enclose a letter

*accede*—to adhere to an agreement, to give consent

*accept*—to receive, to approve

*access*—ability to enter, to approach

*fare*—price of transportation

*further*—additional

*physical*—pertaining to the body or material

*flu*—short for influenza

*flue*—an enclosed passage, a pipe

*formerly*—at a time that has passed

*fourth*—between the third and the fifth

*fowl*—a bird

*farther*—a greater distance

*jester*—a clown

*here*—at this point

*holy*—sacred   *holey*—having holes   *wholly*—completely, fully

*incidence*—act of falling upon or affecting   *incidents*—subordinate actions or events

*interoffice*—from one office to another   *intraoffice*—within one office

*it's*—it is   *its*—of or belonging to it

*jester*—a clown   *gesture*—a motion as a means of expression

*lay*—to put something down, past tense of lie   *lie*—to recline, a falsehood   *lye*—a strong solution

*lead*—to guide, a heavy metallic element   *led*—past tense of lead

*lean*—to incline so as to receive support, thin   *lien*—a claim against property because of a debt

*leased*—property contracted for use   *least*—smallest

*lie*—to recline, a falsehood   *lay*—to put something down, past tense of lie   *lye*—a strong solution

*lien*—a claim against property because of a debt   *lean*—to incline so as to receive support, thin

*loan*—money lent or borrowed   *lone*—situated apart from other things

*loose*—free, unattached   *lose*—to miss from one's possession

*lye*—a strong solution   *lie*—to recline, a falsehood   *lay*—to put something down, past tense of lie

*marital*—pertaining to marriage   *martial*—pertaining to war   *marshal*—an officer

*may be*—might be   *maybe*—perhaps

*pane*—a compartment of a window   *pain*—distress

*parcel*—a package   *partial*—a part only, inclined to favor one person or group

*passed*—having gone by, having completed a test successfully   *past*—a former time

*patients*—persons under a physician's care   *patience*—a quality of being patient, forebearance

*peace*—a state of tranquility   *piece*—a part separated from the whole

*personal*—private   *personnel*—employees

*physical*—pertaining to the body or material   *fiscal*—financial matters

*piece*—a part separated from the whole   *peace*—a state of tranquility

*pole*—a long piece of wood   *poll*—a questioning of persons, a place to vote *practicable*—possible but not fully tested

*practical*—useful

*preceding*—going before

*proceeding*—a transaction, continuing

*presence*—state of being

*presents*—gifts

*quiet*—free from noise    *quit*—to discontinue    *quite*—completely

*raise*—to lift up

*raze*—to destroy

*residence*—a place

*residents*—persons who reside in a place

*respectfully*—marked by respect

*respectively*—each in the order given

*right*—correct, direction    *rite*—a ceremonial act

*wright*—a workman    *write*—to form words with a pen

*role*—a part taken by anyone

*roll*—to turn over and over, a list, bread

*sail*—a part of a sailboat, to glide

*sale*—act of selling

*sealing*—making secure

*ceiling*—overhead part of a room

*sell*—to transfer property for a consideration

*cell*—small room, single unit

*serial*—arranged in a series

*cereal*—a grain product

*sight*—something that is seen    *site*—a place    *cite*—to refer to

*sole*—fish, part of a shoe, the only one

*soul*—spirit

*some*—unspecified amount

*sum*—an amount of money, result of adding

*some time*—amount of time

*sometime*—at some not specified time

*stake*—a marker, prize set in a contest

*steak*—meat

*stationary*—fixed, not moving

*stationery*—letterheads, envelopes

*suit*—clothes    *suite*—a set of rooms, of furniture    *sweet*—pleasing to the taste

*sum*—an amount of money, result of adding

*some*—unspecified amount

*their*—possessive for they

*there*—at that point

*to*—a preposition    *too*—more than enough, also    *two*—a number

*track*—a path, a mark left by something that has passed

*tract*—an area

*two*—a number    *to*—a preposition    *too*—more than enough, also

*uninterested*—not interested

*disinterested*—not affected by

*waive*—to forgo

*wave*—to sway

*wholly*—completely, fully    *holy*—sacred    *holey*—having holes

*wright*—a workman

*write*—to form words with a pen

*right*—correct, direction    *rite*—a ceremonial act

Some words that are frequently misused because of their similar meanings are in the following list:

**among**—use with three or more (The money was divided equally among the three heirs.)

**between**—use with only two, but *at least two* (The money was divided equally between the two children.) NEVER write, "Place a marker between each page."

**amount**—use with things that cannot be counted (A large amount of water poured over the dam.)

**quantity**—use with things that cannot be counted (They bought a large quantity of sugar.)

**number**—use with things that can be counted (A large number of people attended the meeting.)

**any**—use with three or more (Any of the three salesmen will be glad to arrange a demonstration.)

**either**—use with only two (Either of the two salesmen will be glad to arrange a demonstration.)

**balance**—use with financial matters (The balance is due on December 1.)

**rest**—use with nonfinancial matters (The rest of the work can be done next week.)

**each other**—use with only two (The two assistants helped each other.)

**one another**—use with three or more (The three assistants helped one another.)

**fewer**—use with things that can be counted (The typist made fewer errors on this page than on the preceding page.)

**less**—use with things that cannot be counted (The superintendent said that there is less water in this lake than in any of the others.)

**good**—an adjective (The assistant does good work.)

**well**—an adverb (The assistant works well with others.)

**healthful**—serving to promote health (Cheese is a healthful food.)

**healthy**—being in a state of good health (Rebecca is a healthy child.)

**in**—position, used after a verb to indicate movement within an area (My uncle works in a large factory.)

**into**—to enter, used after a verb to indicate movement from one place to another (When the executive walked into his office, he noticed that a window had been broken.)

**majority**—use with things that can be counted (A majority of the employees preferred the new plan.)

**portion**—use with things that cannot be counted (Only a small portion of the work has been completed.)

**neither**—use with only two (Neither the typist nor the stenographer was in the office when I called.)

**none**—use with three or more (None of the six clerks understood the plan.)

**percent**—use after a figure (Almost 8 percent of the office employees attended the meeting.)

**percentage**—use without figures (Only a small percentage of the office employees have adequate life insurance.)

# INDEX